Other McDougall books

THE McDOUGALL PLAN

McDOUGALL'S MEDICINE:
A CHALLENGING SECOND OPINION

THE McDOUGALL HEALTH-SUPPORTING
COOKBOOK, Vol. 1 and Vol. 2

THE
MCDOUGALL
PROGRAM

TWELVE DAYS
TO DYNAMIC HEALTH

THE MCDOUGALL PROGRAM

TWELVE DAYS TO DYNAMIC HEALTH

John A. McDougall, M.D.

WITH RECIPES BY
Mary McDougall

NAL BOOKS

Calculations for nutritional values were made from:
Pennington, J. *Food Values of Portions Commonly Used*. 14th and
   15th Editions. Harper & Row, New York, 1985 and 1989.
Nutritive Value of American Foods in Common Units. Agriculture
   Handbook No. 456. Agriculture Research Services. US Department of Agriculture. 1975.
Composition of Foods. Agriculture Handbook No. 8. US Department
   of Agriculture. Science and Education Administration. Revised
   1976 to 1980.

NAL BOOKS
Published by the Penguin Group
Penguin Books USA Inc., 375 Hudson Street, New York, New York 10014, U.S.A.
Penguin Books Ltd, 27 Wrights Lane, London W8 5TZ, England
Penguin Books Australia Ltd, Ringwood, Victoria, Australia
Penguin Books Canada Ltd, 2801 John Street, Markham, Ontario, Canada L3R 1B4
Penguin Books (N.Z.) Ltd, 182–190 Wairau Road, Auckland 10, New Zealand

Penguin Books Ltd, Registered Offices: Harmondsworth, Middlesex, England

First published by NAL Books, an imprint of Penguin Books USA Inc.

Published simultaneously in Canada.

First Printing, May, 1990
10 9 8 7 6 5 4 3 2 1

 REGISTERED TRADEMARK—MARCA REGISTRADA

LIBRARY OF CONGRESS CATALOGING-IN-PUBLICATION DATA
McDougall, John A.
   The McDougall program : twelve days to dynamic health / by
John A. McDougall with recipes by Mary McDougall.
      p. cm.
   ISBN 0-453-00659-0
   1. Complex carbohydrate diet. 2. Vegetarianism. 3. Health.
I. McDougall, Mary A. (Mary Ann)   II. Title.
RM237.58.M322 1990
613.2′6—dc20   89-13594
                                                          CIP

Printed in the United States of America
Set in Times Roman
Designed by Julian Hamer

To the venturesome pioneers who have blazed lonely
and treacherous trails to bring into practice
principles of sensible nutrition and
conservative medical care.

ACKNOWLEDGMENTS

My gratitude and thanks to:

One dedicated writer, Bill Fryer, who spent a good year of his life helping me put this program on paper. Ozzie Bushnell, Veronica Johnson, and Nellie Sabin, for their help with editing. Wordstar and my IBM personal computer, which never failed to reproduce the words that flowed from my two fingers onto magnetic disk, then to paper. Louise Burk, who typed sections of the manuscript on her computer using all ten fingers.

All the people at St. Helena Hospital and Health Center, and especially Terry Hansen, the vice-president, who recruited me from my warm beachside home in Hawaii to run the McDougall Program in the beautiful Napa Valley of northern California; and to John Hodgkin, M.D., who has lent his support every step along the way.

The McDougall staff: Judy Moore R.N., Ed Haver M.A., Hap Stump Ph.D., Tim Fredrick B.S., Lynn Pizzitola M.F.C.C., Vicki Saunders R.D., M.S., Karin Litzau M.S., and Wanda Whalen, to mention only a few by name; as well as the countless people who provide the education, health care, excellent food, massages, room services, and compassionate warmth that make St. Helena one of the top healing centers in the world.

Both Mary and I want to thank our friends, patients, and the readers of our books and newsletters for all of the valuable lessons you have taught us over the years, and the health and recipe ideas many of you have contributed. Some of the recipes used in this book are from Joanne and Michael Stepaniak, Don and Carol Brown, Pat Hilberg, Lisa Messina, K. Rusk, Winston and Sharon Culp, Elaine French, Vicki Saunders, Wyn Washington, Deb Cheney, and Nancy Koski.

CONTENTS

The doctor of the future will give no medicine,
but will interest his patient in the care
of the human frame, in diet and in the
cause and prevention of disease.

—*Thomas A. Edison*

P·A·R·T
1
THE PROGRAM

1

THE HEALTH PROGRAM

YOU ASKED FOR

Wouldn't you like to get every last vital bit of vigorous living out of your body even in extreme old age? That's what I've always wanted for myself, and it's what I have always wanted to give to every one of my patients. However, after several years of trying the know-it-all doctor's approach, I got wise: Reasoning that other people have ideas too, I decided to ask my patients what *they* wanted in a health program.

Their many different responses made a lot of sense. They asked me for ways to improve their appearance and attain longer life, physical vitality, and freedom from aches and pains. They wanted straightforward and practical methods for gaining those rewards. And, furthermore, they wanted to get them without paying fortunes in doctor's bills.

In this book I present the McDougall Program, a health program you can experience in twelve days' time which offers you all these benefits—and more.

"I Want to Look Great."

Most people do. Physical attractiveness is near the top of any list of human desires. As the father of a teen-age girl, I'm being taught again that this desire is most intense at the onset of puberty. But, even though the passing years may diminish our youthful freshness, we never lose the need to "look great."

Even if prolonged illness and the addition of excess poundage has made you appear less youthful than you want to be, you still sense that underneath your swollen skin and wealth of fatty deposits, sleek curves and rippling muscles are buried, just waiting to be freed. Men and women try widely differing methods (and torments) for improving their appearance, and sex appeal. They attend weight-reducing salons, buy into quickie diet plans, invest in rejuvenation creams, and put their faith in deodorants, perfumes, beauty lotions, vitamin pills, and expensive clothes to cover up all too exuberant flesh. These are all methods of damage control at best, and most of them are of questionable effectiveness. Yet, looking your physical best, without all that fuss, bother, and expense, is easily within your reach.

Imagine a crowd of trim and attractive people. Who do you think of first? Not the waddling, unlovely folks you saw on your last trip to Disneyland, I'll bet.

Among the Chinese, Japanese, Koreans, Malaysians—in their homelands, that is—obesity is almost unknown. The reason for this lies in their diet: Their main food is a starchy plant. You will consistently find that the diets of people who remain slim throughout life are centered around rice, or wheat, or potatoes, or corn, or beans, and other starchy vegetables. Their diets will also provide plenty of fruits and vegetables, but very little (if any) fatty meats and dairy products. And yet, when slender Chinese or Japanese move to San Francisco or New York or your hometown in America, they soon develop a roll of fat bulging over their belts that makes them look very American, indeed. Obesity is not genetic; it's the result of exchanging a starch-based diet for rich, fattening foods.

All right, you say I'll get fat by eating the wrong foods. Does the situation work in reverse?

Of course, it does. Adopting a diet high in starches causes permanent weight loss among those people who continue to eat that way. The idea that eating starches can make you thin will not surprise veteran dieters who are familiar with the calorie contents of foods. A large-size white potato provides a mere 150 calories and a cup of rice 200 calories. It's not the starches, but the butter and the sour cream toppings we pile over them that are fattening.

A starch-based diet is one of the fundamentals of the McDougall Program. Most overweight people who go on the McDougall Program lose six to fifteen pounds of fat a month, while still eating as much as they want of the approved foods.

Being good-looking also means that when you're seventy years

DISEASES *CAUSED* BY
A "RICH" WESTERN DIET

Systemic Diseases	Bowel Disorders	Cancers
Allergies	Appendicitis	Breast
Arthritis	Colitis	Colon
Atherosclerosis	Constipation	Kidney
Diabetes (Adult)	Diarrhea	Pancreas
Gout	Diverticulosis	Prostate
Heart Attacks	Gallstones (cholesterol)	Testicle
Hormone Imbalances	Gastritis	Uterus (body)
Hypertension	Hemorrhoids	
Kidney Failure	Hiatus Hernia	
Kidney Stones	Indigestion	
Multiple Sclerosis	Malabsorption	
Obesity	Polyps	
Osteoporosis	Ulcers	
Strokes		

- Diet is a primary causative factor in all the above diseases and it is *controllable*. (Heredity is also a primary factor, but it is not under our control.) Smoking, alcohol, lack of exercise, and "stress" are secondary factors which are also controllable. A primary factor must be present for a disease to develop; a secondary factor aggravates the disease process after the development has begun.
- *Diet and lifestyle changes are the most effective treatment for chronic forms of the diseases listed in the first two columns*, far surpassing in results any drug or surgical therapy according to scientific and medical literature. This should not surprise you; what causes disease promotes disease. If you eliminate the cause, then the body's healing mechanisms can take over, resulting in improvement or recovery. The effect of diet on cancers is yet to be determined.

old your skin will glow and your smile will be filled with teeth, not empty spaces, or (even worse) phony enameled dentures with shiny pink plastic "gums." That mirror of yours should show you a well-developed, well-preserved, well-nourished you for eighty-five years or more.

"I Want to Live Healthy."

Will you have the chance to reach that age and experience that pleasant state of affairs if you eat the standard American diet? Not very likely. The standard American diet, alas, is hazardous to your health. During the course of this amazing, wealthy, and scientifically advanced twentieth century, Americans and the residents of other industrialized countries have adopted a bizarre rich diet, crammed with fats and cholesterol, unnecessary amounts of sugar and salt, food additives, ultra-refined foods, and oftentimes outright chemical poisons. It's a nutritional nightmare! We go from bacon and eggs at breakfast to a ham and cheese sandwich for lunch, by way of a sugared jelly doughnut for morning coffee break. Then we take a deep breath and, very often, after a martini or two to prepare us for feasting, we plunge our knives and forks into a thick sirloin steak or a deep-fried chicken. The connection between these overrich foods and the medical problems we suffer from is as direct as the connection between half a quart of Kentucky bourbon downed in one session and the next morning's hangover.

Consider, in the United States alone, nearly a million people die from heart attacks and strokes yearly, and thirty-four million adults are overweight. Believe me, that's not what nature intended for us.

"I Want to Feel Well."

Do you recall those far-off happy days when you were a child? You ate as much of everything as you wanted, and never gained weight. You ran and played the whole day through, and never felt tired until you collapsed at bedtime. Your joints were limber, and you never noticed your knees, unless you fell full force on them. You had neither headaches nor muscle aches. You felt so good that you never imagined a time when all this well-being would end. You were almost invincible.

How often do you feel that way now? Often? Once in a while? Never? Perhaps the way you feel now makes you wonder if this very day might not be your last. And no doubt you accept this perpetual misery as a normal part of the process of aging. What else can I expect after fifty? you ask yourself. Or, if you're in an especially bad way, after forty? After thirty . . . ?

If you feel lousy, have a little cheer; you have lots of company. A quick look along the aisles of your local drugstore or in the neighborhood supermarket will show you that there's big business in constipation, indigestion, and post nasal drip; in sinus trouble, fatigue, insomnia, and unrelenting pain. A lot of people out there are hurting.

And yet, in less than a week almost all the people who adopt the McDougall Program, and follow it strictly, end such annoying discomforts, from headaches to bowel irregularity to chronic fatigue.

"I Want to Solve Serious Health Problems."

Some of you will be people whose health problems have reached a life-threatening level. You've stopped complaining about merely mild aches and ordinarily bearable pains. Now your ailments are unrelenting, seriously affecting the quality of your weary days and long nights.

Let's say that when you wake up in the morning your joints no longer simply ache, now they are swollen and red, and they hurt you far beyond the relief you've been winning from half a dozen aspirin tablets. Your doctor calls your condition rheumatoid arthritis, and he tells you there's no chance for a cure. Maybe he's right. But maybe, too, he doesn't know everything. If, as happens all too frequently, his preparation has been limited by a narrow medical education, then his idea of treatment will be restricted to recommending drugs and surgery. A more broadly educated physician, well read in the current scientific literature, will prescribe a self-help program that will address the genuine foundations of good health— your diet and lifestyle—and thus has real prospects of bettering the condition of your joints. This comparison may sound too simple to satisfy you, and those among you who are still looking for serious solutions in high technology may pass by this opportunity with a skeptical shrug.

Possibly your ills are even more alarming than crippling arthritis. What if your chest pains due to a diseased heart are becoming so severe that your cardiologist tells you that bypass surgery is the only way you'll get relief?

You say you'd rather eat cardboard than spend a bloody morning with your chest pried wide open, your heart exposed to the recycled air of the operating room, and your thigh cut open from your groin to your calf. You may have learned from somewhere that there's a better than fifty-fifty chance of suffering brain damage during open heart surgery, as well as a one-in-twenty probability that you won't leave the hospital alive. What can you do about this threat to your heart and soul? You need a mighty powerful program that will get you out of that sort of trouble, and you need it *right now*.

What is my response as a concerned physician to the two examples of patient ailments described above?

First, it's a fact (in spite of the skepticism felt by lots of physicians) that many patients with severe inflammatory arthritis—including rheumatoid arthritis—make extraordinary recoveries within a few days after going on the McDougall Program and giving up eating animal foods, dairy products, and fats.

Next, during the twelve years in which I have been taking care of numbers of heart patients, I have yet to send a single one to bypass surgery. This is not to say that some haven't ended up on the operating table. But, they were the guys who refused to take my advice. So far, all my patients who have adopted a diet that's healthy for the heart have succeeded in avoiding the knife. Does this claim sound boastful to you? I hope that it does not. I say it simply to dramatize the fact that an effective, scientifically supported alternative to heart surgery does exist. It's right here, for the asking.

The McDougall Program is powerful therapy. We're talking about your taking one to five pounds of potent medicine every day—your breakfast, lunch, and dinner. Don't be surprised if the alterations in your diet and lifestyle must be considerable. If you want dramatic changes in your health, then you must make dramatic changes in your diet. Big changes get big results.

Once you begin to eat according to the healthy diet presented in this book, you'll start to feel the effects of better health in as little as a week. If you must repair major damages to your system, you may need three or four months to achieve a complete physical overhaul, but even during the first week the repairs will be exerting their good effect. Don't you think you should begin at once?

"I Want to Stop Medications."

How would you like to stop getting more prescriptions for more medications every time you visit your doctor and instead begin taking new inexpensive agents that need no prescription?

For the past three years I have directed the twelve-day live-in McDougall Program at St. Helena Hospital and Health Center in northern California. Here, most patients stop taking medication, or at least reduce the amounts they take, on the day they start the program. In only a few cases are medications actually required. Often we receive patients who have become emotionally attached to the medications which have been their daily companions for years, if not for decades. I take account of such psychological dependency and gradually wean these patients from their medications.

This approach may seem unorthodox to you, but in time most of you will become comfortable with the radical idea that "less medication is better medicine." For years I have been referred to (in whispers) as "the doctor who takes people off drugs." Yet isn't the proper role of a physician to help you become healthier? That means less dependence on drugs, not more. Now I ask you, when you think of healthy friends and relatives, are they the ones who are taking handfuls of drugs or those needing none at all?

A drug-free state is the natural state for the healthy human body. Your goal is to make your doctor as lonely as the Maytag repairman.

"I Want to Satisfy My Hunger."

While you were grimly sticking to the regime of some low-calorie diet, did you ever have fantasies about encountering a health program that promised that "the more you eat, the thinner you'll be"? Crazy, you may say. Well, when people start on the McDougall Program, I encourage almost all of them to eat as much as they want, as often as they want. The important issue, of course, is *what* you eat. Once you fill up on foods like oatmeal, hash-brown potatoes, bean soup, spaghetti, meatless chili, and burritos, you'll have no room left in your stomach for the high-calorie, fat-filled foods that guarantee you an expanded waistline and a shortened lifespan.

You can't be perpetually hungry when you're eating in the McDougall way. I'm especially proud of this achievement. What can be more annoying than the preaching that's delivered in those stacks of diet books that tell you how you can lose weight by controlling your appetite? Has anyone ever told you to control the amount of air you need to breathe or how much water you should drink? Such cautions are not needed. Well, your body won't need instructions about the amounts of food you'll want to eat either—*if* you eat the right foods.

"I Want to Eat Delicious Foods."

Why not expand your horizons? You might take an expensive world tour during which you sampled the cuisines of every country you visited. Or you might start on the McDougall Program right now.

The McDougall Program's diet includes Italian, French, Mexican, Indian, Spanish, Chinese, Japanese, African, South American, and North American cooking. The ingredients will come in all the colors of the rainbow—an eye-filling spread of green, red, orange, yellow, purple, and brown foods. Some of your favorite spices will give a familiar aroma to the dishes. And some new ones, too, can be added. If your health permits, a bit of salt or sugar *sprinkled lightly* over the surface of the foods will provide the two elemental flavors that everyone desires because of the basic programming of the tongue.

Naturally, you'll need a period of adjustment. Your taste buds will have to learn to recognize flavors other than the fatty, oily, greasy, and salty ones that are the hallmarks of unimaginative Western cookery. This adjustment doesn't take long. Your palate may wonder about your first, or your second, or even possibly your third meal, but it won't resent many experiences after that.

"I Want to Save Money."

Better health, through diet and exercise, also means that your food and medical bills will be wonderfully reduced. America's expenses for health care now amount to 11 percent of the Gross National Product, and this figure is expected to reach 15 percent by the early 1990s. I hope—with selfish indifference to the bankrupting of this country—you're not thinking, "Why should I care? My health insurance will pay the bill." This self-centered attitude has very limited value. Most insurance policies cover only a percentage of the actual health costs, usually about 80 percent. One bout with cancer can soar to a total cost of $100,000—the tidy sum of $20,000 subtracted from your savings account.

Furthermore, if you haven't prepared wisely, poor health could cancel your chance to buy medical and life insurance—and lack of insurance coverage could put you and your entire family into bankruptcy overnight. One heart bypass operation can be expected to set you back about $37,300, unless complications develop—in which event the price tag will really go out of control.

You can carry only so much insurance protection. Being sick means less productivity on the job and sometimes ends in loss of that job and permanent unemployment. Don't forget too: Being grossly overweight, and other such detractions chalked up against your personal appearance, can have a subtly destructive effect on your professional prospects at any time, even before you actually get sick.

All of these are powerful *financial* arguments in favor of being a slim and healthy person. In addition, changing to the kinds of meals recommended by the McDougall Program will reduce your food bills by about 40 percent. You'll spend less money at the grocery store when you shop for these foods, and when you eat out you'll be happy to discover that most restaurants are embarrassed to charge high prices for the kinds of dishes you will order—unburdened with expensive rich ingredients such as meats, butter, imported cheeses, and cream sauces.

"I Want a Program That's Easy to Understand and Follow."

In three short sentences, the McDougall Program asks you to:

1. Follow a diet centered around starches with the addition of fresh or frozen fruits and vegetables.
2. Give up indulging yourself in meats, dairy products, eggs, oils, and other rich foods—except on rare and very special occa-

sions, such as annual feasts like Christmas, Thanksgiving, wedding anniversaries, and family birthdays.
3. Develop the habit of taking some exercise every day. A sensible amount of mild to moderate exertion, such as walking, can help anyone who is leading a sedentary life.

These changes are not hard to make. Cooking, for instance, certainly will not be more difficult. If you've been the kind of cook who burns a piece of flesh on both sides and serves it for dinner, cooking a heap of spaghetti and heating up some frozen vegetables will be no great chore. If you've brought a genuine gourmet's appreciation to your meals and their preparation, then you'll welcome the fun of discovering gourmet cooking à la McDougall. And you'll be delighted with the novel and tasty recipes offered in Part 2 of this book.

As for your "confirmed tastes," they can be changed much more easily than you imagine. Human beings are very adaptable once they're fairly informed about the need for change. After all, with the McDougall Program, you'll be eating many kinds of delicious foods. Your diet just won't include treacherous goodies that you're devouring now—to your disadvantage, even sometimes to the peril of your life.

"I Want the Change to Be Permanent."

Most medical treatments for long-standing diseases can honestly be called patch jobs and temporary fixes. That's the unkind truth, and such makeshift approaches are about all that doctors can do for people who continue to abuse themselves with knives, forks, spoons, and busy fingers. You can't rely on the advertised miracles of medicine to save you from ailments that you yourself are provoking.

One of the major operations of our time for relief of heart disease—bypass surgery—is a classic example of a stopgap solution to a problem that is becoming almost epidemic. A quarter of a million bypass operations are performed annually in the United States alone. Although the operation does relieve chest pains, the unfortunate victim's arteries continue to close at the same or even at an accelerated rate after the surgery. A few millimeters from the obstruction that the surgeons bypassed, lies another equally vulnerable stretch of artery that is being filled up with atherosclerotic plaques made of fats and cholesterol. Unless they stop eating the fats and cholesterol, most patients who survive bypass surgery will develop the same problems within the next decade (if not sooner) and, if they live so long, many will be invited back to the operating table for more temporary relief of pain. Even worse, at any time along the way, they may be so unlucky as to suffer that final, fatal heart attack.

Only one alternative route is available for bypassing this dismal chain of consequences—a sensible change in diet and lifestyle. Many patients in my private practice and at St. Helena Hospital and Health Center have come to me with the symptoms of heart disease. They've wondered if the damage they have done to that most important of all body parts is irreparable. I give them a hopeful message about the marvelous capacity to heal that their tattered and battered arteries possess, and most of those ailing folk are soon convinced that they can begin reversing the situation. The facts are clear and beyond dispute: On a no-cholesterol diet, the amount of cholesterol in the blood usually falls to a safe level, and stays there. After that, within a few short days human arteries begin to heal themselves.

Some of my patients who had high blood pressure before they lowered it as participants in the McDougall Program tested the diet's validity by indulging in a series of high-fat, high-salt meals. They soon found that their blood pressures rose again. The quick return of health problems after a lapse into fatty feasting is one of the best reasons why the McDougall Program is accepted gratefully by people whom it has benefited. Few individuals will risk being sick again when they know how to avoid such episodes of distress.

Not Just Twelve Days, But a Whole New Life

Calling this a "twelve-day program" is not intended as a gimmick, even though the changes I'm introducing to you are meant to be accepted and followed permanently. Twelve days is the minimum amount of time that's needed to convince you of the Program's worth. By the end of twelve days you'll notice undeniable improvements in the way you look and feel. By that time, you will have also adjusted to the recommended foods and to the routine of daily exercise. When you can honestly say "I really like this way of living," then you have made a good start on the path that will guarantee better health for you in the years ahead.

The McDougall Program is a no-nonsense, no-compromise health program that is intended to help you live a better life—the best possible life for you. Most of you will take full advantage of this simple message. Even if you don't do so right now, at least you'll know about a better way to eat and live—and you can think about adopting it soon. After reading this book, you should understand how you can regain your lost health and attractive appearance, and how you can maintain excellent health for a long and comfortable lifetime. *The choice is yours to make.*

2

PHYSICIAN,

HEAL THYSELF

Perhaps you're wondering how I became a doctor interested in nutrition. It was a long process, but I found the reasons for that interest in my own failing body. You see, my body didn't double-cross me—I betrayed it. I too suffered the consequences of the American diet. Because of my experiences, both personal and professional, I have *earned* the right to teach you about this highly effective program for regaining lost health and appearance, discontinuing medications, avoiding surgeries, and maintaining excellent health.

EARNING THE RIGHT

By the time I was six or seven years old, my body was already rebelling against some of the food I was given. I had frequent stomach aches and was constipated so often that I thought everybody in the world had hard, painful bowel movements. Needless to say, neither I nor my parents connected these signs of distress with the meals served in our home.

Our family ate the usual foods of the normal middle-class American family. This was during the 1950s, and my mother thought she was giving the best of care to her children by feeding us eggs and sausages for breakfast; sandwiches prepared with slabs of cheese, bologna, or ham bracketed in slices of white bread all smothered with mayonnaise and topped with a leaf of lettuce for lunch. For dinner we feasted on roast beef, ham, hamburgers, hot dogs, pork chops, or fried chicken always with potatoes—baked, boiled, or mashed—and portions of canned fruits and canned vegetables. And every meal was washed down with big glasses of creamy whole milk.

In those days the importance of dietary fiber was as unknown to the average homemaker as were the hazards of eating excess fats, proteins, table salt, and cholesterol. But our diet certainly wasn't deficient in calories.

When I went off to college food was plentiful, and I helped myself to more of the same all-American meals my mother had been feeding me back home. One morning about three months into my freshman year I woke up feeling confused and weak. When I started out for class I was so disoriented that I had trouble finding my way to the building. By the time I had gone to class and returned to my room in the dormitory I had managed to get hit by two cars. The collisions were minor and did me no harm, but by that afternoon I was unable to lift my left arm and leg.

My condition alarmed some of my dormmates, and they called for help. After an overnight stay in the small campus hospital, I was moved to a large city hospital. There the best specialists gathered around, and began to investigate. They did a cerebral angiogram, and it revealed that a small atherosclerotic plaque had closed a critical artery serving the right side of my brain, in the region that controls movements on the left side of my body. The medical diagnosis was Cerebral Vascular Accident. Most of you know the condition as "a stroke"—something that's supposed to happen only to older people. They're not common among younger folk, but strokes and heart attacks do affect more than a thousand teen-agers every year in the United States.

This stroke completely paralyzed the left side of my body. After a week, my best effort on that side of my body involved moving my left thumb a quarter of an inch. After several months, I recovered partial use of my arm and leg, and from that point on my progress was rapid. I was young; my good fortune allowed other areas of my brain to take over the tasks that the tissues deadened by the stroke were no longer capable of performing. But to this day I still walk with a slight limp.

My experiences in the hospital gave a decisive impetus to my decision to become a physician. In my family, doctors had always been regarded as "gods," and being a doctor had been a goal beyond my wildest dreams. Extensive observations of the work that my dedicated physicians did while I was hospitalized convinced me that they were indeed entirely human, and that what they were doing I could do too.

I returned to classes at the university with a new enthusiasm for learning and a strong purpose in life—medicine. How many eighteen-year-olds face death so closely, and then get a second chance? However, still unaware that the foods I ate were a threat to my health, I continued to eat the same foods I always enjoyed. By the time I entered medical school I was getting fat. And I didn't feel very well.

After graduating from medical school I moved with my wife Mary to the state of Hawaii, to further my education as a surgical resident, and, about that time, the belly pains that had troubled me since childhood became more severe. Often I had to curl up on my bed in the fetal position, desperately hoping for relief. During one three-month period, I was sick every day. I sought a surgical opinion and, as you might expect, I got a surgical solution: That same afternoon I had exploratory abdominal surgery. No clear diagnosis was made at the time, although the surgeons removed my appendix, "just in case."

The reason for my abdominal pains remained a mystery to me and my doctors. Nobody asked what kinds of foods I was eating. I suspect now that if I had told them about the three hot dogs covered with hamburger chili sauce that I usually ate for an evening snack, no one would have raised an eyebrow.

One Frustrated Doctor

Like most medical students, I'd spent my early years in medical school following my teachers around and watching as they directed patient care. Naturally, the decisions they made and the procedures they carried out fascinated me. Eventually, however, I began to notice that their successes—emotionally rewarding though they could be—were far outnumbered by their failures. The successes usually involved the treatment of emergencies caused by violence and the curing of infectious diseases caused by germs.

But what about the failures? These constituted a vast category of patients with chronic degenerative illnesses. Today, I would estimate that 85 percent of the people in the hospital were suffering to one degree or another from the effects of obesity, heart disease, high blood pressure, cancer, diabetes, or stroke. Did we physicians make an appreciable difference in their lives? Not much that I ever saw.

After my year of surgical residency, I declined to continue training in a surgical speciality, as I was expected to do. I was confused about what I had experienced in medicine, and I lacked a strong sense of direction. So for a few days I idled along as an unemployed doctor. Soon after, however, a job opportunity opened on the island of Hawaii, the largest island in the fiftieth state. A sugar cane plantation was looking for a physician. I went. I had no premonition that what lay ahead for me would be a mind-opening experience.

A Real Doctor, Out to Do Good

As a plantation physician living in the village of Honokaa, I was forty-one miles from the island's one big town, Hilo, and the nearest medical specialists. In that isolated location I had to take care of every kind of medical problem from delivering babies at almost any time to doing brain surgery on accident victims in the middle of the night. It was hard work, but unfortunately I soon discovered that the satisfaction I got from saving people's lives in emergency situations was outweighed by my depressing inability to improve the lives of the majority of my patients—those with chronic illnesses. My diabetics went blind, lost kidney function, and suffered heart attacks. My heart patients kept to a steady downhill course and finally died of heart attacks or strokes. Patients with high blood pressure suffered several kinds of side effects from the medications I prescribed, but showed no improvement. I put them on drugs and they stayed on them. As the drug companies' salesmen say, "Once you're on blood pressure medication, you're on for life."

Actually, the scientific evidence, even then, showed that blood pressure pills do no good in most cases, and in almost all patients produce unpleasant and sometimes embarrassing side effects. I remember a twenty-four-year-old man, recently married, who came to me with high blood pressure. I put him on medication, and two weeks later he came back and told me he had noticed one change— he could no longer achieve an erection. I mumbled a little and said, "Well, yes, but think of your health." He never returned. I thought he was foolish. Of course I was wrong.

As is usual in plantation settings, patients received free medical care. My waiting room was full of people who wanted something more from my magical self than Band-Aids and advice. They expected to be given their vials of pills, and, not knowing what else to do, I didn't disappoint them in that.

Success for me, as it should be for most doctors, means watching my patients get healthier. What I saw was that most of my patients were getting sicker. I began to fear that I was a bad doctor, and I fell back on preprocessed explanations. "Your diabetes? Well, your mother had it too, didn't she? What can you expect?" "High blood pressure? It runs in your family." And so on, and so on, with a dismal lack of improvement in my responses—or in theirs.

The reasons I gave them sounded good for a while, at least to me. But then I looked at some of my patients who were victims of several ailments at the same time. Could it really be true that nature had designed them so unsuccessfully as to have heart disease, and diabetes, and gout, and bowel problems, and high blood pressure—all at one and the same time? I was unwilling to believe that genetic defects were the explanation for everything that went wrong in those unhappy people.

I was depressed, and I no longer felt infallible (as a doctor is supposed to do). I began reacting defensively when patients asked me questions. Absurd as it sounds, I can remember barking at one poor man, "Who's the doctor here, you or me?" My arrogance worked: Most of my questioners backed off. I was getting nowhere as a physician, but at least my fragile ego was being protected. Yet, I couldn't feel sure I was protecting my patients nearly as well.

The Turning Point in My Life

In the fall of 1973, I sat in my office one afternoon, after the day's crowd had left. A man about my age, Buzz Hughes, a gentleman-farmer and an astrologer, came in for a chat. We talked for a long time about patients, medicine, and sicknesses. Then Buzz fixed me with a question: "John, do you think that diet has anything to do with the health problems you take care of here?"

"Absolutely not."

"Why are you so sure?"

"I went to one of the best medical schools in the country," I replied (very defensively), "and diet and disease were never mentioned in the same sentence. Don't you think that if this connection existed they would have told me about it?"

"You must admit," Buzz said, unfazed, "that there's a slight possibility you're wrong. Why don't you ask your patients what they eat, and see if you can find any relationship between their eating habits and their diseases?" The challenge was delivered fair and square, and I took it up. During the months that followed, every patient who walked into my office was asked what he or she ate. Soon I acquired quite a reputation—this time as a nuisance. Now, I was the doctor who bothered people with nosy questions about their diets.

Only in Hawaii

Living and working on the Big Island of Hawaii made all the difference to my investigations. In few other places in the world could I have so quickly learned the lessons about health that eventually formed the basis of my practice.

On the island of Hawaii live people of several different ethnic backgrounds and races. Frequently, the living members of a single family span three generations, sometimes even four. The first generation, born in their native lands (mostly Japan, China, and the Philippines), were raised there for the first fifteen to twenty-five years of their lives, and then migrated to Hawaii under contracts to work on the sugar cane and pineapple plantations. There they started families, and often many of their children and grandchildren also became members of the same or a neighboring plantation community.

The first generation's years in their native lands exerted a strong influence on the manner in which they lived after settling in Hawaii. In the home country they had learned to enjoy a diet made up largely of rice and vegetables, supplemented perhaps with a little fish on occasions, but with very little meat. Raised in countries where cows are rare, they never acquired the taste for cow's milk and cheese, or for beef.

But their children, the second generation, born and raised in Americanized Hawaii, were introduced to a whole new style of eating. They learned about a much richer kind of diet, centered around meats and dairy products and refined foods. Their parents' favorite foodstuffs, rice and fresh vegetables, became unimportant side dishes for the children.

For me, Hawaii was a natural laboratory revealing the influence of diet and heredity on a large population of mixed ethnic groups. I observed the effects of different eating habits in successive generations of people sharing the same genetic make-up. If health and disease were the consequences of inherited factors, then no change in those responses should be observed from one generation to the next. But the people of my plantation community did not confirm this theory.

The differences between generations were distinct. Most of my large numbers of older Japanese, Chinese, and Filipinos were in excellent health. Almost all were trim, hard working, few felt aches and pains, needed no medication, had normal blood pressure and low levels of cholesterol, sugar, and uric acid. They felt good and functioned well even in their seventh, eighth, and ninth decades of life. Eighty-five-year-old Japanese ladies could hear someone whispering behind their back. If I placed their charts open on my desk, they could read every word in them while sitting upright in their chairs. Those people were fully functional toward the end of a long and hard life. This was true not just of an occasional individual, but of whole population groups. I never saw good health on such a large scale before (and haven't seen it since).

I found the older Filipino men particularly interesting. A common practice in Hawaii is for the Filipino men to postpone marriage and work for forty years or more on a plantation, saving a good share of their wages all the while. This amounts to a small fortune, in the opinion of their countrymen still living in the Philippines. Then, after he retires, a Filipino man often returns to the Philippine Islands in search of a bride. With his accumulated wealth and the good monthly pension he has earned, he has no trouble finding and marrying a young Filipino woman in her teens or early twenties. She returns with him to the Hawaiian Islands, often to the same plantation village in which he's lived for those many years, and there they start a new family.

Daily, into my office would come such an elderly Filipino gentleman, accompanied by his young wife and several small beautiful children. I found that, in their sixties and seventies, these remarkable men were functioning at a level beyond the capability of younger Filipino (or Japanese, or Chinese, or Caucasian) men still in their forties and fifties. And these elders were fathering children. They also expressed an admirable optimism. They expected to live long enough to see their children grow up and start families of their own—and the majority of them did!

Naturally, I began to wonder if this exceeding youthfulness was a national characteristic limited to Filipinos. I was soon instructed on *that* point. The grown children of those native Filipinos, people who had been born and raised in Hawaii, did not share their parents' enviable health. Before my eyes I saw them developing gout, diabetes, colon cancer, high blood pressure, and heart disease. They were fat. They felt bad. They looked sick. This wasn't the result of the pressures of modern living. The several generations of these Filipino plantation families had been living and working in essentially the same way for almost a hundred years—with one significant exception: there had been a radical change in diet for those who were raised in Hawaii. To me, the impact of this change in diet on their health was indisputable.

BACK TO SCHOOL

After three years of frustration, still unable to help my many patients with their chronic diseases, I returned to advanced study in medicine, taking up a residency in the University of Hawaii's affiliated hospitals in Honolulu, training to become a specialist in Internal Medicine. I was determined to uncover the secrets of effective medicine. After three months I realized I had already learned, during my years in medical school and earlier year of surgical residency, all that the medical profession had to teach me to remedy my patients' long-standing ailments. It seemed that the chronically ill could expect no more miracles, from me or from anybody else.

During the two years of that residency I spent much of my spare time searching the literature in the medical library. I discovered that many other physicians and scientists had already noticed that the current methods of treating chronic diseases were failing to meet the needs of patients. Those observers also saw that improvements in diet and lifestyle were the best ways of preventing and treating most of those chronic conditions.

But all too often the lessons I was learning back in the library stacks directly conflicted with the approaches I was being taught to practice at lectures or bedsides in the hospital.

Trouble on Medical Rounds

As one of the results of my reading, I frequently found myself in trouble with my instructors. If ever I suggested that a change in diet could help a patient, the shocked silence that followed was quickly replaced by something more vigorous. "Unscientific!" "Unorthodox!" "Quack!" were just a few of the epithets that assailed me. This should have kept any self-preserving apprentice from daring to mention such matters again, but I was a slow learner.

Let me tell you about one incident during my residency. I went to see a young man who had just suffered his second heart attack, to perform my routine duties of taking a case history and making a physical examination. He was thirty-eight years old. He had five children. I asked him what he was going to do to prevent the next heart attack.

"I don't know," he answered. "As far as I can tell, I do everything right already. I don't smoke, I don't drink, and I exercise every day."

"What about your diet?"

"Well, my diet is just what my dietitian tells me to eat—margarine instead of butter, low salt, and trim the fat off my meat. I've followed this advice ever since my first heart attack, and it doesn't seem to make any difference."

I suggested—although it seemed radical even to me at the time— that he give up all meats, as well as dairy products.

The next morning I was summoned—not for the first or last time— to the office of my boss, the Chief of Internal Medicine. There, like a naughty schoolboy, I heard that I was interfering with good patient care and was disturbing the patient unnecessarily.

That happened thirteen years ago. If I were studying in a residency today, I would probably be permitted to tell a heart patient to give up eating red meat for a while. I'm afraid that in matters nutritional, the medical profession has not progressed at a very impressive rate.

Once during my residency a very distinguished professor from a mainland medical school gave a series of lectures on the treatment of diabetes. He and his colleagues had done extensive research, showing that diabetics could dramatically improve their condition by eating more carbohydrates, not less, according to the prevailing doctrine. Yet in not one of his lectures in Honolulu did that visiting authority consider the subject of diet as it is related to diabetes.

After his last lecture I stayed to ask him why he did not make that connection. He replied that it was an impractical subject to talk about, because people suffering from diabetes wouldn't change their diet anyway. But, I asked, "Didn't you do research that showed that some diabetics could be greatly improved by changing from a high fat to a high carbohydrate diet? And shouldn't doctors tell them about this good news?"

He admitted this. Then I asked, "Aren't you the head of the nutrition committee that recommends diets for the American Diabetes Association?"

To this, too, he said yes. The conversation ended when I said (very politely, because in those days I was a courteous youth), "I can't understand how you can allow people to think that the high-fat American diet is the only acceptable way to eat when the consequences for them will be illness and premature death." Giving me a patronizing smile, he turned away, without another word. And I—puzzled, no better instructed in the latest word about diabetes, but soon to be wiser in the proper conduct of physicians—wandered back to the wards.

In a matter of hours my Chief of Medicine called me again to his office to inform me once more that I was far too interested in diet and to urge me to be sensible about the practice of medicine in the good old American way. He also warned me that I was close to ending my residency sooner than I'd planned. Lest you think that he was a tyrant toward everyone under his control, let me declare that, in general, he was a reasonably decent man. In his dogmatic way, he was trying to set me straight. I like to think that he cared for me enough to worry about me.

Needless to say, I compromised my beliefs and principles by shutting my mouth for a while after that. Doing so was difficult for me, but I managed it, and I finished my residency. On a day near the end of the term, my Chief of Medicine called me in for a few parting words.

"John," he said, "you're a very good doctor, but I'm concerned that with your crazy ideas about diet, you won't be able to make a living and support your family. All you're going to do is collect a bunch of bums and hippies for patients." And they don't pay their doctor bills, he didn't need to add.

I remember that day very well. What I told him in reply went something like this: "I have to live with my conscience, doctor. I can't practice medicine as I did when I was a general practitioner on the island of Hawaii. I refuse to give my patients useless drugs or send them off for surgeries that do more harm than good." Fairly started, I continued: "I don't think that only bums and hippies will come to see me when I return to practice. I think people just like you will come, people who have good jobs and families, and who work hard. Successful people, who will be failing in one important part of their lives: their health. They'll be fat, they won't feel well, they'll be taking all kinds of medications, and they'll still run the risk of being hit with a health disaster. When they ask themselves why that's so, I'm going to be there ready with an answer. And I'm going to tell them that if they want to regain their health, then they'll have to change their diet and lifestyle. I believe that once they do that, they'll feel good and they'll look good. As every man, woman, and child in this world deserves to. And as *you* deserve too." (I refrained from poking him in his prospering belly.)

I don't suppose my Chief of Medicine was impressed. Besides, there was that other message he may have been trying to give me during our parting conversation. Succinctly put, it is this: *Don't practice medicine in ways the medical system isn't designed to accommodate or you won't be able to earn a living.* Unless I was willing to collect a group of patients who had to come back and see me every thirty days or so for their drug refills, I wouldn't be likely to develop a *successful* medical practice.

And yet I was the one, and not my despairing boss, who was right. Many "successful" people did come to see me. They wanted to know how to enjoy their lives without the strains caused by acute illnesses, chronic miseries, and that worst of intrusions, premature death, which was carrying off too many of their friends and relatives.

MY PERSONAL DIETARY CHANGE

In 1974, just before the birth of our first child, my wife Mary and I were invited to a vegetarian dinner at the home of Buzz Hughes, the man who first set me to thinking about the way my plantation patients were eating. The dishes his wife Susan prepared were attractively presented and didn't taste at all bad (as I was gallant enough to say), but, of course, that gratifying lump of solid meat and slick fat that I found so necessary to my satisfaction was conspicuously absent.

When we got home that night, the first thing I did was rush straight to the refrigerator, reach into the bottom bin, haul out two packages of thinly sliced turkey, and make myself two tall sandwiches with mayonnaise and all the trimmings. I didn't think I could survive till morning without this supplement to Susan's vegetarian dinner.

All the while, however, my education in the relation of diet to sickness was progressing. Each step in knowledge caused personal changes in the life that my family and I led. During the first year of my medical residency I came home from the library one night and told my wife that we would simply have to give up eating red meat. Just like that. It wasn't much of a jolt to Mary, but before long I was saying that chicken and fish had to go too. They are just as loaded with cholesterol as is beef, I preached. Brave woman that she is, Mary took it all in stride. She said she'd wanted to do a number of things with cheese anyway. I'm sure you can guess what I axed next. And after cheese, out went the vegetable oils. All of 'em.

Before long, the four basic food groups in our household became starchy vegetables, green and yellow vegetables, whole grains, and fruits. In less than a year we were transformed from sickly carnivores to healthy vegetarians. My wife soon noticed the difference in herself, and I, being the sicker person, noticed it even more. My stomach aches became sorrows of the past, and so did my constipation. I lost unnecessary weight, my skin became less oily, the cholesterol levels in my blood dropped precipitously, and I had more energy. You'd better believe I was startled and excited. I'd received an education at the dinner table that I couldn't get from textbooks in medicine.

SPREAD THE WORD

After finishing my training in Internal Medicine in 1978 I built a medical practice around what I increasingly came to regard as nutritional common sense. The physical transformations I observed in those patients who followed a healthy diet were so much more remarkable than were the rather feeble improvements that we had been able to achieve with the medications that I was stunned. The major problem I had was getting more people to make those same sensible changes in their diet and lifestyle—and make them be permanent.

Next, I set about spreading the word: the truth according to McDougall. I spoke to interested folks in groups of any size. And, in the early 1980s, I started to write books and discovered a very receptive readership who very much wanted to be slim, trim, energetic, and healthy. Then, in 1986, another dramatic change occurred.

I had long wanted to create a carefully organized program that would convert the majority of people from the standard American diet to the McDougall diet. In order to increase my percentage of success, I needed a live-in setting—a place where people could come for ten or twenty days, and eat the right foods and exercise daily and be lectured at a little bit, just enough so they'd understand what was happening in them and to them.

I found the place I was looking for when the St. Helena Hospital and Health Center in Deer Park, California, asked me to present the McDougall diet at their facilities.

THE MCDOUGALL PROGRAM AT ST. HELENA

The St. Helena Hospital and Health Center is situated in the beautiful Napa Valley of northern California. By bringing patients there, I am able to separate them from the distractions and temptations of their usual life—as well as the settled habits of "customary" behavior and thinking that they and their friends and relatives have accepted uncritically for too many years.

After I'd worked out all the kinks in the enterprise, I came up with a twelve-day program. Patients arrive at the center on a Sunday and for the next twelve days they are involved in a world of new ideas—including new ways to serve the many wonderful foods that most of us don't really know how to enjoy. From the first day our patients eat carefully prepared and mouth-watering meals featuring starches, vegetables, and fruits, all lightly seasoned. Alcohol and caffeine are not permitted, and people who want to smoke do so outside, on the grounds in the fresh air. For those twelve relaxing days our guests are immersed in an environment that is designed to restore good health to ailing bodies and worrying spirits alike.

This is the same twelve-day program that you'll be learning to follow as you read this book. You'll find that surprisingly easily you can do at home everything that the patients at St. Helena do in order to lose weight and regain lost health. Of course, you'll miss the companionship and the sense of a shared adventure that these people enjoy when they do the program together at St. Helena. But you, too, will gain the most important reward: the satisfaction that comes from improving your body day by day—and in noticing all the benefits that you will see and feel.

People in the program at St. Helena participate in talks, lectures, and question-and-answer periods, gaining the background information that's needed to understand why the plan is working for them. You'll find all that information in this book, and you'll be able to go back and refer to it any time you need to do so.

It may be possible for some of you to create satisfactory substitutes for certain aspects of the program that's offered at St. Helena. Certainly, if you can persuade friends or relatives to do the program with you that shared effort will help everyone. You'll be able to talk about your experiences together and encourage each other. But even if you're alone, you'll do just fine, if you can work up the slightest bit of interest in making yourself slimmer and healthier. Once you start, the rest is easy.

A CHANGE THAT YOU CAN SEE AND FEEL

For our patients at St. Helena, the results have been remarkable. In general, overweight patients have lost from two to eleven pounds in twelve days; people suffering from chronic indigestion have usually thrown away their bottles of antacid in less than a week, and patients with advanced atherosclerosis and consequent severe angina pains can take long walks without chest pains before they finish the program.

If you've paid attention to the newspapers during the past ten years, then you must have learned that high cholesterol levels translate into a vastly increased chance of developing heart attacks and strokes. The blood cholesterol levels of some of my patients have fallen 100 mg/dl in twelve days; the average decrease is 28 mg/dl. (Mg/dl stands for milligram per deciliter—or 100 milliliters. In the rest of this book, I'll not feel obliged to mention the actual units, but may simply say, for example, that a patient "lowered his cholesterol by 100 points.")

In twelve days, my patients' blood pressure readings have dropped by an average of 8 percent (for further explanation of blood pressure see Chapter 7 and the section on Hypertension in Part 3). That decrease is still more impressive when you realize two things. First, not all my patients have high blood pressure, and therefore will show little blood pressure change at all. Second, soon after starting

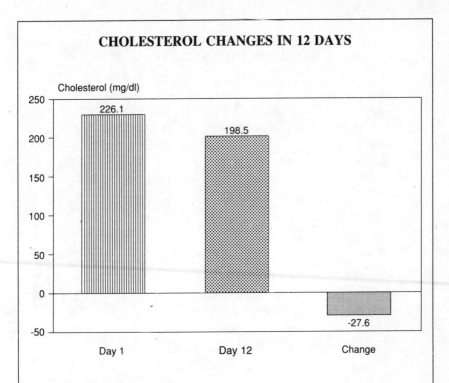

CHOLESTEROL CHANGES IN 12 DAYS

In twelve days on the McDougall Program the average drop in cholesterol is nearly 28 mg/dl, and many people reduce their levels over 100 mg/dl. (Data based on results of 180 participants of the twelve-day live-in McDougall Program at St. Helena Hospital and Health Center, Napa Valley, CA. Participants were not taking cholesterol-lowering medications.)

the Program, almost every patient who does have hypertension is taken off blood pressure medication, and yet blood pressure still continues to fall.

Results Like These Just Don't Happen in the Normal Practice of Medicine

The reason I know I can convince you that a starch-based diet is better for your body than anything you've ever eaten before is that

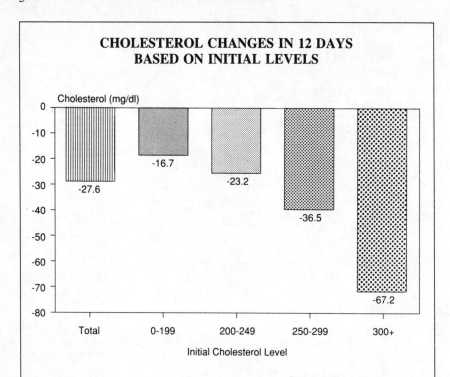

CHOLESTEROL CHANGES IN 12 DAYS
BASED ON INITIAL LEVELS

Cholesterol (mg/dl)

Total: -27.6
0-199: -16.7
200-249: -23.2
250-299: -36.5
300+: -67.2

Initial Cholesterol Level

The worse your cholesterol level when you start the McDougall Program the better the response you can expect at the end of 12 days. Notice that people with cholesterol levels over 300 mg/dl at the beginning dropped on the average over 67 mg/dl. (Data based on results of 180 participants of the twelve-day live-in McDougall Program at St. Helena Hospital and Health Center, Napa Valley, CA. Participants were not taking cholesterol-lowering medications.)

after twelve days you'll *feel* healthier. That prediction is based on the experiences of thousands of my relieved patients. Even young people feel markedly better on the McDougall Program. As for those who are older . . . well, all the clever arguments in creation can't equal the conviction a person experiences when he or she wakes up in the morning and says, "I feel wonderful! I feel better than I've felt in twenty years!" I've had the pleasure of hearing many, many people say exactly that to me.

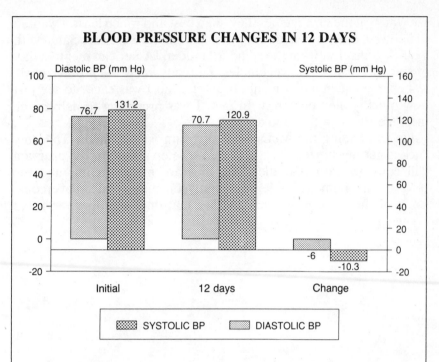

BLOOD PRESSURE CHANGES IN 12 DAYS

At the end of twelve days on the McDougall Program you can expect (on the average) an 8 percent reduction in your blood pressure—the top number, systolic pressure, down 10 mmHg; the bottom number, diastolic pressure, down 6 mmHg. (Data based on results of 180 participants of the twelve-day live-in McDougall Program at St. Helena Hospital and Health Center, Napa Valley, CA. At the beginning of the Program, approximately 20 percent of people were on blood pressure medications vs. almost none at the end.

A PROGRAM THAT WORKS

Working at St. Helena for the past three years has given me the opportunity to refine the program you're going to learn about in this book. When I first devised the McDougall Program I was looking for a system that was practical. I wanted to know how people responded to their new foods, and how best they could be coaxed away from the unwise habit of eating rich foods. I was curious to see which of the new recipes they liked best and which least. I wanted to know whether any negative physical changes were associated with a quick transition from the standard modern American diet to a diet of starches, fruits, and vegetables. I already knew the *positive* physical changes such a diet would promote, but I was eager to see just how quickly they occurred. In fact, I was preparing to deliver the message that's in this book.

Understanding the McDougall Program isn't difficult. The only trick is getting started. The easy step-by-step nature of the program will convince you that the difficulties are merely minor and the rewards are immeasurable. But first, you may need to overcome some of the same misunderstandings that once upon a time I had about "good" nutrition.

3

FOOD FACTS:

COMMON DIETARY

MYTHS DISPELLED

In the last chapter you met a naive young doctor who not too long ago had some very serious misconceptions about diet and health. In those days, I really believed that:

1. Diet had nothing to do with health and disease;
2. The human animal was a creature marvelously designed to survive on any kinds of food he was able to put in his mouth;
3. What little was written about nutrition and health was contradictory and confusing, and therefore undeserving of the time and attention of a very busy doctor.

And although the American Cancer Society, the National Cancer Institute, the American Heart Association, the National Academy of Sciences, the American Diabetic Association, and the U.S. Surgeon General have since reached the conclusion that diet is a leading cause of death and disease, little more is taught about nutrition to medical students now than when I was trained more than twenty years ago. Fortunately for me and for my patients, I discovered for myself the fundamental facts about nutrition. In this chapter I'd like to share some of that basic information with you.

THE NUTRITIONAL LINEUP

Nutrients are substances which are essential for the maintenance, repair, growth, and reproduction of all our body tissues. Our foods contain the following basic nutrients: carbohydrates, fats, proteins, vitamins, minerals, and water.

Carbohydrates, our body's most efficient source of energy and an essential component in the production of many structural and functional materials, are produced by plants in the process of photosynthesis. They are made of compounds of carbon, hydrogen, and oxygen called sugars or saccharides. Molecules of these simple sugars attach together to make long branching chains that are called *complex carbohydrates*. These large carbohydrate molecules are also commonly referred to as starch.

Once you eat them, digestion by intestinal enzymes disassembles these chains back into the simple sugars, which then pass easily through the intestinal wall into the bloodstream, where they journey to the body's tissues. Metabolic processes change these simple sugars into energy, which provides fuel for the body's activity.

Dietary fibers are also long chains of complex carbohydrates. Unlike starch molecules, these fibers resist digestion because of their chemical configurations. Therefore, most fibers eventually end up in the colon and form the bulk of your stool. Most people think that fibers are only the husks of grains and the long stringy components in fruits and vegetables, but actually, dietary fibers are present in all plant tissues. For example, after a potato is peeled, the white matter we eat has plenty of relatively indigestible fibers in it.

Fats, too, are complex molecules made up of carbon, oxygen, and hydrogen. Although they are not as easily digested as sugars are, fats are sources of energy and they provide important structural materials for building different components of the human body. Fats are divided into two categories: *saturated fats* (solid at room temperature), found mostly in animal tissues, and *unsaturated fats* (liquid), found mostly in plant tissues. Most fats can be synthesized by our own bodies from carbohydrates as they are needed. The fats that we can synthesize are said to be nonessential because they are not necessary ingredients in our diet. The only fats we cannot synthesize for ourselves are a few unsaturated fats. They must be provided to us, ready-made, in our foods and therefore are called essential fats.

Proteins provide the raw materials for a large part of the functional and structural components of our bodies. Only as a last resort are they used as a source of energy. The building blocks that make up all proteins are called amino acids. Various combinations of the same twenty-two amino acids, put together as are the letters of the alphabet that can form a whole dictionary of words with different meanings, make all of the proteins in nature. Proteins are found in all foods derived from animals and plants, unless they have been removed or altered by refining processes. Only eight of the twenty-two amino acids are essential to us, because they cannot be made in human metabolism. These eight essential amino acids must be present in sufficient quantities in our food for us to enjoy good health.

Water makes up a large part of our foods. Although it yields no energy, for many reasons water is an essential element for life. It is not just a passive solvent in which salts, compounds, and gasses interact; water participates actively in forming building blocks of cells and is the environment in which cells live. Approximately 60 percent of body weight is water.

Because the four nutrients discussed above—carbohydrates, fats, proteins, and water—make up the largest portion of any foodstuff by weight, they are often referred to as *macronutrients*. Our foods also contain two *micronutrients*—vitamins and minerals—which make up only a tiny percentage of our food by weight.

Vitamins are organic compounds that are synthesized for the most part only by plants and bacteria. Humans and most large animals can synthesize vitamin D (with the help of sunlight), and some animal species can make vitamin C (ascorbic acid). Thus, our supply of vitamins must come from plant foods and our own bowel bacteria. *Vita* means life, and, as the name indicates, vitamins are essential for our existence. Without adequate amounts, disease can develop.

Minerals are also micronutrients, but they come from inorganic matter, primarily the earth. Their presence in adequate amounts in our foods is also essential for our good health. They participate in thousands of metabolic reactions that must take place throughout the body. For instance, iron in the enzyme hemoglobin helps transport oxygen in our red blood cells. Some minerals are important elements in our structural material. Calcium, for example, is a large part of bones and teeth.

Our foods also contain various *non-nutrients*, substances that are not necessary for life or good health. Many of these substances, such as cholesterol, pesticides, herbicides, and additives, present real threats to our health. Even though these non-nutrients make up a small amount by weight of our foods, their health significance can be great, causing problems such as heart disease, cancer and allergies.

THE BEST SOURCES
OF THE BASIC NUTRIENTS

Carbohydrates

Carbohydrates are made by plants and stored in their leaves, stems, roots, and fruits. Plant foods contain both simple and complex carbohydrates in various amounts. Fruits are often more than 90 percent carbohydrate, but most of their carbohydrates are the sweet-tasting simple forms of carbohydrate, such as glucose and fructose. Green and yellow vegetables store most of their calories as complex carbohydrates, but since they contain very few total calories the amount of complex carbohydrate they provide in the diet is small. Whole grains (rice, corn) and the whole grain flours (wheat, rye) and whole grain pastas (wheat, soba) made from them, tubers (potatoes, yams), legumes (beans, peas), and winter squashes (acorn, hubbard) contain large quantities of complex carbohydrates and thus are known as starches. Rice, corn, and other grains and potatoes typically store about 80 percent of their calories in the form of complex carbohydrates. Beans, peas, and lentils are approximately 70 percent complex carbohydrates.

Starches contain sufficient calories to easily meet the energy requirements of the active person, and they are abundant in the proteins (with all their essential amino acids), essential fats, fibers, and minerals required to meet our daily dietary needs. Many starches, such as the maligned potato, have a full complement of vitamins as well. (Grains and legumes need the help of fruits or green and yellow vegetables in order to provide adequate vitamins A and C.)

You have probably heard that marathon runners and other endurance athletes "load up" on carbohydrates before an event, devouring large meals of spaghetti, rice, and potatoes in order to store energy-providing carbohydrates for the long race. Carbohydrate-loading several times a day will give you too the energy to race through your busy life.

The only food from animals in which a carbohydrate is found in significant amounts is milk, which contains a simple sugar called

PERCENT OF CALORIES FOUND AS CARBOHYDRATES IN VARIOUS FOODS:

Almonds	13	Oatmeal	69
Beans (kidney)	72	Oranges	88
Beef	0	Peanuts	10
Bread (whole wheat)	76	Peanut Butter	10
Brussels Sprouts	70	Pork	0
Cabbage	77	Potatoes	83
Carrots	36	Rice (brown)	87
Cheddar Cheese	2	Spaghetti (whole wheat)	81
Chicken	0	Sugar	100
Corn	80	Sweet Potatoes	92
Eggs	2	Tofu	12
Grapefruit	90	Tomatoes	76
Lobster	6	Turkey	0
Milk (whole)	30		

When we hear or read the word *sugar*, most of us think of granular white table sugar. Unlike the simple sugars found in ripe fruit, this kind of sugar should be eaten only in limited quantities. After the refining process, it contains no fibers, proteins, essential fats, vitamins, or minerals. It is purely concentrated sugar. Nothing could better deserve the descriptive term "empty calories," because calories are all it provides. Although refined sugar can provide energy, too much refined sugar in the diet can lead to tooth decay, contribute to obesity, and raise triglycerides. A nutritional imbalance, weakening the body's defense and repair systems making us susceptible to disease processes from infection to cancer, may result when "empty calories" make up a substantial part of the diet.

---

lactose. However, lactose cannot be digested by most adults,* and consequently, when they drink milk, they suffer assorted evidences of indigestion, such as diarrhea, stomach cramps, and hurtful amounts of gas.

---

* Lactose intolerance is found in 90 percent of adult Asians and blacks, 60 percent of Mexicans and Eskimos, and 20 percent of whites.

In the sense of total amount of carbohydrates in their diet, Americans eat far too few calories from this source—only about 40 percent of their diet is carbohydrate. To make things worse the kinds of carbohydrates commonly eaten are mostly "empty calories" in the form of white sugar, corn syrup, and fructose. A healthy diet, like the McDougall diet, is more than 80 percent carbohydrate from nutritious foods—starches, vegetables and fruits.

Surmount the Anti-Starch Myth

MYTH: *Starches will make me fat.*

FACT: Of all the misconceptions I once held about nutrition, the idea that starches are fattening was the easiest for me to correct. Let's look at some of our commonest starches. A large-sized potato yields 150 calories, a cup of rice gives 200. By contrast, two tablespoons of mayonnaise means 200 calories, a cup of grated Cheddar cheese is 450 and a cup of creamed chipped beef is 420. In order to function well, the average woman needs to eat foods that will give her about 2200 calories in a day, the average man about 3000. Can you calculate how much rice you'd have to eat each day in order to gain weight? Once you complete that calculation, you'll know why there are so many slender Chinese in China. As for potatoes, the only way to gain weight from them is to cover them with butter, melted cheese, sour cream, or bacon bits.

Fibers

Fibers are made only by plants and found only in vegetable foods. There is no fiber in beef, pork, chicken, lobster, cheese, egg, or other animal-derived foods.

An Outdated Myth Bites the (Saw) Dust

MYTH: *Fiber is a waste component in foods.*

FACT: Once upon a time, fiber was removed from whole grains and discarded because it was considered to be a valueless substance.

GRAMS OF CRUDE FIBER* PRESENT IN PORTIONS OF FOOD THAT YIELD 100 CALORIES:

Beans (kidney)	1.5	Peanuts (with skin)	0.8
Bread (whole wheat)	0.7	Peanuts (without skin)	0.3
Brussels Sprouts	4.4	Potatoes (with or	
Cabbage	4.3	without skin)	0.6
Carrots	2.3	Radishes	4.1
Cauliflower	3.7	Rice (brown)	0.2
Corn	0.7	Scallions	2.0
Green Beans	4.0	Soybeans	1.4
Grapefruit	0.8	Spaghetti (whole wheat)	0.6
Kale	3.4	Sweet Potatoes	0.6
Oatmeal	0.3	Tofu	0.1
Oranges	0.9	Tomatoes	2.3
Peas	2.4	Yams	0.9

* Crude fiber values are not as relevant as dietary fiber, but data for dietary fiber is sparse.

It's still being processed out of many of the foods you buy from supermarket shelves, but the industrial giants that commit this robbery are no longer operating under the benign delusion that their actions are without consequences. They are well aware that the refining processes that produce white flour and white rice remove most of the fiber from these foods (as well as many of the nutrients) and render them less fit for human consumption. And nowadays the big companies are happy to sell you the separated fibers in packages labeled "bran" or even—so daringly—"dietary fiber." In the past, however, nutritionists and food manufacturers genuinely could not see the value in fiber, because it provided neither calories nor any recognized nutrients. In fact, most dietary fiber does not remain in the body, but only passes through it.

Even so, fiber has many positive effects on your health. Most noticeably, since it absorbs water, it increases the size and ease of passage of your stools. Fiber also binds and removes heart-disease-causing cholesterol as well as certain other chemicals that are known to be cancer-causing. Because fibers in the intestinal tract tie up some of the sugars we eat, releasing them only slowly into the bloodstream, they help to lower and stabilize blood sugar levels— a great benefit for diabetics. Incidentally, the nondigestible chains of complex sugars that make up these ingredients we call fiber are microscopic; don't think of them as if they were the bristles of a brush scraping the lining of your intestines clean as they journey through the digestive tract.

A diet including lots of plant foods provides about 60 grams of fiber daily. The typical American diet—loaded with animal products and refined foods—is woefully fiber-deficient and provides only about 10 grams of dietary fiber a day. This is why a significant proportion of the American population is chronically constipated. You cannot pass a comfortably large stool when your diet condemns you to turning out rabbit pellets for your bowel movements.

Check your high-fiber breads. In a misguided effort to return fibers to our foods, some manufacturers have added wood fiber from sawdust, known as cellulose, to white bread. However, wood fiber does not have the beneficial properties of food fibers such as lowering cholesterol and blood sugar. Even the movement of the fecal material is *not* normal with wood fiber.

Fats

Fats are abundant in foods from plants as well as in those from animals. Essential fats are made only by plants; approximately one third of all of the fats found in plants are of the essential kinds. Herbivorous animals, having eaten plant foods, do store some of the essential fats in their tissues, but the amount varies, depending on their diet.

As long as the need for an essential fat is met by eating plant foods, the likelihood of having too little fat in the diet is never a problem. On the contrary, too much fat is our national health hazard. In the average American diet, 45 to 55 percent of the calories will be from fats. The American Heart Association, the American Cancer Society, and the American Diabetic Association now recommend eating 30 percent fats or less. These recommendations are tempered, however, by the recognition that people are creatures of habit and will not willingly lower the amount of fats in their diet (so why ask too much of them?). Uncompromised by fear of asking too much from you, I recommend a diet in which not more than 10 percent of the calories consumed daily are derived from fat. Here I'm assuming that you want to get a lot of good health out of the efforts you will put into improving your diet.

PERCENT OF CALORIES FOUND AS FATS IN VARIOUS FOODS:

Almonds	75	Milk (whole)	49
Beans (kidney)	2	Oatmeal	15
Beef	74	Oranges	4
Bread (whole wheat)	8	Peanuts	72
Brussels Sprouts	9	Peanut Butter	72
Cabbage	6	Pork	58
Carrots	4	Potatoes	1
Cheddar Cheese	73	Rice (brown)	5
Chicken (skinned)	39	Spaghetti (whole wheat)	5
Corn	8	Sweet Potatoes	2
Eggs	65	Tofu	54
Grapefruit	2	Tomatoes	8
Lobster	6	Turkey (skinned)	32

Don't Swallow Myths About Fats

MYTH: *Vegetable oil is a health food.*

FACT: This myth has recently gained wide acceptance in the popular culture because unsaturated fats, which most vegetable oils consist of,* do not contain cholesterol and will also *lower* cholesterol in your blood, thereby reducing your risk of heart disease, whereas saturated fats, which butter and lard and the other animal fats consist of, raise your cholesterol level. Sadly, the myth that vegetable oil is health food isn't true. Although most vegetable oils do have a beneficial effect on your cholesterol level because of the unsaturated fats they contain (and the saturated fats they lack), choosing between dropping some butter or pouring some olive oil into your frying pan is, nutritionally speaking, like choosing whether you want to be shot or hanged.

Here's why. *All fats*—saturated and unsaturated—*are involved in the growth of certain kinds of cancer cells.* Scientific research begun in the 1930s on animals has consistently shown that a higher consumption of fats will produce a higher incidence of cancer. What's worse, the unsaturated fats in such highly touted vegetable oils as

* Coconut oil, palm oil, and cocoa butter contain large amounts of saturated fats. In addition, any vegetable oil that has been "hydrogenated" or "partially hydrogenated" (to increase the oil's stability and shelf life) has been altered to become more saturated.

corn oil, safflower oil, and olive oil, and the margarines made from them, are the fats that most promote the growth of cancer. They're much better at this double-crossing deal than are the saturated fats that are so bad for your arteries and heart.

Moreover, a large amount of any type of fat affects your circulation and energy level. What happens immediately after you eat a meal high in vegetable or animal fats? First, you suffer a metabolic slowdown. Surely, you've noticed how after a big business lunch you often want to take a two-hour nap? That's because after you've eaten a meal high in any type of fat, your blood cells stick together in clumps. These clumps crowd your blood vessels so that the flow of blood gradually slows down, and many smaller blood vessels are actually blocked. As a result, tissues and organs receive a decreased amount of essential nutrients and oxygen. Chest pain (angina) may occur in patients with heart disease, blood pressure rises due to increasing resistance to the flow of blood, and all the organs, including the brain, function less efficiently. Naturally, you feel sluggish and dull—you would rather sleep than think or work. Vegetable oils cause just as severe blood sludging and clumping as animal-derived fats do.

And finally, vegetable oils, like animal fats, are also extremely fattening because of their high calorie content, and they can make the skin and hair oily. All in all, they're a bad bargain in any shape, at any time.

MYTH: *Tofu is a perfectly healthy meat and dairy substitute.*

FACT: People in search of better health often replace meat and dairy products with soybeans and products derived from soybeans such as tofu, soy cheese, soy milk, miso, and tempeh. Soybeans are about one third protein, one third fat, and one third carbohydrate. Thus, though they are indeed an excellent (even excessive) source of protein, they contain far too much fat for regular use by most people, especially anyone trying to lose weight or recover from an illness.

Tofu, the most popular soyfood, is even a little worse than the original soybean. To make tofu, soybeans are ground, then filtered, separating the liquid from the fiber. The liquid is then solidified into blocks of tofu, which is now one half fat (54 percent) and deficient in fiber (from 1.4 grams to 0.1 grams of fiber per 100 calories from soybeans to tofu). Obviously, tofu is a rich, high-fat, low-fiber food that should be used sparingly.

Soyfoods are not the only high-fat plant foods to watch out for. Others are seeds (85 percent fat), nuts (80 percent fat), avocados (88 percent fat), coconuts (87 percent fat), and olives (96 percent fat). If you know any vegetarians who are overweight and greasy-skinned, you can assume that their diet is filled with these high-fat plant foods—hardly a good representation for the health benefits of vegetables.

If you are in good health and you want to include a small amount of these high-fat plant foods in your diet as special treats, there will likely be no significant adverse consequences. But *special* is the key word here. Children, pregnant women, athletes, and people needing to eat more calories may find these concentrated-calorie foods helpful in moderation.

Proteins

Proteins are abundant in foods derived from both plants and animals. The eight essential and fourteen nonessential amino acids are all found in plants in generous amounts. Animals, such as cows, chickens, and pigs eat plants and then use the essential and nonessential amino acids they have eaten to build various tissues, such as muscles, which is why meats are rich in proteins.

Protein deficiency is almost unknown in humans worldwide, but protein excess is a real problem in developed societies. When the protein content of the diet exceeds 15 percent of calories consumed, the body's liver and kidneys are burdened with the task of removing the excessive amounts of proteins. Under this strain, the liver and kidneys enlarge and the physiology of the kidneys changes, causing the loss of significant amounts of calcium from our bones into the urine. Foods from animals lead to this problem not only because they are higher in protein content than are most vegetable foods, but also because the proteins they contain cause more calcium loss than do equal amounts of vegetable proteins. (This is an effect of sulfur-containing amino acids, which are more plentiful in meats.) Thus, kidney beans (which are 26 percent protein) are much easier on the body than is beef (which is 26 percent protein).

PERCENT OF CALORIES FOUND AS PROTEINS IN VARIOUS FOODS:

Almonds	12	Milk (whole)	21
Beans (kidney)	26	Oatmeal	16
Beef	26	Oranges	8
Bread (whole wheat)	16	Peanuts	18
Brussels Sprouts	21	Peanut Butter	18
Cabbage	17	Pork	42
Carrots	10	Potatoes	11
Cheddar Cheese	25	Rice (brown)	8
Chicken (skinned)	61	Spaghetti (whole wheat)	14
Corn	12	Sweet Potatoes	6
Eggs	33	Tofu	34
Grapefruit	8	Tomatoes	16
Lobster	88	Turkey (skinned)	68

Forget the Myth Proteins Are Found Only in Animal Foods

MYTH: *If I ate only fruits, vegetables, and starches, I'd soon become protein-deficient.*

FACT: It's actually extremely hard for anyone to become protein-deficient. Unless you gave up eating altogether, I don't see how you'd ever manage to do it. Virtually all unrefined foods are loaded with proteins. Rice is 8 percent protein, oranges 8 percent, potatoes 11 percent, beans 26 percent. We don't need large intakes of proteins: This is demonstrated by the fact that we drink human breast milk (which is 5 percent protein) only in infancy, at the time in life when we are growing fastest and require more protein in our diet than we ever will need again. The unfortunate reality is that most Americans consume enormous quantities of unnecessary—and maybe excess—proteins, which must be excreted through the kidneys, harming them and the rest of the body in the process.

Another Popular Protein Myth Is Debunked

MYTH: *Vegetable foods are not complete protein.*

FACT: You might once have learned that "complete proteins," with sufficient amounts of all amino acids, are not found in vegetable foods, or that you have to make careful combinations of foods such as beans with rice in order to make the protein complete. Fortunately, scientific studies have plainly debunked this complicated nonsense.

Nature designed and synthesized our foods complete with all the essential nutrients for human life long before they reach the dinner table. All the essential and nonessential amino acids are represented in *single unrefined starches* such as rice, corn, wheat, and potatoes in amounts in excess of every individual's needs, even if they are endurance athletes or weight lifters.

Common sense tells you this would have to be true for the human race to have survived on this planet. Throughout history the food-providers went out in search of enough rice or potatoes to feed their families. Matching beans with rice was not their concern. We have only the hunger to relate to food; there is no drive to tell us to mix and match protein sources to make a more ideal amino acid pattern. There is no need for such a drive because there is no more ideal protein and amino acid composition than that found in natural starches.

Vitamins

Vitamins are synthesized by plants and by some kinds of bacteria. Eleven of the thirteen recognized vitamins are made by plants (A, B_1, B_2, B_3, B_6, Pantothenic Acid, Biotin, Folic Acid, C, E, K). The other two vitamins are vitamin D, which your body synthesizes with the aid of sunlight, and vitamin B_{12}, which is made by bacteria. Most vegetables and fruits are plentiful in the eleven vitamins they make. Legumes and whole grains are low in vitamin A and C. Although storage, cooking, freezing, and canning all rob foods of vitamins, nature endowed these gifts so well that vitamin deficiency among Americans is almost unknown.

Don't Worry About the Vitamin B_{12} Myth

MYTH: *If I don't eat meat, I'll develop a vitamin B_{12} deficiency, since B_{12} is found only in animals.*

FACT: This is the only myth discussed in this chapter that has a smidgen of truth in it. Vitamin B_{12} is synthesized by some bacteria and a few species of algae, and animals store it in their tissues. Since plants do not make or contain B_{12}, theoretically you could develop a deficiency if you follow an all-vegetable diet. (Certain fermented soybean and yeast products do contain B_{12}, but sometimes the amount is not dependable.)

B_{12} deficiency is rare but not unknown. Two kinds have been observed. The more common is due to malabsorption of this vitamin as a consequence of diseased conditions of the stomach or of the small intestine. It has nothing to do with the amount of B_{12} present in the diet, so it is treated with injections of B_{12}. The other kind of B_{12} deficiency is found very rarely among people who take essentially no B_{12} in their diet. Less than a dozen cases of this type of B_{12} deficiency have been reported among the tens of millions of vegetarians in the world. One reason it's so uncommon is that B_{12} is made by the bacteria naturally present in the human mouth and intestines.

However, it's better to be safe than sorry, and I'm sure that neither you nor I would want you to be the thirteenth person to get B_{12} deficiency because you've turned vegetarian. Therefore, I suggest that after you've been off animal foods for a few years, you take a B_{12} vitamin pill periodically. The average American has stored so much B_{12} in his body's tissues, and the vitamin is used so slowly, that twenty to thirty years must pass before you run out of it. But, to avoid the very small risk of this deficiency, use B_{12} supplements after you've been off meats for three years, or if you're pregnant or a nursing mother. Five micrograms per day, which is found in most nutritional supplements, provides generously for vitamin B_{12} dietary needs. Those who prefer not to take supplements can have their serum B_{12} levels checked annually to be assured of adequate body stores (an adequate level is greater than 180 pg/ml).

Minerals

All minerals, including calcium, sodium, iron, and zinc, originate in the earth. Plants absorb them in water solutions through their roots and store them as components of complex substances in their roots, stalks, leaves, and fruits. Therefore, foods from plants contain an abundance of minerals. People, cows, horses, apes, and other herbivorous animals then eat the plants and receive these minerals.

The more vegetables you eat, the more minerals you consume. Grandmother told you that years ago.

Minerals present, and sometimes concentrated, in the outer coat of a grain seed are often removed by refining processes. Realizing the seriousness of possible mineral deficiencies being caused by refining flours, rice, and other grain derivatives, manufacturers will often enrich their products by coating them with the same vitamins and minerals taken away in the refining mills. However, adding a few vitamins and minerals back does not return the food to its original quality. Therefore, you should choose the unrefined natural products.

MILLIGRAMS OF IRON IN 100 CALORIES OF FOOD:

Asparagus	3.0	Egg	1.3
Bananas	0.4	Fish (salmon)	0.4
Beans (white)	2.6	Kale	5.8
Beef	2.0	Milk	0.1
Broccoli	3.4	Pears	0.4
Carrots	1.5	Rice (brown)	0.5
Cheese	0.1	Rice (white)	0.2
Cherries	1.7	Rice (enriched)	0.9
Chicken	0.6	Yogurt	0.1

When we think of sodium, we usually think of table salt, which is the most commonly used seasoning in the world. Although sodium is an essential nutrient in small amounts, too much sodium chloride has been linked to hypertension, stomach cancer, and edema. Excess sodium is especially burdensome for people with heart, liver, and kidney disease. Therefore, use of table salt should be limited. 2000 milligrams of sodium a day is considered safe for a healthy adult; ½ teaspoon of table salt equals about 1150 milligrams. Most people on the McDougall diet can sprinkle ½ teaspoon daily over the surface of their foods if they choose—providing a familiar flavor without harm. It has been estimated that the average American eats about 5000 milligrams a day!

The Milk Myth Topples

MYTH: *My bones and teeth will soon be weakened by a lack of calcium if I don't drink milk.*

FACT: The National Dairy Council would like you to think that without milk you'd soon become calcium-deficient and little more than a quaking mass of jellylike flesh, but the truth is almost the opposite. Where does a cow or an elephant get the calcium needed to grow its huge bones? From plants, of course. *Only plants.* And that's where you can get yours, too. People in Asia and Africa who consume no milk products after they're weaned from their mother's breast grow perfectly healthy skeletons in the normal size for their race. A consistent conclusion published in the scientific literature is clear: *Calcium deficiency of dietary origin is unknown in humans.*

Dairy products contain large amounts of animal proteins. This excess protein removes calcium from the body by way of the kidneys. Knowing the physiological effects on calcium metabolism of eating excess protein explains why societies with the highest intakes of meat and dairy products—the United States, England, Israel, Finland, and Sweden—also show the highest rates of osteoporosis, the disease of bone-thinning. Osteoporosis is rare in Asian and African countries, where meat and milk products (animal proteins and calcium) are a much smaller portion of the people's diet.

Non-Nutrients

Non-nutrients that are harmful to our health are most abundant in animal products. Pesticides, herbicides, and chemicals wasted from modern technical processes are distributed throughout the world, and are found now even in the deepest parts of the oceans. They cannot be totally avoided, but the amounts of them we consume can be markedly reduced if we eat things "low on the food chain." These polluting chemicals appear first on vegetables and grains, which then are eaten by fish, cows, pigs, chickens, etc. Most pollutants are fat-soluble, which means they are absorbed and concentrated in fats. Therefore, the fats of animals that consume these harmful substances concentrate the chemicals in amounts thousands of times greater than was originally present in the plants upon which they fed. When you eat starches, vegetables, and fruits, chances are good that you will eat much smaller amounts of these hazardous substances.

Additives intended to preserve, stabilize, flavor, and color are found extensively in processed foods ranging from breath mints and candies to soda crackers and breakfast cereals. Growth hormones are found in most red meats. Dairy products and poultry flesh can contain residues of several antibiotics. Natural plant foods are free of these additives.

Perhaps the most notorious non-nutrient is cholesterol. Plants do not contain cholesterol; only animal foods do. Actually, the human body makes cholesterol itself. Cholesterol is a fatlike, waxy substance that serves several important purposes in our bodies. It is used in making cell walls, sex hormones, vitamin D, and bile acids. We can't live without it. But our bodies can synthesize all that we need of it. Therefore, the cholesterol we get in food is not a nutrient. We don't need to eat it. When we eat more of it than we excrete, usually cholesterol is deposited along the lining of the arteries, forming arterial plaques, creating the condition known as atherosclerosis. These plaques, as they evolve, can block circulation of the blood, eventually leading to heart disease and strokes, two of the most common complications of atherosclerosis.

Don't Swallow the Red Meat Myth

MYTH: *I can lower my cholesterol level by eating chicken and fish instead of beef and pork.*

FACT: Virtually all animal foods we eat contain exceedingly high levels of cholesterol. In the popular notion of what causes heart disease, red meat has been getting a raw deal. Consider the milligrams of cholesterol in a 3½ ounce portion of the following foods:

Beef	85	Pork	90
Chicken (white meat, skinned)	85	Smelt	89
Lamb	82	Trout	73
Lobster	72	Turkey	82
Haddock	74	Veal	88
Mackerel	75	All plant foods	0

All these muscle foods contain relatively comparable amounts of cholesterol. Why shouldn't they? A muscle is a muscle, whether it flips a tail, flaps a wing, or moves a leg. They are totally deficient in fibers and carbohydrates, but high in fats or proteins, and high in cholesterol. Being near the top in the food chain, they are all usually contaminated with disconcerting (and often illegal) amounts of pesticides, herbicides, drugs, and other toxic chemicals introduced into our environment by agribusinesses and industries. Other commonly consumed foods which have very high levels of cholesterol are eggs, lobster, shrimp, crab, and liver.

How did the idea get started that one should stay away from eating red meat and eat poultry and fish instead? The justification for this notion is that red meat contains approximately twice as much saturated fats, which promote the production of cholesterol in the body. However, the effect of all these meats is pretty much the same. Studies show that when beef and pork are exchanged for fish and chicken, blood cholesterol levels hardly change. Doctors and nutritionists well read in the scientific literature are well aware of this fact.

NUTRITIONAL CONCLUSIONS

Foods That Threaten Our Health

Meats, fish, eggs, dairy products, lard, vegetable oils, and refined foods all fail as health-supporting foods for human nutrition. The fact that they are lacking in complex carbohydrates, fibers, many vitamins, and essential minerals is a serious concern, but one can usually obtain enough of the necessary nutrients in other foods to survive. The problem is that these foods contain excessive amounts of the potentially good nutrients, and harmful quantities of fundamentally unhealthy non-nutrients. A diet centering around these foods continuously assails us with imbalances and excesses of many kinds, and the body soon reacts with signs of distress that we recognize as diseases.

Foods from animals contain excessive quantities of fats, which can lead to obesity, heart disease, and cancer. The burden of coping with surplus proteins damages the kidneys, liver, and bones. As for processed and refined foods, they are at best nutritionally empty;

at worst, they supply unhealthy oils and large amounts of salt and sugar which tax the body without benefiting it.

By the time they're thirty years of age, most Americans are already suffering serious effects from overconsumption of animal products and refined foods. Many Americans never reach their fifties and sixties—they've succumbed to early death by diet-caused diseases.

Foods That Support Good Health

Starches (rice, corn, potatoes, beans, pasta), green and yellow vegetables, and fruits provide us with large quantities of clean-burning, high-energy "fuel"—carbohydrates. Those sensible foodstuffs furnish us with all the essential fats we need, the ones that our bodies cannot synthesize from carbohydrates. They give us ample, but usually not excessive, quantities of proteins. They provide large quantities of fibers that help prevent or cure our intestinal problems. They supply us with all our vitamins except vitamin D, which we ourselves synthesize, and vitamin B_{12}, which we can obtain from natural bacteria in our bodies or by supplementing with pills. They offer abundant sources for the minerals we require. Just as important as what they provide is what they withhold: Starches, vegetables, and fruits contain the smallest possible quantities of undesirable non-nutrients.

The Optimum, Health-Supporting Diet

By now it should be clear: A healthful diet should be based around starches—which contain all the calories an active person needs, plus adequate but not excessive amounts of carbohydrates, proteins, essential fats, minerals, and vitamins—supplemented with fresh or frozen fruits and vegetables.

Why is a plant-based diet so healthy for humans? Because from the beginning our bodies were designed for such fare. Consider the animals. You must have observed the great variations in the way they eat. Have you ever known your cat to dine on a carrot? Did you ever hear of a horse that liked steak? Our fellow creatures don't choose their meals by accident; their bodies are superbly adapted by evolution to particular types of foods.

Carnivorous animals—meat eaters—have claws and sharp teeth for tearing apart raw meat. Herbivores—plant eaters—have hands for gathering foods (unless they're hoofed animals), and they have flat teeth (resembling most of yours and mine) for grinding grains, fruits, and vegetables. They have (as do we) a long intestine, which keeps the food in the body long enough to allow it to digest the raw materials that release the nutrients that are present in plants. Carnivores, on the other hand, have short intestinal tracts that rapidly digest flesh and excrete the putrescent remnants. Carnivores also pant to cool their bodies, and lap water when they drink. We, and other plant eaters, sweat to cool ourselves and sip water. Very significantly, we can excrete only a small quantity of cholesterol from our bodies because of the design of our livers, whereas carnivores have an unlimited capacity to excrete ingested cholesterol, thereby preventing it from clogging their arteries. All carnivorous animals synthesize vitamin C, ascorbic acid. Humans, guinea pigs, and monkeys do not; they are obliged to obtain this vitamin from their diet. Fortunately, although vitamin C is essentially not present in meats or dairy products, it is abundant in plant foods.

Furthermore, look at the eating patterns of human beings worldwide. Our rich American diet of meats and dairy products is an eccentricity, a glaring example of conspicuous consumption that is all but suicidal. In almost every region of the world, a starch-based diet has been the norm throughout history. In Asia, the staple is rice; in New Guinea, sweet potatoes; in South America and Africa, different grains and beans; among the Indians of North and Central America, corn; and in Europe, before the modern era, breads made from unrefined flours prepared from many kinds of grains.

Our state of health is intimately related to eating the foods that nature has designed us to eat. Obviously, however, we are not fragile creatures. Human beings are survivors—and many of us can live for quite a long time on cigarettes, whiskey, and greasy fast foods. But for these foolishnesses we pay the penalty, sooner or later. I hope that you're tired of testing your limits of survival, and that that's why you're reading this book.

THE BIGGEST MYTH OF ALL

I've had patients who assume I must be crying wolf when I talk about the importance of a good diet, because (they say) overall

America is such a healthy society and its citizens are getting healthier all the time. If you believe that myth, then you may see no reason at all to make improvements in the way you live and eat. That's why the statistics must be closely examined. "Lying with statistics," as someone said long ago, is a favorite game among people out to make a fast buck.

If I were to tell these patients that in a sense we're living a whole lot worse than people did a hundred years ago, they'd have a very commonsensical reply. "Don't you know that when our grandparents were young, people's life expectancies were much shorter than they are today? How can you say that we're doing worse than ever?"

I have two reasons to support my belief. First, the difference in life expectancy doesn't mean exactly what it sounds like it does. Second, for the most part we're suffering from entirely different diseases than people did in times past.

If you look at the vital statistics for the period from 1870 to 1970, you'll find that although our life expectancy today is twenty-three years longer than it was one hundred years ago, that's largely because of decreases in rates of infant mortality and maternal death during childbirth. In 1870 the infant mortality rate was almost fifteen times what it is today, and the increase in life expectancy I'm quoting is an increase in life expectancy *at birth*. But what if you're not an infant anymore and you're past the age of childbearing? This is where the nasty surprise comes in. If you were over the age of forty-five, your life expectancy in 1970 was only *six years* greater than it was in 1870. Statistics, alas, often cover up simple truth under mountains of misleading figures.

You may find this conclusion hard to understand. During the last seventy-five years, scientists have developed vaccines and antibiotics that can save us from typhoid fever, cholera, smallpox, yellow fever, bubonic plague, most venereal diseases, tuberculosis, and most of the other epidemic killers. These are very possibly the greatest discoveries in the history of Western medicine, and naturally they caused a very significant decrease in the general death rate. Improvements in public sanitation and the adoption of sterile procedures in hospitals were other important factors in the war against germs. The result should have been a far greater rise in life expectancy for people over age forty-five than six years. Unfortunately, during that same period Americans changed the way they ate. The result: a radical increase in heart disease, stroke, cancer, and diabetes; a radical shortening in life expectancy.

If you haven't thought about it, you may find this a startling bit of news. People ate *differently* in the past. Only the aristocrats gorged themselves on meat and cheese. The vast majority of people were either farmers or workers. Unless they were poor and starving, the food they ate was simple and healthy—starchy vegetables, whole grains, fresh fruits and vegetables. And the breads our ancestors ate were made from unrefined whole grains. Meat was something they ate only in small amounts, once or twice a week, if they could afford to buy it. In those days, there were no Big Macs for the average man. Even cheese was a bit of a luxury. Milk was the food they breast-fed infants; milk from cows and goats was devoted to feeding their own young or swine in order to ready them for market. As for the plethora of fatty, greasy, processed, chemicalized, sweet and salty garbage that clogs the supermarket aisles and the fast-food drive-ins nowadays, none of it had even been invented. Heavens, those people in the old days were lucky!

But soon after World War I came the dramatic changes, the biggest changes in human diet since life began on this planet. This change in diet has had an enormous significance for human health and appearance. Fortunately, with the McDougall Program, you can easily and safely back out of the problems modern man has raised for himself, and you can do it without feeling any hunger or the slightest distress.

4

WHAT THE
PROGRAM INVOLVES

In this chapter I will outline exactly what the McDougall Program involves, including specific guidelines for eating and advice about exercising. Then in the next five chapters I will take you through the preparation process and the twelve-day diet step by step so you can see how it all works.

THE ESSENTIALS OF THE PROGRAM

As we have seen, the McDougall Program combines:

- A health-supporting twelve-day diet in which you eat starches, vegetables, and fruits high in complex carbohydrates and fiber and low in fat, and
- Judicious daily exercise (see Exercise, below).

You will need to:

- Check with your doctor before you begin if you have any health problems (e.g., heart disease, high blood pressure, diabetes, arthritis), both about the diet and about your exercise program (see Medical Considerations, below).

You will be allowed:

- Unlimited amounts of the right foods
- Unlimited healthful snacks

You will not be allowed:

- Animal foods (meats, fish, poultry, eggs, milk, cheese, yogurt, etc.)
- Oils
- Refined foods (see Chapter 3)
- Alcohol and caffeine (except in extreme circumstances—see Chapter 5)

You will be limited to:

- Almost no fat (no animal fat; no added vegetable fat; no high-fat plant foods)
- Reduced sugar
- Reduced salt

But the McDougall Program is more than just a twelve-day regimen; it is a whole new lifestyle. At the end of twelve days, you can expect to feel younger and more energetic, look better, and see measurable improvement in your weight, blood pressure, and laboratory blood tests. I hope this will convince you to continue the Program for the rest of your life.

FOOD GUIDELINES

Although the outline above looks specific, it needs some elaboration. What exactly can you eat? Are all nonanimal foods allowed? Can you eat nuts? What about tofu? In order to get the most from the diet, it is best to be sure, so I have included a list of foods you must avoid. You may find some things there that surprise you. Brand names of packaged and canned products acceptable for the diet are listed on pages 100–114.

DON'T EAT:	Possible Substitutes:
Milk (for cereal or cooking)	Low-fat soy milk (e.g., Vanilla Edensoy,* Rice Milk (recipe page 196), fruit juice, water (use extra when cooking hot cereal or pour over cold cereal)
Milk (as beverage)	None; drink water, juice, herb tea, or cereal beverages
Butter	None, or Corn Butter (recipe page 189) as spread
Cheese	None,† or Melty Cheese if made with potato (recipe page 264)
Cottage cheese	None†
Yogurt	None
Sour cream	None†
Ice cream	Banana-Strawberry Freeze (recipe page 181), pure fruit sorbet, frozen juice bars; see also below†
Eggs (in cooking)	Ener-G Egg Replacer (for binding)
Eggs (for eating)	None†
Meat, poultry, fish	Starchy vegetables, whole grains, pastas, and beans; see also below†
Mayonnaise	None†
Vegetable oils (for pans)	None; use Teflon, Silverstone, or silicone-coated (Baker's Secret) pots and pans
Vegetable oils (in recipes)	None; omit oil or replace with water, mashed banana, or applesauce for moisture
White rice (refined)	Whole grain (brown) rice or other whole grains
White flour (refined)	Whole grain flours

* Most soy milks are high in fat (45% fat). Low-fat soy milk, like the vanilla flavor of Edensoy, is only 12% fat and so is acceptable on the diet. More low-fat soy milks should be coming on the market. If you can't find a low-fat soy milk, dilute regular soy milk with 3 cups water for every 1 cup soy milk.
† See below for richer foods allowed sparingly after the twelve-day diet.

Refined and sugar-coated cereals	Any acceptable hot or cold cereal (list pages 100–102)
Coconut	None
Chocolate	Carob powder
Coffee, decaffeinated coffee, and black teas	Non-caffeinated herb tea, cereal beverages, hot water with lemon
Colas and un-colas	Mineral water or seltzer (flavored or plain)

NOT ALLOWED ON THE TWELVE-DAY DIET, BUT ALLOWABLE OCCASIONALLY AFTERWARD:

These high-fat plant foods (high in natural vegetable oils) can be used occasionally and/or in small amounts after you have completed the twelve-day diet and regained your health and appearance.

Soybeans
Soybean derivatives (tofu, tempeh, miso, high-fat soy milk)
Nuts and nut butters
Seeds
Olives
Avocado

SOY-BASED SUBSTITUTES TO BE USED SPARINGLY AFTER THE TWELVE-DAY DIET:

For:	Use:
Cheese	Soy- and nut-based cheeses (Chapter 12)
Cottage cheese	Crumbled tofu (mashed with fork) for cooking
Sour cream	Tofu Sour Cream (recipe page 263)
Mayonnaise	Tofu Mayonnaise (recipe page 263)
Ice cream	Lite Tofutti
Eggs (for eating)	Scrambled Tofu (recipe page 258)
Meat, poultry, fish	Tofu "meat" recipes (Chapter 12)

Salt and Sugar

Salt and sugar are tolerated by most people when used in reasonable amounts. Most flavor for the least amount is had when they are sprinkled over the surface of the food where the tongue has potent contact. When buried in the food the tastes are hidden so more is needed. In the Program, very little salt and sugar is used in cooking. If you want, you may sprinkle a small amount lightly on the surface of your food. If you add a combined total of about ½ teaspoon of table salt to all the dishes you eat daily, your intake will be about 1500 mg. Your local hospital's coronary care unit serves its heart attack victims 2000 mg daily with their meals. If you limit yourself to two teaspoonsful of sugar, this will be precisely 32 calories out of the total of 2000 to 3000 calories you should eat every day.

Please note: People with sugar sensitivities (including those with hypoglycemia, high triglycerides) should avoid all sugar, even the natural sugars found in honey, molasses, maple syrup, and fruits. People sensitive to salt (including those with heart disease, high blood pressure, and kidney disease) must avoid as much sodium as possible.

Some improvement is made by making these substitutions:

For:	*Use:*
Table salt	Salt-free or low-sodium seasoning mixes, low-sodium soy sauce
Table sugar	Honey, pure maple syrup, no-sugar pure-fruit spread

HOW THE TWELVE-DAY DIET WORKS

Getting used to a new way of eating and cooking is not easy. To help you learn what is involved I have prepared menus for the twelve days of the diet. If you want to avoid having to make any decisions about foods or meals while you're beginning the Program, just follow the suggested menus. However, if there are certain dishes that don't appeal to you, you can make substitutions. Or, if there are dishes you especially like, then repeat them as often as you like. You can pick and choose among the dishes and rearrange them in any combination you wish. Feel free to add whole grain bread and/or additional vegetables to any meals (bread is higher in calories than most starches, so to lose weight rapidly don't eat too much). Some of you may find the desserts too rich in simple sugars—simply omit them.

Recipes for the suggested menus are given in Chapter 10. All the dishes are easy to prepare. If you like, you may also choose from among the more elaborate recipes in Chapter 11. However, do *not* use the richer recipes in Chapter 12, "Transition Treats," until you have completed the diet.

If you enjoy going out to eat, or need to do it for your job, you'll find Chapter 13, on eating out, particularly helpful. Eating out can be as healthy as eating at home as long as you're willing to make the effort to do some preliminary research, choose your dishes carefully, and tell the restaurant staff your wishes.

Suggested Menus for the Twelve-Day Diet

(Recipes and instructions for preparations appear in Chapter 10.)

DAY 1

Breakfast: Fresh Fruit or Fruit Juice
Quick Oatmeal
Herbal Tea

Lunch: Fast Pizza
Fresh Fruit
Water or Soda Water

Dinner: Spicy Chili Beans
Brown Rice (make extra rice for tomorrow's breakfast)
Fresh or Frozen Corn or Peas
Strawberry Frozen Fruit Dessert
Hot or Iced Herbal Tea

DAY 2

Breakfast: Fresh Fruit or Fruit Juice
Breakfast Rice and Fruit
Herbal Tea

Lunch: "OLT" Sandwich
Fresh Fruit
Water or Soda Water

Dinner: Spaghetti with Marinara Sauce
Tossed Green Salad with Low-Sodium,
  Oil-Free Italian Salad Dressing
Sunbeam Tapioca
Hot or Iced Herbal Tea

DAY 3

Breakfast: Fresh Fruit or Fruit Juice
Frozen Hash-Brown Potatoes with Ketchup,
  Salsa, or Barbecue Sauce
Herbal Tea

Lunch: Quick Pasta Salad
Cucumber Vinaigrette
Fresh Fruit
Water or Soda Water

Dinner: American Vegetable Stew
Brown Rice (make extra rice for the next two days)
Steamed Broccoli with Lemon
Microwaved Apple Wedges
Hot or Iced Herbal Tea

DAY 4

Breakfast: Fresh Fruit or Fruit Juice
Hot 7 Grain Cereal or Hot Apple Granola
Herbal Tea

Lunch: Whole Grain Bread Sandwich with Vegetables
Fresh Fruit
Water or Soda Water

Dinner: Bean and Rice Burritos
Tossed Green Salad with Low-Sodium,
  Oil-Free Russian Salad Dressing
Sunshine Fruit Dessert
Hot or Iced Herbal Tea

DAY 5

Breakfast: Fresh Fruit or Fruit Juice
Whole Wheat Toast with Corn Butter
Herbal Tea

Lunch: Pita Bread Stuffed with Kidney Beans
Fresh Fruit
Water or Soda Water

Dinner: Minestrone Soup
Rice and Corn Salad
Whole Wheat Bread
Easy Fruit "Gelatin"
Hot Herbal Tea

DAY 6

Breakfast: Fresh Fruit or Fruit Juice
Quick "Fried" Potatoes
Herbal Tea

Lunch: Quick Garbanzo Bean Soup
Sliced Tomatoes with Salsa
Whole Wheat Bread or Pita Bread
Fresh Fruit
Water or Soda Water

Dinner: Cajun Rice (make extra rice for the next two days)
Tossed Green Salad with Low-Sodium,
    Oil-Free French Salad Dressing
Frozen Fruit "Sorbet"
Hot or Iced Herbal Tea

DAY 7

Breakfast: Fresh Fruit or Fruit Juice
Multi-Mix Cold Cereal with Rice Milk
Herbal Tea

Lunch: Baked Potato Salad
Fresh Fruit
Water or Soda Water

Dinner: Vegetable Burritos
Red and White Salad
Fruit Delight
Hot or Iced Herbal Tea

DAY 8

Breakfast: Fresh Fruit or Fruit Juice
Microwaved Baked Potato with All the Permitted
    Toppings *or* Hot or Cold Cereal
Herbal Tea

Lunch: Pita Bread Stuffed with White Beans
    and Vegetables
Fresh Fruit
Water or Soda Water

Dinner: A La King Sauce on Whole Wheat Toast
Quick Broiled Zucchini
Rice Pudding
Hot or Iced Herbal Tea

DAY 9

Breakfast: Fresh Fruit or Fruit Juice
Hot Breakfast Quinoa
Herbal Tea

Lunch: Quick Saucy Vegetables
Whole Wheat Bread or Pita Bread
Fresh Fruit
Water or Soda Water

Dinner: Pasta Primavera
Saucy Cauliflower
Easy Fruit Pudding
Hot or Iced Herbal Teas

DAY 10

Breakfast: Fresh Fruit or Fruit Juice
Fruity Bran and Oats
Herbal Tea

Lunch: Pita Bread Stuffed with Spicy Beans
    and Vegetables
Fresh Fruit
Water or Soda Water

Dinner: Bean Burrito Casserole
Mexican Corn on the Cob
Tossed Green Salad with Low-Sodium,
    Oil-Free Creamy Cucumber Dressing
Sparkling Minted Fruit
Hot or Iced Herbal Tea

DAY 11

Breakfast: Fresh Fruit or Fruit Juice
Cold Breakfast Cereal (see list page 100) with
    Fruit Juice, Rice Milk, or Low-Fat Soy Milk
Herbal Tea

Lunch: Peasant Salad
Fresh Fruit
Water or Soda Water

Dinner: Split Pea Soup
Broiled Tomatoes
Quick Apple Pie
Hot or Iced Herbal Tea

DAY 12

Breakfast: Fresh Fruit or Fruit Juice
Rice Cakes or Whole Wheat, Oil-Free Bagels
    with No-Sugar, Pure-Fruit Jam
Herbal Tea

Lunch: Kale Sandwich
Sliced Tomatoes
Fresh Fruit
Water or Soda Water

Dinner: Gingered Vegetable Soup
Seasoned Potatoes
Peach Pie
Hot or Iced Herbal Tea

MEDICAL CONSIDERATIONS

Establishing Your Physical Baseline on Day 1

Proofs of change that can be shown in numbers are the most convincing evidence of the effectiveness of the Program. Therefore, I always advise even perfectly healthy McDougall dieters to measure everything they can about their body on the Program's first day, or as close before it as possible, and then record their physical changes on the last day. If this seems to be unnecessary to you, and you're in good health, then you can certainly ignore my recommendation and do the Program anyway. However, most people find it rewarding to track their progress in a measurable way.

Establishing a physical baseline involves:

- Weighing yourself
- Having your blood pressure taken (or, if you wish to buy an inexpensive blood pressure cuff, doing it yourself)
- Getting blood tests to determine your levels of cholesterol, triglycerides, glucose, uric acid, and everything else your doctor may deem important.

The most significant findings from your blood tests will be:

- *Cholesterol level:* If your level is above 180 mg/dl, you should consider this a warning sign of potential circulatory problems. (This refers to your total cholesterol level. Sometimes the findings are broken down into HDL ["good"] and LDL ["bad"] cholesterol levels, but I feel the total cholesterol is the most significant—see the appendix, Interpretation of Laboratory Tests.)
- *Triglyceride level:* This measures the amount of fats floating along in your blood. Probably it will be between 50 and 200 mg/dl. Higher levels sludge the blood, cause resistance to insulin activity, and are associated with an increased risk of heart disease.
- *Glucose (blood sugar) level:* Normal level is between 70 and 120 mg/dl. Higher levels indicate diabetes.
- *Uric acid level:* Normal is less than 7 mg/dl. A higher figure indicates a risk of developing gout and/or kidney stones.

The significance of the data from all these tests is explained in more detail in the appendix of this book, Interpretation of Laboratory Tests.

Your doctor can arrange for the blood tests for you, or you can arrange for them yourself at a reputable laboratory (you should be able to obtain them for less than fifty dollars). "Mini laboratories" are springing up throughout the United States that will draw blood without a doctor's prescription and send you the results; they're often found in shopping malls (look in your yellow pages under "Laboratories—Medical").

Consulting Your Doctor

Mentioning your diet plans to your doctor is always wise, even if you are feeling fine. If you have established a relationship with your doctor from the beginning and problems crop up, you will have an expert familiar with your situation to consult. You may experience weakness, fatigue, or new aches and pains that could be a coincidence or could be related to the dietary and lifestyle changes you are making and/or medications you take. Your doctor will help you sort out these new developments. Your doctor is also the expert professional best qualified to help you interpret tests based on his knowledge of your health condition. Having a medical pro on your team will give you peace of mind. It may also teach your doctor about the benefits of a good diet and a little exercise.

If you are in good health—just a little overweight, or constipated, or suffering from the aches and pains you have attributed to being a stressed-out human being—then it is not absolutely necessary to see your doctor. However, if you have been feeling rundown or have a hint that you may have something serious going on with your health, then you should be cautious and go to your doctor for a baseline evaluation. He or she may need to order additional tests beyond the routine blood tests, such as liver function tests, kidney function tests, thyroid function tests, "cbc" (a complete blood count, which provides information on anemia and infection), and/or a "ua" (urinalysis, a chemical and microscopic examination of the urine to determine the health of the urinary system and metabolic functions of the entire body). These tests are discussed in detail in the appendix.

If you have a known health problem and/or you're on medication, you must have a doctor's examination before starting the twelve-day Program. This examination should include a detailed history and a thorough physical examination as a baseline evaluation. The doctor should order any necessary tests and review their results with you. Special problems may indicate the need for further tests. For example, if you are a heart patient, you may need a recent treadmill stress test and possibly other heart exams to evaluate the severity of your condition and your tolerance for exercise.

Obviously, in such cases as this you'll be working together with your doctor each step of the way. He'll need to decide when you can reduce your medications in response to the improved state of your body. Believe me when I say that significant changes can occur within just a few days.

I can't stress enough the importance of working with a doctor if you take medication. Consider, if you take diabetic pills or insulin and you change your diet and exercise, your need for these drugs will diminish or may vanish. If you continue them at the same dose (or at all), then your blood sugar may fall to dangerously low levels and you could be hurt. Powerful blood pressure medications must be reduced in a timely manner or you could become faint as your pressure falls naturally when the salt and fat are removed from your diet. Medications used to treat symptoms such as chest pain, arthritis, and even headaches should be stopped when indicated because they can cause side effects (and are expensive).

Your doctor should be an expert on the effects of medications and should have no trouble adjusting the dosages as your health improves. Laboratory tests (like blood sugar) and clinical findings (like blood pressure) will be his guides for making decisions on proper dosages of medications.

If Your Doctor Is Skeptical

I don't know what attitude your doctor will have toward your change in diet. All too often doctors regard a dietary approach to health as just a lot of nonsense. Nevertheless, you ought at least to be able to convince him that nothing you're planning can do you any harm. If your doctor wants to think he's humoring an eccentricity of yours, then let him think that. If he's a tyrant strongly opposed to change, then find another opinion from another doctor.

If you don't find a doctor that is helpful, or at least cooperative, by asking friends, nurses, doctors, and at your local health food store, then call your county medical society and ask if they can refer you to a doctor who might share your interests. These days, finding a helpful doctor should not be too great a task. Interest in diet and disease is growing in the medical profession and doctors are more open-minded than a few years ago. Keep looking.

If your doctor is skeptical about your new dietary program, this can be a ticklish time in your relationship with him. Be gentle and courteous. Let him down easy.

One of my patients was Sid Hellman who, at the age of sixty-two years, had crippling arthritic problems and was 120 pounds overweight. He had tried every diet known to the paperback book industry, and estimated that he had lost a total of 600 pounds during the course of thirty years of attempts at dieting. Sid was so huge that when he traveled he occupied two airplane seats, and because the seat belts were always too short, he brought along his own seat belt extender.

The unique complication to Sid's case grew out of his relationship with his doctor; they had been best of friends for more than thirty-five years. The doctor had watched Sid try all those different diets, had no doubt encouraged him, at least occasionally, and had been disappointed every time, just as Sid was. When Sid heard about the McDougall Program at St. Helena and mentioned it to his physician-friend, the doctor sighed, reached into his desk, and handed Sid a sheet of paper with a standard low-calorie diet printed on it. This was his way of saying, *Why waste your money on McDougall? The secret of weight loss is self-control. Without that, Sid, you're never going to lose weight.*

Sid came to St. Helena anyway, lost eleven pounds in twelve days and a total of sixty-six pounds during the next six months, greatly lessened his arthritic pain (he actually put away his walking stick), got off all his medications, and lowered his high blood pressure, high cholesterol, triglyceride, and blood sugar levels.

His only problem was that at the same time he was achieving all these medical successes he was developing a rift in his personal relationship with his doctor-friend. In fact, they hardly spoke anymore. Sid talked to me about it, and I said, "Sid, you have to realize that he probably feels he let you down before you tried my Program. He was never able to cure your problems with his approach, and he even tried to discourage you from going to the people who did cure them. You have to talk to him, ask him if that's how he feels, make him understand that you don't look at it in that way." Sid did this and eventually they got their friendship back on track. So be comforted—you're not likely to have problems with your doctor that will be nearly as personal or as delicate as Sid's.

Just remember, although ignoring your doctor's advice could be risky, the final decision should be yours. After all, you are the one to gain or lose most by whatever course you take, right? Use your doctor as a valuable consultant. Ask questions and become informed. Your decision will be the right decision if you have taken the trouble to become an educated health care consumer.

EXERCISE

Exercise is an important part of the Program, and it should be an enjoyable part as well. I'll be frank with you—if you were never to exercise at all, you'd still see remarkable improvements resulting from your change of diet. You'd probably gain up to 80 percent of the benefits the Program has to offer. But, isn't it better to go for 100 percent? I think that deep down inside yourself you know that exercise can do wonderful things for you. Have you ever in your life felt physically happier than when as a child you ran and seemed not to be tied down to earth by the force of gravity? Wouldn't you like to regain that exhilarating feeling? If you still have the use of your limbs, then I think it's possible to regain a portion of that physical grace that now seems to have been lost forever.

Of course, many people consider moving their muscles to be about as appealing as having root-canal work done. I object to this view of exercise. If the heaviest bout of exercise you've given yourself lately is hoisting a can of beer to your lips while you lounge in an armchair, that still doesn't mean that exercise should be a terrible strain. It's not. Don't believe those who say so sagely, "No pain, no gain." If you want to see results, then just exercise a little more than you're already doing. And then, a little more. Go out and take a walk. Five blocks, six blocks, ten blocks, twenty blocks. If no health problems prevent you, walk vigorously. Then come back home. What do you find? That you feel better than you did when you left, with fewer aches and pains to moan over—after you work the stiffness out of your unused muscles—and a sense of accomplishment that has you smiling at yourself in the mirror.

You may already be involved in an exercise program more vigorous than the one I just described. You should continue those physical activities that have been making you feel so fit. There is no reason to change a successful routine unless you're not enjoying your exercise or the physical activity is doing you some physical harm. Many people tell me that they experience an increase in their endurance soon after they start the McDougall Program—they can walk an extra mile or two without tiring, and nothing has changed but their fuel. I'm not surprised. Accomplished athletes have been taking advantage of improved performance gained by a high-carbohydrate diet for many years.

Why Exercise?

Here's a short list of the benefits from exercise:
- More appropriate appetite
- Increase in muscle tissues, and thus a better ratio of lean body tissue to fat
- Loss of excess weight
- Burn more calories
- Improved muscle tone and flexibility
- More energy, less fatigue
- Some improvement in circulatory system
- Improved digestion
- Better mood—including less depression and anxiety
- Fall in blood pressure
- Lower triglyceride and blood sugar levels
- Higher HDL ("good") cholesterol level

Most of these are quite moderate physical improvements, but they're still well worth having. The first two entries on that list represent intriguing and by no means obvious advantages of an exercise program. Certainly you would expect to be *more* hungry when you burn up energy in exercising, but the truth is that the "appestat" (the body's mechanism that controls appetite) sets itself at a lower level than expected when a person takes regular periods of physical exertion. People who hardly exercise at all, by contrast, have a higher appestat setting and are frequently hungry to a degree that's entirely inappropriate to their body's actual needs.

The formation of more muscle tissue is also an advantage to a person who wants to lose weight, because the many mitochondria (energy-producing structures) that are found in muscle cells consume considerably greater quantities of fuel than do the few mitochondria in the rather inert fat cells of the body. Thus, your own body will be burning more of the calories you bring into it by eating if you improve the ratio of muscle tissue to fat tissue on your frame.

You can see from these examples that slimness is a self-reinforcing physical state. If fat were fashionable, a person who ate the healthy foods of the McDougall diet, and exercised as little as thirty minutes a day, would have great difficulty in achieving the culturally desirable pudgy profile.

Establishing an Exercise Program

What Form of Exercise Should You Do?

I suggest you begin by choosing—realistically—the kind of exercise you feel most comfortable with. *If you have a health problem, you should consult your doctor about what would be appropriate and safe for you.* The least you can do is walk, swim, or bicycle, and, for you sedentary types, that isn't a bad beginning. If you're in good enough condition for more strenuous athletics, you can play handball or tennis or basketball. You could learn how to ski or windsurf, or take up fencing or aerobic dancing. Or join a health club and work out with weights. You may want to purchase a stationary bicycle or treadmill to exercise indoors. This is especially helpful in bad weather or if it is unsafe to exercise outdoors in your area. Barbell weights and calisthenics (floor exercise) are also good for indoor conditioning.

You have probably heard that exercise can be classified as either aerobic or anaerobic. The distinction between the two is not a clear one. Aerobic activities are ones that require a great consumption of oxygen on the exerciser's part. Examples include walking, jogging, swimming, bicycling, dancing and rowing. Anaerobic exercise refers to exertions that do not require a large, continuing supply of newly breathed oxygen to perform. Examples are sprint running, weight lifting, and carrying heavy objects—most manual labor, in fact.

There's some evidence to suggest that aerobic exercise is better for the heart and the circulatory system. Anaerobic exercise, on the other hand, builds muscle mass and power and that too has its advantages. Men and women who go in for exercises that increase strength, like body building, not only get a better-looking body from the work but get also a better functioning one. That ratio between lean muscle tissue and fat tissue that I mentioned earlier is obviously thrown strongly toward the muscle side by such activities.

The things that you can do for exercise are limited only by your inventiveness and personal inclinations. You don't need to stick to one favorite exercise; add interest to your life by varying your routine. Don't be guided by other people's tastes or opinions. If something is fun (and safe) for you, just do it.

How Much Should You Do?

You should feel physically good when you finish an exercise session. Pain—apart from the muscle aches following a long layoff—isn't a necessary part of any exercise program undertaken for good health. If you're already in good physical shape, you'll know how much exercise is right for you. If you've been leading a basically sedentary life, then I suggest you begin with a very modest exercise program. As you grow accustomed to it, you can gradually increase the amount and intensity of your activity. *Be careful about overdoing it*, especially if you're over thirty. In our society, most people have acquired some degree of disease by that age. It wouldn't be wise for you to push your body to the limit.

If you haven't been feeling very energetic *or if you have any question about a specific health risk, have a checkup before undertaking vigorous exercise.* Remember that extremely vigorous exercise is hard even on the athlete's body. Not only does he risk the danger of injury, but studies have shown that marathon runners, who are perhaps overstressing their bodies, have somewhat impaired immune systems in the days following such a strenuous race and are very susceptible to colds and infections caused by other viruses.

Some people who exercise energetically count their pulse rate to see if they're overdoing it. I think a less difficult and more reliable way to judge a safe top level of exercise is to observe the labor of your breathing. If uncomfortable effort is required to supply your body with adequate air, then you've reached the time to rest. You have labored enough. Later, as you condition yourself over a period of time, your wind will improve.

Setting Aside the Time

You should consider exercising at the same time each day. Once you've set aside a definite block (or blocks) of time for the purpose of physical fitness, keeping to your program will be easier. Many people find that they do well by exercising in the early morning. If that's the case with you, then lay out your clothes each night before you go to bed. When the alarm rings in the morning, don't brush your teeth, don't take time to have a hot drink, simply jump up, get dressed, and get started.

Many people tell me they don't have time for exercise, but I think that's just a delaying tactic. Once one understands the overwhelming importance of something, one does it. You say your life is over-crowded? I say, straighten out your priorities. If you choose to exercise in the morning, you may have to go to bed earlier at night. That may mean skipping some late-evening television programs or reading less of the newspaper. You know your schedule better than I do, but I already know how much time most of you have. There are 168 hours in each week. Consider a typical use of that time:

- 40 hours for gainful employment
- 5 hours to commute to and from work
- 49 hours to sleep
- 5 hours to eat

This leaves you with 69 hours of uncommitted time—almost 10 hours a day. Do you really think it's impossible to fit a mere 30 minutes for exercise into that span each day?

KEEPING TRACK OF YOUR PROGRESS

It is useful to keep track of your progress every day. Duplicate on a copy machine and use the chart below as a diary to help you organize your meals and keep you from forgetting to exercise; fill in these two sections before the day begins. Document any physical, mental, laboratory test, and medication changes that you are experiencing—including the cessation of problems or symptoms (e.g., headaches, diarrhea). As well as being encouraging for you, this record will be particularly helpful for your doctor if a problem crops up.

DAY: _____

MEALS:

  Breakfast: _____

_____

_____

  Lunch: _____

_____

_____

  Dinner: _____

_____

_____

EXERCISE: _____

_____

_____

PHYSICAL STATUS: _____

_____

_____

MENTAL STATUS: _____

_____

_____

TEST RESULTS: _____

_____

_____

MEDICATIONS:_____

_____

_____

5

PREPARING FOR

THE BIG CHANGE

You can't drive a car without first turning on the motor. In almost everything we do in life, there's a logical and efficient way to proceed. In this chapter I'll show you the logical way to begin your new diet. This will involve you in psychological, practical, and social preparations for the big change. Consider taking these important steps:

- Asking yourself why you're doing the Program;
- Making a firm resolution to carry it out conscientiously and strictly;
- Deciding what, if anything, you're going to do about other unhealthy habits, such as drinking, smoking, and taking drugs;
- Setting goals;
- Telling your family and friends about your intentions;
- Choosing a convenient date for beginning the Program—and sticking to that date.

Logical? I think you'll find it is.

YOU WON'T BE THE FIRST PERSON TO WALK THIS WAY— MEET THE WATERMANS

Before we start, I'd like to introduce you to some people whose experience will help you along the way.

I can't explain this process of making the dietary change without citing the examples, good and bad, of people who've gone before you. More than likely, among them you'll run into someone who bears a close resemblance to you. However, I don't intend to tell you merely a series of entertaining and encouraging anecdotes. If you are to understand the Program, then you should see how it affected at least one person during the course of twelve days. I began looking through my medical files, talking to my patients, and wondering who that person might be. Eventually, I decided on not one person but on two, a couple from northern California, where I'm currently practicing. For the purposes of this book, I'm going to call them Sam and Sally Waterman.

Many things led me to pick them. First, they kept a very detailed record of what happened to them, including a health diary and a list of the foods they ate, and they were willing to share that information with me. Second, I had a very close and cordial relationship with them, so I knew a good deal about their day-to-day reactions to the Program. Third, they were typical in so many respects that I knew I couldn't find better examples of converts who were helped most successfully by the Program. What happened to the Watermans will probably match fairly closely what you, too, can expect.

Sam and Sally Waterman came to my office more than a year ago. Sally was a petite, fine-boned woman, slim from the waist up, who had a quiet but inquiring air about her. Sam was a big man with sandy hair streaked with gray, a hearty voice, and a firm handshake. He seemed to be a person who was in the habit of making decisions. The Watermans were interested in trying the Program but didn't want to spend twelve days at St. Helena. After only a short conversation I agreed that they could do the Program at home.

In our initial conversation I learned that Sally Waterman was a forty-eight-year-old travel agent who'd been fighting an on-again, off-again battle with her weight since she was twenty. Sam was a fifty-year-old executive with a large insurance company who had never paid any attention to his body until he started having chest pains. The Watermans' children were grown, both Sally and Sam seemed happy with their work, and they recognized no particular kind of stress.

Sally and Sam had different reasons for trying the McDougall Program, and met different experiences while they were on it. In just one way were they similar: *They wanted a better life. And when they got it, they were both so happy with the results they'd achieved on the McDougall Program that they've never gone back to eating the way they used to B.P.* (which means "Before the Program").

As we consider the basic steps that will bring you to your first day on the Program, where appropriate, the Watermans' experiences with the Program will be brought in as illustrations.

PSYCHOLOGICAL PREPARATION

What Are Your Reasons for Changing Your Diet?

Let me ask you right now the basic questions: Why are you reading this book? What's in it for you?

The Watermans definitely had their several reasons when they first came to see me.

Sally Waterman was moderately overweight, and suffered from persistent constipation, frequent headaches, and permanent fatigue. She felt that she weighed about twenty pounds too much. At certain times in her life by strenuous dieting she had gotten down to a trim body weight—for a month, or two months, or rarely even for three. But always the pounds came back. Each later attempt at dieting was just a little bit harder than the one before, and had less good results. Sally had been dieting since her college days, and she reckoned that she had been hungry during at least half of her adult life. Is that any way to live? I asked, and she agreed. Sometimes it seemed to her that she could never have a comfortingly full, satisfied stomach without turning pudgy in the blink of an eye.

Sam's problem was somewhat different from Sally's. Oh, yes, he too was overweight by at least fifty pounds—but he didn't particularly care about that. What he did care about was the chest pains he'd been having for over a year. They scared him, and when he found out that he had high blood pressure and his doctor put him on blood pressure medication, that reinforced his expectation of doom. If he took the medication regularly and at full strength, he felt very tired. In addition, he found that it was almost impossible to get an erection. This failure can be pretty demeaning and depressing, especially if you're enjoying what, in other respects, is a satisfying marriage.

As an executive in the insurance industry, Sam saw statistics in front of him every day about how many middle-aged men die of heart attacks. He knew that 50 percent of all heart attack victims are dead within twenty-four hours of the attack. Sam did not like to think about this. But Sally did think about it and she nagged him.

Sam's response was to drink an extra martini before dinner. And then, three weeks before they came to see me, as he was taking out the garbage one morning, Sam had chest pains so severe that he almost called an ambulance. They understood that the time to do something useful had come. Because the Watermans had a neighbor who had taken the McDougall Program at St. Helena with good results, they decided to call me.

You too must have reasons for wanting to do the McDougall Program. No one changes the way he lives and eats just for the sheer fun of it. Back in the days when I was a sickly carnivore, I never would have done anything about my eating habits if I hadn't been overweight and tired and disgusted with the condition of my ornery stomach. (As a doctor I had one more reason: I felt I had to set a good example and change my diet so I could recommend such changes to my even sicker patients.)

If you want to think in more detail about some of the many reasons for making the changes recommended in this book, read carefully the information summarized below.

SOME REASONS FOR MAKING THE CHANGE:

1. *Illness:* Always think first of this life-preserving reason: Abundant and ever-mounting evidence shows that the continuous consumption of rich foods increases your risk of developing heart disease, high blood pressure, diabetes, some forms of cancer, and other degenerative diseases (see Part 3).

2. *Pain:* I hope you don't yet suffer from the pain of serious illness, but even the lesser pain that comes with headaches, mild arthritis, constipation, and fatigue is no laughing matter. You'll find that diet is usually closely related to such problems.

3. *Ugliness:* If you suffer from a weight problem, your chance of controlling it on a diet high in fats is as poor as you've always suspected it to be. Increased body odor and oily skin are also consequences of the diet Americans take for granted. One patient of mine was a woman whose husband threatened to divorce her because he said she "stunk." After she changed her diet, she smelled as sweet as a basketful of fresh fruit.

4. *Money:* Once you get settled into the McDougall diet (and the initial expense of stocking up on the items you'll need), you'll discover that

you spend a good deal less on food. Moreover, remember that the costs of medications and medical care verge on the catastrophic. I suggest that you make every effort to stay healthy and thereby avoid the financial tragedy that accompanies most medical tragedies.

5. *Taste:* Although this doesn't apply to most of you, many people eat meat and dairy products only because they've been told they ought to for the sake of a "balanced diet." Some people find the taste of beef or of fish repugnant, others just don't get excited about any sort of meat or eggs or smelly cheese. If you're one of these long-suffering people victimized by foods rather than helped by them, here is your chance to change to a diet that will discard the things you've never really liked.

6. *Ecology:* If you are concerned about the fate of the world's starving poor, then you'll want to avoid eating animal foods. To produce the amount of meat and dairy products that will feed one American, a single cow must consume each day grain that could be used to feed seven people. Consider, too, that the so-called "greenhouse effect," which threatens all parts of the earth, is caused not only by the release of industrial wastes into the air but also by the destruction of our planet's forest cover. Brazil, for example, is rapidly destroying thousands of square miles of its rain forest, primarily in order to convert those bared areas to grazing areas for great cattle herds, in order to sell beef to wealthy industrialized countries. Cocaine from South America we don't need, and neither do we need more beef.

7. *Philosophy:* The religious teachings of Mormons and Seventh Day Adventists oppose the eating of meat of any kind, and many Eastern religions hold similar views. Although vegetarianism has not been a part of the Judeo-Christian tradition, you will find a passage in *Genesis* that reads, ". . . every seed-bearing plant on the face of the whole earth and every tree that has fruit with seed in it. They will be yours for food." That verse does give one food for more than thought. In addition, many people's personal beliefs include an objection to the killing of animals.

Resolving to Do It

You must, of course, make that initial resolution to do the Program. If you have any hesitation about sticking with it, think about the rewards it will give you. Good health and good looks aren't mere abstractions. A life that includes them is incomparably richer and happier than one without them. Don't be like the woman who signed up to take the program and came all the way from Texas to attend it. On the day she arrived at St. Helena, she turned around and went home again: The prospect of making the change was simply too terrifying for her to endure.

One other suggestion is needed: *Don't be half-hearted about the deal we're arranging.* Some of you are quietly thinking: "I'll try out McDougall's program—sort of." You're planning to give it a one- or two-day trial and then cheat the moment you're tempted. Please don't do that. You'll hurt yourself more than you'll cheat me. Of course, for a while you'll miss the familiar taste of meats and cheese, chocolates and doughnuts, but that's no reason to merely reduce the amounts of these rich foods you eat. To continue eating old favorites in smaller quantities is a form of slow torture that will lead you back to eating the way you used to. And, you'll never be able to judge the Program fairly—or yourself, as a willing experimenter—if you don't follow it strictly for twelve days.

I believe not only that everyone deserves to have a slim and healthy body, but that everyone who reads this book—and follows faithfully the Program it describes—can achieve that goal. Right here and now, for your own sake, resolve to do the Program strictly for twelve whole days. It can be the most important resolution you'll ever make.

PRACTICAL PREPARATION
Choosing the Best Possible Day to Begin

It is important to decide in advance when you are going to begin so you have time to make all the necessary preparations discussed below. If you've no compelling reason to do otherwise, I suggest that you plan to start the Program on a weekend or a Monday. That way you'll have extra time to learn how to shop and prepare some of your new dishes over the weekend while you're relatively free of pressure. Furthermore, if by sad chance you can't locate any restaurants close to where you work that can serve a healthy low-fat lunch, you'll have time to figure out what to tuck into that brown bag when you go to the office. Monday is the beginning of a new work week for most of us; therefore, psychologically Monday may be a good day to begin any new program.

If you were to plan to start the diet during the week and you got very tense at work, you might say to yourself, "Well, I haven't started this program yet, so I'll wait till tomorrow or until next week." That great day may never come.

Seeing Your Doctor and Arranging for Lab Tests

Before you begin, you will need to make an appointment to see your doctor to discuss going on the Program and arrange to have lab tests done on your first day or as close beforehand as possible (see Chapter 4). Don't leave this until the last minute; it is sometimes difficult to set appointments at short notice.

Setting Goals

Before they began, I talked to Sam and Sally Waterman about their twelve days on the Program, and advised them to set some very modest goals for themselves. Here is what they came up with:

Sam:

- Relieving some of the chest pain
- Losing five pounds (in the twelve days)
- Reaching a normal blood pressure
- Getting off some of the medications
- Stopping burning acid indigestion
- Ending bouts of diarrhea

Sally:

- Losing five pounds (in the twelve days)
- Relieving stiff, painful joints (arthritis)
- Ending constipation
- Ending nagging sinus headaches and postnasal drip
- Feeling more energetic
- Getting away from caffeine (she had two big mugs in the morning and at least a cup in the afternoon)

Both Sam and Sally:

- Learning to like the new kinds of foods
- Satisfying hunger at every meal
- Getting used to taking daily exercise
- Having the change go smoothly

I told them that they had developed goals that they could feel good about and that they could expect to achieve.

As you read this, write down the goals *you* would like to achieve on the McDougall Program. These can range from the relatively trivial—getting rid of acne or oily hair—to the momentous—ending chest pains and high blood pressure.

Expect to see real and good changes in your body in less than two weeks. Proper diet with exercise does that. On the other hand, if losing weight is your main goal, don't pile up foolish hopes. You're not going to lose thirty pounds in twelve days unless a surgeon removes a tumor the size of a watermelon from your tummy. My advice is kinder and gentler: Take off weight slowly and steadily. That's the way to take it off and keep it off. Consider this: If you lose two pounds a week, in one year at that rate you'll have lost 104 pounds. I have treated thousands of people for whom being overweight was a critical problem. Not too many of them had more weight to lose than those 104 pounds.

If you have serious health problems, then your goals are easily understood: You want to feel well, you want to reduce or get off your medications (you certainly should want to do that, medications are always a poor alternative to good health), you want to see certain specific symptoms disappear. If, for instance, you have adult-type diabetes, then on your first day on the McDougall Program you will find yourself able, with the help of your doctor, to cut your dose of insulin in half. Very soon after that you'll learn that your blood sugar levels are coming down and that you're feeling markedly better, having less swelling of the limbs, more energy, fewer aches and pains. If you're tortured by the pain of angina, you can expect it to be much lessened, if not ended, in twelve days. If severe indigestion is the cause of your heartache, then a good deal less than twelve days should ease, if not end, your symptoms.

To understand what the Program can do for specific serious health problems, refer to Part 3 of this book. But remember, if you have a health problem you should not undertake the Program without consulting a doctor, as Sam consulted me.

If you don't have specific health problems, then your goals for the twelve days might be as broad as losing a couple of pounds, feeling more energetic, improving digestion.

Defining your goals clearly before you start is important. It gives you a sense of purpose which helps keep you on course. Moreover, when your goals are reached you will feel the pride of accomplishment from your efforts. Those who skip this step don't know where they're going or when they get there.

Dealing with Unhealthy Habits

Before you go on the Program I urge you to think about any aspects of your lifestyle that could harm your health and give them serious attention. Smoking tobacco, drinking coffee, drinking alcohol, and using addicting prescription medicines or recreational drugs are all health-damaging problems that you should correct as soon as possible.

Most people who do the McDougall Program at the St. Helena Center try to change all their unhealthy habits while they're there.* But among the pilgrims we do find some exceptions. On the average, one person in every program will grab a smoke out on the balcony whenever the opportunity arises. As far as I know, however, no one has continued to drink alcohol or coffee. Neither of these addictive beverages is provided at the center, and no one is allowed to bring them onto the grounds.

Of course, it is easier to give up these habits when you are in a new and supportive environment, away from the pressures, patterns, and responsibilities of your usual life. When you go on the Program at home it may be too difficult to try to solve these problems while you are also changing your diet radically and beginning an exercise program. You are going to suffer withdrawal symptoms when you

---

* St. Helena Hospital and Health Center also has live-in programs dedicated just to helping people resolve particular serious health problems. Anyone attending the twelve-day live-in McDougall Program at St. Helena who is dependent on tobacco, alcohol, prescription medications, or recreational drugs is provided education and counseling by the professional staff from the appropriate program. The Smoking Cessation Program has made thousands of most hardened nicotine addicts permanent nonsmokers. The Alcohol and Chemical Recovery Program encourages people to look at their use of alcohol and/or drugs and how it has affected their lives. After detoxification, the twelve-step programs of Alcoholics and Narcotics Anonymous become a vital part of the treatment philosophy.

stop smoking, and even when you stop drinking alcohol or coffee. If you have a heavy habit it may take time to wean yourself from it—you will probably not be able to stop "cold turkey." And quitting smoking is a major project for most people. Ideally you should take care of these problems now, but don't try to do it now if it gets in the way of adjusting to your new diet.

A well-known West Coast radio talk show host came to the Program to correct some intestinal problems that were so advanced as to require surgical attention. He adapted easily to the dietary change and ended the persistent stomach cramps and diarrhea that had for many months past kept him practically chained to the nearest men's room from fear of uncontrolled distress. He also lost thirty-five pounds and lowered his cholesterol level by forty-two points after about three months on the McDougall diet.

But then he decided to quit smoking. After three weeks of torment, the added stress of nicotine withdrawal caused him to abandon his new diet. M & M candies and shrimp creole moved to the nutritional forefront once more. The result was a fifteen-pound gain in weight and early indications that he was eroding the improvements he had made in his relationship with his intestinal tract. So he took up smoking again, but the added weight stayed with him. Eventually he had courage enough to return to the St. Helena Center and to the security and comfort that the diet restored in him.

Remember, lifestyle and diet change are not "all or nothing" arrangements. Allow each change to come naturally, and then to become ingrained in you as part of your preferred way of living and eating, before going on to the next contest. Don't consider yourself a failure if you can't make all your improvements at once. By following the McDougall Program, you're taking major steps toward gaining the kind of better health that most people spend their lives only dreaming about. Those first steps are the important ones, so don't make the going too difficult for yourself.

If you do decide to deal with your unhealthy habits, take advantage of professionals and dedicated programs in your community. If you want to stop smoking, try attending a no-smoking clinic. If you have a drug or alcohol dependency you wish to break, do not try it alone. Begin by visiting your doctor for advice and guidance. He may suggest you attend a dedicated program in your area. When the addiction is very powerful, suddenly discontinuing alcohol, street drugs, or doctor-prescribed narcotics or tranquilizers can result in serious illness and occasionally death. In some cases, to be safe, hospitalization and physician-supervision detoxification are required.

If you decide to stop coffee, alcohol, tobacco, or drugs during the twelve days of the McDougall Program, then make doing so a specific goal.

Dealing with Stress

People are often told that stress is at the root of their health problems—that if they changed their lifestyles their health problems would go away—but in my experience, stress-caused illness is actually very rare. As a doctor I get to ask people almost anything and, by and large, I think they give me honest answers. I've come to the conclusion that for most of us life is perpetually difficult. We have bills to pay, people to get along with, jobs to finish, impossible hopes to dream up, disappointments to endure, and troubles to resolve during each and every day. Yet we survive by just plugging along—or as GIs say, by putting one foot in front of the other. Perhaps to a few people life has dealt such unusually severe physical and emotional problems that their health is adversely affected by the extraordinary pressures they must bear. But for most of us life's difficulties are manageable—unless we choose to use them as excuses for not making changes in diet or lifestyle or for explaining health problems we don't understand.

The important diseases that afflict people in the industrialized nations of the West were almost unknown to mankind anywhere in earlier ages. Pilgrims to the New World had never heard of heart attacks or colon cancer. And they certainly were not free of stress. People in the Middle Ages saw many of their children die from infectious diseases, or from famine, or in war. They, like we, had to deal with infidelity, and tax collectors, and financial failure. Yet stress in these people did not produce ulcers, or colitis, or constipation.

If you doubt the reliability of our records for people so distant in time, then look at underdeveloped Asian and African societies today. The people of those countries have the stresses peculiar to their cultures, but what they do not show is significant numbers of deaths from the diseases that the U.S. Surgeon General tells us are caused by our faulty diet. You may find that stress is unpleasant, but stress alone will not make you sick or kill you, except in the rarest of cases, where a person endures almost intolerable torment until he finally breaks. *Unless*, of course, you use stress as an excuse that, as you say, drives you to drink more coffee and more alcohol, to smoke more cigarettes, and to eat lots more greasy food. *Then* you're opening yourself up to destruction by a deadly assassin, not by stress.

Stress can be a complicating factor nagging at you from the sidelines; however, there are simple ways to relieve much of the discomfort you feel from stress. Mild exercise relieves anxiety and elevates the mood, and a high-carbohydrate diet decreases hyperactivity and relieves depression.

If stress isn't your enemy, then could it be a friend? Pressures you feel from within and without cause you to take action: to get problems resolved and jobs finished. Most people really like to work hard, and find the difficulties they meet exciting challenges that keep their lives interesting. These successful people are relieved to learn that the pressures from their chosen career are not the roots of their poor health. Early retirement will not prevent the next heart attack—unless you now work as a food taster at a commercial bakery.

Stocking Up

You'll also need to stock up on some new foods for the diet. Before doing so, browse around in your local markets to discover what's available, where. The next chapter is devoted to that subject. Chapter 10 contains shopping lists specifically for the sample diet; you'll need to purchase the staples and the items necessary for the first four days the day before you begin. You may also want to invest in some nonstick cookware (see Chapter 6).

SOCIAL PREPARATION

Patients often ask me about the social implications of a diet change. I understand what they're getting at. For some people a meatless, greaseless diet is a genuine cultural problem. It can send the wrong message to friends and relatives. Patients are afraid they're going to be thought of as leftovers from some hippie commune, circa 1968, or as the newly recruited followers of an Indian guru. They wonder if business associates, too, and casual acquaintances aren't going to think them weird for eating "that crazy McDougall style."

Well this may have been a legitimate worry ten or fifteen years ago. In those days, you'd have been an odd duck indeed if you went out to Rambo's Steak House with the gang and ordered a fruit salad. But people have changed a lot since then. The health craze that began in the seventies with jogging is moving over into nutrition as well. People no longer regard killing yourself through self-indulgence and neglect as a tremendously classy and stylish thing to do. You must have noticed the new attitudes toward smoking. The habit of puffing the old weed is becoming a social embarrassment. When they see a heavy smoker, most folks may not say anything (provided they can tolerate the smoke), but the word that zips across their minds is *dumb*. I'm betting that in a few more years that's exactly how people will react when they see someone stuffing his precious body with fats and cholesterol.

The honest truth is that most people admire someone who's making an extra effort to take care of his or her body. You don't need to go up to them and talk about the healthy changes you're making in your lifestyle, but you don't need to hide these good deeds either. Some people will want to ask you about them. You may be surprised to learn how many of your acquaintances would like to do something positive to improve their own physical condition.

Preparing Your Family and Friends

Before you start the McDougall Program, you'd best explain to your family and anyone else close to you what you're planning to do. They'll certainly find your intention very interesting, if not a turn they'd want to try for themselves. They may think you're being very wise to be taking these steps or, alternatively, they may think you're being taken in by some sort of "quackery." Let them think what they like. Just don't let their contrary opinions put you off the track you've chosen to follow. Tell them to wait and see.

If your immediate family doesn't want to try out this new style of eating with you, then you'll have to make some adjustments in your approach to it. I think you should take a reasonable and tolerant attitude toward your spouse and children, if they don't want to start suddenly to eat in a way they've never tried before. After all, why should they? I don't mean that they shouldn't do so for their own health's sake, but I do mean that you can't expect them to be convinced of its value just because you are. Instead of pressuring them, think of meal plans that will allow all of you to eat the same dishes up to the point where the meat and the cheese are added and serve the meat and cheese separately as add-ins. (Advice on how to share your meals with people who aren't on the Program appears on page 162.) If you're doing the cooking, after ten or twelve days, when they've had a chance to see the tremendous progress you've made toward renewed health, you might just leave out the meat, explaining that you didn't have time to fix both parts of the meal. By that time, after seeing the change in you (and having tasted a number of healthier foods during the week), they may be more than willing to give permanent approval to your new way of eating.

Sally and Sam Waterman made the change quite easily, because they were doing the Program together, and their children were no longer living with them. Their married daughter Heather, in fact, took up the McDougall Program herself, once she saw what it did for her parents. Their son has been more resistant. When he comes to the family house for dinner, sometimes he brings along a sort of reverse doggie bag, stuffed with cold cuts and hard-boiled eggs. But I had told Sally and Sam that varied responses were only to be expected, people being what they are, and the Watermans feel happy to have converted one of their offspring to this healthier way of eating.

LAST-MINUTE PREPARATIONS— REMOVING TEMPTATION

Now that you're so close, there's no sense torturing yourself by keeping forbidden food in the same house you'll be inhabiting. Clear out your fridge and even your freezer. Send those steaks and eggs and cheeses and milk off to an unconverted friend. Donate the canned pork and beans to your local charity. You have twelve days of new-style eating ahead of you. It's much easier to stay with the new diet if you don't have to move a pepperoni pizza to get at your meatless spaghetti sauce. (Of course, if family members are not going on the program, you will have to keep these foods around, but you can make it easier for yourself by at least designating separate shelves in refrigerator and pantry for the forbidden fare.) Consider taping a snapshot of the trim healthy-looking you, from way back when, on the refrigerator door to remind you of your goals.

YOUR LAST SUPPER

Here you are on the eve of change. No doubt you're clinging to your last hours of riotous carnivorous feasting. You wouldn't be human if you're not tempted to indulge yourself with some forbidden treats. My advice, if you must have a last fling, is not to overdo it. A heart attack brought on by overindulgence in fatty foods would be a particularly lousy way to start my program, or anybody else's.

A little over a year ago, a man named Jim Answell took the McDougall Program at St. Helena. On his first day there, I noticed that he looked pale and a bit uncomfortable. He wasn't eating much of anything, and I wondered why. Jim didn't really want to talk about it, but after a while he admitted he was getting over a very bad bout of indigestion. The night before he had invited a few friends over to celebrate "the condemned man's last meal." He had fixed it in the Californian's usual outdoor barbecue style, and he personally had swallowed two charcoal-broiled steaks, a hot dog with all the trimmings, uncounted handfuls of potato chips, and a few glasses of wine. By the time his friends went home, Jim was glad to see them go. He made straight for the Alka Seltzcr. It had been a bad night. I raised an eyebrow and tried not to smile.

The next day, I checked Jim's lab reports. His cholesterol was 376 (more than twice what I'd regard as a safe level), his blood sugar was 286, and his blood pressure was a whopping 166/102. The man was fifty-two years old, a big, strong fellow with biceps as thick as hams, and with four kids. He probably never would have come to see me if he hadn't been taking three different kinds of blood pressure medication which made him dog tired, and if he hadn't had a younger brother who'd died of colon cancer six months before, and finally, if he hadn't had a worried wife who wouldn't stop fussing at him about the condition he was in. He looked as sturdy as an ox, but I had a pretty good idea what condition his arteries were in: They were setting him up for the last ride to the morgue. There's only one good thing I can say about Jim Answell's way of preparing for the McDougall Program—not only was he going to feel a heck of a lot better after twelve days on my diet, he was going to feel better even after one day of St. Helena's tender care.

SAM AND SALLY TAKE THE PLUNGE

The Watermans spent almost a week preparing themselves for the Program. They practiced a few mental exercises. Can we do it? Is it worth the trouble? Will it really be worth the bother and expense?

Sally—who did not have the advantage of reading this book, remember—had lots of major doubts when she thought of all the diets she'd tried before. None of them had worked over the long haul. After each trial, she gained all her weight back and then some. But, as I explained to her many times, this wasn't just another diet she was thinking about starting—and ending after a while, whenever she felt like quitting. This was to be a complete change in her basic lifestyle.

Sam had always felt that as long as his body could get him out of bed in the morning and carry him to work, worrying about it was effeminate. Now he had to admit that when those chest pains hit him he was scared stiff. He had gone to a cardiologist and was popping nitroglycerin pills as often as the pains came. They eased the pain all right, but not the fear.

In the end, Sally and Sam faced the honest truth: "Look at the shape we're in. If we can start losing weight, and start getting healthy too, in just twelve days, what are we waiting for?"

They were almost ready to begin the Program when Sam thought he should worry some about the restaurants where he generally goes to lunch. Were they going to be able to feed him anything at all, if he wasn't going to eat any more meat, fish, cheese, or eggs? He made a few phone calls and discovered what he'd never taken the trouble to notice before: most restaurants already serve at least one meatless dish (and even at the ones that don't do so, he could always order a big salad and a baked potato). What's more, one or two of Sam's favorite restaurants were perfectly ready to make a special dish for him, upon request. And the Italian restaurants he went to were already equipped to serve spaghetti and marinara sauce without the meat or the olive oil. (See Chapter 13 for a full discussion of eating out.)

Sally thought that for her, eating at restaurants would be less of a problem, partly because she ate out less often, and partly because

she already knew several places where she could get a good slenderizing salad. And since the travel agency at which she worked was
only half a mile from home, she could easily go home for lunch
whenever she felt like it.

These two pilgrims in hope of health were running out of excuses
for postponing the big event. One morning they called me up and
said they were starting that very next Monday. "No more putting
it off," Sally announced.

6

SHOPPING

AND COOKING,

MCDOUGALL STYLE

My patients at St. Helena sit down at the table and their dishes for each meal of the day are placed in front of them. But you, eating in the quiet of your own home, will have to do some shopping and cooking before you can sit down to the fare you'll prepare.

Most of you will start by checking out your local grocery stores to see whether they stock the foods the Program requires you to eat. Why not begin with "perimeter shopping," because there, along the outside walls of your stereotypical supermarket, you'll find the fresh fruits and vegetables. Here in America, we're not faced with any shortage in amounts or variety. Go past the old familiar apples, bananas, potatoes, and corn. Heft a Hubbard squash, examine a pineapple. Notice the many new exotic names and flavors on the shelves, awaiting your discovery—chayote squash, cocozelle, kale, mangoes, kiwis. The box on the facing page lists some of the unfamiliar fruits and vegetables you'll want to try. Although you may not have tasted them before, I'll bet that some of them will be promoted to the status of favorites within just a few weeks.

Unfamiliar Fruits and Vegetables to Look For

Fruits:

carambola
cherimoya
guava
kiwifruit
kumquat
loquat
lychee
mango

papaya
persimmon
pomegranate
passion fruit
pummelo
quince
soursop

Vegetables:

aduki beans
arugula
bok choy
broccoli de rabe
burdock
celeriac (celery root)
chicory (curly endive)
cocozelle
collard greens
daikon
endive
fava beans
garbanzo beans (chick-peas)
Jerusalem artichoke
  (sunchoke)

jicama
kale
kohlrabi
radicchio
salsify
sprouts (alfalfa, lentil, mung
  bean, wheat)
Swiss chard
taro root
turban squash
waterchestnuts
watercress

After you look over the novel and exotic fruits and vegetables, check out some of the new starchy foods you'll be eating, such as triticale wheat, bulgur, and quinoa. The starch staples are listed on pages 94 and 95.

Starch Staples

The following starchy foods are high enough in calories that they can serve as the center of a meal:

Whole Grains

barley
brown rice
buckwheat
bulgur (cracked wheat)
couscous (refined wheat)
corn
millet

oats
quinoa (pronounced "keen-wa")
rye
triticale
wheat berries
wild rice

Unrefined Flours

barley
buckwheat
corn
garbanzo bean
lima bean
oat
potato

rice
rye
soy
triticale
wheat
whole wheat pastry

Egg-Free Pastas
(Pastas come in many shapes including spaghetti, macaroni, lasagna noodles, flat noodles, spirals, wheels, alphabet noodles.)

artichoke pasta
corn pasta (no wheat)
spinach pasta

tomato pasta
whole wheat pasta

Oriental Noodles

bean threads
buckwheat soba
rice noodles

somen
udon

Roots

burdock
celeriac (celery root)

sweet potatoes
tapioca

Roots (contd.)

Jerusalem artichoke (sunchoke)	taro root
jicama	waterchestnuts
parsnips	white potatoes
rutabaga	yams

(Carrots, beets, turnips, daikon, and salsify are low in carbohydrates and calories and so are not considered starch staples.)

Squashes

Winter squashes:	butternut
acorn	Hubbard
banana	pumpkin
buttercup	turban squash

(Summer squashes usually cannot serve as the center of a meal because of their low calorie content. They are also lower in carbohydrates than winter squashes.)

Legumes

Beans

aduki (azuki)	red kidney
black	mung
fava (broad)	navy
garbanzo (chick-peas)	pink
great northern	pinto
limas	white kidney (cannellini)

(Soybeans cannot be considered a starch staple because they are too high in fat to be allowed on the diet routinely.)

Lentils

brown	red
green	

Peas

black-eyed	split yellow
split green	whole green

BUYING PACKAGED AND CANNED FOODS

Label Shopping

As you continue your tour through the supermarket, check out the labels on the boxes, bottles, cans, and jars. The packaged foods that the industry sells in supermarkets are loaded with hidden sugars, oils, and chemicals of dubious safety. You don't want to be avoiding known nutritional catastrophes such as meats and cheeses and yet be eating cereals and breads that are like fields mined with explosives.

It's almost impossible to be utterly safe from all of the threats to your well-being. Most of us will be forced to buy some packaged foods occasionally, and that means we are never going to escape entirely from additives, "food fresheners," and preservatives. But you can minimize your risk by buying only the foodstuffs that hold as few of these chemicals as possible. The way to succeed in doing this is to read each label carefully. You want to eat genuine wheat or oats or corn, not one of those famous popular foods to which twenty or so other alien substances have been added. And you want all the components of the food to be wholesome. The main components should be mentioned first, at the head of the list on the label, because, by law, the manufacturer must name the major ingredients first, and list all the other components in the order of diminishing weight. If too many magical chemical names follow the important one you're interested in (or precede it), then put the package back on the shelf and go on to another brand for the unadulterated food you want.

Recheck the labels on the foods you eat frequently. Your friendly industrial foods giant is not going to send you a form letter reading: "Important Notice—We have just added three new helpful chemicals and a hefty dose of corn syrup to your whole wheat bread" every time he decides to "improve" his product. "Never trust a food technologist" is a motto that should hang in every kitchen.

Watch for "Hidden" Salt and Sugar

Salt and sugar are often added to packaged foods in large amounts as flavor enhancers. Salt is also added to many foods as a preservative. Be aware when you check labels that the food industry is not above playing tricks on us trusting types. Very seldom will you look at the list of ingredients on a package and see sugar listed as second or third. Instead, the manufacturer hides behind the names of several kinds of sugars. He has maltose, sucrose, dextrose, fructose, and corn syrup to choose among and, by listing them separately, he can keep them well down on the label. Combined, they might shoot the sugar content up toward the top of the list and scare the wary buyer into choosing another brand. The same thing can happen with salt, which is found on labels not only in various different forms of the word *sodium*, but also in ingredients that don't mention the word for example, carrageenan, soy sauce, bouillon, and mustard).

Stay Away from Oils and Fats

In your shopping according to label, avoid all foods that contain added fats and oils. All oils—be they saturated or unsaturated—are harmful to your health. Consumer pressure is changing the types of oils used in processed foods from saturated to unsaturated. Don't be fooled into thinking this is a healthy change. Keep a particularly sharp lookout for coconut oil and palm oil. These tropical oils are put into most cookies and crackers manufactured commercially in America, and in the amounts used, flood the eater with colossal quantities of saturated fats. The effect is intensified if these oils are hydrogenated. Do your body a favor and avoid such genuinely appalling, heart-damaging junk foods.

Avoid Sulfur Dioxide and MSG

I'd also suggest that you avoid eating products containing sulfur dioxide or MSG (monosodium glutamate). Many people have allergic reactions to these ingredients. Sulfur dioxide and also sodium metabisulfate and potassium metabisulfite, called sulfiting agents, are used as preservatives on light-colored, dehydrated (dried) fruits such as apples, apricots, bleached raisins, pears, and peaches and in wines (even nonalcoholic wines) and beer. They are also commonly used in restaurants to preserve the fresh look of salads, uncooked vegetables, avocado dips, and shrimp. Salad bars can keep greens from wilting and turning brown for days with a few sulfite sprayings. You may get a hint of whether or not the salad ingredients are preserved with these chemicals by the amount of ice used around the salad bowls—the more ice, the less likely sulfites have been used. But to be safe, ask. Some people have severe reactions to these substances that can result in asthma attacks, weakness, tightness of the chest, and—rarely—shock and coma.

MSG is a sodium salt of one of the most common amino acids found in proteins. It is used as a flavoring agent in cooking and in a wide variety of processed and packaged foods. The most common unpleasant reactions to MSG are headache, nausea, lightheadedness, increased salivation, fullness, and heartburn. Less frequent symptoms include tingling and pain of the chest, arms, neck and/or face; warmth (burning), tightness, weakness, thirst, sore throat, asthma, and psychiatric reactions. Cooks in some Chinese restaurants use this flavor enhancer liberally; thus, the reaction is commonly known as "Chinese Restaurant Syndrome."

Canned or Frozen?

Next, there's the question of canned foods and frozen foods. For the most part, avoid canned foods, although you may have no choice but to eat tomato paste and other tomato products and beans put up in cans. Food preserved in cans by heat treatment tends to have altered constituents—fewer vitamins, denatured proteins—and a host of additives, including salt and sugar. You're also getting small amounts of metal contaminants—iron, lead, tin, aluminum—leached from the cans.

Frozen foods, on the other hand, are almost as good as fresh. Just check the labels so you can steer clear of unwanted sauces, preservatives, sugars, and salt, added to what's supposed to be a natural product.

Buying Bread

The best bread is made at home or by the local bakery. If you ask—and especially if you're willing to order several loaves—most bakers will make you fresh tasty breads with all the right ingredients, and without salt.

When purchasing commercial bread, be sure it does not contain oil or dairy products of any kind, including milk, skim milk, and whey. It should be made from whole grains and/or whole grain flour (labels will say such things as "stone-ground flour," "no flour, sprouted grains," or "unrefined, whole wheat flour"). Additives abound in breads; look for breads with the shortest list of chemicals. If you want a bread with a sweeter taste, choose one with a natural sweetener such as honey, malted barley, or raisin syrup added. Salt will be found in small amounts in most commercial breads.

Most French, sourdough, and pumpernickel breads are made without oils, although the flour used in French and sourdough breads may be highly refined. Pita bread and bagels are also made without oil, but the fiber content of their flour will vary between the whole wheat and white varieties. (Bagels and breads are high in calories, so if you're trying to lose weight you should limit them during the twelve-day diet.) Breads made with refined flours are acceptable in most people's diets when used in small amounts, for unlike oils and dairy products, they are not actually harmful to the body.

Choosing Cereals

Hot and cold cereals should have the simplest ever list of ingredients, preferably only one ingredient, like "100% Natural Rolled Oats" (Quaker Oats Co.) or "100% Natural Whole Wheat" (Nabisco Shredded Wheat). Certainly listed first should be the whole grain (whole wheat, oats, oat bran, brown rice, corn, barley). After this you may find a natural sweetener like malted barley, rice syrup, or fruit juice. Salt and yeast may appear occasionally on the cereals you're looking for. However, if there is more listed, like coconut or tropical oils, hydrogenated soybean oil, safflower oils, sugar, coconut, BHA, sorbitol, gelatin, and other suspicious additives, return the package to the shelf.

Acceptable Packaged and Canned Foods

McDougall okayed Packaged Products are low-fat; they contain no added oils or fats, or high-fat plant foods such as nuts. However, some do contain significant amounts of salt and sugar, and an occasional additive, so read the labels carefully if you have any special health restrictions. Manufacturers have been known to change ingredients; therefore you should reread labels periodically.

This list does not contain all the packaged products you will need for McDougall-style cooking. Some common items, such as canned waterchestnuts, pimientos, and chilies are not listed because they are usually found packed only in water—no special brand is necessary. This list is far from complete. You will find other acceptable products on the grocery shelves if you look carefully.

I have listed the manufacturer and brand specifically because many similar products may contain unhealthy ingredients. For example, horseradish will usually contain dairy cream or oil, but the brands I list are made only of ground horseradish, vinegar, sugar, and salt.

Most of the items are available nationally in large supermarkets and in natural food stores. With the growing interest in health around the country, many large markets are adding health food sections. If you cannot locate a product, ask the store manager if he will order it for you.

MCDOUGALL OKAYED PACKAGED AND CANNED PRODUCTS

Manufacturer/Distributor   Variety

COLD CEREALS

Cold cereals are whole grain, low in salt, sugar, and additives, and contain no added fats or oils.

Manufacturer/Distributor	Variety
Nabisco	Shredded Wheat
Post	Grape-nuts
Nature's Path Foods	Manna (Millet Rice Flakes, Multi-Grain Flakes)
	Fiber O's
	Corn Flakes

MCDOUGALL OKAYED PACKAGED AND CANNED PRODUCTS

Manufacturer/Distributor   Variety

COLD CEREALS (*contd.*)

Manufacturer/Distributor	Variety
Kolln	Oat Bran Crunch
Health Valley Foods	100% Natural Bran Cereal
	Oat Bran Flakes
	Oat Bran O's
	Blue Corn Flakes
	Stone Wheat Flakes
	Raisin Bran
	Fruit Lites
U.S.Mills	Uncle Sam
	(Erewhon) Crispy Brown Rice
	(Erewhon) Raisin Bran
	(Erewhon) Wheat Flakes
	Skinner's Raisin Bran
	Skinner's Low-Sodium Raisin Bran
Perky Foods	Crispy Brown Rice
	Nutty Rice
Barbara's Bakery	Brown Rice Crisps
	Breakfast O's
	Breakfast Biscuits
	Raisin Bran
Kellogg Co.	Nutri-Grain (Corn, Wheat, Nuggets, etc.)
Weetabix Co.	Grainfields (Wheat Flakes, Raisin Bran, Corn Flakes)
Arrowhead Mills	Wheat Flakes
	Bran Flakes
	Oat Bran Flakes
	Corn Flakes
	Puffed Wheat
	Puffed Rice
	Puffed Millet
	Puffed Corn
New Morning	Fruit-e-O's
	Super Bran
	Oatios

MCDOUGALL OKAYED PACKAGED AND CANNED PRODUCTS

Manufacturer/Distributor   Variety

HOT CEREALS

Hot cereals are whole grain, low in salt, sugar, and additives, and contain no added fats or oils.

Manufacturer/Distributor	Variety
Quaker Oats Co.	Quaker Oats
	Quick Quaker Oats
U.S. Mills (Erewhon)	Instant Oat Meal
	Barley Plus
	Brown Rice Cream
Stone-Buhr Milling	Hot Apple Granola
	7-Grain Cereal
Golden Temple Bakery	Oat Bran
Barbara's Bakery	14 Grains
Kashi Company	Kashi (some sesame seeds)
Arrowhead Mills	Bear Mush
	Oat Bran
	Instant Oatmeal
Maple Leaf Mills	Red River Cereal (Original, Creamy Wheat and Bran)

FROZEN POTATOES

Frozen potatoes have no added fats, oils, or salt. Most have sugar (dextrose) and a preservative added (Mr. Dell's contain only potatoes).

Manufacturer/Distributor	Variety
Ore-Ida Foods	Hash Browns
	Potatoes O'Brien
Bel-air	Hash Browns
Mr. Dell Foods	Hash Browns
J.R. Simplot Co.	Okray's Hash Brown Potato Patties

POPCORN

Unprocessed popcorn (with no added ingredients). You can pop any natural popcorn yourself in an air popper or in the microwave.

Manufacturer/Distributor	Variety
H.J. Heinz Co.	Weight Watchers (microwave popcorn)
Nature's Best	Nature's Cuisine (natural popcorn)

MCDOUGALL OKAYED PACKAGED AND CANNED PRODUCTS

Manufacturer/Distributor	Variety

RICE CAKES

Rice with other whole grains and seasonings, but no added fats or oils. Some have salt added.

Quaker Oats Co.	Rice Cakes (lightly salted)
	Corn Cakes
H.J. Heinz Co.	Chico San (Millet, Buckwheat, etc.)
Hollywood Health Foods	Mini Rice Cakes (Teriyaki, Apple Cinnamon)
Pacific Rice Prod.	Mini Crispys (Apple Spice, Raisin N' Spice, Italian Spice, Natural Sodium)
Westbrae Natural Foods	Teriyaki Rice Cakes
Lundberg Family Farms	Rice Cakes (Wild Rice, Wehani, Brown Rice, Mochi Sweet)
	Brown Rice Chewies, Brown Rice Crunchies
Glenn Foods	Brown Rice Treat

CRACKERS

Rice, wheat, rye, and other whole grains with seasonings but no added fats or oils. Some have salt added.

San-J International	Tamari Brown Rice Crackers
Westbrae Natural Foods	Brown Rice Wafers
Ralston Purina Co.	Natural Ry-Krisp
Edward & Sons Trading Co.	Baked Brown Rice Snaps
Parco Foods	(Hol-Grain) Brown Rice Lite Snack Thins, Whole Wheat Lite Snack Thins
O. Kavli A/S	Kavli Norwegian Crispbread
Barbara's Bakery	Crackle Snax
	Lightbread
Sandoz Nutrition Corp.	Wasa Crispbread (Lite Rye, Hearty Rye)
H.J. Heinz Co.	Weight Watchers Crispbread (Harvest Rice)

MCDOUGALL OKAYED PACKAGED AND CANNED PRODUCTS

Manufacturer/Distributor	Variety

CRACKERS (*contd.*)

Shaffer, Clarke & Co.	Finn Crisp
Lifestream Natural Foods	Wheat & Rye Krispbread

PRETZELS

No added fats or oils. Most are high in salt and refined flours.

Laura Scudder's	Mini-Twist Pretzels
	Pretzel Sticks
	Bavarian Pretzels
Anderson Bakery Co.	Oat Bran Pretzels
Snyder's of Hanover	Sourdough Hard Pretzels (salted and unsalted)
Granny Goose Foods	Stick Pretzels
	100% Natural Bavarian Pretzels (salted and unsalted)

BREADS

Baked with whole wheat, sprouted wheat, rye, or other whole grains with no added oil or dairy products, such as whey. Low in sugar, and sodium. Most breads, bagels, and tortillas are baked locally. You may find several acceptable choices on your supermarket shelves.

Cedarlane Foods	Whole Wheat Lavash Bread
Lifestream Natural Foods	Essene Bread
Nature's Path Foods	Manna Bread
Grainaissance	Mochi (Plain, Raisin Cinnamon, Mugwort, Organic)
International Baking Co.	Mr. Pita
Garden of Eatin'	Bible Bread (regular and salt-free)
	Thin-Thin Bread
Breads for Life	Sprouted 7-Grain Bread, Sprouted Wheat with Raisin, Sprouted Rye Bread
Interstate Brands	Pritikin Bread (Rye, Whole Wheat, Multi-Grain)
French Meadow Bakery	French Meadow Brown Rice Bread

MCDOUGALL OKAYED PACKAGED AND CANNED PRODUCTS

Manufacturer/Distributor	Variety

BREADS (*contd.*)

New England Foods Co.	Whole Wheat Milldam Pouch Bread
Food For Life	Sprouted Grain Breads

SOUPS

Soups have no meat, dairy products, or added fats and oils. Many are high in salt.

Dry Packaged:

Nile Spice Foods	Cous-Cous (Tomato Minestrone, Lentil Curry)
Westbrae Natural Foods	Ramen (Whole Wheat, Onion, Curry, Carrot, Miso, Seaweed, 5 Spice, Spinach, Mushroom, Buckwheat)
	Instant Miso Soup (Mellow White, Hearty Red)
Sokensha Co.	Soken Ramen
Eden Foods	Buckwheat Ramen
	Whole Wheat Ramen
Hain Pure Food Co.	Natural Classic Onion
	Natural Classic Potato-Leek

Canned:

Thompson Kitchens	Pritikin Lentil Soup (not every Pritikin soup is acceptable— some have dairy products: whey, etc.)
Hain Pure Food Co.	Split Pea Soup
Real Fresh	Andersen's Soup—Split Pea

BURGER MIXES

Mixes contain no added fats, oils, dairy products, or soybean products. Most tell you to fry in oil—*Don't*; cook on a nonstick griddle.

Fantastic Foods	Fantastic Falafil
	Nature's Burger (Barbecue Flavor)
Richter Bros.	Fritini (Vegetable Patties)

MCDOUGALL OKAYED PACKAGED AND CANNED PRODUCTS

Manufacturer/Distributor   Variety

EGG-FREE PASTAS

Pastas are egg-free and low in sodium with no added oils or fat. Most are made of flour and water.

Manufacturer/Distributor	Variety
Health Valley Foods	Spaghetti Pasta (Spinach, Whole Wheat, Amaranth, etc.)
Westbrae Natural Foods	Spaghetti Pasta (Spinach, Whole Wheat)
	Lasagna Noodles (Spinach, Whole Wheat)
	Whole Wheat Somen
DeBole's Nutritional Foods	Curly Lasagna, Elbows, Spaghetti
	Corn Pasta (Wheat-free)
Quinoa Corp.	Quinoa Spaghetti (Wheat-free)
Golden Grain Macaroni Co.	Spaghetti, Macaroni, Rotini, Lasagna, Manicotti
A. Zerega's Sons	Antoine's Pasta—Fusilli Tri Colori
Eden Foods	Udon (Japanese Noodles)
	Soba (buckwheat)
	Pasta (many shapes)
Nanka Seimen Co.	Chow Mein Udon
Sokensha Co.	Soken Jinenjo Noodles
Health Foods	MI-del (Spaghetti, Macaroni, Alphabets)
Best Foods, CPC Int.	Muellers (Twist, Spaghetti, Linguine)
Creamette-D, Borden	Spaghetti, Fettuccini, Rotini, Shells
Reese Finer Foods	Da Vinci Pasta
Ferrara Foods	Gnocchi with Potato
Ronzoni Foods Corp.	Radiatore-79
	Linguine
	Fusilli
	Rotelle
	Spaghetti

MCDOUGALL OKAYED PACKAGED AND CANNED PRODUCTS

Manufacturer/Distributor   Variety

PACKAGED MIXES

Packaged mixes contain whole grains and vegetables only; no added
fats or oils.

Quinoa Corp.	Quinoa
Continental Mills	ala—cracked wheat bulgur
Lundberg Family Farms	Rizcous (grain mixture; don't follow cooking directions— omit butter and olive oil)
Fantastic Foods	Brown Basmati Rice
	Whole Wheat Couscous
Arrowhead Mills	Wholegrain Teff
	Quick Brown Rice
Thompson Kitchens	Pritikin Pilaf Brown Rice
	Pritikin Spanish Brown Rice
Near East Food Prod.	Spanish Rice
	Wheat Pilaf
	Taboule
Sahara Natural Foods	Casbah-Wheat Pilaf
	Casbah-Spanish Pilaf
Nile Spice Foods	Rozdali (Vegetable Curry)
Health Valley Foods	Oat Bran Pasta with Sauce (Fettucini Marinara, Fettucini Primavera)
Will-Pak Foods	Pinto Bean Flakes
Fantastic Foods	Potatoes Country Style
	Quick Pilaf (Three Grain with Herbs)
Barbara's Bakery	Mashed Potatoes (instant—add water only)

SALAD DRESSINGS

Salad dressings have no added dairy products (whey, buttermilk, etc.),
fats, or oils. Many state clearly "No-oil." Should also say low-sodium.

Thompson Kitchens	Pritikin No-oil Dressing (Ranch, Tomato, Italian, Russian, Creamy Italian, etc.)
WM Reily & Co.	Herb Magic (All No-oil—Vinaigrette, Italian, Gypsy, Zesty Tomato, Creamy Cucumber)

MCDOUGALL OKAYED PACKAGED AND CANNED PRODUCTS

Manufacturer/Distributor   Variety

SALAD DRESSINGS (*contd.*)

American Health Products   El Molino Herbal Secrets (All
                                    No-oil—Herbs & Spices, etc.)
Cook's Classics Ltd.   Cook's Classics (Italian Gusto
                                    only)
Kraft   Oil Free Italian (high salt)
H.J. Heinz Co.   Weight Watchers Dressing (To-
                                    mato Vinaigrette, French)
Hain Pure Food Co.   No Oil Dressing Mix (Italian,
                                    French, Natural Herb)

SPAGHETTI SAUCE

Spaghetti sauces contain no meat or dairy products and also no olive
oil, or any other oils or fats.

Pure & Simple   Johnson's Spaghetti Sauce
Trader Joe's   Trader Giotto's Italian Garden
                                    Fresh Vegetable Spaghetti
                                    Sauce
Westbrae Natural Foods   Ci' Bella Pasta Sauce—No Salt,
                                    No Oil
Thompson Kitchens   Pritikin Spaghetti Sauce
H.J. Heinz Co.   Weight Watchers Spaghetti
                                    Sauce with Mushrooms

SOY SAUCES

Soy sauces contain no MSG (monosodium glutamate). They are all high
in sodium, even though salt-reduced.

Kikkoman Foods   Kikkoman Lite Soy Sauce
Westbrae Natural Foods   Mild Soy Sauce
San-J International   Tamari Wheat Free Soy Sauce
Live Food Products   Bragg Liquid Aminos

MCDOUGALL OKAYED PACKAGED AND CANNED PRODUCTS

Manufacturer/Distributor   Variety

OTHER SAUCES

Sauces contain no oils, fats, or MSG. Many have salt and preservatives. Most are very spicy and can burn. Worcestershire sauce should have no anchovies. Horseradish should have no added dairy products.

Manufacturer/Distributor	Variety
New Morning	Corn Relish
Nabisco Brands	A.1. Steak Sauce
St. Giles Foods Ltd.	Matured Worcestershire Sauce
McIlhenny Co.	Tabasco
Gourmet Foods	Cajun Sunshine
Durkee-French Foods	Red Hot Sauce
Baumer Foods	Crystal Hot Sauce
B.F. Trappey's Sons	Red Devil Louisiana Hot Sauce
J. Sosnick & Son	Kosher Horseradish
Reese Finer Foods	Prepared Horseradish

SALSAS

Salsas contain vegetable ingredients only, with no oils. Some have preservatives. Many have sugar and/or salt.

Manufacturer/Distributor	Variety
Hain Pure Food Co.	Salsa
Pet	Old El Paso Salsa
Tree of Life	Salsa
Nabisco Brands	Ortega Green Chile Salsa
Pace Foods	Picante Sauce
La Victoria Foods	Chili Dip
	Salsa Jalapena, etc.
Artichoke Industries	Cara Mia-Artichoke Hearts Picante
Ventre Packing Co.	Enrico's Salsa
Thompson Kitchens	Pritikin Mexican Sauce

SALT-FREE SEASONING MIXTURES

Salt-free seasoning mixes are made with no added salt, but there is a small amount of natural sodium in them. They are made of dehydrated vegetables and spices. (Watch for added salt and oils in any seasoning mixes you buy.)

Manufacturer/Distributor	Variety
Alberto-Culver Co.	Mrs. Dash (Low Pepper-No Garlic, Extra Spicy, Original Blend, etc.)

MCDOUGALL OKAYED PACKAGED AND CANNED PRODUCTS

Manufacturer/Distributor   Variety

SALT-FREE SEASONING MIXTURES (*contd.*)

Modern Products	Vegit All-Purpose Seasoning
	Onion Magic
	Natural Seasoning
Parsley Patch	Parsley Patch (All Purpose, Mexican Blend, etc.)
Maine Coast Sea Vegetables	Sea Seasonings (Dulse with Garlic, Nori with Ginger, etc.)
Estee Corp.	Seasoning Sense (Mexican, Italian)
Hain Pure Food Co.	Chili Seasoning Mix
Bernard Jensen Products	Broth or Seasoning Special Vegetable Mix

BAKING INGREDIENTS

Baking ingredients contain no aluminum and a minimum of additives.

The Rumford Co.	Rumford Baking Powder
Sandoz Nutrition	Featherweight Baking Powder
Ener-G Foods	Egg Replacer (a binder for baking)

HOT DRINKS

Drinks contain no caffeine or other strong herbs that you might be sensitive to. Any noncaffeinated tea is acceptable.

Modern Products	Sipp
Libby, McNeill & Libby	Pero
Worthington Foods	Kaffree Roma
Richter Bros.	Cafix
General Foods Corp.	Postum

CANNED BEAN PRODUCTS

Canned beans contain no added fats and oils, and are low in sodium and preservatives. Any low-sodium, water-packed plain beans are acceptable. The cans are made of metals that leach into the foods unless they are coated, so those in glass jars are preferable.

Eden Foods	Great Northern Beans (glass jars)
	Pinto Beans (glass jars)

MCDOUGALL OKAYED PACKAGED AND CANNED PRODUCTS

Manufacturer/Distributor   Variety

CANNED BEAN PRODUCTS (*contd.*)

	Adzuki Beans (glass jars)
Whole Earth	Baked Beans
Health Valley Foods	Boston Style Baked Beans
Hain Pure Food Co.	Spicy Vegetarian Homestyle Chili
Bush Bros. & Co.	Bush's Deluxe Vegetarian Beans
Bruce Foods Corp.	Casa Fiesta Mexican Style Chili Beans

CANNED TOMATO PRODUCTS

Canned tomato products contain no added salt. Metals leach from cans unless they are coated.

Health Valley Foods	Tomato Sauce (coated lead-free can)
Del Monte USA	Tomato Sauce—No Salt Added
	Original Style Stewed Tomatoes (with onions, celery, green peppers)—No Salt Added
	Tomato Paste
Beatrice/Hunt-Wesson	Hunt's All Natural Tomato Paste, No Salt Added
	Hunt's All Natural Tomato Sauce, No Salt Added
	Hunt's Stewed Tomatoes, No Salt Added
	Hunt's All Natural Whole Tomatoes, No Salt Added
Contadina Foods	Tomato Puree
	Tomato Paste
Pet	Progresso Tomato Paste
	Progresso Tomato Puree

CANNED FRUIT PRODUCTS

Canned fruits are not packed in sugars or fruit syrups, just plain fruit and maybe some natural fruit juice. Metals leach from the cans.

Dole Packaged Foods Co.	Pineapple Chunks (in unsweetened juice)

MCDOUGALL OKAYED PACKAGED AND CANNED PRODUCTS

Manufacturer/Distributor	Variety

CANNED FRUIT PRODUCTS (*contd.*)

	Crushed Pineapple (in unsweetened juice)
	Pineapple Slices (in unsweetened juice)
S & W Fine Foods	Nutradiet (Grapefruit, Apricot Halves, Pear Halves, Sliced Peaches, Peach Halves)
	Mandarin Oranges (Natural Style, in its own juice)
	Grapefruit (Natural Style, in its own juice)
Tri Valley Growers	Libby's Lite (Sliced Peaches, Pear Halves)

ACCEPTABLE MILKS

Acceptable milks are dairy-free and low in natural vegetable fat. They are not to be used as beverages, but on cereals and in cooking.

Grainaissance	Amazake Rice Nectar
Eden Foods	Edensoy Vanilla Soy Milk (low-fat)

RICHER FOODS

These richer foods are high in simple sugar and/or salt, so some caution must be used in adding them to your diet.

FRUIT SNACKS

Fruit snacks are made of pure fruit, but are concentrated.

Sunfield	Nature's Choice—Real Fruit Bars
Barbara's Bakery	Apples, and that's all
Stretch Island Fruit	Tropical Fruit Ripples (Mandarin Cherry, Banana)
	Fruit Leather

MCDOUGALL OKAYED PACKAGED AND CANNED PRODUCTS

Manufacturer/Distributor   Variety

FRUIT CANDIES

Fruit candies are concentrated natural fruit with no added sugar.

Panda Factory	All Natural Bar
Sokensha Co.	Plum Candy
Erewhon	Plum Sweets
	Cinnamon Sweets
Edward & Sons	Natural Temptations Rice Malt Candies

JELLIES, JAMS, AND SYRUPS

Jellies, jams, and syrups should have no added sugar, corn syrup, or other sugars, and few preservatives. Any pure honey or pure maple syrup is acceptable.

Clearbrook Farms	Fruit Spreads
M. Polaner	All Fruit (Jams)
Robertson Foods Int.	Pure Fruit Conserve
The J.M. Smucker Co.	Smucker's Simply Fruit (Red Raspberry, Strawberry, Blueberry, etc.)
Sorrell Ridge Farm	Sorrell Ridge Fruit Only (Apricot, Grape, etc.)
Knudsen & Sons	All Fruit Fancy Fruit Spreads (Concord Grape, Blueberry, Cranberry, etc.)
	Syrups (Raspberry, Boysenberry, Fruit N' Maple, Blueberry, Strawberry)
Westbrae Natural Foods	Brown Rice Syrup
Eden Foods	Barley Malt

BARBECUE SAUCES AND KETCHUPS

These sauces contain no added fats or oils, but most have salt and sugar and some have preservatives.

Beatrice/Hunt-Wesson	Hunt's All Natural Thick & Rich Barbecue Sauce
	Hunt's No Salt Added Tomato Ketchup
Ridg's Finer Foods	Bull's Eye Original Barbecue Sauce

MCDOUGALL OKAYED PACKAGED AND CANNED PRODUCTS

Manufacturer/Distributor   Variety

BARBECUE SAUCES AND KETCHUPS (*contd.*)

Robbie's   Robbie's Sauce (Barbecue—mild
                                & hot, Sweet & Sour Ha-
                                waiian Style)
                                Ketchup
Hain Pure Food Co.   Catsup
Kingsford Products   K.C. Masterpiece Original Sauce
Mrs. Renfro's   Mrs. Renfro's Barbecue Sauce
Westbrae Natural Foods   Fruit Sweetened Catsup
                                Unsweetened Un-Ketchup
Health Valley Foods   Catch-Up Tomato Table Sauce
Ventre Packing Co.   Enrico's Ketchup
Pure & Simple   Johnson's Ketchup

ICE DESSERTS

Ice desserts are made from fruit and concentrated fruit juice, with no added dairy products (whey) or oils.

Dole Packaged Foods Co.   Fruit Sorbet (no dairy products)
                                Fruit N' Juice Bars
                                Dole Sun Tops—Real Fruit Juice
                                Bars
Eskimo Pie Co.   All Natural Pops (Fruit Punch,
                                Cherry, Orange)
Frozfruit Corp.   Frozfruit (strawberry, raspberry,
                                lemon, cantelope, lime,
                                orange, cherry, pineapple)

Help us update this list. Please send packages and labels that identify packaged products that make healthful eating easier. This list was compiled in September 1989.

For an updated package list send with SASE to:
McDougalls
P.O. Box 14039
Santa Rosa, CA 95402

STOCKING UP FOR THE DIET

Now that you've finished your shopping tour, you may want to buy some of the foods you'll need when you begin the diet. To make things easier for you, itemized shopping lists for the sample diet menu plan are included in Chapter 10. Whether or not you plan to follow the sample diet exactly, you will need the staples listed there and can buy them now. You may also want to sample some of the starch staples and unfamiliar fruits and vegetables listed on page 93.

Putting Together a Survival Kit of Seasonings and Snacks

Seasoning is an important element of a starch-based meal. You may find it helpful to put together a "survival kit" of seasonings acceptable for the Program both to use at home and to take with you when you go to work, eat out, or travel. Old spice jars are excellent portable containers for carrying individual servings of dressings and sauces. (See Chapter 13 for a discussion of eating out, McDougall style.) You can choose among low-sodium, oil-free salad dressings, oil-free barbecue sauces (though they contain a little sugar and salt), or any other condiments acceptable to your individual health plan. Soy sauce contains lots of salt, so only use a recommended low-sodium variety (500 mg sodium, as opposed to 800 mg in regular soy sauce). Mustard is high in fat content and should be used sparingly (but it's only 4 calories per teaspoon). Ketchup is high in sugar and should be used sparingly.

Snacking is encouraged in the Program, as long as you do it McDougall style. It's best to plan ahead to stock up on snacks so you have them at hand when you get the urge. Fortunately, there are a lot of munchies available that are all right to eat between meals. Easiest to find are leftovers from the night before. Or you can make "smoothies" of blended fresh or frozen fruit, or heat up

Survival Kit

Check the list of McDougall Okayed Packaged Products on pages 100–114 for acceptable brands.

TOPPINGS AND SEASONINGS:

low-sodium, oil-free salad dressings
lemon juice (bottled)
vinegar (try Balsalmic vinegar as a salad dressing)
low-sodium ketchup
mustard
salsa (oil-free)
hot pepper sauces
horseradish (oil- and dairy-free)
low-sodium soy sauce
barbecue sauces (bottled; no oil)
spaghetti sauce (bottled; no oil)
salt-free vegetable seasonings and seasoning mixes
sugar, honey, molasses, syrup
no-sugar, pure-fruit jams

HANDY SNACKS:

rice cakes and rice crackers
pretzels
whole wheat crackers (oil-free)
popcorn (Spice this up by sprinkling it with garlic, chili, curry, or
  onion powder, poultry seasoning, or diluted Tabasco sauce. If
  you're not salt sensitive, spray soy sauce on it or moisten the
  popcorn with water and sprinkle it with table salt.)
fresh fruit and fruit snacks
sliced raw vegetables
seaweed
whole grain and sprouted wheat breads, whole wheat pita, and
  bagels (oil-free; avoid if you're trying to lose weight)
instant oatmeal
baked potatoes (leftover, eaten cold or microwaved)
frozen hash-brown potatoes
dry packaged or canned soups
canned beans
herbal teas and other noncaffeinated hot drinks
soda water (low-sodium; flavored or unflavored) or mineral water

a can of soup or beans. When going to work or traveling, carry your snacks in zip-lock plastic bags or airtight plastic containers or jars in your briefcase, purse, or a brown paper bag.

COOKING FOR THE PROGRAM

The McDougall style of cooking and eating, or McDougalling as some people refer to their new diet, is not restrictive but rather expands your enjoyment of eating. You will discover that food can taste delicious when cooked without oil or added salt and sugar. In fact, these crude gustatory stimulations, which so many Americans rely on, often mask the natural flavors of fresh foods.

Familiar cooking methods—primarily steaming, boiling, sautée-ing, baking, and broiling—are used, but with water and other fat-free liquids instead of butter, lards, or cooking oils. Flavor-furnish-ing fat-free liquids include low-sodium soy sauce, tomato juice, lemon juice, grape juice, and wine or sherry, which can be mixed with just the right amounts of onion powder, garlic, dill, paprika, oregano, and/or other favorite spices.

Cookware for Oil-Free Cooking

If I'm not supposed to use vegetable oils, you may ask, how am I going to keep foods from sticking to my pots and pans? The answer is to use containers that have nonstick synthetic coatings like Teflon or Silverstone, or that are silicone-coated (Baker's Secret). Buy high-quality nonstick cookware to avoid having the surface coat flake off. A light oiling when you first get a Teflon or Silverstone imple-ment will help to prevent sticking. Your iron wok and cast-iron pots and pans should be "seasoned" occasionally by coating them lightly with oil and heating them, then wiping off any excess oil.

Seasoning

Oil, salt, and sugar are potent flavor-enhancers. When you cook without them you have to rely more on the quality of your ingre-dients, careful cooking procedures, and a judicious use of other interesting flavoring agents such as herbs, spices, onion, garlic, peppers, vinegars, and pungent condiments such as mustard.

Whatever your experience with cooking, when you first begin the diet you will want to rely on flavors that have been old favorites in the past. For most people the amount of seasoning in the diet recipes will be just right. Others of you will knowingly add less when you start each recipe and those of you who like spicy foods will increase these enjoyment-enhancing ingredients automatically. Those sauces and gravies you thought could only be made with the disgusting drippings left behind after cooking one animal part or another can be made delicious with accustomed smells and flavors by adding your favorite spices to vegetable stocks. The liquid to be thickened is heated to a boil and an arrowroot or cornstarch paste is stirred in. Soon, gyrations with your spoon are rewarded by a smooth, creamy sauce just asking to be poured over spinach spaghetti, baby potatoes, or wild rice. Many recipes can be quickly thickened by stirring in instant oatmeal or instant mashed potatoes—try this with soups and stews. Mistake-proof recipes for sauces and other toppings are provided in the recipe section of this book.

Flavoring Precautions

Some sensitive people must avoid even small quantities of sugar and spices, and may have to strictly limit the amount of salt they consume. Persons with intractable high blood pressure (a very rare condition), or who suffer from heart or kidney failure, or who experience edema—persistent swelling of the tissues of the legs, feet, or other body parts—must limit their salt intake. Individuals with tendencies toward high blood levels of triglycerides (see page 59) or suffering from hypoglycemia may jeopardize their health quite seriously by consuming foods containing simple sugars, such as white sugar, honey, maple syrup, molasses, or even fruit juice. Some people are harmed even by the sugar found in natural fruits, and must limit their consumption. People with intestinal problems (indigestion, hiatus hernia, gastritis, esophagitis, colitis, diarrhea, and painful or itchy anus) should be very careful with spices. The most irritating spices for people with these problems come from the pepper family—chili, the pepper components in curry powders, and preparations of black, white, and red peppers. Some exceptionally unfortunate individuals are allergic to almost all spices.

SUMMARY OF FLAVORFUL PRECAUTIONS

AVOID SALT	AVOID SUGAR	AVOID SPICE
if you have:	*if you have:*	*if you have:*
high blood pressure	high triglycerides	gastritis
most heart muscle failure	hypoglycemia	colitis
most kidney disease		other GI conditions
swelling (edema)		allergy

Some Time-Saving Techniques

I know many of you are busy people and want to cut down on the time you spend preparing meals. The basic ingredients used in McDougall cooking can be shopped for in large quantities, saving you trips to the store, because some (like dried beans and rice) have long shelf lives and others (like fruits and vegetables) last when refrigerated. You can save time by cooking extra beans and rice, and freezing the leftovers for use in another meal. Or double a recipe and save half. Also, once cooked, the dishes themselves refrigerate and freeze well. Because there are no meat or dairy products, spoilage is much less of a problem. Your meatless, oilless spaghetti sauce will taste fresh-made when thawed two months later.

SHARING MCDOUGALL-STYLE MEALS WITH NONDIETERS

If you have family at home who are not participating in the Program, you will find that you can share your McDougall meals easily with them with a little creative planning. Simply provide the "forbidden" ingredients they require on the side for them to add to the basic dishes. Make Spaghetti with Marinara Sauce, for instance, put a can of Parmesan cheese on the table, and cook meatballs separately for the others to add. Make A La King Sauce or Cajun Rice and offer shredded chicken or turkey for them to stir in. Offer diced ham to put in the split pea soup, cheese or meat slices to add to vegetable sandwiches, hard-boiled eggs to slice over a salad, grated cheese to sprinkle over hot soups, casseroles, or stews. It won't be easy for you to see these things on the table—you may have to use all your will power to resist them and you may have trouble quieting your concern for your family's health. But at least you and your family will be able to eat together.

These same suggestions will allow you to have unconverted friends and relatives for dinner without going off the Program. Choose dishes that are similar to favorite traditional dishes and allow your guests to embellish them if they choose. If you have completed the twelve-day diet and regained your health, you can serve the richer dishes from Chapter 13 for the special occasions when you have company.

THE WAY THE WATERMANS ATE

I gave Sally and Sam the same sort of advice I've just given you. They were very interested in starting the Program, but they still hesitated, wondered about attempting a diet that would deny them every trace of meat and fish, every drop of milk, every slice of cheese and dribble of vegetable oil—not just a moderate diet but a diet radically low in fats and cholesterol. I told them what I tell all my patients: *If you want big improvements, you must make big changes*; if you want small improvements, then make small changes. The small improvements are hardly worth working for, unless you're in almost perfect shape already.

Sally and Sam knew that perfect they weren't. They shopped around for a couple of days before starting the Program. They strolled through their local supermarkets, looked into a couple of health food stores, and found an Oriental grocery. All this meant a bit of work, but also quite a lot of fun. They discovered the numerous kinds of egg-free pasta you can buy these days and tried out four or five new kinds of fruits even before they started the Program. Sally realized she had always been very fond of fruits but had never eaten many of the new kinds that have appeared in the American markets recently.

Sam still insisted that he wanted to feel full after a meal. I told him, "Wait until you find out all the different ways for making starch foods delicious—all the vegetable stews that can be served with rice, all the different marinara sauces that can be put on so many different kinds of pasta. You could take six months to get acquainted with all the possibilities for gourmet health foods."

I knew, of course, that some mild shocks were in store for Sally and Sam. They had been raised on picture-perfect American meals, and they had raised their children on them. Sam usually had eggs and bacon in the morning. When he was rushed he ate a cold cereal. Sally always ate buttered toast for breakfast. They both drank juice and coffee. For lunch Sam mostly ate out. Red meat, poultry, or fish was the main dish for those meals. On weekends he would fill up on sandwiches made from cold cuts or on leftovers from the previous night. Sally's lunches were more varied—sometimes a sandwich, sometimes a salad, sometimes a restaurant meal not much different from the ones Sam ate. Sally also had a sweet tooth and tended to hit on the jelly doughnuts and the cakes with sugary frostings. Their dinners were usually an ultratraditional combination of meat, vegetable, and starch. Their biggest concession to dietary change had been two years ago, when they stopped eating red meat two or three times a week. Now they had it only about once a month. From this you'll guess that Sally had heard about the dangers of too much cholesterol. Sam, who didn't know cholesterol from a camel, stopped pooh-poohing that move when his chest pains started up about six months later.

Needless to say, my two model patients were going to be making some big changes.

7

THE PROGRAM BEGINS:

Days 1–4

You climb out of bed, glance in the mirror, groan, and head toward the kitchen. You've committed yourself to doing the McDougall Program. This is to be your first day. *How do you feel?*

"Physically? Just the way I've always felt."

Exactly. If you were overweight yesterday, you're still overweight today. If you usually wake up with a headache, or sore joints, or chest pains, you still will feel those morning miseries. That's the physical condition you've made for yourself by eating both unwisely and too well of the foods included in the standard American diet. Whatever age you are, if you're willing to begin eating according to the recommendations of a healthy diet, you're about to start the second and better half of your life. Some weeks later, Sally Waterman admitted to me that she was tremendously excited on the morning she started the Program—she felt like she was buying a new car or about to take a trip. But she was skeptical, too. She remembered saying to Sam, "I don't know if I can believe everything Dr. McDougall told us. But I figure a lot of it will turn out to be true—otherwise he must be the biggest liar in creation."

Sally and Sam were setting sail, hoping to cross unknown seas, toward a new goal. That will be your situation on Day 1.

THE AGENDA

As we describe Sam and Sally's first four days of the Program, we'll be covering the following important subjects:

- Choosing an agreeable menu plan
- Physical changes during the first few days
- Rapid improvement in blood pressure and the need for reducing medication levels
- Improvement in arthritis on the Program
- What to expect after your first four days on the Program

T·H·E W·A·T·E·R·M·A·N·S

DAY 1

Breakfast: Oatmeal and cantaloupe (Sam ate two bowls with extra hot water and lightly sprinkled with raisins; Sally had one bowl with a little low-fat soy milk)
Lunch: Fast Pizza / apple / soda water (ate at work)
Dinner: Chili / brown rice / Strawberry Frozen Fruit Dessert

EXERCISE: Sam walked 5 minutes in the morning and 10 minutes in the evening, but stopped frequently due to chest pain. Sally walked 20 minutes in the morning but only 10 minutes in the evening, because she came back home with Sam.

PHYSICAL STATUS: Sam: BP 158/104. Weight 213 lbs. Frequent chest pains, recurrent acid indigestion, diarrhea four times. Sally: BP 100/60. Weight 135 lbs. One, rock-hard, difficult-to-pass BM today. Headaches (both sinus and caffeine withdrawal), postnasal drip, arthritic pains, and "rundown" tired-out feeling most of day.

MENTAL STATUS: Sam is determined to get well. He figures there is no place left to turn for the kind of help he wants—to get his health back. Sally is far from convinced the diet will work. For too many years she has believed that diet therapy is quackery.

TEST RESULTS: Sam visited his cardiologist for a check-up and went to the laboratory for blood tests. Sally went for her blood tests. Sam: Cholesterol 246 mg/dl. Triglycerides 275 mg/dl. Blood sugar 180 mg/dl. Sally: Cholesterol 218 mg/dl. Triglycerides 104 mg/dl. Blood sugar 98 mg/dl.

MEDICATIONS: Sam: Dyazide (a diuretic) twice a day, Inderal (a beta-blocker) 10 mg four times a day, Calan (a calcium blocker) 80 mg three times a day. 10 nitroglycerin tablets today. Sally: 2 aspirin four times today for relief of headaches and arthritic pain.

DAILY LESSON: In order to change, you first have to learn what to do. Practice what you've learned. In the beginning a little faith helps.

THE WATERMANS' FIRST DAY

Sally and Sam Waterman started the Program on a Monday. Over the weekend they had done their shopping and told their children and a few good friends about their plans, in hopes that they would offer encouragement and support. Sunday night they ate a couple of pork chops for dinner and then, in a very good sense, kissed meat good-bye. Monday they woke up committed to the McDougall Program, ate oatmeal and cantaloupe for breakfast, and went off to work.

Sam had arranged an appointment with his cardiologist for late in the morning of this first day to have his blood pressure taken. Both Sam and Sally had arranged for blood tests to be done prior to breakfast. They had weighed themselves on their bathroom scale, which they had checked for accuracy by comparing their readings with the doctor's scales. Both took Fast Pizza with them to work and warmed it in microwave ovens in their employees' lounges. When the work day was done, both went home a little early, and, together in the kitchen, they prepared a chili and rice dinner. Before going to sleep, they shared a summing-up of the day. Sally wasn't feeling too well. She was having a new kind of headache—more generalized, all over her head instead of just in her forehead like she usually had. She figured it was from caffeine withdrawal, which I had warned her about. Sam felt okay except that he was still hungry even though he had eaten a lot of chili and rice for dinner—he planned to eat a rice cake with some pure fruit jam before bed. His chest pain was the same; he'd taken a nitroglycerin tablet after breakfast, two around noon, some in the afternoon, and then one around five o'clock just before leaving work, and he was still taking them. As he put it, "You can't expect anything sensational to happen on the first day, and besides, McDougall was probably exaggerating about how fast we'll see changes."

Sam and Sally's Exercise Program

Sally and Sam began their athletic stint in a modest style, taking separate walks on Monday morning and walking together after dinner on Monday night. They were coming off a fifteen- to twenty-year exercise break and naturally had some sore muscles the next morning.

But, suffering as he did from the symptoms of heart disease, Sam

Waterman had a much bigger problem to handle. He could walk only short distances, and rather slowly at that, because after a few minutes in the straight-away his chest pain would strike. If the pain was bearable, he sat down for a little while until it eased off. If it felt more severe, he took a nitroglycerin tablet, and the pain was usually gone in about a minute. I told Sam to take things slow and easy. It would have shown poor medical judgment to suggest he exercise right through the pain.

I remember when Sam and I first talked about exercise, and suddenly he looked at me with a slightly shamefaced expression and said, "You know, doc, sometimes I feel ridiculous struggling down the street like somebody who's almost ready for a wheelchair. I used to play football in college, and we'd go for a two-mile run at the start of every practice session. It seems like just yesterday. But yesterday—I'm talking about the real yesterday now—I had to go to the toilet in the worst possible way. I was talking to some clients at the door to the elevator. I shook hands all around and showed them into the elevator and then I ran for the men's room. I hadn't gone ten feet when I thought I was going to have a heart attack, right there in that hallway. I had to lean against the wall, panting, until the chest pain subsided. What's happened to me?"

What could I tell him? The answer was easy, "Sam, if you want to do so, you can be running two miles a day again in two to four months. There's nothing on God's green earth to stop you."

THE WATERMANS' DAY 2

On their second day Sally took Sam's blood pressure at home. Sam had bought a blood pressure cuff, with stethoscope, at the local drugstore. He had tried electronic blood pressure monitors before but found them inaccurate. He could take his own blood pressure, but he preferred to have Sally do it—he felt more relaxed, and he enjoyed the extra attention from her.

That day Sally only packed lunch for herself—just soda water, a banana, and an "OLT" sandwich stuffed with lettuce, onion, and tomato. Sam went out to eat at an expensive restaurant called the Equus, where he sometimes took important clients. He had made an advance call to the maitre'd that morning, and was served a steamed vegetable platter mixing broccoli, cauliflower, carrots, zucchini, and several small salad potatoes all seasoned with a blend of spices and herbs, but untouched by butter or cheese. Even that old carnivore Sam had to admit it was delicious.

T·H·E W·A·T·E·R·M·A·N·S

DAY 2

Breakfast: Breakfast Rice (warmed up from the night before) with sliced bananas and blueberries

Lunch: Sally: Packed an "OLT" sandwich with lettuce, sliced tomatoes, and sliced onions and a banana. Sam: Ordered a steamed vegetable platter at the Equus restaurant and had a plate of assorted sliced fruit for dessert.

Dinner: Spaghetti (egg-free spinach pasta) with marinara sauce / tossed green salad with Italian dressing / Sunbeam Tapioca Pudding

EXERCISE: Sam walked 5 minutes in the morning with one episode of severe chest pain and 15 minutes in the evening with frequent halts. Sally walked 20 minutes in the morning and 15 minutes in the evening.

PHYSICAL STATUS: Sam: BP 148/90. Weight 211 lbs. His indigestion is much better. No diarrhea—two formed BMs in the morning.
Sally: Weight 135 lbs. No constipation—one large easy-to-pass BM, though she is now having mild bowel cramps. Sinus headaches are a little better and her postnasal drip may be a little less. Her caffeine-withdrawal headaches worsen, and her joints are still stiff. Her energy is up—less fatigue.

MENTAL STATUS: Sam has no unrealistic expectations—it took many years to get him in the poor shape he is in now; he expects it will take more than two days to get out of trouble. Sally is most worried about Sam's health. Even though she is pleased at the rapid relief of her constipation, she is still distressed about her headaches, arthritis, and postnasal drip.

TEST RESULTS: No new tests today.

MEDICATIONS: Sam: 8 nitroglycerin tablets and his regular doses of Dyazide, Inderal, and Calan.
Sally: 2 aspirin four times today.

DAILY LESSON: Although this is not an all-or-nothing health plan, you need to know the best you can do, so you can make a real choice for the level of health you want to enjoy.

Choosing Your Own Personal Menu Plan

I didn't leave Sally and Sam entirely on their own in the matter of the food they ate. After getting some idea of their tastes, I gave them the same menus for their twelve days on the Program that you found in Chapter 4. When you look at the boxes in this and the following chapters that describe what they actually did each day, you'll notice that they didn't always follow the suggestions I'd offered. For instance, since Sam often ate out at lunchtime, I knew he wouldn't always be sticking to my menu plan at this midday meal. I'd told Sally and Sam to feel perfectly free to pick and choose among the items on the menus, to switch the order of the days, or to repeat any meals that they particularly liked. In short, the suggested menus were simply models that they could follow at their convenience. When you make up your own twelve-day meal plan, you should look at it in that way too. The purpose of the suggested menus is to get you most easily through twelve days of eating healthy foods so that at the end of twelve days you'll see the results of the Program.

Physical Changes in the First Few Days

Caffeine Withdrawal

By the middle of the second day, Sally's headaches had become worse. It's perfectly normal for people to get headaches when they withdraw from coffee or from anything that has a good deal of caffeine in it.

Although for most people giving up coffee isn't as important as eating a healthy diet free of oil, meat, and dairy products, it's a very useful step, and I encourage all my patients to take it. Caffeine certainly can be enjoyable: it gives a pleasant high. But the stimulation you get from it is both good and bad. In addition to the mental stimulation we look forward to, caffeine stimulates the stomach membranes and causes indigestion, stimulates the bowels and causes diarrhea, and increases the heart rate, thus producing higher blood pressure and an irregular heartbeat. Some women even notice increased tenderness of the breasts and breast lumps as a result of drinking caffeine.

Improved Bowel Function

Both Sally and Sam had large, easy bowel movements on the morning of the second day. Although I had predicted this, they were a little surprised. Sally had been constipated for years—a typical result of the standard low-fiber American diet. Fibers should form the bulk of any stool, and when fiber-deficient foods like meat and cheese, white bread and white rice, are the major part of a person's diet, the intestine produces small, hard stools that can be passed out of the body only by harmful straining.

Sam often had diarrhea, which is a less common response to the Western diet but by no means infrequent. The grease in Sam's high-fat diet would cause his liver to produce excess bile acids. These acids often irritated his colon, causing it to secrete fluids that liquefied the contents in that part of the intestine. For years Sam made sure that he learned the location of the nearest men's room any time he went to a place he hadn't been in before.

Of course, all this talk about bowels is a trifle indelicate, but for people who have these problems this is a very important subject. Amazingly, most people have never heard that they can correct such problems by eating a starch-centered diet. It's almost impossible not to have a good bowel movement if you're eating the foods recommended by the McDougall Program. It is possible, however, that during the first few days, you'll have too much of a good thing and will experience frequent unformed stools—not quite diarrhea, but still too soft for comfort. This is a short-term problem that lasts only while your intestines are adjusting to the sudden introduction of a high-carbohydrate, high-fiber diet.

Indigestion

Other problems in the early days are an increased passage of bowel gas and, somewhat less commonly, stomach cramps. This is caused by the sudden introduction of a large amount of fiber into an intestine unaccustomed to such food. Fortunately, thc bowel adjusts quickly. The problem gas, however, may continue for as long as two weeks, while the bacteria in your colon are changing in both kind and number in response to new components to digest. Think of this stage as part of your initiation ceremony into better health, and if it bothers you, eat fewer beans, peas, and lentils, for they do tend to produce gas—on any diet.

Increased Energy

On the positive side, you're probably already feeling less tired, more energetic. The effort of digesting and utilizing meats and dairy products is quite a drag on the body. Sally, too, was already feeling more energetic, especially in the afternoons when she used to feel like lying down for a nap.

Hunger

One surprising consequence of your new diet may be hunger. Amazing, when you think of all those bulky fruits and plump potatoes you've been eating. The reason for your hunger is in part unfamiliarity with the new dishes. The sensation of fullness you get from a starch-centered meal is different from the kinds of fullness produced when you consume those great lumps of muscle and fat that are the centerpieces of a typical Western meal. After a few days on the new diet, you'll find that your stomach has adjusted.

The primary reason for your hunger is that you have not yet discovered what and how much you need to eat of your new diet to feel satisfied. You must work this out by trial and error. Fruits and vegetables pass from the stomach much more quickly than the heavier items on the standard American diet, and to prevent a quick return of hunger, you may wish to eat at more frequent intervals. Eat all you want and as often as you want—as long as you eat the right stuff. You're not going to get fat on a starch-based diet.

T·H·E W·A·T·E·R·M·A·N·S

DAY 3

Breakfast: Orange juice / Hash-Brown Potatoes with
barbecue sauce
Lunch: Quick Pasta Salad and Cucumber Vinaigrette
(packed in plastic bowls) / grapes
Dinner: American Vegetable Stew / Brown rice /
broccoli / Microwaved Apple Wedges

EXERCISE: Sam walked 5 minutes in the morning and 10 minutes
in the evening. Sally walked 20 minutes in both morning and evening.

PHYSICAL STATUS: Sam: BP 140/88. Weight 208 lbs. Thinks he
has less chest pain. He notices orange juice makes his indigestion
worse. No diarrhea—two large, easy-to-pass stools in the morning.
Sally: Weight 135 lbs. One BM passed without straining, bowel
cramps gone. Both sinus and caffeine withdrawal headaches are less
frequent and intense. Less postnasal drip. Arthritis is better. She had
no afternoon letdown today—energy definitely up.

MENTAL STATUS: Sally finds the adjustment to these new foods
quite agreeable, but Sam is not sure he'll be able to live forever on
this new diet. On the other hand, he'd rather eat cardboard than die
or have heart surgery. Besides, he's committed himself to twelve days
and he keeps his promises.

TEST RESULTS: No tests today.

MEDICATIONS: Sam visited his cardiologist today to discuss progress and medication adjustments. Stops Dyazide; cuts Inderal in half
(to 5 mg four times a day), continues Calan. Took 3 nitroglycerin
today.
Sally: Took 2 aspirins in the morning for her arthritis and 2 in midafternoon for a mild headache.

DAILY LESSON: Paradoxically, you will end up enjoying your
walk or turn on the bicycle most on those days you woke up and
initially thought you really didn't want to exercise today.

THE WATERMANS' DAY 3

By the end of the third day, Sally and Sam were noticing changes.
Sally's headaches had diminished considerably, and her constipation
and bowel cramps were gone. Sam's blood pressure was way down,
he hadn't had diarrhea in two days, and his chest pains had notice-

ably decreased—he had only needed three nirtroglycerin tablets all day. Sam hadn't had acid indigestion since they'd started the diet. Did this mean he could throw out the Alka Seltzer and stop buying Tums? I replied that if he intended to go on following the McDougall diet, he could do just that.

That evening while they worked in their kitchen tossing a green salad and cooking spaghetti, they discussed their next-door neighbors, who had been eating McDougall-style for six months, and agreed they looked five years younger and as if they had the energy of twenty-year-olds. Sam declared enthusiastically, "I'm next on the road they're traveling if things keep on the way they have so far."

Rapid Improvement in Blood Pressure on the Program

On Day 1, Sam's blood pressure was quite high—158/104 mm Hg (millimeters of mercury raised on the blood pressure machine). A normal blood pressure is about 110/70 mm Hg. When the bottom number is over 80, the risk of having a fatal heart attack is doubled, and when it's over 95, the risk of a stroke is increased seven times over that in a person with normal blood pressure levels. Sam's cardiologist was providing him not only with nitroglycerin tablets but also with three different medicines that attempted to lower his blood pressure: a diuretic (Dyazide) to reduce amounts of water in his tissues; a beta-blocker (Inderal) to slow the action of his heart and thus reduce the blood pressure and decrease the angina pain; and a calcium-blocker (Calan), which also relieves chest pain and reduces blood pressure by relaxing the arteries. Sam felt he was doing what he had to do to stay alive. However, from the things he said to me, I don't think he fooled himself. He knew his pharmaceutical potions were not cures.

Before he started the Program, I told him we would gradually take him off his blood pressure medication. High blood pressure falls very quickly on the McDougall Program. In fact, within hours of a person's beginning to eat a diet low in sodium and saturated fat (i.e., a diet that bears no resemblance to the typical American diet), blood pressure begins to fall. One reason is that arteries and veins are no longer clogged with blood cells that clump together because fat coats their surfaces. These clumps begin to form within an hour after a high-fat meal is eaten. Fats also cause the vessels to constrict in spasms that retard the flow of blood. This clumping or sludging slows the flow of blood sufficiently so that the heart is forced to pump harder to move the blood along. One expected response is higher blood pressure. Without the fats in the diet, the blood flows smoothly through relatively unclogged vessels and the pressure drops. Another reason for an improved blood pressure is less sodium (from salt), which means less fluid for the heart to pump along. With a decrease in the work the heart must do, the pressure lowers.

By his third day on the diet, Sam's blood pressure was 140/88 mm Hg and I asked him to stop his diuretic (Dyazide) and cut in half his beta-blocker medication (Inderal). I couldn't improve Sam's diet and leave him on his blood pressure medication simultaneously; he would have suffered from low blood pressure and that would have caused weakness and dizziness. As a matter of fact, on Thursday morning, Sam's fourth day on the diet, that was exactly what happened: His blood pressure dropped to 90/50, and he felt dizzy. I realized I had left him too long on his calcium-blockers and after consulting his cardiologist, I instructed Sam to halt that medication. By evening his blood pressure was back up to 110/70.

There was nothing out of the ordinary about these changes in Sam's blood pressure. The body heals quickly if it's given half a chance. Most of the desirable drop in blood pressure occurs within two days of starting the McDougall Program. To you, this rapid change for the better may seem unbelievable. However, from a physiological point of view it's easy to understand; the blood is no longer sludging under the influence of fats and so the resistance to blood flow decreases and blood pressure drops. (About 10 percent of cases with high blood pressure will not respond so dramatically because of extensive blood vessel and/or kidney disease.)

Improvement in Arthritis on the Program

Sally had a problem that we haven't said much about yet—arthritis. Her aches and pains had been getting worse for several years, and quite often when she got up in the morning some of her joints were swollen. On certain days the only way she could relieve the pain and stiffness was to take aspirin tablets, as many as eight a day. Sally's condition wasn't what could be called alarming, but year by year it was getting worse, and she was still a relatively young woman.

Arthritis is a complex condition that very often is related to foods of one kind or another. The reason the McDougall Program so often produces notable improvement in arthritic people is that dairy products and fats are eliminated from their diets. Certain foods to which a person is allergic can cause arthritis. Cow's milk proteins are among the most common offenders. Also, the fats in one's diet can impair the immune system in a way that contributes to arthritis. Very serious forms of arthritis, including rheumatoid arthritis and lupus, can dramatically benefit from a change in diet that eliminates these offending components in foods.

THE WATERMANS' DAY 4

Sam's quick return to a normal blood pressure of 110/70 mm Hg that evening filled him with hope. This was a great improvement over his condition on Day 1, and it had been gained even though he had stopped taking a diuretic and a calcium-blocker, and, since the third day of the Program, was taking only half of his beta-blocker, Inderal.

What made Sam happiest, of course, was the fact that he had felt less chest pain during the past two days. He still got some symptoms of pain serious enough to make him reach for his nitroglycerin tablets, but the attacks came less often, and he thought they were less severe. Was this just a fluke? Sam wondered. He certainly intended to hang in there and find out.

The Watermans' Exercise Program Continues

By the fourth day, Sam and Sally were becoming fond of their exercise sessions. So far they'd done only simple walking. In fact, walking is an excellent form of exercise. It's beneficial to people at any age and in almost any physical condition. It limbers the muscles, it's good for the cardiovascular system, and most people find that it improves their general mood.

As I've said earlier, it makes very good sense to exercise at the same time every day and not attempt more than you can finish easily. Sam and Sally took separate walks in the morning. Sally walked vigorously until she was about ten blocks from their house, and then she walked back, jumped into her car, and drove off to work. Sam left his car in a parking lot about a quarter of a mile from where

T·H·E W·A·T·E·R·M·A·N·S

DAY 4

Breakfast: Hot 7-Grain Cereal and sliced peaches
Lunch: Sally: Whole Grain Bread Sandwich filled
  with tomatoes, alfalfa sprouts, grated carrots, and
  sliced radishes / apple. Sam (ate out with friends):
  2 baked potatoes / green salad with vinegar /
  honeydew melon
Dinner: Bean and Rice Burritos / tossed green salad
  with Russian dressing / Sunshine Fruit Dessert

EXERCISE: Sam is up to 10 minutes of walking in the morning and 20 minutes in the evening with only one long halt. Sally stays at 20 minutes of walking twice a day. Sally uses the exercise bike at a vigorous pace, but Sam pedals slowly.

PHYSICAL STATUS: Sam: BP drops to 90/50 and he becomes weak and a little dizzy. Medication reduced. BP up to 110/70 by evening. Weight 210 lbs. (up because he stopped diuretic the day before and regained water weight). A few mild chest pains—definitely less than before. No diarrhea.
Sally: Weight 134½ lbs. Developed a bit of indigestion after lunch from all the raw vegetables in her sandwich. No bowel cramps; one easy-to-pass large BM in the morning. Less postnasal drip or slight sinus headache today. Her generalized caffeine withdrawal headaches are gone. Arthritis much better. Felt energetic all day.

MENTAL STATUS: Sam is starting to appreciate the ability of his middle-aged body to recover. He never thought he had that potential. Having solved most of her minor physical problems, Sally's chief concern now is to lose weight.

TEST RESULTS: No tests today.

MEDICATIONS: Sam: Stops Calan entirely. Took 5 mg Inderal four times and 2 nitroglycerin tablets. Sally: 2 aspirin in the morning to get her joints loosened up.

DAILY LESSON: "Eat to live, not live to eat" is a fine formula, but it doesn't mean you have to suffer. Delicious meals are still possible even without meats and cheeses.

he worked and then walked slowly to the office. After the first few days, he discovered, to his considerable surprise, that he enjoyed that little bit of time to himself.

In the evenings after dinner Sally and Sam took a walk together. At least they called it a walk. At first, they spent about half the time sitting on benches or leaning against trees, while Sam tried to relieve his chest pains.

Trying to think of what else they could do, the two of them dug out a dusty exercise bike they'd been storing in their garage. Sally had tried it once or twice years before, but stopped using it because to her this kind of exercise was very boring. I advised Sam to do no more than a little leisurely pedaling on the bike until his angina was better.

What Four Days Did for the Watermans

The One-Third Point Recheck

On Friday morning, the start of their fifth day, Sally and Sam were more than one third of the way through the Program, and, at my suggestion, they had blood tests done that morning in order to measure their progress.

Sam's lab reports were much more dramatic than Sally's, all the way down the line. His cholesterol level, which hadn't gone below 225 mg/dl in the two years he'd been having it measured, fell from 246 to 200 mg/dl in four days. Sam felt like a kid who's always failed algebra and then (after suitable effort, of course) gets his report card with a big bright A. He wanted to know why his cardiologist had had the laboratory report only his overall cholesterol level, instead of breaking it down into the "good" (HDL) and the "bad" (LDL) types. The cardiologist told him, "With the total levels you've got, Sam, you know you're in trouble. Why waste your time trying to figure out if your percentage of good cholesterol is a little better than average. It's always going to be only a fraction of the total, and its going to go up and down as your total cholesterol goes up and down." Sam thought about that and thought about his 46 mg/dl drop in four days, and his questioning turned to elation. And he was right to be delighted. His cholesterol drop was much better than is the average drop for people who do the McDougall Program at the St. Helena Hospital and Health Center. Also, Sam's blood sugar fell 58 mg/dl (from 180 to 122 mg/dl)—an improvement that would soon remove "adult-type diabetes" from his health records.

The only negative factor revealed by Sam's tests was that his triglycerides had gone up from 275 to 325 mg/dl since he started the Program. This usually means that a patient is particularly sensitive to sugar and is being affected by the sugars present in fruits, fruit juices, and jellies. Since he started the diet, Sam had been eating much more fruit than he had before the Program, having it not only with meals but often in midafternoon and evening for a snack. I told Sam that for a while he would be eating only starches and vegetables without fruit juices and fruits, and that once we got his triglycerides down to a proper level, I would start easing fruits back into his meals and see how much of those he could consume without elevating his trigylceride levels excessively.

All of Sally's blood tests improved, but the cholesterol drop was the important one: Cholesterol down 48 mg/dl; Triglycerides down 14 mg/dl; blood sugar down 4 mg/dl.

What about weight? Sam had lost a remarkable five pounds by the third day, but most of that was excess water. He gained three pounds back almost as soon as he stopped taking his diuretic pills on Day 3. By Day 5 he showed a net loss of two pounds. Sally's progress was unbearably slow, which I was sorry to hear, not because it had any special significance but because I knew it depressed her. Sally said to me, "If I squint at the scale, it sort of looks as if I've lost half a pound." One possible reason for such slow loss for Sally is the change in water retention that occurs with a woman's menstrual cycle. With the approach of a period women will often gain two to three pounds of water, which will hide any loss of body fat.

Nonetheless, in general Sally was far from downcast. She was overjoyed about Sam's improvement in blood pressure and chest pains. As for herself, she was quietly satisfied to have put a lifetime of constipation behind her. Furthermore, she noticed that those miserable caffeine-withdrawal headaches had ended and, better still, she was having fewer headaches of any kind, period. What's more, the midafternoon fatigue she often experienced after a high-fat lunch simply wasn't there anymore. This relief is important to career people. If you're trying to get ahead in your profession, you can't afford to be weary and weak after lunch each day.

You Will See Very Similar Results

Your first four days on the Program will be a rather quiet time. Since Americans are an impatient people, you may think I owe you fast and dramatic changes, but don't fret: They're coming, and the new diet will do its wonders quickly. Obviously, four days of healthy eating won't be enough to overcome instantly the results of many decades of less healthy or even horribly unhealthy eating. But the first signs of improvement are already showing up. Your blood pressure has gone down, you probably have lost that first pound or two (on the average men lose two to three pounds and women one to two pounds the first week), your bowel function is excellent, your energy level is up. You're coming along nicely. And—I promise—bigger, happier, more satisfying changes await you.

8

CONTINUING TOWARD

YOUR GOALS: Days 5–8

After four days, you'll be pretty well acquainted with the McDougall Program and the ideas underlying it, and you'll have begun to see results. You'll soon be telling your friends what good the new diet is doing you and how much you like it.

THE AGENDA

In this chapter, while we follow Sam and Sally for four more days, we will discuss:

- Vegetarianism
- Why most weight-loss diets are unsuccessful
- Why McDougall is stricter than Pritikin
- Having guests and being a proper guest
- What kinds of physical changes you'll notice after eight days on the Program

THE WATERMANS' DAY 5

For Sam and Sally Waterman the fifth day was a Friday. They reported to the laboratory for their blood tests (discussed in the last chapter) and then went off to work. Sally joined her colleagues in the employees' lounge after lunch and, as she told me later, immediately found herself the center of a fascinating discussion. She had no idea that so many people knew she was "eating differently." But, she recalled, at least half the women she knew and a quarter of the men were regularly trying to diet, according to the rules of one system or another.

What was this one like, her colleagues wanted to know. Were McDougall's meals tasty? Did she long for meat? Did she think she could keep this up? No milk, either? Now *that* was interesting! Then,

T·H·E W·A·T·E·R·M·A·N·S

DAY 5

Breakfast (after blood tests): Sally: Orange juice / whole wheat toast with Corn Butter. Sam: Instant oatmeal with extra hot water, topped with sliced banana and cinnamon
Lunch: Pita bread stuffed with kidney beans / banana
Dinner: Minestrone Soup / Rice and Corn Salad / Easy Fruit "Gelatin" (Sally only; Sam skipped the dessert because he found out this afternoon simple sugars have raised his triglycerides)

EXERCISE: Sam has no trouble with 15 minutes of walking twice today. Now he parks his car farther from the office for his morning walk and takes a short spin on the exercise bike at home. Sally walks 20 minutes twice today and watches half the evening television news program while pedaling on the exercise bike.

PHYSICAL STATUS: Sam: BP 110/70. Weight 211 lbs. (up because he stopped diuretic on Day 3). Chest pains only occasionally and mild. No indigestion or diarrhea.
Sally: Weight 134 lbs. One soft BM without straining today. Only very faint headaches. Postnasal drip seems to be gone. Her arthritis feels a lot better. No longer tired in the afternoon.

MENTAL STATUS: Sam thinks he is better, but he's worried that this is "only a coincidence." Sally's convinced she's getting healthier, and is looking forward to some substantial weight loss. Optimism grows in both.

TEST RESULTS: Sam: Cholesterol 200 mg/dl (down 46 mg/dl); Triglycerides 325 mg/dl (up 50 mg/dl); Blood Sugar 122 mg/dl (down 58 mg/dl).
Sally: Cholesterol 170 mg/dl (down 48 mg/dl); Triglycerides 90 mg/dl (down 14 mg/dl); Blood Sugar 94 mg/dl (down 4 mg/dl).

MEDICATIONS: Sam only on Inderal, 5 mg four times a day. Took no nitroglycerin today. Sally took 2 aspirin in the morning for her arthritis pain and stiffness.

DAILY LESSON: Moderate diets, restricting you to small portions of old favorites, provide too much temptation for most people. Strict rules assure success.

how do you get your protein? Your calcium? Sally Waterman didn't have the answers to all these questions, but she did know some of them, because I had told her many of the same things that you read about in Chapter 3. What's more, Sally realized that she might be in the forefront of a new field of discovery, like somebody who had dared to take up running way back in 1970.

Are McDougall Dieters Vegetarians?

That evening, the Watermans' bachelor son came home to pick up his skis. As usual, he had a few male and female friends in tow. Sally and Sam had just finished dinner, and they sat with the young folk for a while in the living room chatting and sharing a selection of snacks the visitors brought with them. They ate vegetable slices dipped in salsa, salt-free Bavarian pretzels, and rice cakes.

It was obvious to everyone that Sam and Sally did not partake of the cheese spreads, the spiced meats, and the oil-rich salty crackers, and of course, the guests wondered how they could resist such goodies. Everyone was surprised to hear about the Watermans' experience during the past five days. One of the young ladies exclaimed, "That's great! I'm a vegetarian too. I never eat anything but chicken and fish." And their son's girlfriend told them that her sister had been a fruitarian (a person who eats only fruits) for several months in the previous year, and how that diet had made her sick. All the young visitors agreed (though they put it more tactfully) that it was great to see old folks doing something so unusual.

In my early years, I never liked to be called names. The word *vegetarian* has meanings in our society beyond describing a person who avoids eating meat. Many uninformed (and uncharitable) people consider vegetarians to be slightly mad, part of the radical fringe. Those close-minded people are prejudiced, of course. To escape having this vegetarian label pinned on me, I have made a point of having roast turkey on Thanksgiving Day, and sometimes on Christmas, too. Needless to say, I advertise this as evidence of being "normal," and therefore "thoroughly American."

When you start the McDougall Program, think of yourself as someone who is eating the foods that best support human health. The master plan for human beings was designed many millions of years ago, and naturally, it included a diet appropriate for people.

I did not create this diet, I merely recognized a simple truth: People function best on a diet of whole grains, vegetables, and fruits.

Weight-Loss Diets

After all the young people left the Watermans' home (including the enlightened "vegetarian" who dined on fish and chicken), Sally thought about all the different kinds of diets she'd heard of people trying over the years, and she wondered how anyone could possibly make sense out of all that confusion of opinions. Men and women with different sorts of bodies, trying different sorts of diets, and getting different sorts of results—but mostly not getting good results. Did any of it make any sense at all? Was the McDougall Program any more apt to work than any of the others? These are perfectly legitimate questions for anyone to ask. Let's talk about weight loss.

You're on the McDougall Program now. Probably you've tried other diets before this one, and either they failed you or you failed them. But you're not unique in this. You must have heard as many calamitous stories about failures as I have. There's neighbor Jones, for example, who lost ten pounds the first month skimping on calories and then gained them all back the second month by eating cake. And there's teacher Smith who drank little cans full of protein powder and was actually losing weight until his heart rhythm became so erratic that his doctor had to rush him off to the hospital. And surely you remember cousin Sarah, who ate nothing but grapefruit several times a day for ten whole days and finally concluded that chronic diarrhea was the reason why she lost most of the weight during that session. They're all fat now, and still searching for the diet that will guarantee their return to the form divine.

Most people set out on a diet course with the unexpressed intention of making a fool of that poor old darling Mother Nature.

If you've ever tried a diet that's not based on a permanent change in lifestyle, then somewhere in your mind when you started was the notion that excess weight was just an accidental accumulation of poundage that somehow sort of crept up on you before you noticed it. This inconvenient (and unsightly) bulge, acquired over the ten or twenty or thirty years since you were a teen-ager (you said to yourself), wasn't really a part of the real you, or of your way of life. Therefore, in a few weeks or months of sustained effort, you're simply going to drop it over the side, so to speak, get rid of it once and for all. Many people harbor this secret fantasy: In two or three months they'll lose all the extra weight they've attracted over the course of twenty years, and, once it's gone, well then, by gosh, another twenty years must pass before they put it back on again. But the game never seems to work that way. From the point of view of health, it's a good thing that it doesn't because since quickie quack diets don't work, you have to adopt healthy ones.

Dealing with the Hunger Drive

In the previous chapters I've explained why the McDougall Program works for continued good health. Let me tell you now the basic reason it is also such a spectacularly effective diet for losing weight.

The essential fact about the satisfaction of hunger is that it is almost a purely mechanical response: Once the stomach gets filled of almost any kind of food, you won't feel hungry any longer (for a while). Common sense will tell you that if one large potato (about 6 ounces) yields only 150 calories and one bacon and egg sandwich (6 ounces) yields 538 calories, then it's going to be a lot easier to fill your stomach *and still lose weight* on a meal of potatoes than on one of bacon and eggs. Consider these basic facts, which are really two sides of the same coin:

- Starches, fruits, and vegetables eaten in amounts that are equal in bulk to a meal of rich foods will yield far fewer calories.
- For a helping of healthy food to yield the same number of calories as a helping of rich food, the serving of healthy food will have to be much larger in bulk and therefore will fill the stomach more satisfyingly.

To eat so many fruits, vegetables, and starches that you'd get fat on them would take hard work on your part, and lots of time. An average active adult male burns about 3000 calories a day. To maintain his weight solely on large potatoes, he would need to eat twenty of them a day. On the balanced and interesting diet you'll be eating for this Program, you'll be losing weight (and satisfying your hunger) without having to put up with the boring prospect of a marathon potato orgy. And, in addition, you'll find that once you've attained your ideal weight, stabilizing at that level will be easy, even while eating all the healthy foods you'll want for that happy, full feeling.

The Three Basic Types of Weight-Loss Diets

Hundreds (if not thousands) of different diet plans have been sold to an eager public during the course of this century, and yet, whatever individual quirks and enticements may have been added to them, there are really only three particular ways to deal with the hunger drive. Let's consider how those three approaches work.

Starve Your Fat Away

The first of the three basic methods to help people to lose weight is what I would call a low-food/low-calorie diet. This is your standard "eat less" plan. On this diet, you don't consume a lot of calories, because you don't take in much food. It is a perfectly effective method for the one person in a thousand who can stay on it. But it has a simple and infamous drawback: *It hurts*. In order to maintain the low-calorie part of this diet while continuing to eat typical high-fat American foods, you have to eat less of them than your stomach craves. The only way to go on eating roast beef and bacon, chicken and cheese, butter and vegetable oils, and still stay thin is to have a stomach that's permanently only half full. Result: You feel hungry all the time, and you suffer. This kind of long-term semistarvation is unreasonable, and should be permitted only to masochists. Don't let anybody tell you that if you don't like starving, then you're some sort of shameful, guilty glutton. Most people who try a low-food/low-calorie diet eventually go back to eating the way they did before, which simply proves that they would rather be fat than in pain.

This sort of diet includes the 500- and 1000-calorie programs prescribed by all kinds of "authorities," from eminent physicians to registered dietitians to hired movie stars, and also the various surgical procedures to make you eat or absorb less, such as stomach stapling, balloons in the stomach, and intestinal bypass. Health consequences as serious as death may result from these surgeries designed to reduce the intake of food. Most often their results are only temporary because the surgery needs to be reversed because of failing health, or the patient devises ways to sabotage the purpose of the surgery, such as having frequent liquefied meals in order to get large quantities of calories past a stomach reduced in size by surgery (stomach stapling.)

Burn Your Fat Away

The second basic diet method is the typical Western diet taken to an extreme: what's known as a *very* low carbohydrate diet. Carbohydrate foods, including whole grains, vegetables, and fruits, are minimized, and consumption of meat, fish, poultry, eggs, and cheese is emphasized. You would think you would get even fatter from eating all these fat-filled foods, but low-carbohydrate diets take advantage of a natural adaptive mechanism that suppresses your appetite so that you actually eat less. Carbohydrates are the human body's preferred choice for sources of energy. Your brain alone needs approximately 400 calories each day to perform its functions. Under the strain of carbohydrate deprivation, the body responds as it does when you're ill or fasting: It burns body fats to obtain energy. This low-carbohydrate condition of the body is called ketosis (because chemical waste products called ketones are released from the fats), and ketosis suppresses the appetite. As a result, you eat less, and you suffer less from hunger. Of course, you lose weight, too.

Well, you ask, isn't that what diets are for? Unfortunately, and as always, hidden costs must be reckoned with. The price you pay if you stay on a low-carbohydrate diet is long-term overconsumption of cholesterol, proteins, and fats, which leads in time to heart disease, cancer, and osteoporosis, to name only a few health disasters. If you go off the diet, then, of course, you quickly gain back the weight you've lost. Among the best known low-carbohydrate diets are those proposed by Atkins and Stillman.

Convenient, but even more extreme in their effects, are variations of this ketosis-producing approach that are known as "liquid protein diets." The label promises that you simply have to open a can of the product and drink the contents in order to simulate the conditions of ketosis otherwise seen in cases of illness and prolonged fasting. Liquid protein diets are much more dangerous than are ordinary low-carbohydrate diets. The most serious complication seen in people on the liquid protein program is fatal irregularities of the heart rhythm, which can develop after as short a time as two months, even if the dieter is under close supervision by a physician.

Eat Your Fat Away

The third basic diet plan is the kind I am proposing to you in the McDougall Program and I consider it a high-food/low-calorie diet.

This diet is a high-carbohydrate diet of whole grains, vegetables, and fruits, so you can eat all you want of *the right foods*. The underlying thought is that you will learn to like the foods that are both healthy and slenderizing for you. The Kempner Rice Diet, the Pritikin Diet, and macrobiotics are also this type.

When I was first studying what could be done for the human body through nutrition in the middle seventies, all three of these programs made a big impression on me. The Pritikin diet is a terrific diet, but it allows a little meat and dairy products every day. Theoretically, there's not an awful lot wrong with eating just two ounces of meat a day, but in practice it's another matter. It's a whole lot easier to be faithful to a diet that provides you with black and white rules about which foods you can eat and which you can't. It's easy to let a little bit of meat and cheese a day balloon into a lot. More important, it's really very hard not to eat foods you grew up on if they stare you in the face every time you open the refrigerator. When you go to the kitchen for a snack on the McDougall diet, you're not confronted with that leftover chicken breast or a slice of beef, so you can't backslide as effortlessly.

The Kempner Program, from Duke University's Medical School, is one of the earliest medically tested diets used to "cure" high blood pressure, diabetes, heart disease, kidney disease, obesity, and many other serious ailments. This highly effective therapy based around rice and fruit was started in the early 1940s by Dr. Walter Kempner, and is still one of the most successful programs at Duke's Medical School. If you think the McDougall Program is tough, Dr. Kempner would ask you to eat rice and fruit for your recovery. White rice is used (because of palatability) and sugar is often added to the diet in order to provide calories and at the same time reduce the amount of protein found naturally in the rice and fruit. The program is spartan, but very effective.

Macrobiotics is based on sixteenth-century Japanese philosophy, and shrouded by teachings that are often hard for Americans to relate to, such as the concept of "Yin and Yang." Brown rice is the center of the meal plan, and most other vegetables are eaten. Night shade plants (white potato, tomato, eggplant, and green pepper) and often fruits are restricted from the diet. Salt and oil are used in amounts I feel are too great for many people with illnesses. In general, however, the macrobiotic approach has a sound foundation for good health, even though the foods are not familiar to most Westerners and therefore are hard to adapt to for many of us.

T·H·E W·A·T·E·R·M·A·N·S

DAY 6

Breakfast: Grapefruit for Sally / Quick "Fried" Potatoes (Sally had barbecue sauce on hers, Sam had his favorite salsa)

Lunch: Quick Garbanzo Bean Soup / sliced tomatoes with salsa stuffed in pita bread

Dinner: Cajun Rice / tossed salad with French dressing (at home): Assorted vegetables for hors d'oeuvres / salad with lemon juice / green beans / baked potato (at dinner party)

EXERCISE: Sam and Sally walked together for 20 minutes twice during the day. Both used the exercise bike for half an hour. Sally still peddled more enthusiastically than Sam, but he was catching up.

PHYSICAL STATUS: Sam: BP 120/76. Weight 209 lbs. Very mild chest pains. No indigestion and good BMs.
Sally: Weight 133 lbs. Two easy-to-pass BMs today. No headaches of any kind today. No postnasal drip. Notes freedom of joints and plenty of energy to spare.

MENTAL STATUS: Sam feels a new responsibility for his own health and for the first time is participating in his medical care, using his doctor as a specialized health consultant. Sally is finding the foods easy to fix. She reasons if you are the kind of cook who burns a piece of flesh on two sides and calls it dinner, you can just as easily on the McDougall Program microwave potatoes and boil frozen vegetables for dinner. She was always a gourmet cook and puts just as much effort into McDougall-style cooking as she did before.

TEST RESULTS: No tests today.

MEDICATIONS: Sam called his cardiologist and cut his Inderal in half to 5 mg twice a day. No nitroglycerin needed. Sally took no aspirin today.

DAILY LESSON: "People food" is whole grains, vegetables, and fruits.

The high-food/low-calorie diet approach—the one you'll be follow-ing on the McDougall Program—is the only approach that causes weight loss without pain and simultaneously promotes good health.

Sam and Sally Become More Confident

Sally and Sam Waterman were already practically convinced. That's not uncommon for people who are almost halfway through the Program. Here was Sally, after six days, having no headaches, no constipation, no postnasal drip, fewer joint aches, and less of the fatigue she'd been suffering for years. It's amazing how quickly a human body responds to positive efforts on its owner's part.

As for Sam, ending attacks of diarrhea and acid indigestion was all very nice, but curing his angina was really the heart of the matter (pun intended), and he was convinced that his chest pains were lessening. As expected, Sam was forthright with me: "You know, doctor, if the chest pain doesn't get better, I don't really care about anything else, and I'm going back to eating the way I always have."

I admired his honesty. I had a strong feeling that when his chest pain went away permanently, Sam was going to give up eating rich foods—forever.

THE WATERMANS' DAY 6

Having Guests

That first Saturday the Watermans went for a walk—this time together. Now that Sam was moving more quickly, Sally felt she could take an occasional morning walk with him and still get her exercise. As they walked, Sally told Sam she was worried about their friends' reactions to their diet. "Some of them are going to think it's mighty strange, coming to our house for dinner and being served a McDougall meal—even if we fix separate meat or cheese for them." Sam sensibly replied, "Look, if people are going to be upset at finding us eating in a healthy way, maybe they're just not our friends. And if it's too hard on them to eat what we eat, then we can invite them over for after-dinner snacks, liquid refreshments, and all that sort of stuff. The truth is, if they are smart, they'll get on this Program too."

Being a Proper Guest

At noon a couple of old friends stopped by to invite Sam and Sally out for a pizza, but they bravely refused because they knew they were going to need all their courage for later that evening. They were going to a dinner party; the hostess was a great cook and temptations were going to be offered everywhere. Sally had called the week before and explained about their new diet. The hostess had said that wouldn't be any problem for her; she'd serve plenty of vegetables, fruits, and potatoes. She was a bit sad they'd not be able to try her new marinated steak tartare, but at least they'd be present at the party. Sally thought that matter had all been very nicely and intelligently handled on both sides, but when she remembered how delicious the food in that house usually was, her insides ached.

The solution to this crisis was simple: If you're not hungry, you're not tempted. The Cajun rice they ate before they went to the party was spicy and filling enough.

Sally and Sam got to the dinner party about 7:30 p.m., stayed for three hours, and resisted every temptation with ease. It was a triumph of will power, and they were justifiably proud of themselves. (Further advice on being a guest is offered in Chapter 13.)

THE WATERMANS' DAY 7

Sam Is Convinced

The next morning, they sat down with large bowls of Multi-Mix Cold Cereal. Sam was thinking about his body.

SAM: You know, I can't believe how easy it was to pass up those crabmeat appetizers last night.

SALLY: That's because there were so many other things to eat. I munched on raw vegetables and mushrooms all the time we were there. Although, you must admit, Sam, that steak tartare looked great.

SAM: Sure did, but I feel so much better on the new food that I've got to think it was more fun looking at dinner than eating it.

T·H·E W·A·T·E·R·M·A·N·S

DAY 7

Breakfast: Multi-Mix Cold Cereal with Rice Milk / a
banana for Sally (Sam still avoided fruit because of
triglycerides)
Lunch: Baked Potato Salad / apple for Sally
Dinner: Vegetable Burritos / Red and White Salad /
Fruit Delight (Sally only)

EXERCISE: Both Sam and Sally walked 20 minutes twice today,
and used their exercise bike.

PHYSICAL STATUS: Sam: BP 100/70. Weight 208 lbs. Two faint
chest pains. Bowels functioning well. No indigestion.
Sally: Weight 132½ lbs. One easy-to-pass BM. No headaches. No
postnasal drip. Less joint stiffness, almost no pain. Lots of energy.

MENTAL STATUS: Both are convinced something wonderful is
happening. The objective results they are seeing are providing them
with undeniable proof of the benefits of a sensible diet and moderate
exercise.

TEST RESULTS: No tests today.

MEDICATIONS: Sam: Inderal 5 mg twice a day. No nitroglycerin.
Sally: No aspirin.

DAILY LESSON: What causes disease promotes disease. The way
to cure most chronic illnesses is simply to stop the cause. For most
people a change in diet and a little exercise is *too* simple. A magic
placebo pill could be sold along with the Program to make it more
believable for some people raised in this world of modern science
and technology.

SALLY: Oh, so you've become a new man, have you?
SAM: Not yet, but I will. And don't tell me you don't feel better
too, Sal. You were getting so grouchy with your headaches and
your stiff joints that I never knew if it was safe to talk to you.
SALLY: Well, you used to be so sleepy after dinner that I never
thought you noticed my moods. You know, I got us started on
this thing and now you're more excited about it than I am. How
was the chest pain yesterday?
SAM: Definitely better. That's what really excites me about this

diet. You know, I didn't work for twenty-five years, getting ahead in the insurance business, just so I could drop dead as soon as it really starts to pay off. Look at Dan Dempsey, two years older than me, and everyone knew he was going to make senior V.P. when promotions came around this fall. Well, he keeled over the other day while getting on a flight to Boston and was dead before they ever got to the hospital. I thought, *that could have been me.* Well, if McDougall's right and that's what eating the way we used to eat does to a guy, then I've finished with that kind of meal. I don't care if they never sell another steer in Texas.

Would you have the nerve to argue about this with Sam? Besides, he was right.

THE WATERMANS' DAY 8
Day 8 was a Monday—the start of their second work week on the McDougall Program. They hadn't lost a lot of weight, they probably didn't look any different than they did before they began, but they already felt they were doing something right. Their stomachs felt better, their lower intestines worked great, Sally's headaches were gone, and her breathing passages were clear, her joints ached less, and Sam's chest pain had improved. I didn't have a hard time convincing them to hang in there.

Cure Means Stopping the Cause

In most people, after eight days on the McDougall Program, most health problems at least start getting better, if they're not resolved completely. The human body is a self-regenerating organism. If you cut your hand with a knife, you don't have to wonder whether or not it will heal. It always does—usually in as little as a week.

This kind of healing miracle has happened to me. Nearly twenty years ago, I suffered from a serious lung disease. I coughed and wheezed, and yellow gunk came up out of my lungs every now and then. I remember times when I coughed with such distress that I had to stop the car at the side of the road. This lung trouble went on for several years. I couldn't walk up a small hill without stopping to catch my breath. I took cough syrups and wheezing pills (bronchodilators), and drank gallons of water. I was sick like that for ten years. Then on October 20, 1972—an unforgettable day!—I quit smoking. Within a week my breathing was easier, my cough was

T·H·E W·A·T·E·R·M·A·N·S

DAY 8

Breakfast: Orange juice for Sally / Microwaved
Baked Potato with toppings (Sam poured some
leftover spaghetti sauce from Day 2 on his, and
then sprinkled some chopped scallions; Sally put
leftover chili from Day 1 on hers)
Lunch: Pita Bread with White Beans and Vegetables
Dinner: A La King Sauce on Whole Wheat Toast /
Quick Broiled Zucchini / Rice Pudding (Sally only)

EXERCISE: Sam increases walks to 20 minutes three times a day.
Sally walks with him twice. Exercise bike in use for both.

PHYSICAL STATUS: Sam: BP 126/80. Weight 207 lbs. Possibly
one or two faint chest pains. No indigestion and good BMs.
Sally: Weight 132½ lbs. Great bowel function. No headaches. She
woke with no pain and only a little stiffness in her hands this
morning—arthritis appears to be going. Plenty of energy to spare
during the day, yet she sleeps well at night.

MENTAL STATUS: Sam is beginning to wonder if there are any
limits to how much health he can regain. As terrible as this may
sound, Sally is much less worried about waking up next to a dead
body in the morning.

TEST RESULTS: No tests today.

MEDICATIONS: Sam: Inderal 5 mg twice a day. No nitroglycerin.
Sally took no aspirin.

DAILY LESSON: Good health does not mean taking more and
more medications. Sick people take medications.

gone. I had stopped my sickness in the simplest possible way: I
eliminated its cause. The same principle works for most chronic
illness. This is already happening to you if you're on the McDougall
Program.

Swelling in feet and hands diminishes

If you were swollen from edema, you will already be noticing a
decrease in the accumulation of fluid in the tissues about your ankles,

feet, and fingers. You've removed the cause—because now less salt and less fat is present in the foods you're eating.

Arthritic pains lessen

The aches and pains in your joints ought to be lessening. If you had serious arthritis, you should already be experiencing a reduction in the inflammation in the joints. Improvement will be gradual, while the intestine is clearing itself of the old foods that caused the arthritis. This process takes from four to seven days. If it takes longer, be patient. Eventually you may have to make further refinements in your diet. Most people with inflammatory arthritis react to animal products, especially dairy foods, but some people are allergic to certain vegetable foods, usually wheat, corn, or citrus fruits.

No more daily irregularity

By now, your bowels should be moving comfortably and regularly. I have yet to see constipation go unrelieved by a healthy diet (except for people I have cared for with nerve damage affecting the colon). Remember, bowel function is not necessarily a daily occurrence, but whenever it does happen, it should come without pain or strain and should produce a soft fecal mass. Added help can be gained by drinking more water each day, eating more fruit (including those time-honored prunes), and as a last resort, adding Miller's bran and flax seed to your menu. Be sure you have eliminated all dairy products from your diet. Even a little skim milk can bind the bowels up in some sensitive people.

If you had bowel cramps and/or diarrhea, they should be ended by now. Once the amount of fats in the diet is reduced, less colon-irritating bile acids are produced and the watery diarrhea they provoke will stop. Another factor is dietary proteins. Some of them—especially dairy proteins—can cause abdominal pain and cramps. Since you're off these foods now, your bowels should be quiet and comfortable. If you're still having trouble at this stage, then consider eliminating the wheat from your diet—wheat proteins could be the cause of the trouble. (That means no wheat bread, no whole wheat cereals, no wheat pasta. Too bad about that, but you'll adjust to the prospect and the benefits can be assessed within a week.)

Remember also that a few people are very sensitive to certain spices. On rare occasions, even in the moderate amounts I recommend, these can irritate the colon and cause frequent, uncomfortable bowel movements. Elimination of the suspect spices will help you detect the culprit.

Normal blood pressure and no medications

Most people have reached a low blood pressure and are off medications after the first few days on the McDougall Program. We'll hope that this has been the case with you. Your goal is to have your pressure close to 110/70. Even if you haven't reached that yet, almost everybody does better without medications prescribed for hypertension when their diastolic (the lower number) is below 100. Consistent readings above this number do warrant medication. Remember, however, that elevated blood pressure does its damage only over a long time, measured in months to years, and right now, a few days (even a few months) without medication will do you no harm in most cases. Get your doctor's reaction to this suggestion.

If you are interested in the medical changes that occur during these first twelve days, and thereafter, then turn to the medical guide in Part 3. Your doctor, too, might want to read the medical sections that pertain to you, in order to become familiar with the physical changes in you that will be caused by proper foods and exercise. Both of you will also learn about adjustments in medications that may be indicated by your progress toward health.

The physical pain from exercise diminishes

If you're like many of my patients, daily exercise was not simply a chore when you started eight days ago, but was actually painful to your muscles and joints. You have moved muscles these past eight days that have been resting, almost unused, for many years. Moderately sore muscles can give you a good honest feeling, not unpleasant at all if you understand why they are complaining. Blood tests taken at this time might show an elevation in the amount of the enzyme that is released when muscle tissues are injured by a blow or some other damage. Your lazy-man's muscles have been in such poor condition for so long that an activity as simple as fast walking has damaged them, causing the release of the muscle enzyme called creatine kinase (abbreviated CK or CPK). An elevation in CK level is only temporary. And as your muscles become conditioned to the activity, the pain will stop.

This moderate exercise will be producing many positive benefits. You will be losing stored fat and gaining muscle tissue. Blood pressure and blood levels of triglycerides and sugar will fall. Exercise adds an extra support system to back up the other positive changes that your new diet is producing.

Stick with It—Your Taste in Food Will Change

After eight days Sally and Sam definitely felt healthier. You probably will too. But don't become cocky at this important point. Remember how tired you are of being overweight? Remember how miserable you felt all over a little more than a week ago? Let's say your blood pressure used to be 145/90 and now it's down to 115/70. Don't be foolish now and say to yourself, "If I've done this once in less than a week, I can lower it again next month. Right now I want to head out to the Rancho Notorious Steak House and sink my molars into a few sirloin tips, charcoal-broiled." Do you really want the state of your health to go up and down like a kid's yo-yo, dancing at his whim?

Hold it! Hold on to what you've gained. Stop cheating yourself with fantasies like that. The worst of all the difficult days are behind you. Don't throw them away now. Perhaps you're marveling at how you could so quickly have adjusted to such a considerable change in the way you eat. Most of my patients ask about that. And I tell them that rarely is a sensible dieter, with his mind set on the goal, unable to make the adjustment—or to stay with it through all the years ahead.

When people change from eating the rich foods of the standard American diet to eating those of a starch-based diet, their taste for oils and fats diminishes after four or five days of doing without them. As that's happening, their tastebuds begin clamoring for a satisfying substitute. In an emergency like this, the body wastes no time. Even if you've positively despised fruits, vegetables, and starches, you'll find them highly appealing after a few days of having nothing else to eat. This may seem like a rather severe way to change your taste in foods, but it is actually less painful than any other method I know of.

9

REAPING THE REWARDS:

Days 9–12, and

One Year Later

On his ninth day on the McDougall Program, Sam Waterman went off to work having received an unusual compliment from his wife: She told him he didn't snore anymore. That's a common improvement gained from a diet that excludes dairy products, because dairy proteins often act as allergens that cause the airway passages in the nose and throat to swell and partially obstruct the flow of air.

THE AGENDA

In this chapter, while we look at Sam and Sally's last four days on the Program, we're going to cover these subjects:

- The addictive effects of exercise
- Sam and Sally's progress in nine days
- Dairy-protein allergies
- Converting other people to the Program
- Sharing a diet meal with nondieters
- The results of Sam and Sally's twelve-day program
- Feasting on special occasions
- Designing special modifications for your own diet
- Sam and Sally one year later

T·H·E W·A·T·E·R·M·A·N·S

DAY 9

Breakfast: Grapefruit (Sally only) / Breakfast Quinoa
Lunch: Sally: Went home for Quick Saucy Vegetables over whole wheat bread and a peach. Sam: Lunched at Jose's Mexican Restaurant near his office: an oil-free corn tortilla topped with beans, tomatoes, lettuce, and salsa
Dinner: Pasta Primavera / Saucy Cauliflower / Easy Fruit Pudding (Sally only)

EXERCISE: Sam walked 20 minutes three times today (with umbrella) and parked his car half a mile from the office. Sally walked 30 minutes at a fast pace through the shopping mall. She also spent some extra time on the exercise bike in order to encourage a little more weight loss.

PHYSICAL STATUS: Sam: BP 125/80. Weight 206 lbs. He has had no chest pain for 24 hours. Everything is feeling and functioning well. He notes that his skin and hair are much less greasy than before he started the Program. Sally notes that he's stopped snoring.
Sally: Weight 132½ lbs. Feeling great. Arthritis pain and stiffness are completely gone.

MENTAL STATUS: Sam has decided that a healthy diet and lifestyle are a good foundation for business success. When he feels well he thinks clearly and with optimism. On his walks, he is amazed by how many thoughts come into his mind that strike him as being proof of pure genius. In no time at all, he crowed (but only to himself), he'd be rich as well as healthy. Sally is still a bit puzzled as to why she has only lost 2½ lbs., but she realizes this rate translates into 6 to 10 lbs. of weight loss each month; and she only has 20 lbs. to lose altogether.

TEST RESULTS: No tests today.

MEDICATIONS: Sam telephones his cardiologist and stops Inderal altogether. No nitroglycerin. Sally takes no aspirin.

DAILY LESSON: Count your blessings. Everything may not be corrected yet, but this is the first time in your adult life that in matters of health you're going uphill instead of down.

THE WATERMANS' DAY 9

The Addictive Effects of Exercise

The ninth day was rainy, so Sally didn't take her morning walk. When lunchtime came, she drove to a nearby shopping mall and walked through its long, broad indoor corridors for half an hour. Sally wasn't going to be deprived of her exercise just because of a little problem like the weather. These walks made her feel good while she was doing them as well as after she was done, and this, more than a sense of duty, made her reluctant to go without them.

I hope that all of you are making exercise a part of your new approach to life. Even if you—like the Watermans—have never exercised much before, you'll soon find the balance of pleasure and pain starting to shift in the direction of pleasure. Of course, exercise is good for your stretching muscles and loosening joints, and if you choose the right exercise it can be entertaining too. But there's also a chemical reason for the pleasure it brings. Exercise causes your tissue cells to release endorphins, a natural narcotic related to morphine that is not only soothing but safe. The only thing it makes you addicted to is more exercise.

An interesting example of the addictive effects of exercise is a woman named Reva, who did the program at St. Helena Hospital and Health Center in 1987. Reva had avoided exercise for almost all her adult life because she tired so quickly. I understood the reason for that trouble the first time I saw her out walking. She was trying to cover half a mile in less than ten minutes. The exercise physiologist at St. Helena persuaded her to move more slowly, and to talk with him while they walked. Thus, she had to conserve enough breath for walking and for talking. Gradually, this rather immoderate woman learned to take exercise in moderation, and, as a result, she exercised more. At the end of twelve days she was able to walk a mile and a half in less than forty minutes. That was the farthest she had walked in many years, and the accomplishment did a great deal for her self-esteem. She was amazed to learn, at last, that she could benefit from a pace that didn't exhaust her. Now she calls often, to say she still walks thirty minutes a day—regardless of the weather. She walks on Thanksgiving and Christmas days, and she even walked on the day of her eighty-ninth birthday party!

Sam Walks On

On the eighth day of the Program, Sam extended his exercise sessions and began to take a twenty-minute stroll during the lunch hour. Now he walked three times a day; and on the ninth day he changed his car to a parking garage half a mile from his office, abandoning the garage he'd been using that was only a quarter of a mile away. During the first five days, Sam had usually had a chest pain before he covered one or two blocks. Now, walking at a moderate pace, he often completed an entire twenty- or thirty-minute stroll without a single angina attack. One day he said to me, "You know, doc, thanks to you I feel like a free man again."

I guess you won't have any trouble in believing that hearing patients say things like that is one of the great satisfactions of being a doctor.

Sam's Progress in Nine Days

On the sixth day Sam had cut his Inderal (the beta-blocker) in half again, and now, on the ninth day, his second Tuesday on the diet, he eliminated the drug entirely. For the first time in almost two years, he was off all medications. His blood pressure was completely under control. It varied daily from approximately 110/70 up to a high of 125/80. He had a young man's blood pressure, as all of us should have, at any age. His chest pains were more manageable. He hadn't taken a nitroglycerin tablet since Friday. When he did feel some pain, he waited for a few moments to see if it would get worse. Usually it subsided. On Days 7 and 8 the chest pains, when they did hit, had been faint and infrequent, and he hadn't been tempted to reach for the nitroglycerin. A skeptical doctor might grumble "placebo effect" at this point—meaning that Sam wanted desperately to believe in the treatment and so had convinced himself that the pain was less. Well, Sam was willing to be patient and to wait and see.

Sam had another small personal success. He had always had an obsession about having clean skin and hair. Unfortunately, he is one of those men who looks like he's dumped half a bottle of hair oil over his head each morning even though he's never used the stuff. Two showers and two shampoos a day hardly helped his appearance. In the younger Sam, this oily condition had contributed to a socially devastating case of acne, but now he had only a few red blemishes on his back. A pleasant surprise for Sam: After nine days on a very low-fat diet he was no longer greasy. He shouldn't have been surprised. The way he made his dog's coat shine was by adding the equivalent of two tablespoons of pure lard to the dog chow every day. Now he's following the opposite procedure, avoiding the lard and all other oils and removing the shine from his face and fur.

Sally's Progress in Nine Days

Much of Sally's progress had come in the first week, but she was still seeing changes. From Days 5 to 8, she had noticeably less inflammation of her joints in the morning. By Day 9 all the pain and stiffness was gone. All her headaches were gone, both the ones she had become used to before she started the Program and the ones the Program had caused by taking her off caffeine, and that alone cheered her considerably.

But just as Sam had a primary reason for wanting to try the McDougall Program—ridding himself of chest pains—so did she have one that was more important than all others—losing weight. And Sally wasn't showing the same good results that Sam had achieved; she had lost only two and one-half pounds so far. She thought that she'd put in an awful lot of effort for so small an effect. I spent a fair amount of time on the phone encouraging Sally, because this slow progress bothered her.

"You're acting," I scolded, "like a schoolgirl who receives a report card with five As and one C. The one average grade overshadows the praise you should be giving yourself for all your other accomplishments. Remember, your menstrual period is due this week, and so you're probably carrying around two extra pounds of water. Tell me if anything else has become better."

Indeed, many things did get better for Sally. The postnasal drip she had suffered with for years went away. For years she had suspected it might be caused by an unidentified allergen in the air, but in fact, she was allergic to dairy products. I've found that more than 75 percent of the time a person with this problem will end it by eliminating dairy products from the diet. Sally had also had itchy red eyes on occasion and that too was cured now. Giving up dairy and egg products will do that for many people. (Not for everyone, though. Allergic responses are a complex subject of study, and problems such as red eyes and postnasal drip can be caused by many other kinds of foods—for example, wheat and corn. Furthermore, medications and airborne allergens can also be the cause of allergic conditions.)

THE WATERMANS' DAY 10

Don't Be a Missionary— Food Is Personal Business

On the tenth day of his new diet, Sam had his first encounter with one of the drawbacks to a successful change in lifestyle. Having passed five days without a chest pain significant enough to make him reach for the nitroglycerin tablets, he went into the office of an associate with whom he'd been working on exceedingly friendly terms for more than a decade and tried to convince him of the merits of the McDougall Program. I remember Sam's puzzled phone call.

"Hey, doc, I hope you've never been shot down like I was. From the way Jack lit up, you'd think I'd tried to persuade him to fly to Libya and sell a life insurance policy to Qaddafi. He not only told me to mind my own business, he told me that (a) he was not a rabbit and didn't intend to eat like one, and (b) I wasn't going to live any longer on my new diet; it was just going to seem longer to me— eating all that fodder—and to everyone around who had to listen to me."

What had gotten into Sam's friend? Maybe Sam was overzealous, like any devoted missionary, but some people will always react that way to well-meant advice. The foods they eat are as personal to them as are their religious beliefs or their politics. The wise convert to a new diet must tread warily in spreading the good word, and evangelize slowly.

You'll find yourself having a bigger effect if you don't say a word about your great discovery and just let people notice the changes in you. Arousing others with your enthusiasm would be nice, but the facts are what really excite them. When they look at the slim, perky, bright-eyed, clear-skinned, and vital you, they're going to

T·H·E W·A·T·E·R·M·A·N·S

DAY 10

Breakfast: Fruity Bran and Oats / orange juice for
   Sally, herb tea for Sam
Lunch: Pita Bread with Spicy Beans and Vegetables /
   grapes for Sally
Dinner: (at home, with their daughter and son-in-law)
   Bean burritos / Minted Fruit Mix (Sam abstained)

EXERCISE: Sam walked 20 minutes three times again today. Sally
walked her usual 20 minutes twice at a fast pace. That evening they
went to the neighborhood YMCA for a swim in the pool instead of
using the exercise bike.

PHYSICAL STATUS: Sam: BP 110/70. Weight 205 lbs. Feeling
great; no chest pains. Intestines functioning well.
Sally: Weight 132 lbs. Great bowel function. She is free of all aches
and pains.

MENTAL STATUS: Sam feels like he's the sole discoverer of a
miraculous cure for a malignant disease that's suffered by millions of
victims. He doesn't know what to do with his newfound knowledge—
or his new-gained energy. Sally is feeling mentally and physically
twenty years younger.

TEST RESULTS: No tests today.

MEDICATIONS: None for Sam or Sally.

DAILY LESSON: Example, not preaching, is the best teacher.

wonder, "Why not me too?" Then, and only then, when they ask
you how you arranged that marvelous change, you can let them
know how the magic transformation came to you.

A Mixed Family—
Sharing a Meal with a Meat Eater

That evening the Watermans' married daughter, Heather, arrived
for dinner with her husband, Pat. Heather had been interested in

healthy eating ever since she discovered as a teen-ager that her complexion was clearer and her weight easier to control when she avoided oily foods, but Pat was a meat-and-potatoes man—heavy on the meat and proud of it. Sam, still suffering hurt feelings from his earlier encounter with Jack, was not yet ready for another confrontation over his changed eating habits.

Everyone but Sally was a bit apprehensive about the meal. She, however, was confident they all would enjoy this evening because of her thoughtful planning. She knew Mexican food was everyone's favorite. Before she left for work that morning she started a pot of beans in her slow cooker. Since she preferred to visit with her guests than spend time in the kitchen, she prepared the rest of the meal right after work. At dinner time, five minutes' warming time in the microwave was all that was required.

Sam and Sally, Heather and Pat—a family with mixed eating habits—sat down to a large bowl of mashed pinto beans seasoned with onion powder, garlic powder, and chili powder, several small individual bowls of chopped lettuce, scallions, tomatoes, and chili peppers, a plate of alfalfa sprouts, three different salsas (mild, medium, and hot)—*and* bowls of grated cheese and seasoned hamburger meat that Sally had prepared with Pat in mind. They began their dinner by passing around a basket filled with corn tortillas and whole wheat flour tortillas. Over this tortilla foundation each person built a mouth-watering meal from the smorgasbord of tasty ingredients set before them. This freedom of choice allowed them all to eat in the way they each felt best, and to enjoy each other's company without the slightest distress.

Later that evening, when Heather and Pat had left, Sam turned to Sally and exclaimed, "Dinner was great! Pat was happy, and I wasn't even tempted by all that cheese and meat. Let's do this again soon!"

T·H·E W·A·T·E·R·M·A·N·S

DAY 11

Breakfast: Nutri-Grain Cereal, with Apple Juice for
Sally and low-fat soy milk for Sam
Lunch: Sam: Peasant Salad (in the office). Sally:
Chinese vegetables and sweet-and-sour pork at a
Chinese restaurant
Dinner: Split Pea Soup / Broiled Tomatoes / Quick
Apple Pie (Sally only)

EXERCISE: Sam walked 20 minutes three times today. Sally walked
her usual 20 minutes twice at a fast pace. Both spent a good deal of
time on the exercise bike.

PHYSICAL STATUS: Sam: BP 106/76. Weight 204 lbs. No chest
pains. 2 normal BMs this morning.
Sally: Weight 132 lbs. One normal BM in the morning. Stomach
cramps and diarrhea 3 hours after that Chinese lunch. No headaches
or joint pains.

MENTAL STATUS: Sam almost feels guilty because he has had
the fortune to feel so good. Sally now understands—and will never
forget—that the principles of good health apply to her too. The diarrhea and stomach cramps that can follow a greasy meal are hard facts,
never to be dismissed.

TEST RESULTS: No tests today.

MEDICATIONS: None for Sam or Sally.

DAILY LESSON: Follow the McDougall Program only on days
when you want to feel good. Otherwise, break the rules—and see
what punishment fits your crime.

THE WATERMANS' DAY 11

What Happens When You Break the Diet Rules

When the final two days arrived, Sally and Sam were excited—
and maybe a little restless too. Sam wanted to see what his blood
tests would show on Day 12, and Sally wanted to see some more
weight loss right there on the scale, clear and undeniable.

On Day 11 at lunchtime, Sally foolishly did something that wasn't going to help her diet at all. She hopped into her car and drove a few miles to a Chinese restaurant to meet some friends. She couldn't imagine how one meal off the diet could make any big difference. There she settled down to enjoy what her fancy yearned for: a feast of sweet and sour pork. The results were disastrous. The meal didn't taste as good as she'd dreamed it would, because she was already out of the habit of eating so much salt and grease. It hit her stomach like a truckload of overlarded bricks. Even before the afternoon ended, she was bent over with stomach cramps, and had diarrhea. "McDougall's Revenge," she called it, and rightly so. After that speedy penance she decided that a long time would pass before she'd challenge her stomach (or McDougall) again in such a stupid way. Being noble, not to say charitable, I refrained from saying "I told you so."

THE WATERMANS' DAY 12

The Twelve-Day Report

Sam and Sally, about to become graduates of the Program, had blood tests done in the morning and treated themselves to lunch at Sam's favorite Italian restaurant.

In the afternoon, Sam picked up the test results. In those figures Sam and Sally were seeing numerical representations of major physical changes in their bodies that had taken just twelve days to achieve. Sam's cholesterol, which had been at 246 when he began, had fallen to 156. Sally's had dropped from 218 to 178. Sam's triglycerides were only slightly more than half of what they had been when he began the Program. His blood sugar had decreased from 180 to 98 mg/dl. His initial high level could have meant trouble for him later, possibly the complications of diabetes, which can include blindness, kidney disease, and a still greater likelihood of heart disease.

Sam's changes in those several tests were more impressive than Sally's because to begin with he had been a much sicker person. Still, she had every reason to be proud of that forty-point cholesterol change; it was good for her health, and it's a bigger reduction than is the twenty-eight point *average* that my group of patients at St.

T·H·E W·A·T·E·R·M·A·N·S

DAY 12

Breakfast: Cantaloupe (Sally only) / rice cakes with
raspberry jam for Sally; 2 plain bagels microwaved
to freshness and spread with Corn Butter for Sam
Lunch (at a restaurant): Sam had spaghetti with marinara sauce and Italian bread; Sally ate a vegetable
salad with zesty tomato dressing she brought with
her in a spice jar.

Dinner (at a steak house): salad bar / baked potato /
steamed vegetables (no butter, no cheese) / lots of
other (acceptable) goodies

EXERCISE: Sally and Sam walked together twice today for half an
hour each time and Sam had no trouble keeping up. They spent their
usual time on the exercise bike.

PHYSICAL STATUS: Sam: BP 118/78. Weight 203 lbs. (down 10
lbs.). No chest pains. Bowels function normally; no indigestion. Skin
and hair are no longer greasy. He visits his cardiologist for follow-
up.
Sally: BP 100/60. Weight 132 lbs. (down 3 lbs.). Feeling great—
recovered quickly after yesterday's lunch.

MENTAL STATUS: Sam and Sally realize they've found a sensible
diet and exercise program. They're no longer worrying about sliding
downhill into a miserable old age and a housebound retirement. Now
they're looking forward to living, playing, and working more enjoy-
ably than ever. Sam plans a new insurance program, based on lower
rates for people who reduce their health risks by sensible adjustments
to diet and lifestyle.

TEST RESULTS: Sam: Cholesterol 156 mg/dl (down 90 mg/dl and
close to ideal); Triglycerides 140 mg/dl (down 135 mg/dl from the
first test and 185 mg/dl from the test on Day 5, by eating no fruits);
Blood Sugar 98 (down 82 mg/dl,and now normal).
Sally: Cholesterol 178 mg/dl (down 40 mg/dl); Triglycerides 80
mg/dl (down 24 mg/dl); Blood Sugar 98 mg/dl.

MEDICATIONS: None for Sam or Sally.

DAILY LESSON: Your goal is to live as fully and functionally as
you can for as long as you can—enjoying both the improved quality
and the extended quantity of life.

Helena will show. (Although at St. Helena larger improvements in individuals are quite common: Some people drop their cholesterol levels by more than 100 mg/dl in twelve days. The average age of St. Helena patients is more than a decade older than Sam and Sally.)

Recent research has shown that each 1 percent decrease in cholesterol in individuals is associated with a 2 to 3 percent decrease in chances of dying from heart disease. According to these figures, Sam, having reduced his cholesterol level by 37 percent, has reduced his risk of dying from heart disease by at least 70 percent. Sally's 18 percent improvement represents at least a 36 percent reduction in risk. Needless to say, these improved health prospects are achieved not merely by reaching a good cholesterol level, but also by *staying* at that good level.

The readings of the Watermans' blood pressure tests that morning were excellent. Sam's was 118/78, and Sally's was 100/60. No surprises there. One of the easiest and quickest problems to correct

Summary of the Watermans' Laboratory Tests

	Sam	Sally
Cholesterol Readings:		
Day One	246	218
Day Five	200	170
Day Twelve	156	178
Difference	−90	−40
Percentage	37%	18%
Triglyceride Readings:		
Day One	275	104
Day Five	325	90
Day Twelve	140	80
Difference	−135	−24
Blood Sugar Readings:		
Day One	180	98
Day Five	122	94
Day Twelve	98	98
Difference	−82	0

with the low-sodium, high-carbohydrate McDougall diet is high blood pressure.

Finally, there's the matter of weight. In twelve days Sam had lost ten pounds, but Sally had lost just three. Lots of reasons can explain her slowness to part with unwanted pounds, among them that ill-fated Chinese lunch on Day 11 and the latest phase in her menstrual cycle. A good deal of the weight loss for Sam (probably three or four pounds of it) was in the form of water, which he had accumulated because of his diseased heart and the years of eating too much salt in all those rich foods he loved. If we subtract those pounds of discarded water, Sam still lost twice as much weight as Sally did, but Sam was fifty pounds overweight to begin with, and when you're that big, you can lose weight more easily. Sally was only twenty pounds over her ideal weight, and losing weight can be slow when you're that close to normal. I thought Sally did well to lose three pounds, and assured her that if she stayed on the diet, I expected her to lose five to eight pounds a month. At that rate, she'd be trim within two to four months. The McDougall method of weight reduction doesn't work as fast as eating only grapefruit does, but (a) you stay healthy while doing it, (b) you're never hungry, (c) you don't gain the weight back once you've lost it, and (d) all the time you eat a wide variety of delicious foods. (And an added bonus— you don't end up hating grapefruit for the rest of your life after such overexposure to it.) Those are all advantages hard to deny.

Not All Physicians Appreciate Medical Miracles

After getting the results of the tests, Sam went to see his cardiologist. The doctor declared that the changes were impressive, but confessed that he couldn't understand how they had happened so fast. This was certainly an unusual experience for a physician who was accustomed to seeing his patients' health decline with the passing of months and years.

"I knew he was considered a good doctor," Sam told me later on the phone, "and I'd always felt he was doing the best he could for me, but I wondered what the story was here, with my responses to your diet. I'd been seeing him for eighteen months and during all that time I did nothing but get worse. He'd put me on three maintenance medications to lower blood pressure, with a fourth (those nitroglycerin tablets) to be kept in reserve, 'for emergencies.' He'd already hinted once or twice that probably a heart bypass operation awaited me down the road a piece. 'That's the only way you can be sure to relieve those chest pains,' he said. Well! What was all that nonsense about, I ask you, if all I had to do to get well was to eat differently, and walk a few minutes a day. And in less time than it takes to enjoy a two-week vacation, to feel like a new man? Frankly, I'm disappointed in the guy!"

To make matters worse a heart surgeon colleague of the cardiologist stopped in, listened to the history of Sam's extraordinary progress with a patronizing smile, and told Sam that (a) you can't judge such short-term results, (b) nobody sticks to diets, (c) the results were temporary and he'd need bypass sooner or later and, (d) diets were just fads. Sam was furious.

I spent a full ten minutes cooling him down. Did he have any right to feel so angry? you might ask. Frankly, I think he did, although there was nothing unusual or unethical about his doctor's treatment.

It's hard (and unwise) for one doctor to criticize other physicians, because most of them are caring people, dedicated to the welfare of their patients. But, unfortunately, too many of them stop learning after they leave medical school and the few years of hospital training that follow. The one hopeful sign I can see for the future comes out of publications that have appeared during the last decade. Enough has been published about nutrition, not only in professional journals but also in newspapers and popular magazines, to establish a genuine continuing education program for doctors (as well as laymen). The Surgeon General of the United States, The American Heart Association, The American Cancer Society, The National Cancer Institute, The National Academy of Sciences, and the American Diabetic Association all have reached the conclusion that faulty diet is the major cause of enormous numbers of cases of deaths and disabilities among the American people.

The Surgeon General's report on *Nutrition and Health*, released in 1988, should be as revolutionary a document as was the 1964 Report of the Surgeon General on *Smoking and Health*. The report notes that dietary factors play prominent roles in five of the ten leading causes of death in the United States (including heart disease, cancer, and stroke); dietary diseases are killing over one million of the two million people who die each year in the United States. Referring to the need for new ideas in the way we eat, the Surgeon

The Watermans Review Their Original Goals

On Day 1, Sally and Sam had high expectations of the Mc-Dougall Program. Now the twelve days of testing were concluded. Did they consider that the Program had helped them?

GOALS	ACCOMPLISHED?
Sam:	
Relieving some of the chest pain	All chest pains gone
Losing five pounds	Lost 10 pounds
Reaching a normal blood pressure	Reached normal BP without drugs
Getting off some of the medications	Off all medication
Stopping burning acid indigestion	Comfortable stomach
Ending bouts of diarrhea	Quiet bowels
Sally:	
Losing five pounds	Lost only 3 pounds
Relieving stiff, painful joints (arthritis)	Pain-free
Ending constipation	Easy BMs
Ending nagging sinus headaches	Headaches gone
Ending postnasal drip	No more drip
Feeling more energetic	Feels like she was twenty
Getting away from caffeine	No more addiction
Both Sam and Sally:	
Learning to like the new kinds of foods	Love their foods
Satisfying hunger at every meal	Eat more than ever before
Getting used to taking daily exercise	Look forward to it
Having the change go smoothly	Smooth, but difficult

General writes, "Of highest priority among these changes is to reduce intake of foods high in fats and to increase intake of foods high in complex carbohydrates and fiber." Further on, he writes, ". . . clinical evidence . . . has established the relationship between high blood cholesterol and CHD [coronary heart disease]. The relationship is strong, continuous, and graded." In another place, the Surgeon General says, "Dietary fat increases the risk of cancers of the breast, colon, rectum, endometrium [uterus], and prostate." That the highest medical authority in the land should deliver this message should make doctors stand up and take notice.

Growing Old Gracefully

Sam and Sally decided to have their final meal on Day 12 at the Sizzler Steak House to celebrate their success. They got there around 4:45 p.m. and seeing a large crowd of senior citizens, realized that those lucky folk received a special discount if they showed up before 5:00 p.m.—a promotion to get people to come earlier to eat.

They ordered a few special items to be prepared for them. By the time they'd visited the salad bar and the pasta bars they found their table filled with all kinds of dishes: baked potatoes, rice pilaf, steamed vegetables without butter, tossed salad with mushrooms, peppers, and tomatoes, and varicolored pasta with marinara sauce. They'd piled up so much delectable food that they felt embarrassed. While they ate they watched the older people around them. Many were quite feeble and even crippled.

SAM: It would be nice to get old with a little style, wouldn't it? And in good health too, of course.

SALLY: Well, why shouldn't we? I used to think one didn't have any power over the way one aged. You just went steadily downhill, like everybody else. But now McDougall's given me the idea that we do have a lot of power over the way our bodies change. That's pretty amazing, isn't it?

SAM: You don't have to tell me. I hardly think of chest pain anymore. It seems to be gone.

SALLY: Of course it is. Unless we go back to eating the way we used to. Do you think we will?

SAM: Not a chance. We've been stuffing ourselves with what McDougall calls rich foods for fifty years. Well fine, we've had our big blast; we did ourselves proud. We've feasted enough for a lifetime. I don't feel like dying too soon just because I want to go on feasting. There's absolutely nothing wrong with the foods we eat now. Most of it's delicious. We'd be crazy to go back.

Can McDougall Dieters Ever Feast Again?

Of course, my best answer is no, you should avoid all feasts, because that's safest and the most sensible path to health. However, I do see a place for feasting on holidays and limited special occasions, as long as it's done with moderation. The fact is, if you choose to take risks, you must also take the responsibility—and the chance of sudden death that always accompanies risks of that kind. Many patients have asked me if I could fix them up with a "less pure" form of the diet. I answer that there's no point to doing that. If you want to compromise with the rules, you can do that all by your grown-up self. You can decide when you want to feel well and when—and for how long—you're willing to be sick. Consider how many meals fit for a king an American who doesn't know about the McDougall diet will have consumed in his lifetime. Where do you fit in this table?

Number of Feasts to Date*

Your Age	Total Number of Feasts	Your Age	Total Number of Feasts
5	5475	50	54750
10	10950	55	60225
15	16425	60	65700
20	21900	65	71175
25	27375	70	76650
30	32850	75	82125
35	38325	80	87600
40	43800	85	93075
45	49275	90	98550

* Based on the usual three meals of rich foods a day, you would have approximately 1095 feasts per year. A little past the age of ninety-one you could celebrate your 100,000th feast—with another and bigger feast to mark the day (in the unlikely event that you've survived all those years of food-gorging).

Special Modifications for Your Own Diet

Will all people on the McDougall Program experience similar benefits to those Sam and Sally enjoyed? The answer is pretty much an unqualified yes, but because each individual's body is a little different from all others of the species, I want to discuss a few particular problems that may arise.

1. Are You Losing Weight Too Fast?

As the word indicates, individuals are highly individual. This is especially true when we consider the many elaborate kinds of mechanisms that run each one of us, the sum of which we call our metabolism. Even when they're eating the foods included in the standard American diet, some people will still be slim enough so that they don't want to lose weight and might even prefer to gain some.

Gaining weight is hard to do when you're eating the healthy, high-carbohydrate foods of the McDougall diet, but it can be done. Bread is the starch food with the highest calorie content (e.g., the cooked natural wheat grain yields only ½ calorie a gram, but after refining and baking, wheat bread yields 2½ calories a gram). When you eat lots of bread you should be able to maintain your weight. If that's not sufficient, and you are otherwise in good health, you can add dried fruits (apricots, raisins, dates, apples, etc.) to your menu. Be careful, however, that their high concentrations of natural sugars don't raise your triglyceride level too high or otherwise upset your metabolism. If even that doesn't work, you can eat moderate amounts of high-fat plant foods such as avocados, nuts, seeds, peanut butter, olives, tofu, and soybeans. Using these high-fat vegetable foods, I can easily design a diet that exceeds the number of calories provided by the famous heavy and greasy American diet. I hesitate to recommend them, however, because the high concentration of fats in such foods might raise your long-term risk of developing cancer or gallbladder disease.

2. Are You Losing Weight Too Slowly?

A few people do find that significant loss of weight while they're on a healthy diet is a very slow process. If you're sixty or seventy pounds overweight and you're losing only a pound or so a week, you may be impatient as well as discouraged. In that case, you should concentrate on eating the starches having the lowest calorie yields until your weight has dropped appreciably. Use potatoes, rice, squash, and corn as the starch center for your meals. Stay away from bread. Limit fruits to three or less a day. Concentrate on green and yellow vegetables (onions, carrots, celery, lettuce, green beans, wax beans, zucchini), all of which have very low calorie concentrations. Avoid the high-calorie plant foods mentioned in the paragraph above. And *above all, exercise!* This activity does burn up calories, and even a small increase in the amount of exercise you do, combined with a healthy low-calorie diet, makes the whole process of shedding weight go more quickly.

3. Do You Still Have Indigestion?

Many kinds of foods can cause indigestion. Raw onions, cucumbers, radishes, and green and red peppers are common culprits. Cooking will often change the irritating components enough so that you'll be able to tolerate the altered foodstuff. Acid fruit juices (orange, lemon, tomato, passion fruit, pineapple, and apple) make many people feel the burning sensation in the stomach and esophagus that is known as "heartburn." Ironically, the raw fruits themselves seldom have this effect, and sometimes they can even be used to relieve indigestion. Hot foods (peppers, kim chi, chili, salsa) are certainly not advisable for people with sensitive stomachs. Even very common spices can cause trouble. If you suffer often from an upset stomach and if ceasing to eat fats, coffee, and alcohol doesn't entirely stop that misery, then you'll have to do some careful observation to learn the identity of the specific foods that affect you so badly. Rarely does anyone who avoids the troublesome foods mentioned in this paragraph get indigestion (unless, of course, he is still eating the standard American diet).

4. Do You Still Have Bowel Problems?

The first thing to remember is that the frequency of your bowel movements is not too important. After you've been on a high-carbohydrate diet for a few days, you're likely to have from one to three bowel movements a day. This frequency has a lot to do with what you eat and how much you eat. Some people will have a bowel movement only once every two days. The important thing is that you pass a soft, large stool. Constipation is exceedingly rare on a high-fiber diet, but if you have diarrhea after twelve days on the diet, consider the possibility that you may be sensitive to wheat, barley, or rye, all of which contain a protein called gluten that many people are sensitive to. If, after taking all these precautions, you still have bowel problems while you're following the McDougall diet, then you should see your physician.

5. Other Problems

For information about other physical problems—or, indeed, for more thoughts about the problems mentioned above—turn to the medical guide in Part 3.

The Benefits Don't Stop After Twelve Days

Sally and Sam finished the twelve-day diet more than a year ago, and they have never gone back to eating the foods of the standard American diet. They have found a number of favorite vegetarian dishes that they repeat often. Sam, keeping track on a desk calendar in his study at home, had his last chest pain seventeen days after he started the McDougall Program. He no longer sees his cardiologist because he no longer has a heart problem. He no longer has a heart problem because he doesn't eat foods that damage his arteries. It's as simple as that. Sam weighs 170 pounds now, which means he's about ten pounds overweight. He's still thinking of trimming that last layer of flab away (some day!) and he may well do it, although with his big appetite and rather quiet lifestyle (not totally sedentary, however, because he still walks thirty minutes a

T·H·E W·A·T·E·R·M·A·N·S

One Year Later

FAVORITE MEALS

Breakfast: Sam: Oatmeal / hash-brown potatoes / bananas (Sam can eat three fruits a day now and his triglycerides stay normal). Sally: Whole wheat bagels with a thin spread of no-sugar raspberry or strawberry jam

Lunch: Sam: Green salad and 2 baked potatoes / low-sodium oil-free French dressing over both potatoes and salad. Sally: Pita bread stuffed with onions / tomatoes / lettuce / salsa

Dinner: Sam: Spaghetti / Bean Burritos / Chili / "Meat" Loaf. Sally: Rice and Greens / Pasta Salad / California Stew

FAVORITE EXERCISE: Walking for both Sally and Sam. They often hike in the country on the weekends. They also ride bikes outside, swim in the summer, and ski in the winter.

PHYSICAL STATUS: Sam: BP 110/70. Weight 170 lbs. No chest pains. Bowels function like clockwork.
Sally: BP 100/60. Weight 115 lbs. Feeling well in every way.

MENTAL STATUS: Both Sam and Sally consider their way of living to be natural and comfortable. They're fit, healthy, and happy.

TEST RESULTS: Sam: Cholesterol 138 mg/dl; Triglycerides 130 mg/dl. Blood Sugar 90 mg/dl. Sally: Cholesterol 124 mg/dl; Triglycerides 70 mg/dl. Blood Sugar 78 mg/dl.

MEDICATIONS: None for Sam or Sally.

LIFELONG LESSONS: You are what you eat. You don't need to eat rich foods to be happy—you've done enough of that in the past. Now's the time to get on with healthy, happy living.

day) there was bound to be a little resistance to losing those last few pounds. Also, he has found the "transitional treats" in Chapter 12 hard to resist. Special occasions for Sam, the Reformed Gourmand, come at least once a week. Still and all, he's kept himself free of any health trouble, and he keeps a very close watch on his cholesterol level.

Sally on the other hand, after all that anguish over a slow start toward sylphlike slimness, has reached precisely the weight she's always wanted to be, which is 115 pounds. And she is feeling great.

All the improvements in health and well-being that Sam and Sally made during their first twelve days on the Program they've kept ever since. They're still walking, and they're fitter physically and mentally than they've been since they were in their twenties. And they're happier with their bodies than they've been since they were in their twenties as well.

The Watermans' story is not uncommon. It could be yours.

P·A·R·T

2

EATING, MCDOUGALL STYLE: RECIPES AND SPECIAL MEALS

10

RECIPES FOR THE

TWELVE-DAY DIET

In this chapter I give recipes for the twelve-day diet menus presented in Chapter 4. To make your change in eating habits easier, these recipes are all quick and easy to prepare. You may want to follow the menus exactly, but that is not necessary. You can pick and choose among the recipes and rearrange them in any combinations you wish, repeating your favorites as often as you like. You may also want to browse through the more elaborate recipes in the next chapter and use the ones that look good to you and your family. But, please remember the basic principle: Keep to the guidelines given in Chapter 4.

To help you through the big change, I have included shopping lists on pages 216–221 for those who plan to follow the menus as they're listed. If you're going to repeat favorite breakfasts, lunches, and dinners, or use recipes from Chapter 11, then you'll have to prepare your own shopping lists. A list of acceptable packaged and canned products appears in Chapter 6.

Many of the recipes call for already-cooked beans or rice. You may find it helpful to cook large amounts of beans and rice ahead and freeze them in conveniently sized batches. Most of the recipes call for dried herbs, but feel free to substitute fresh herbs any time. If you do, increase the amount by one quarter to one half; dried herbs are more powerful than fresh.

NOTE: Wherever stewed tomatoes are called for in a recipe, low-sodium whole tomatoes, chopped, may be substituted.

DAY 1

BREAKFAST

QUICK OATMEAL

Follow the directions below, not those on the package. Use no salt. You may want to add some dried fruit during the cooking.

SERVINGS: 1
PREPARATION TIME: 1 MINUTE
COOKING TIME: 5 MINUTES

½ cup quick-cooking oatmeal   *1 cup water*

Place water in saucepan. Add quick oats, bring to a boil, and stir. Boil for one minute, stirring occasionally. Cover, remove from heat. Let rest a few minutes. Stir again and serve at once. Sprinkle on nutmeg, mace, or cinnamon, in any combination.

LUNCH

FAST PIZZA
SERVINGS: 1
PREPARATION TIME: 10 MINUTES
COOKING TIME: 10 MINUTES
---

1 pita bread   *⅛ teaspoon dried basil*
¼ cup low-sodium tomato sauce   *⅛ teaspoon dried oregano*

Toppings (choose as many or as
*   few as you wish):*
⅛ cup chopped yellow onions   *4 sliced fresh mushrooms*
⅛ cup chopped scallions   *⅛ cup alfalfa sprouts*
⅛ cup chopped green peppers

Cut the pita bread in half by separating it into two circles. Spread each half with tomato sauce. Sprinkle on the basil and oregano and add the toppings of your choice. Bake at 300° for 10 minutes, or heat in toaster oven for 5 minutes at 250° setting.

DAY 1

DINNER

SPICY CHILI BEANS

Canned beans cannot be used in this recipe; the cooking liquid from the dry beans makes a rich, flavorful broth that forms the base for the chili. If you soak the beans overnight you can cut the cooking time in half. Freeze any leftover chili for a fast meal later. Serve over brown rice (make ¾ cup per serving extra rice for tomorrow's breakfast).

SERVINGS: 4–6
PREPARATION TIME: 10 MINUTES
COOKING TIME: 4 HOURS

---

2 cups dry red kidney beans
5 cups water
2 yellow onions, chopped
1 green pepper, chopped
2 stalks celery, chopped
2 cloves garlic, crushed
1 cup low-sodium tomato sauce

1 15–16 ounce can low-sodium
* stewed tomatoes*
4 tablespoons chili powder
2 teaspoons ground cumin
¼ teaspoon crushed red pepper
⅛ teaspoon cayenne

Place the beans and water in a large pot. Bring to a boil, cover, reduce heat, and simmer for 2 hours. Add the remaining ingredients and cook an additional 2 hours.

STRAWBERRY FROZEN FRUIT DESSERT

SERVINGS: 8
PREPARATION TIME: 10 MINUTES
(PLUS 15–30 MINUTES FREEZING TIME)
COOKING TIME: NONE

1½ cups canned crushed pineapple
* with juice*
3 frozen bananas*

3 cups frozen strawberries
(1 16 ounce bag)

Place the crushed pineapple and juice in the blender. Add the frozen fruit a little at a time, blending between each addition. Scoop ½ cup servings into dessert dishes and freeze for 15 to 30 minutes. (If frozen for longer period of time, remove from freezer a few minutes before serving to soften.)

---

* *To freeze bananas*, peel, wrap securely in plastic wrap, and place in freezer for at least 12

DAY 2

BREAKFAST

BREAKFAST RICE WITH FRUIT
SERVINGS: 1
PREPARATION TIME: 5 MINUTES
COOKING TIME: 1 MINUTE IN MICROWAVE,
5 MINUTES ON STOVE (COOKED RICE NEEDED)

¾ cup cooked brown rice
1 banana, peeled and chopped

½ cup unsweetened applesauce
dash nutmeg (optional)

Warm the rice in a microwave about 1 minute on high, or place in a small saucepan with a small amount of water and warm on the stovetop for about 5 minutes, stirring frequently. Place the banana in the blender with the applesauce and process until smooth. Spoon over the warmed rice. Sprinkle nutmeg on top for extra flavor, if desired.

LUNCH

"OLT" SANDWICH (ONION, LETTUCE, AND TOMATO)
SERVINGS: 1
PREPARATION TIME: 3 MINUTES
COOKING TIME: NONE
---

2 slices whole wheat bread
1 tomato, sliced
1 red onion, sliced

lettuce leaves
low-sodium, oil-free Russian or
*   Italian salad dressing*

Toast the bread. Spread some dressing on each slice, layer the tomatoes and onions on one slice, top with lettuce leaves, and close the sandwich.

DAY 2

DINNER

MARINARA SPAGHETTI SAUCE

Make the sauce earlier in the day, if desired, and reheat just before serving. About 15 minutes before serving, drop ½ to 1 pound egg-free whole wheat or spinach spaghetti noodles into 4 quarts boiling water and cook until tender, about 10 minutes. Serve the sauce over the noodles.

SERVINGS: 4–6
PREPARATION TIME: 10 MINUTES
COOKING TIME: 1 HOUR

---

1 yellow onion, finely chopped
½ pound fresh mushrooms,
  cleaned and finely chopped
2 cloves garlic, crushed
1 15–16 ounce can low-sodium
  stewed tomatoes
1 8 ounce can low-sodium
  tomato sauce

1 15–16 ounce can low-sodium
  tomato puree
1 teaspoon dried basil
1 teaspoon dried oregano
2 tablespoons parsley flakes

Sauté the onions, mushrooms, and garlic in a small amount of water for 10 minutes. Add the remaining ingredients. Simmer over low heat 1 to 2 hours, until sauce thickens, breaking up the tomatoes as they cook. Do not cover.

SUNBEAM TAPIOCA

SERVINGS: 4
PREPARATION TIME: 15 MINUTES
(PLUS 2 HOURS CHILLING TIME)
COOKING TIME: 5 MINUTES

---

3 tablespoons instant tapioca
1 cup pineapple juice
1 cup orange juice
1½ tablespoons lemon juice

½ cup canned mandarin orange
  sections, drained
1 cup canned pineapple,
  crushed or tidbits, drained

Combine the instant tapioca, pineapple juice, and orange juice in a saucepan. Cook and stir over medium heat until the mixture comes to a boil. Remove from heat; add the lemon juice. Cool, stirring occasionally. Add the fruit and chill until firm.

DAY 3

BREAKFAST

FROZEN HASH-BROWN POTATOES

Frozen hash-brown potatoes are frozen diced potatoes. Sometimes they come as patties. Look for hash-browns that contain potatoes only, or potatoes with dextrose (sugar) but no oil (see list of acceptable packaged products on pages 100–114).

SERVINGS: 1
PREPARATION TIME: 2 MINUTES
COOKING TIME: 20–25 MINUTES

1 package frozen hash-browns (use as many as you desire)

Place the frozen patties in a dry nonstick skillet or griddle. Cook over medium-to-high heat for 15 minutes, then turn and cook 10 minutes on the second side, until brown. Cover with ketchup, barbecue sauce, or other acceptable topping (see staples, pages 216–217).

LUNCH

QUICK PASTA SALAD

This dish is very adaptable. It can be served hot or cold and can be different every time you serve it depending on the vegetables you choose.

SERVINGS: 2
PREPARATION TIME: 10 MINUTES
COOKING TIME: 10 MINUTES

1 cup uncooked whole wheat or spinach elbow macaroni, shells, or spirals
1½ cups chopped vegetables (scallions, green or red peppers, broccoli, celery, carrots, pimientos—alone or in any combination you want)

¼ to ½ cup low-sodium, oil-free salad dressing

Cook the macaroni in boiling water until just tender, 8 to 10 minutes. Mix with the vegetables, add dressing, and toss to coat.

DAY 3

CUCUMBER VINAIGRETTE
SERVINGS: 2–4
PREPARATION TIME: 10 MINUTES
(PLUS 2 HOURS OR OVERNIGHT CHILLING TIME)
COOKING TIME: NONE
---

2 unpeeled cucumbers, thinly sliced
1 scallion, sliced
1 tablespoon frozen apple juice
concentrate

¼ cup white vinegar
⅓ teaspoon celery seed
dash ground black pepper

Mix all the ingredients in a bowl and chill for at least 2 hours or overnight.

DINNER

AMERICAN VEGETABLE STEW

Serve over brown rice (make 3 cups extra rice to use on Days 4 and 5).

SERVINGS: 4
PREPARATION TIME: 15 MINUTES
COOKING TIME: 45 MINUTES

1 yellow onion, coarsely chopped
1 clove garlic, crushed
1 white potato, scrubbed and
chunked
1 carrot, scrubbed and sliced
1 stalk celery, sliced
1 zucchini, sliced
½ cup chopped broccoli
1 leek, trimmed, washed,
and sliced

2 cups low-sodium tomato sauce
1 tablespoon parsley flakes
½ teaspoon paprika
½ teaspoon dried basil
½ teaspoon chili powder
¼ teaspoon dry mustard
¼ teaspoon ground cumin
⅛ teaspoon ground black pepper

Cook the onions, garlic, potato, carrot, and celery in a small amount of water in a large saucepan for 10 minutes. Add the remaining ingredients and cook over low heat until the vegetables are tender, about 35 minutes.

DAY 3

STEAMED BROCCOLI WITH LEMON

SERVINGS: 4
PREPARATION TIME: 10 MINUTES
COOKING TIME: 15 MINUTES

1 pound broccoli, cut into
flowerettes

1 lemon, cut into wedges
garlic powder (optional)

Steam the broccoli over 1 inch of boiling water just until tender. Drain. Place the broccoli into a covered serving bowl, squeeze the lemon juice over it, and sprinkle with garlic powder, if desired. Cover and allow to set for 5 to 10 minutes to absorb flavors.

MICROWAVED APPLE WEDGES

SERVINGS: 2
PREPARATION TIME: 5 MINUTES
COOKING TIME: 2 MINUTES

1 teaspoon sugar
¼ teaspoon ground cinnamon
⅛ teaspoon ground ginger

⅛ teaspoon ground cloves
1 large unpeeled apple, cored and
cut into 8 wedges

Combine the sugar, cinnamon, ginger, and cloves in a small bowl and mix well. Press the cut sides of the apple into the spice mixture. Place four wedges on a paper plate, cover with waxed paper, and microwave on high for about 45 seconds. Repeat with the remaining wedges. Serve at once.

VARIATION: *To make this in a conventional oven*, place the wedges in a small casserole dish and bake, covered, at 250° for about 15 minutes.

DAY 4

BREAKFAST

HOT 7 GRAIN CEREAL
(OR HOT APPLE GRANOLA)

SERVINGS: 1
PREPARATION TIME: 2 MINUTES
COOKING TIME: 5 MINUTES

---

2 cups water
1 cup 7 Grain Cereal, or Hot Apple
  Granola

chopped fruit: bananas, apples,
  or pears

Bring the water to a boil in a saucepan. Add the cereal, stir, reduce heat to low, and cook until done, about 5 minutes. Top with fresh fruit, or if you prefer, a sweetener such as pure maple syrup or honey.

LUNCH

WHOLE GRAIN BREAD SANDWICH
WITH VEGETABLES

SERVINGS: 1
PREPARATION TIME: 5 MINUTES
COOKING TIME: NONE

---

2 slices whole grain bread
Dijon or prepared mustard
  (optional)

Choice of any combination of
  vegetables:
sliced onions
sliced tomatoes
sliced cucumbers
sliced radishes

sliced green peppers
sliced carrots
lettuce
alfalfa sprouts

Toast the bread and spread each slice lightly with mustard if desired. Layer the vegetables on one slice of bread and close the sandwich.

VARIATION: Spread the bread with Garbanzo Spread (page 227) or Pimiento Spread (page 227) instead of mustard.

DAY 4

DINNER

BEAN AND RICE BURRITOS

This is a quick and easy recipe to fix for those days when you're too busy to spend much time in the kitchen.

SERVINGS: 2–3
PREPARATION TIME: 10 MINUTES
COOKING TIME: 10 MINUTES (COOKED RICE NEEDED)

Filling:
1 28 ounce can low-sodium, water-packed pinto beans, drained and rinsed

6 whole wheat tortillas
Toppings:
1 head iceberg lettuce, chopped and dried

1–2 cups cooked brown rice
dash each: chili powder, garlic powder, and cumin
3/4 cup water

1 bunch scallions, chopped
1 ripe tomato, chopped
low-sodium, oil-free Mexican salsa

Place the beans in a saucepan and mash with a potato masher. Add the cooked rice, spices, and water. Heat 5 to 10 minutes. Meanwhile, prepare the vegetables. Heat the tortillas quickly (just to soften) in a preheated skillet, a toaster oven, or a microwave. Place a line of bean mixture down the middle of each tortilla. Top with lettuce, scallions, tomato, and salsa. Tuck in the top and bottom edges, roll into a burrito, and serve immediately, topped with additional salsa if desired.

SUNSHINE FRUIT DESSERT

This recipe uses only part of a fresh pineapple. Wrap and freeze the remaining portion for use in the Day 6 dessert.

SERVINGS: 4
PREPARATION TIME: 15 MINUTES
COOKING TIME: NONE

1/4 fresh pineapple, cut in chunks
1 banana, sliced
1/2 pint fresh strawberries, sliced
3/4 cup fresh blueberries

1/8 cup frozen orange juice concentrate
1/8 teaspoon nutmeg

Mix all the ingredients together lightly in a serving bowl and chill.

DAY 5

BREAKFAST

WHOLE WHEAT TOAST WITH CORN BUTTER

If you prefer, you can omit the Corn Butter and simply spread the toast with no-sugar, pure-fruit jam.

SERVINGS: 1
PREPARATION TIME: 1 MINUTE
COOKING TIME: 2 MINUTES

Whole wheat (or whole grain)
bread

Corn Butter (recipe below)

Toast the bread and spread with Corn Butter while hot.

CORN BUTTER

Keep this on hand in the refrigerator as a butter substitute for spreading on bread or toast or melting over hot vegetables. It keeps about a week.

MAKES 1½ CUPS
PREPARATION TIME: 5 MINUTES
COOKING TIME: 5 MINUTES (FOR CORNMEAL)

¼ cup cornmeal
1 cup water
¼ cup additional water

1–2 teaspoons lemon juice
1 teaspoon no-salt seasoning blend

Place the cornmeal in a saucepan, add the 1 cup water, and cook, stirring constantly, until smooth and thick. Place the cooked cornmeal and all the remaining ingredients in the blender and process until smooth. Add more water if necessary to reach desired spreading consistency.

DAY 5

LUNCH

PITA BREAD STUFFED WITH KIDNEY BEANS

Leftover chili from Day 1 dinner could be used in this recipe instead of the spread.

SERVINGS: 2
PREPARATION TIME: 5 MINUTES
COOKING TIME: NONE

---

2 pieces whole wheat pita bread
1 cup Kidney Bean Spread (recipe below)

low-sodium, oil-free Mexican salsa (optional)

Topping options:
chopped green pepper
sliced cucumber
grated carrot
chopped tomato
alfalfa sprouts

chopped lettuce
chopped scallions
chopped yellow onion
low-sodium corn relish

Fill the pita with bean spread and the vegetable toppings of your choice. Drizzle with salsa if you wish.

KIDNEY BEAN SPREAD

Store leftover spread in the refrigerator to use another day as a sandwich spread or as a snack on crackers.

MAKES 1½ CUPS
PREPARATION TIME: 10 MINUTES
COOKING TIME: NONE (COOKED BEANS NEEDED)

1½ cups cooked and drained
kidney beans, or 1 15–16 ounce
can low-sodium, water-packed
kidney beans, drained and rinsed
1 clove garlic
½ teaspoon cumin seeds

½ teaspoon Tabasco sauce
½ tablespoon cider vinegar
2 tablespoons water
2 tablespoons fresh cilantro or parsley

Place all the ingredients in a food processor or blender and process until smooth.

DAY 5

DINNER

M I N E S T R O N E   S O U P

SERVINGS: 6
PREPARATION TIME: 20 MINUTES
(PLUS OVERNIGHT SOAKING TIME)
COOKING TIME: 2½ HOURS

---

1 cup dry kidney beans, soaked
   overnight in water to cover
½ teaspoon crushed garlic
1 yellow onion, chopped
2 quarts water
1 stalk celery, sliced
1 carrot, scrubbed and sliced
1 white potato, scrubbed and
   chopped
1 cup fresh or frozen green beans
   (sliced into 1-inch pieces)
1 8 ounce can low-sodium tomato
   sauce

2 tablespoons parsley flakes, or
   ¼ cup chopped fresh parsley
¼ teaspoon celery seed
½ teaspoon dried marjoram
1½ teaspoons dried basil
1½ teaspoons dried oregano
¼ teaspoon ground black pepper
1 zucchini, chopped
1 cup shredded cabbage
½ cup uncooked egg-free whole
   wheat elbow macaroni

Drain the soaked beans, then place with the garlic, onion, and water in a soup pot and cook for 1 hour to make a rich stock. Then add the celery, carrot, potato, and green beans, plus the tomato sauce and all the seasonings. After 30 minutes, add the zucchini. Cook another 30 minutes and add the cabbage and elbow macaroni. Cook until tender, 20 minutes or so.

VARIATIONS: Add 1 15 ounce can low-sodium, water-packed garbanzo beans, 1 10 ounce package frozen chopped spinach, and/or 1 15–16 ounce can low-sodium chopped tomatoes about 20 minutes before the end of the cooking time. Stir well and heat thoroughly before serving.

DAY 5

RICE AND CORN SALAD

SERVINGS: 4
PREPARATION TIME: 20 MINUTES
(PLUS 2 HOURS CHILLING TIME IF POSSIBLE)
COOKING TIME: NONE (COOKED RICE NEEDED)

---

1 cup frozen corn kernels
1 cup cooked brown rice
1 tomato, coarsely chopped
1/4 cup chopped green pepper

1/4 cup chopped scallions
1/8 cup finely chopped fresh
cilantro, parsley, or dill

Dressing:
1 tablespoon wine vinegar
1 tablespoon water
1 tablespoon low-sodium soy sauce

1/4 teaspoon Dijon mustard
several dashes Tabasco sauce
(optional)

Thaw the corn in a colander under cold running water. Mix with the brown rice, tomato, green pepper, scallions, and cilantro, parsley, or dill in a serving bowl. In a small jar or bowl, mix the dressing ingredients together thoroughly. Pour the dressing over the salad and mix well. For best flavor, cover and chill for at least 2 hours before serving. If you're in a rush, the salad may also be served soon after mixing.

EASY FRUIT "GELATIN"

SERVINGS: 12 SQUARES
PREPARATION TIME: 5 MINUTES
(PLUS 2 HOURS CHILLING TIME)
COOKING TIME: 5 MINUTES

---

1 6 ounce can frozen apple juice
concentrate
3/4 cup unsweetened applesauce

1/3 cup cornstarch
1 teaspoon vanilla extract

Mix the juice, applesauce, and cornstarch in a small pan. Cook over medium heat until thickened and clear, stirring constantly. Add the vanilla. Stir and pour into an 8-inch-square nonstick pan. Chill. When cool, cut into squares.

DAY 6

BREAKFAST

QUICK "FRIED" POTATOES

SERVINGS: 1
PREPARATION TIME: 10 MINUTES
COOKING TIME: 10–15 MINUTES

*1 or 2 white potatoes, scrubbed and
   thinly sliced (do not peel)*
¼ cup chopped green pepper
1 small yellow onion, chopped

*½ tablespoon low-sodium
   soy sauce (optional)*
½ cup water

Place all the ingredients in a nonstick skillet. Cook and stir until water is boiled off and ingredients are tender. Serve plain, or sprinkle with a small amount of Tabasco, hot pepper sauce, ketchup, seasoning powders, etc., if desired.

LUNCH

QUICK GARBANZO BEAN SOUP

This is a quick and easy soup for those days when you are too busy to spend much time cooking.

SERVINGS: 4
PREPARATION TIME: 10 MINUTES
COOKING TIME: 30 MINUTES

*1 small yellow onion, finely
   chopped*
1 cup minced fresh parsley
½ cup minced red or green pepper
2 large cloves garlic, crushed
1 teaspoon ground cumin
¼ cup water

*3 15 ounce cans low-sodium,
   water-packed garbanzo beans,
   undrained*
½ cup water
¼ cup fresh-squeezed lemon juice
cayenne

In a large soup pot, sauté the onion, parsley, pepper, garlic, and cumin in the ¼ cup water until the vegetables are tender. Meanwhile, place the garbanzo beans and their liquid in a blender or food processor and puree. Add to the vegetables along with the ½ cup water and lemon juice. Simmer, covered, for 20 minutes. Add cayenne to taste before serving.

DAY 6

SLICED TOMATOES WITH SALSA

SERVINGS: 2–4
PREPARATION TIME: 10 MINUTES
(PLUS 3–6 HOURS CHILLING TIME IF POSSIBLE)
COOKING TIME: NONE

---

alfalfa sprouts   *sliced tomatoes*

Salsa:
½ cup minced green pepper   *⅛ teaspoon ground cumin*
⅛ cup minced scallions   *¹⁄₁₆–⅛ teaspoon crushed red pepper*
½ tablespoon minced fresh cilantro *1 clove garlic, crushed*
* or parsley*   *1 teaspoon cider vinegar*

Combine the salsa ingredients, stir well, and chill for 3 to 6 hours, if possible. To serve, place some sprouts on individual salad plates, arrange tomato slices over the sprouts, and top with salsa.

DINNER

CAJUN RICE

SERVINGS: 4
PREPARATION TIME: 10 MINUTES
COOKING TIME: 15 MINUTES (COOKED RICE NEEDED)*

---

1 yellow onion, chopped   *¼ cup chopped green chilies*
1 green pepper, chopped   *1 teaspoon chili powder*
1 bunch scallions, chopped   *1 teaspoon Cajun spice mix (see*
2 cloves garlic, crushed   * Note)*
½ pound fresh mushrooms,   *¼ cup chopped fresh cilantro or*
* cleaned and sliced*   * parsley*
1 15–16 ounce can low-sodium   *dash or two Tabasco sauce*
* stewed tomatoes*   *4 cups cooked brown rice*

Sauté the onion, green pepper, scallions, garlic, and mushrooms in a small amount of water for 5 to 10 minutes. Add the remaining ingredients (except for the rice) and mix well. Stir in the cooked rice, heat through, and serve.

NOTE: Some commercial Cajun spice mixes are now available. *To make your own Cajun spice mix*, combine 3 tablespoons paprika, 2 teaspoons onion powder, 2 teaspoons ground black pepper, 2 teaspoons ground white pepper, 2 teaspoons cayenne, 1 teaspoon ground dried oregano, 1 teaspoon ground dried thyme, and ½ teaspoon celery seed. Mix together and store in a tightly covered container. Makes about ⅓ cup.

* Make extra rice for Day 7 and 8.

DAY 6

FROZEN FRUIT "SORBET"

This dessert uses frozen fresh pineapple. Use the frozen pineapple left over from Day 4, or freeze 2 cups pineapple at least a day before using.

SERVINGS: 6
PREPARATION TIME: 10 MINUTES
COOKING TIME: NONE

1 cup pineapple juice
1 frozen banana (see page 181)
½–1 cup frozen blueberries or
  strawberries

2 cups frozen fresh pineapple

Put the juice into the blender. While the blender is running, add pieces of frozen fruit through the feed tube. Blend until the mixture attains a "soft-serve" consistency. Pour into individual serving dishes. Serve immediately or hold in the freezer for a short time before serving.

DAY 7

BREAKFAST

MULTI-MIX COLD CEREAL
WITH RICE MILK

If you prefer, you can omit the Rice Milk and use low-fat vanilla soy milk or apple juice instead.

SERVINGS: 1
PREPARATION TIME: 5 MINUTES
COOKING TIME: NONE (COOKED RICE NEEDED)

⅓ cup cooked brown rice
⅓ cup quick-cooking oatmeal
⅓ cup Grape-nuts
½ sliced banana

1 tablespoon raisins
dash cinnamon
¼ cup Rice Milk (recipe below)

Combine the rice, oats, and Grape-nuts in a small bowl and mix well. Top with cinnamon, raisins, sliced banana, and a little Rice Milk.

RICE MILK

A milk substitute to use on cereal or in cooking. Store in the refrigerator; it lasts five days.

MAKES 4 CUPS
PREPARATION TIME: 5 MINUTES
COOKING TIME: NONE (COOKED RICE NEEDED)

---

1 cup cooked brown rice
4 cups water

1 teaspoon vanilla extract
(optional)

Place the rice in the blender with the water and vanilla (if desired) and process until thoroughly liquefied.

DAY 7

LUNCH

BAKED POTATO SALAD

SERVINGS: 2
PREPARATION TIME: 10 MINUTES
COOKING TIME: 10 MINUTES (IF USING MICROWAVE)

---

2 white baking potatoes, scrubbed
2 cups coarsely shredded lettuce
1 tomato, chopped
¼ cup thinly sliced celery
¼ cup thinly sliced radishes

¼ cup chopped scallions
¼–⅓ cup low-sodium, oil-free
Italian, French, or Russian
salad dressing

Scrub the potatoes, prick with a fork, and microwave on high about 10 minutes, until tender. (If you don't have a microwave, bake at 400° for 50 to 60 minutes.) Combine the lettuce, tomato, celery, radishes, and scallions. To serve, slice the baked potatoes in half lengthwise, then cover each half with some salad mixture. Top all of this with your choice of dressing.

DAY 7

DINNER

VEGETABLE BURRITOS

SERVINGS: 6
PREPARATION TIME: 30 MINUTES
COOKING TIME: 30 MINUTES

6–8 whole wheat flour tortillas

Sauce:
1 small yellow onion, chopped
1 clove garlic, crushed
¼ cup water
¼ cup chopped canned green chilies
½ tablespoon chili powder
½ teaspoon ground cumin

¼ teaspoon ground coriander
dash cayenne
1 8 ounce can low-sodium tomato sauce
¼ cup low-sodium tomato paste
1 cup water

Filling:
1 small yellow onion, chopped
½ cup chopped green pepper
¼ pound fresh mushrooms, cleaned and chopped
½ cup water

½ cup corn kernels
1 cup chopped zucchini
1 teaspoon chili powder
½ teaspoon ground cumin

Sauce: Sauté the onion and garlic in the water for 5 minutes. Add the green chilies and spices, stir, and sauté a few minutes. Add the remaining ingredients, mix well, and simmer for 15 minutes. Set aside.

Filling: Sauté the onion, green pepper, and mushrooms in the water for 5 minutes. Add the corn, zucchini, and spices, sauté about 10 more minutes, and set aside.

Preheat the oven to 350°. Place about ⅓–½ cup filling down the center of each chapati or tortilla and roll up. Spread 1 cup sauce over the bottom of a covered casserole dish. Place the burritos seam-side-down in the casserole. Pour the rest of the sauce over the burritos, cover, and bake for 30 minutes.

VARIATION: *For "Cheese" Burritos*, use potato-based Melty Cheese (recipe page 264) instead of the sauce given here.

DAY 7

RED AND WHITE SALAD

SERVINGS: 4
PREPARATION TIME: 10 MINUTES
COOKING TIME: NONE

2 extra-large tomatoes, sliced
1 sweet onion, thinly sliced
1 small cucumber, thinly sliced
⅛ cup cider vinegar or low-
sodium, oil-free Italian dressing

dash Tabasco sauce (optional)
dash ground black pepper
(optional)

Layer the sliced vegetables in a bowl. Pour the vinegar or dressing over them. Sprinkle with Tabasco sauce or pepper, if desired. Chill until serving time.

FRUIT DELIGHT

SERVINGS: 4
PREPARATION TIME: 15 MINUTES
COOKING TIME: 15 MINUTES

2 bananas, chunked
2 teaspoons lemon juice
1 8 ounce package frozen
unsweetened strawberries or
raspberries, thawed (reserve
juice)

1 cup water
¼ cup instant tapioca

Place the bananas and lemon juice in the blender and blend until smooth. Place the mixture in a saucepan and add the thawed fruit with its juice. Add the water and tapioca. Mix well and let stand for 5 minutes. Heat to boiling, stirring frequently. Remove from heat. Let stand for 15 minutes. Stir and pour into individual serving dishes. Chill until served, preferably 2 hours.

DAY 8

BREAKFAST

MICROWAVED BAKED POTATO
WITH ALL THE TOPPINGS

If you don't have a microwave oven, cook the potatoes in a conventional oven at 350° for 1½ hours the night before, and serve them cold for breakfast.

SERVINGS: 1
PREPARATION TIME: 1 MINUTE
COOKING TIME: 8 MINUTES

---

1 or more white baking potatoes,
  scrubbed

Topping options:
low-sodium, oil-free salad dressing   *Tabasco*
low-sodium soy sauce   *hot pepper sauce*
lemon juice and/or vinegar   *low-sodium, oil-free Mexican salsa*
no-salt vegetable seasoning   *chopped chives or onions*
low-sodium corn relish   *Corn Butter (recipe page 189)*

Puncture the potatoes several times with a fork and place in a microwave. Cook on high for 7 to 8 minutes, depending on the size of the potato and the number of potatoes cooked, or until tender. Eat plain or with your choice of toppings.

DAY 8

LUNCH

PITA BREAD WITH WHITE BEANS AND VEGETABLES

SERVINGS: 2
PREPARATION TIME: 5 MINUTES
COOKING TIME: NONE

---

2 pieces whole wheat pita bread
1 cup White Bean Spread (recipe below)

low-sodium, oil-free Mexican salsa (optional)

Topping options:
chopped green pepper
chopped cucumber
grated carrot
chopped tomato
alfalfa sprouts

chopped lettuce
chopped scallions
chopped yellow onion
low-sodium corn relish

Fill the pita with bean spread and the vegetable toppings of your choice. Drizzle with salsa if you wish.

WHITE BEAN SPREAD

Refrigerate leftovers for later use. Try it as a sandwich spread or as a dip for pita triangles.

MAKES 1½ CUPS
PREPARATION TIME: 5 MINUTES
COOKING TIME: 15 MINUTES
(COOKED BEANS NEEDED)
CHILLING TIME: 2 HOURS

---

1 small yellow onion, finely chopped
1 clove garlic, crushed
2 tablespoons chopped green chilies
⅛ teaspoon cayenne

1½ cups cooked and drained white beans, or 1 15–16 ounce can low-sodium, water-packed white beans, drained and rinsed
1 tablespoon low-sodium soy sauce
2 tablespoons sherry or apple juice

Place the onion, garlic, and green chilies in a saucepan with a small amount of water. Cook and stir until the onion is very soft. Add the cayenne and mix in well. Add the beans and cook, mashing them with either a bean masher or a fork as they cook. Add the soy sauce and sherry. Cook and stir for several minutes. Transfer to a bowl, cover, and refrigerate for at least 2 hours.

DAY 8

DINNER

A LA KING SAUCE

Serve over whole grain toast, brown rice, baked potato, or pasta.

SERVINGS: 4
PREPARATION TIME: 20 MINUTES
COOKING TIME: 30 MINUTES

---

1 yellow onion, chopped
1 green pepper, chopped
1/2 pound fresh mushrooms,
   cleaned and sliced
1 stalk celery, sliced
1 8 ounce can sliced waterchestnuts
1/2 cup frozen peas
1 cup water
1/2 cup whole wheat flour
3 cups low-fat soy milk or Rice
   Milk (recipe page 196)

1 2 ounce jar diced pimientos
1/8 teaspoon ground white pepper
2 tablespoons low-sodium soy sauce
1 tablespoon Worcestershire sauce
2 tablespoons cornstarch or
   arrowroot
1/4 cup cold water

In a large pan, cook the onion, green pepper, mushrooms, celery, waterchest-nuts, peas, in water for 10 minutes. Stir in the flour and continue to cook for a few minutes, stirring constantly. Slowly add the milk, while stirring. Cook, stirring frequently, until the mixture boils. Stir in the pimientos. Add the white pepper, soy sauce, and Worcestershire sauce. Mix the cornstarch or arrowroot in the cold water. Gradually add to the pan while stirring. Cook and stir until mixture boils and thickens.

QUICK BROILED ZUCCHINI

SERVINGS: 2
PREPARATION TIME: 5 MINUTES
COOKING TIME: 10–15 MINUTES

---

2 zucchini, cut in half lengthwise

no-salt seasoning blend

Preheat the oven to broil. Place the halved zucchini on the broiler pan, sprinkle with seasoning, and broil 8 inches from heat 10 to 15 minutes, or until tender.

DAY 8

RICE PUDDING

SERVINGS: 4
PREPARATION TIME: 10 MINUTES
COOKING TIME: 45 MINUTES
(COOKED RICE NEEDED)

2 cups cooked brown rice
1½ cups low-fat soy milk
½ cup raisins or currants

2 tablespoons honey
1 teaspoon vanilla extract

Combine all the ingredients, pour into a casserole, cover, and bake at 325° for 45 minutes. May be served hot or cold.

DAY 9

BREAKFAST

HOT BREAKFAST QUINOA

Quinoa, a newly available grain that can be found in most health food stores, needs to be rinsed well before using to eliminate a slightly bitter taste.

SERVINGS: 1
PREPARATION TIME: 2 MINUTES
COOKING TIME: 7 MINUTES

½ cup quinoa
1 cup water
¼ cup chopped apples
¼ cup raisins

¼ teaspoon cinnamon
¼ cup low-fat soy milk, Rice Milk
(recipe page 196), or fruit juice

Rinse the quinoa well, then place in a saucepan with the water, bring to a boil, reduce heat, and simmer for 5 minutes. Add the remaining ingredients and simmer until the water is absorbed. Top with soy or rice milk or fruit juice.

LUNCH

QUICK SAUCY VEGETABLES

Serve this sauce over whole wheat toast or over whole grains or pasta. It may also be made with fresh vegetables cut into small pieces.

SERVINGS: 2
PREPARATION TIME: 5 MINUTES
COOKING TIME: 20 MINUTES

2 cups frozen mixed vegetables
1 cup water
2 tablespoons low-sodium soy sauce

1 tablespoon cornstarch or
arrowroot
¼ cup water

Seasoning options:
1. *½ teaspoon turmeric*
   ½ teaspoon ground cumin
   ½ teaspoon Cajun spice mix
   (see page 194)

2. *½ teaspoon dried basil*
   ½ teaspoon dried dill
   ½ teaspoon paprika

3. *½ teaspoon dried thyme*
   ½ teaspoon dried rosemary
   ½ teaspoon dried marjoram

Cook the vegetables in the 1 cup water until tender, about 8 to 10 minutes. Add the soy sauce and optional seasonings of your choice. Mix the cornstarch or arrowroot in the ¼ cup water. Add to vegetable mixture while stirring. Cook and stir until thickened.

DAY 9

DINNER

PASTA PRIMAVERA

SERVINGS: 6
PREPARATION TIME: 15 MINUTES
COOKING TIME: 30 MINUTES

Sauce:
1 cup low-fat soy milk
1½ cups water
1 tablespoon low-sodium soy sauce
1 teaspoon dried basil or
  1 tablespoon fresh basil
¼ teaspoon dried dill or 1 teaspoon
  fresh dill
¼ teaspoon freshly ground black
  pepper
3 tablespoons arrowroot or
  cornstarch

Vegetables:
¼ cup water
1 tablespoon low-sodium soy sauce
4 cloves garlic, crushed
1 carrot, scrubbed and sliced
1½ cups broccoli, broken into
  small flowerettes
1½ cups zucchini, cut in half
  lengthwise, then sliced
1 cup snowpeas, cut in half
2 cups cleaned and sliced fresh
  mushrooms

Pasta:
1 pound uncooked egg-free whole
  wheat or spinach fettucine or
  linguine noodles
3 quarts boiling water

Garnish:
½ pint cherry tomatoes, sliced in
  half
freshly ground black pepper
(optional)

To make the sauce, combine the soy milk, water, soy sauce, basil, dill, pepper, and arrowroot or cornstarch in a saucepan and cook, stirring, over medium heat until thickened, about 7 minutes. Remove from heat.

To cook the vegetables, heat the water in another pan, add the soy sauce and garlic, and stir well. Add the carrot and broccoli. Cover, stirring occasionally. After 3 to 4 minutes, add the zucchini and snowpeas. After 2 to 3 minutes, add the mushrooms. Cook 2 minutes more. Turn off the heat and cover.

Cook the pasta in boiling water until just tender, about 8 minutes. While the pasta is cooking, warm up the sauce over very low heat. When pasta is done, drain well and pour into a medium-sized bowl. Stir the sauce into the pasta well, tossing it. Add the vegetables and toss again to mix well. Garnish with tomatoes and sprinkle with some freshly ground black pepper, if desired.

DAY 9

SAUCY CAULIFLOWER

SERVINGS: 4
PREPARATION TIME: 10 MINUTES
COOKING TIME: 20 MINUTES

---

1 pound cauliflower, cut into
flowerettes

¼ cup low-sodium, oil-free Italian
dressing

Steam the cauliflower over 1 inch boiling water until tender, about 15 minutes. Drain. Place the cauliflower in a serving bowl, pour the dressing over it, and toss gently to mix. Serve hot or cold.

EASY FRUIT PUDDING

SERVINGS: 4–6
PREPARATION TIME: 5 MINUTES
(PLUS 1 HOUR CHILLING TIME)
COOKING TIME: 5 MINUTES

½ cup instant tapioca
3 cups water
1 12 ounce can unsweetened frozen
fruit juice concentrate

1 tablespoon lemon juice

Combine all the ingredients in a saucepan. Cook and stir over medium heat until the tapioca is clear and the pudding is thickened, about 5 minutes. Chill at least 1 hour before serving.

DAY 10

BREAKFAST

FRUITY BRAN AND OATS

This will keep for several months in an airtight container.

MAKES 3 CUPS (¾ CUP = 1 SERVING)
PREPARATION TIME: 5 MINUTES
COOKING TIME: NONE

¾ cup uncooked wheat bran
½ cup uncooked oat bran
1¼ cups uncooked regular rolled
  oats
⅛ cup chopped dried apricots
  (optional)

⅛ cup chopped dried apples
  (optional)
⅛ cup raisins (optional)

Combine all the ingredients and mix well. To serve, pour low-fat soy milk or Rice Milk (page 196), apple juice, or hot water over the cereal. Stir, let rest for a couple of minutes, and enjoy.

LUNCH

PITA BREAD WITH SPICY
BEANS AND VEGETABLES

SERVINGS: 2
PREPARATION TIME: 5 MINUTES
COOKING TIME: NONE
(COOKED BEANS NEEDED)

---

2 pieces whole wheat pita bread
1 cup Spicy Bean Spread (recipe
  below)

low-sodium, oil-free Mexican salsa
  (optional)

Topping options:
chopped green pepper
chopped cucumber
grated carrot
chopped tomato

alfalfa sprouts
chopped lettuce
chopped scallions
chopped yellow onion

Fill the pita bread with Spicy Bean Spread and your choice of vegetable toppings. Drizzle with salsa if desired.

DAY 10

SPICY BEAN SPREAD

This is quite highly spiced, too much so for some people; cut the amount of spices in half if you like less spicy foods. It is also good as a sandwich spread, on whole wheat flour tortillas, or as a dip for wedges of pita or raw vegetables.

MAKES 1½ CUPS
PREPARATION TIME: 10 MINUTES
COOKING TIME: NONE
(COOKED BEANS NEEDED)

*1½ cups cooked and drained
   kidney or pinto beans, or 1
   15–16 ounce can low-sodium,
   water-packed beans, drained
   and rinsed
½ yellow onion, chopped
1 tomato, chopped*

*1 clove garlic
1 tablespoon low-sodium soy sauce
½ tablespoon chili powder
½ tablespoon ground cumin
½ teaspoon paprika
½ teaspoon dried oregano*

Process all the ingredients in a food processor, blender, or food mill until smooth. A little water may be added if necessary during processing.

DINNER

BEAN BURRITO CASSEROLE

This may be made without the brown rice; use 5 cups mashed cooked and drained beans instead. The sauce can also be used in other Mexican recipes.

SERVINGS: 6
PREPARATION TIME: 30 MINUTES
COOKING TIME: 37 MINUTES
(COOKED RICE AND/OR BEANS NEEDED)

*12 whole wheat tortillas
3 cups mashed cooked or canned,
   rinsed, and drained pinto beans*

*2 cups cooked brown rice
1 cup chopped scallions*

Enchilada Sauce (makes 5 cups):
*2 cups low-sodium tomato sauce
3 cups water
¼ teaspoon garlic powder
½ teaspoon onion powder*

*3 tablespoons chili powder
4 tablespoons cornstarch or
   arrowroot*

To make the enchilada sauce combine all the ingredients in a saucepan and cook, stirring constantly, until the mixture boils and thickens, about 7 minutes.
    Preheat the oven to 350°. Spread 1 cup of the enchilada sauce in the bottom

of a covered casserole dish. Take one tortilla at a time and spread some beans, rice, and scallions down the center. Roll up and place seam-side-down in the casserole dish. Repeat until all ingredients are used. Pour the remaining enchilada sauce over the rolled-up tortillas, cover, and bake for 30 minutes.

MEXICAN CORN ON THE COB

SERVINGS: 1
PREPARATION TIME: 5 MINUTES
COOKING TIME: 3 MINUTES

1 ear fresh or unthawed frozen
  corn
1 tablespoon low-sodium, oil-free
  Italian dressing

⅛–¼ teaspoon chili powder

Place the corn on a heavy-duty paper plate. Drizzle dressing over all sides of the corn and sprinkle with chili powder. Cover the entire plate tightly with plastic wrap and microwave on high for 2½ to 3 minutes, rotating the plate halfway through cooking time. Let stand, covered, for 5 minutes. Serve warm.

VARIATION: *To prepare on the stove,* boil the corn until tender (about 5 minutes) and then drizzle with dressing and sprinkle with chili powder.

SPARKLING MINTED FRUIT

SERVINGS: 6
PREPARATION TIME: 10 MINUTES
CHILLING TIME: 30 MINUTES

1½ cups chopped peeled apple
1½ cups fresh pineapple chunks
1 cup halved seedless red grapes

1 tablespoon chopped fresh mint
1 cup peeled, sliced kiwi
¾ cup chilled sparkling apple juice

Combine the first four ingredients in a bowl, toss gently, cover, and chill for 30 minutes. Just prior to serving, line six individual dessert bowls with kiwi. Spoon the fruit mixture over the kiwi and drizzle each serving with about 2 tablespoons sparkling apple juice. Serve at once.

DAY 11

BREAKFAST

COLD CEREAL BREAKFAST
SERVINGS: 1
PREPARATION TIME: 2 MINUTES
COOKING TIME: NONE
---

1 cup cold cereal (see page 100 for
  acceptable cereals)
¼ cup fruit juice, low-fat soy milk,
  or Rice Milk (recipe page 196)

¼ cup sliced bananas,
  strawberries, or blueberries
  (optional)

Pour the cereal into a bowl, add juice, soy milk, or Rice Milk, and top with fruit, if desired.

LUNCH

PEASANT SALAD
SERVINGS: 2
PREPARATION TIME: 10 MINUTES
COOKING TIME: NONE
---

2 tomatoes
1 cucumber, unpeeled
1 yellow pepper
1 small mild yellow or red onion
⅛ cup lightly packed chopped fresh
  basil leaves

1 tablespoon capers
1 clove garlic, crushed
½ cup low-sodium, oil-free Italian
  salad dressing
½ loaf oil-free French-style bread

Cut the tomatoes, cucumber, yellow pepper, and onion into bite-sized pieces. Place in a large bowl and stir in the remaining ingredients except for the bread. Cut the bread into bite-sized pieces, add to vegetable mixture, and toss gently to coat with dressing.

DAY 11

DINNER

SPLIT PEA SOUP
SERVINGS: 4
PREPARATION TIME: 15 MINUTES
COOKING TIME: 2½ HOURS

---

4 cups water
½ cup dry split green peas
¼ cup dry lima beans
⅛ cup uncooked barley
1 yellow onion, chopped
1 bay leaf
½ teaspoon celery seed
1 carrot, scrubbed and chopped
1 stalk celery, chopped

1 white potato, scrubbed and
 chopped
¼ teaspoon paprika
1 tablespoon parsley flakes, or
 ¼ cup chopped fresh parsley
½ teaspoon dried basil
⅛ teaspoon ground black pepper
dash ground white pepper

Place the water in a large soup pot. Add the peas, limas, barley, onion, bay leaf, and celery seed and cook for 1½ hours. Add the remaining ingredients and cook an additional 45 to 60 minutes.

BROILED TOMATOES
SERVINGS: 2
PREPARATION TIME: 5 MINUTES
COOKING TIME: 3–4 MINUTES

---

2 tablespoons whole wheat bread
 crumbs (see Note)

1 clove garlic, crushed
2 fresh tomatoes, halved

Brown the bread crumbs and garlic in a nonstick pan, stirring constantly so they don't burn. Sprinkle on top of tomatoes and brown under broiler for 3 to 4 minutes.

NOTE: *To make bread crumbs,* break up 1 slice whole wheat bread and process in blender or food processor until finely chopped, or chop finely with a sharp knife.

DAY 11

QUICK APPLE PIE

SERVINGS: 6
PREPARATION TIME: 10–20 MINUTES
COOKING TIME: 60 MINUTES

½ cup Grape-nuts cereal
6 large Delicious apples, thinly
  sliced
⅓ cup frozen apple juice
  concentrate, thawed

½ teaspoon ground coriander
1 tablespoon cinnamon

Preheat the oven to 400°. Crush the Grape-nuts with a rolling pin and spread over the bottom of a covered casserole dish. Mix the apples, juice, and spices in a bowl. Spread the apple mixture over the cereal in the casserole and pour any juice left in the bowl over the apple slices. Sprinkle with additional cinnamon, if desired. Cover and bake for 45 minutes, or until apples are tender. Remove cover and return to oven to allow pie to brown for 10 to 15 minutes longer.

DAY 12

BREAKFAST

RICE CAKES OR BAGELS AND JAM

This is a simple, fast breakfast for busy days. Corn Butter (page 189) can be used instead of jam if you like. Those who are trying to lose weight should choose rice cakes rather than bagels, which are high in calories.

SERVINGS: 1
PREPARATION TIME: 2 MINUTES
COOKING TIME: NONE

---

rice cakes or whole grain, oil-free   *no-sugar, pure-fruit jam*
 bagels

Toast the bagels or rice cakes, if desired, and spread with jam.

LUNCH

KALE SANDWICH

Surprisingly delicious.

SERVINGS: 1
PREPARATION TIME: 5 MINUTES
(PLUS 1 HOUR CHILLING TIME)
COOKING TIME: 5 MINUTES

2–3 large whole kale leaves,   *2 tablespoons Dijon or spicy brown*
 washed and trimmed   *mustard*
dash lemon juice   *1 whole wheat pita bread*
dash garlic powder

Steam the kale for 2 minutes and drain off any liquid. Do not chop—keep the leaves in large pieces. Sprinkle with lemon juice and garlic powder and chill. When ready to serve, cut the pita bread in half, spread each pocket with mustard, and then stuff with the cold seasoned kale.

DAY 12

DINNER

GINGERED VEGETABLE SOUP
SERVINGS: 4
PREPARATION TIME: 15 MINUTES
COOKING TIME: 50 MINUTES

---

1 yellow onion, sliced
1 stalk celery, sliced
1 green pepper, sliced
¼ teaspoon crushed garlic
2 teaspoons grated fresh ginger
  root
½ cup water
4 cups additional water
1 8 ounce can low-sodium tomato
  sauce

2 white potatoes, scrubbed and
  cubed
1 teaspoon dried basil
1 teaspoon paprika
⅓ teaspoon ground black pepper
1 zucchini, cut in half lengthwise,
  then sliced
2 cups fresh or frozen corn kernels

Sauté the onion, celery, green pepper, garlic, and ginger root in the ½ cup water for 5 minutes. Add the 4 cups water, tomato sauce, potatoes, and seasonings and cook over low heat for 30 minutes. Add the zucchini and corn and cook an additional 15 minutes, or until all vegetables are tender.

SEASONED POTATOES
SERVINGS: 4
PREPARATION TIME: 15 MINUTES
COOKING TIME: 50 MINUTES IN OVEN,
15 MINUTES IN MICROWAVE

---

4 large white potatoes, scrubbed
1 small yellow onion
⅛ cup low-sodium soy sauce

dash ground black pepper
dash paprika

Peel the potatoes if you wish, and slice into ⅛-inch slices. Slice the onion thinly and separate into rings. Place the potatoes in a large covered casserole dish and lay the onions over them. Season with a few sprinkles of soy sauce, some black pepper, and a little paprika. Cover and bake in a 350° oven for 45 to 50 minutes, or microwave on high for 10 to 15 minutes.

DAY 12

PEACH PIE

SERVINGS: 8
PREPARATION TIME: 30 MINUTES
COOKING TIME: 45 MINUTES

Filling:
4 cups sliced fresh peaches
1/3 cup no-sugar apricot preserves
2 teaspoons lemon juice

1/8 teaspoon nutmeg
3 tablespoons whole wheat flour

Topping:
1 tablespoon pure maple syrup
1/2 teaspoon vanilla extract

1/4 cup quick-cooking oatmeal
1 tablespoon cornmeal

Preheat the oven to 375°. Place the sliced peaches in a 9-inch pie plate. Stir the preserves, lemon juice, and nutmeg together and spoon over the peaches. Sprinkle with flour and toss gently. Bake for 30 minutes.

Meanwhile, make the topping. Combine the maple syrup and vanilla, pour over the oats and cornmeal, and mix well. Reduce the oven to 350° and remove the peach filling. Crumble the topping mixture over the filling and return the pie to the oven for 15 minutes. Serve warm or cold.

SHOPPING LISTS FOR THE TWELVE-DAY DIET

If you plan to follow the menus as outlined, then every food item you need to buy is listed here for you. Nonperishable items that you will need throughout the twelve days are listed as staples. If you don't already have these on hand, purchase them on your first trip to the supermarket and health food store. You may also want to stock up on the healthy snacks listed on page 116.

I have divided the rest of the list into four-day segments so your shopping will be easier, the expense will be divided, and your fruits and vegetables will always be fresh. Some items such as garlic, dried beans, and juices may carry over from one four-day block to the next. The quantities are based on two people: If you are feeding more than two, check the recipes and adjust the quantities you purchase appropriately. Brand names of acceptable canned and packaged goods are listed on pages 100–114—don't buy unacceptable foods if you want the diet to work.

STAPLES

Baking Powder (no aluminum)
Baking Soda (no MSG)
Cornmeal (1-lb. bag)
Cornstarch or Arrowroot (16-oz. box)
Soy Milk (low-fat)
Whole Wheat Flour (5-lb. bag)
Honey
Lemon Juice (bottled)
Sherry (optional)
Soy Sauce (low-sodium, no MSG)
Vanilla Extract
Vinegar (white, wine, and cider)
Fresh Fruits
Dried Fruits (apples, apricots, currants, raisins)

Seasonings and Condiments:
No-Salt Seasonings
Barbecue Sauces (low-sodium, oil-free)

Fruit Jams and Preserves (pure-fruit, no-sugar)
Maple Syrup (pure)
Mustard
Mustard, Dijon
Salad Dressings (low-sodium, oil-free): Russian, Italian, and
  French
Corn Relish (low-sodium)
Salsa, Mexican (low-sodium, oil-free)
Tabasco Sauce
Hot Pepper Sauce
Tomato Ketchup (low-sodium)
Worcestershire Sauce

Herbs (dried) and Spices:

Allspice
Basil
Bay Leaves
Black Pepper
Cayenne
Celery Seed
Coriander (ground)
Chervil
Chili Powder (no salt)
Cloves (ground)
Cinnamon
Cumin (ground)
Cumin Seeds
Dill
Garlic Powder
Ginger (ground)

Italian Seasoning Blend
Mace
Marjoram
Mustard (dry)
Nutmeg
Onion Powder
Oregano
Paprika
Parsley Flakes
Rosemary
Red Pepper, Crushed
Tarragon
Thyme
Turmeric
White Pepper

Beverages:

Cereal Beverages
Soda Water or Seltzer (no salt)
Herbal Teas (no caffeine)

Days 1–4

1 24-oz. box quick-cooking oatmeal
1 21-oz. bag 7 Grain Cereal or Hot Apple Granola
1 8-oz. box instant tapioca
1 pkg. whole wheat pita bread (6)
1 loaf whole wheat bread
1 pkg. whole wheat tortilla (6)
1 16-oz. pkg. egg-free whole wheat or spinach spaghetti
1 16-oz. pkg. egg-free whole wheat or spinach elbow macaroni,
   shells, or spiral pasta
1 16-oz. bag dry red kidney beans
1 5-lb. bag brown rice
1 16-oz. bag frozen corn kernels
1 24-oz. box frozen hash-brown potatoes
1 6-oz. can frozen orange juice concentrate
1 6-oz. can frozen apple juice concentrate
1 16-oz. bag frozen strawberries
1 16-oz. can low-sodium tomato puree
2 16-oz. cans low-sodium stewed tomatoes
5 8-oz. cans low-sodium tomato sauce
1 28-oz. can low-sodium, water-packed pinto beans
1 32-oz. jar unsweetened applesauce
1 4-oz. jar chopped pimiento
2 16-oz. cans crushed pineapple
1 8-oz. can mandarin oranges
1 quart jar pineapple juice
1 quart jar orange juice
1 quart jar apple juice
2 heads garlic, or 1 jar crushed or minced garlic
1 5-lb. bag white potatoes
1 3-lb. bag carrots
7 yellow onions
1 red onion
3 green peppers
2 bunches scallions (sometimes called green onions)
1 lb. fresh mushrooms
1 bunch celery
1 bunch green-leaf lettuce
4–6 tomatoes
2 cucumbers
1 zucchini

1 leek
1 large bunch broccoli
1 box alfalfa sprouts
1 head iceberg lettuce
1 bunch radishes
1 lemon
1 pineapple
1 large bunch bananas (10)
1 pint box fresh strawberries
1 pint box fresh blueberries
2 Delicious apples

Days 5–8

1 16-oz. box Grape-nuts cereal
1 pkg. whole wheat pita bread (6)
1 loaf whole wheat bread
1 16-oz. bag dry red kidney beans
2 bags whole wheat tortillas (6)
1 5-lb. bag white potatoes (if others are gone)
1 6-oz. can low-sodium tomato paste
1 15-oz. can low-sodium stewed tomatoes
1 16-oz. bag dry white beans, or 1 15-oz. can low-sodium, water-packed white beans
1 15-oz. can low-sodium, water-packed kidney beans
3 15-oz. cans low-sodium, water-packed garbanzo beans
2 8-oz. cans low-sodium tomato sauce
2 4-oz. cans chopped green chilis
1 8-oz. can waterchestnuts (sliced)
1 2-oz. jar pimientos
1 6-oz. can frozen apple juice concentrate
1 16-oz. bag frozen corn kernels
1 16-oz. bag frozen peas
1 12-oz. bag frozen blueberries
1 12-oz. bag frozen raspberries or strawberries
1 bunch bananas (6)
3 lemons
1 bunch fresh parsley
2 large bunches fresh cilantro (coriander leaves; if unavailable, use fresh parsley)
1 box alfalfa sprouts
1 head iceberg lettuce
1 small cabbage

¼ lb. fresh green beans, or 1 10-oz. pkg. frozen sliced green beans
9 yellow onions
1 sweet onion (for slicing)
5 green peppers
7 tomatoes (2 extra-large)
1½ lbs. fresh mushrooms
2 bunches scallions
6 zucchini
2 cucumbers
1 bunch green-leaf lettuce

Days 9–12

1 24-oz. box regular rolled oats
1 12-oz. box quinoa
1 12-oz. pkg. wheat bran
1 12-oz. pkg. oat bran
1 pkg. whole wheat pita bread (6)
1 loaf oil-free French bread
1 bag rice cakes or oil-free whole wheat bagels
1 10-oz. jar no-sugar apricot preserves
1 16-18 oz. box Shredded Wheat (or other healthful cold cereal—
  see pages 100–101)
1 16-oz. pkg. egg-free spinach fettucine or linguine
1 8-oz. jar low-sodium, oil-free Italian dressing
3 8-oz. cans low-sodium tomato sauce
1 15-oz. can low-sodium, water-packed pinto or kidney beans, or
  1 16-oz. bag dry pinto beans
2 28-oz. cans low-sodium, water-packed pinto beans, or 1 16-oz.
  bag dry pinto beans
1 16-oz. bag dry split peas
1 16-oz. bag dry lima beans
1 8-oz. bag barley
1 4-oz. jar capers
1 liter jar sparkling apple juice
1 16-oz. bag frozen mixed vegetables
1 16-oz. bag frozen corn kernels
1 6-oz. can frozen apple juice concentrate
1 12-oz. can frozen fruit juice concentrate (your choice)
2 pkgs. whole wheat tortillas (6)
1 5-lb. bag white potatoes (if others are gone)
2–4 ears fresh (or frozen) sweet corn
1 piece ginger root

1 head cauliflower
1 bunch celery
1 cucumber
1 yellow pepper
1 green pepper
1 bunch broccoli
3–4 zucchini
1 bunch kale
6 yellow onions
6 tomatoes
2 bunches scallions
½ lb. fresh mushrooms
¼ lb. snowpeas
fresh basil leaves
fresh mint leaves
½ pint cherry tomatoes
10 Delicious apples
8 peaches
4 kiwis
1 pineapple
1 bunch red seedless grapes

11

MORE HEALTHFUL

RECIPES

If preparing the foods for the twelve-day diet has been enjoyable for you, then probably you are ready to graduate to some more elaborate starch-based recipes. Many are based on traditional dishes that have already been favorites. I have no doubt that you will soon develop a new repertoire of McDougall-style favorites, for this new way of cooking combines foods and spices so as to serve them up with more color, flavor, texture, and aroma than you may have thought possible in such a diet plan.

Remember, acceptable packaged and canned products are listed in Chapter 6.

BREADS AND BREAKFASTS

BROWN'S WHOLE WHEAT WAFFLES

Serve with pure maple syrup, unsweetened applesauce and cinnamon, or no-sugar, pure-fruit jam.

MAKES 8 WAFFLES
PREPARATION TIME: 15 MINUTES
COOKING TIME: 7 MINUTES EACH WAFFLE

2 cups whole wheat pastry flour
3 teaspoons baking powder
1 teaspoon baking soda
½ teaspoon salt (optional)
1 teaspoon active dry yeast

¼ cup water
1 teaspoon honey
½ cup cooked oat bran*
1 cup low-fat soy milk
1 teaspoon lemon juice

Combine the first four ingredients and set aside. Combine the yeast, water, honey, and cooked oat bran and let rest a few minutes. Then add the soy milk and lemon juice, mix well, and combine with the dry ingredients. Pour into a hot waffle iron and cook for 7 minutes.

VARIATION: *After you have completed the twelve-day diet*, for a special treat you may add 2 tablespoons tahini with the soy milk.

* *To make ½ cup cooked oat bran*, cook ¼ cup uncooked oat bran in ¾ cup water for 2 minutes.

CHUNKY APPLE SPICE MUFFINS

Serve with Corn Butter (recipe page 189).

MAKES 12 MUFFINS
PREPARATION TIME: 20 MINUTES
COOKING TIME: 25 MINUTES

1 cup whole wheat flour
1 cup oat bran (or another cup of whole wheat flour)
2 teaspoons baking powder
½ teaspoon allspice
2 teaspoons cinnamon
¼ teaspoon ground cloves
¼ teaspoon powdered ginger

1 teaspoon arrowroot
¼ cup honey
½ cup unsweetened applesauce
2 tart apples, peeled and cut in small dice
½ cup water
½ teaspoon vanilla extract

Preheat the oven to 400°. Mix the dry ingredients and wet ingredients *separately*. Combine them and mix thoroughly. Spoon into nonstick muffin tins and bake for about 25 minutes, until golden brown on top.

FAVORITE PANCAKES

These pancakes are wonderful with a little unsweetened applesauce spread over them and sprinkled with cinnamon. Or try pure maple syrup or no-sugar pure-fruit jam.

MAKES 12 PANCAKES
PREPARATION TIME: 10 MINUTES
COOKING TIME: 20 MINUTES

1 cup whole wheat flour
1½ teaspoons baking powder
1¼ cups diluted low-fat soy milk
1¼ cups unsweetened applesauce
½ teaspoon vanilla extract

1 teaspoon Egg Replacer, well
  mixed with 2 tablespoons water
  and beaten until frothy

Mix the flour and baking powder together. Mix the wet ingredients together, including the Egg Replacer mixture. Combine the wet and dry ingredients and beat until well blended. Pour the batter onto a hot nonstick griddle. When bubbles form on top and the edges are beginning to dry out, turn to bake the other side.

POTATO SCRAMBLE

SERVINGS: 2
PREPARATION TIME: 10 MINUTES
COOKING TIME: 30 MINUTES

1 medium yellow onion
1 carrot, scrubbed and thinly sliced
¼ cup water
2 white potatoes, scrubbed and
  thinly sliced

¼ pound fresh mushrooms,
  cleaned and sliced
½ tablespoon low-sodium soy sauce
  (optional)

Cook the onions and carrots in the water for 5 minutes. Add the potatoes and mix well. Cover the pan to steam. Stir occasionally. Add more water if necessary to prevent sticking. Steam 15 minutes, then add the mushrooms and soy sauce. Cook another 10 minutes. Serve hot.

OATMEAL MUFFINS

MAKES 10 MUFFINS
PREPARATION TIME: 15 MINUTES
COOKING TIME: 15 MINUTES

*1 cup uncooked quick-cooking
  oatmeal
1 cup apple juice
1 cup whole wheat flour
3 teaspoons baking powder
1/8–1/4 teaspoon salt (optional)*

*1 teaspoon cinnamon
1 teaspoon Egg Replacer, well
  mixed with 2 tablespoons water
  and beaten until frothy
2 tablespoons honey
2 tablespoons apple or orange juice*

Preheat the oven to 400°. Combine the oatmeal and apple juice in a large mixing bowl and let stand for ten minutes. Sift the flour, baking powder, salt, and cinnamon together in a separate bowl. After the oatmeal and apple juice have stood 10 minutes, add the Egg Replacer, honey, and orange or apple juice and combine the wet and dry mixtures. Mix until just moistened. Fill nonstick muffin cups with the batter and bake for 15 minutes, until golden brown on top.

VARIATIONS: Add 1/3 cup chopped nuts, waterchestnuts, or raisins to the dry ingredients. Substitute 1 tablespoon molasses for 1 tablespoon of the honey. Add 1/4 teaspoon of ginger to the dry ingredients. If your muffins stick, you may need to lightly oil the muffin cups before using.

BANANA-APPLESAUCE BREAD

MAKES 1 LOAF (8'' × 4'' × 3'')
PREPARATION TIME: 10 MINUTES
COOKING TIME: 60 MINUTES

*1/2 cup mashed banana (about 2
  medium bananas)
3/4 cup unsweetened applesauce
1/4 cup honey
1/2 cup water
1 tablespoon lemon juice
2 cups whole wheat pastry flour*

*1/2 teaspoon baking soda
2 teaspoons baking powder
1 teaspoon dried grated lemon peel
1 teaspoon vanilla extract
2 teaspoons cinnamon
1/2 cup raisins*

Preheat the oven to 350°. Stir and blend together the wet ingredients. In a large bowl combine the dry ingredients and raisins. Pour the wet ingredients into the dry and mix thoroughly. Pour into nonstick 8" × 4" × 3" loaf pan and bake for about 1 hour, or until a cake tester tests dry.

WHOLE WHEAT BREAD

SERVINGS: MAKES 2 LOAVES (9 ¼'' × 5 ¼'' × 2 ¾'')
PREPARATION TIME:
1 HOUR (PLUS 4 HOURS RISING TIME)
COOKING TIME: 50 MINUTES

2½ cups warm water
2 tablespoons honey
2 tablespoons active dry yeast

3–4 cups unbleached white flour
3–4 cups whole wheat flour
cornmeal

Pour the warm water into a large bowl. Add the honey and stir to mix. Sprinkle the yeast on top of the honey and water. After about 3 minutes the yeast will begin to react and produce bubbles. Stir in 1½ cups of the unbleached white flour and 1½ cups of the whole wheat flour. Beat well until the dough becomes smooth, about a hundred strokes. Cover and let rise in a warm place for 1½ hours.

Add the remaining flour 1 cup at a time, mixing well after each cup. Knead in the bowl until the dough does not stick to the sides, then turn out onto a floured board or countertop. Flour your hands well. Knead, push, and fold, adding flour as necessary to prevent the dough from sticking to the board or counter. Don't put flour on top of the dough while kneading, put it on the board and then knead the dough on top of it. Continue kneading until the dough is soft and springy and does not stick to your hands or the board. Return the dough to the bowl. Cover with a damp towel and set in a warm place. Allow to rise until double in bulk, about 45 minutes. Remove the towel, punch the dough down with your fist, cover, and let rise again.

Remove dough from bowl, divide in half, shape into oblongs, and place into 9¼" × 5¼" × 2¾" nonstick loaf pans that have been sprinkled with cornmeal. Preheat the oven to 325°. Cover the loaves and let rise until double in size, about 20 minutes. Bake for 50 minutes. When the bread is done, it should be golden brown and sound hollow when tapped. Remove from the pans immediately and cool on wire racks.

VARIATION: *This dough may also be made into dinner rolls* (one loaf of bread dough will make about twelve to fifteen rolls). Form one loaf of bread dough into a log shape about 2 inches in diameter. Section this log into equal-sized pieces. Shape the pieces into rolls. *For plain rolls:* Place the sectioned pieces on a nonstick baking sheet sprinkled with cornmeal. *For cloverleaf rolls:* Divide each section into three pieces, shape each piece into a ball, and place the three balls into a nonstick muffin cup sprinkled with cornmeal. *For spiral rolls:* Roll each section into a 6-inch length, roll it up, and place it in a nonstick muffin cup sprinkled with cornmeal. To complete the rolls, cover and let rise for 20 minutes, then bake at 350° for about 25 minutes, until nicely browned.

LUNCHES

Spreads

GARBANZO SPREAD OR DIP

This is better made the day before you plan to serve it and refrigerated. Use as a sandwich spread or as a dip for pita bread.

MAKES 1½ CUPS
PREPARATION TIME: 5 MINUTES
COOKING TIME: NONE

¼ cup water
1 15–16 ounce can low-sodium,
*   water-packed garbanzo beans,*
*   drained and rinsed*
1–2 cloves garlic

1–3 teaspoons ground cumin (to
*   taste)*
2 tablespoons lemon juice
*   (optional)*
chili powder to taste

Combine the ingredients in a blender and process until smooth.

PIMIENTO SPREAD

MAKES ABOUT 2 CUPS
PREPARATION TIME: 15 MINUTES
(PLUS 1 HOUR CHILLING TIME)
COOKING TIME: 5 MINUTES
(COOKED RICE NEEDED)

---

4 tablespoons agar agar flakes,*
*   soaked in 1 cup cold water*
*   5 minutes*
¾ cup water
1 cup cooked brown rice

1 4 ounce jar pimiento
1 tablespoon lemon juice
1 teaspoon low-sodium soy sauce
¼ teaspoon onion powder
⅛ teaspoon garlic powder

Place the soaked agar agar flakes in a saucepan and simmer over low heat until clear; remove from heat. Place the water in a blender. Add the remaining ingredients (except the agar agar) and process until smooth. Leave the blender running and slowly add the agar agar mixture. Pour into a container and refrigerate for at least an hour, until the mixture thickens to spreading consistency.

* Agar agar is a seaweed product that is a substitute for gelatin (which is animal-based). It is commonly available in health food stores. Emes Kosher gelatin can also be used.

Salads

STUFFED TOMATO SALAD

SERVINGS: 12
PREPARATION TIME: 20 MINUTES
COOKING TIME: NONE
(COOKED RICE AND BARLEY NEEDED)

1 cup cooked barley
3 cups cooked brown rice
½ cucumber, diced
1 stalk celery, diced
1 red onion, diced
1 green pepper, diced
12 tomatoes
2 tablespoons lemon juice

1 teaspoon honey
½ teaspoon garlic powder
½ teaspoon dried dill
1 carrot, cut into "flowers"
  (see Note)
fresh parsley

Combine the barley, rice, cucumber, celery, onion, and green pepper. Cut the tops off the tomatoes, hollow them, and set aside. Reserve the pulp. Dice all twelve tomato tops and the pulp of four tomatoes (about 1½ cups of pulp) and place in a mixing bowl. Mix together the honey, lemon juice, garlic powder, and dill and add to the tomato mixture. Add the grain and vegetable mixture and toss. Stuff the tomatoes with this mixture and garnish with carrot "flowers" and parsley.

NOTE: *To make carrot "flowers,"* scrape the carrots, then cut lengthwise into *very thin* slices. Roll up and fasten with toothpicks. Chill in a bowl of ice water. Remove the toothpicks before serving.

CARROT-PINEAPPLE SALAD

SERVINGS: 6-8
PREPARATION TIME: 15 MINUTES
(PLUS 2 HOURS CHILLING TIME)
COOKING TIME: NONE

3½ cups finely grated carrots
1 20 oz. can crushed pineapple

¼ cup raisins
2 teaspoons orange juice

Mix all the ingredients well in a serving bowl. Chill for at least 2 hours before serving.

WALDORF SALAD

SERVINGS: 6
PREPARATION TIME: 15 MINUTES
(PLUS 2 HOURS TO CHILL DRESSING)
COOKING TIME: 5 MINUTES

5 cups unpeeled apples, diced
1 cup diced celery
½ cup chopped walnuts, roasted

½ cup raisins
½ teaspoon lemon juice

Dressing:
1½ cups pineapple juice

2 tablespoons cornstarch

To make the dressing, combine the pineapple juice and cornstarch in a saucepan and mix well to dissolve. Bring the mixture to a boil over medium-high heat and continue to boil for 1 minute or until thickened and clear, stirring occasionally. Chill for 2 hours. Combine the salad ingredients, pour the chilled dressing over the salad, toss thoroughly, and let stand a few minutes before serving.

MIXED BEAN SALAD

SERVINGS: 12
PREPARATION TIME: 20 MINUTES
(PLUS 6–8 HOURS OR OVERNIGHT CHILLING TIME)
COOKING TIME: 5 MINUTES
(COOKED BEANS NEEDED)

¾ pound fresh green beans, cut into 1-inch pieces
½ cup sliced celery
½ cup sliced purple onion
1½ cups cooked and drained red kidney beans, or 1 15 ounce can low-sodium, water-packed red kidney beans, drained and rinsed

1½ cups cooked and drained garbanzo beans, or 1 15 ounce can low-sodium, water-packed garbanzo beans, drained and rinsed

Dressing:
½ cup cider vinegar
½ cup unsweetened apple juice
1 tablespoon honey

2 tablespoons prepared mustard
1 tablespoon cornstarch
¼ teaspoon ground black pepper

Steam the green beans over boiling water for 6 minutes, until crisp-tender. Rinse in cold water and drain well. Combine with the celery, onion, kidney beans, and garbanzo beans. Toss gently and set aside.

Combine the dressing ingredients in a small saucepan. Cook over medium heat for 5 minutes, stirring frequently, until thickened. Pour over the bean mixture and toss gently to coat. Cover and chill for 6 to 8 hours or overnight.

HINT: Frozen green beans may be used instead of fresh. Use 1 10-ounce package, thawed under cold water.

CHINESE BEAN THREAD SALAD

This is a popular dish at buffets in Hawaii, where bean thread noodles and rice vinegar can easily be found in any supermarket. Here, they are available in Oriental markets in major cities, or you may find them in your natural food store.

SERVINGS: 6
PREPARATION TIME: 20 MINUTES
(PLUS OPTIONAL 2-HOUR CHILLING TIME)
COOKING TIME: NONE

8 ounces dry bean thread noodles
2 quarts boiling water
1/3 cup rice vinegar
3 tablespoons low-sodium soy sauce
1/2 cup sliced scallions
1/3 cup chopped fresh cilantro or
parsley

1–2 tablespoons grated fresh ginger root
2–4 cloves garlic, minced
1 small unpeeled cucumber, seeded and cut into thin 3-inch slivers

Place the noodles in a large bowl, cover with the boiling water, stir, and let stand for 15 to 20 minutes, until the noodles are softened. Drain and cut into 6- to 8-inch lengths. Mix together the vinegar, soy sauce, scallions, cilantro, ginger root, and garlic and pour over the bean threads. Add the cucumber. Toss gently to mix. Serve immediately, or cover and chill for 1 to 2 hours before serving.

Soups

VEGETARIAN VEGETABLE SOUP

All the vegetables should be chopped bite-size, but not too small.

SERVINGS: 8–10
PREPARATION TIME: 30 MINUTES
COOKING TIME: 3 ½–4 HOURS

½ pound dry kidney beans
½ pound dry navy beans
¼ pound dry split peas
8–10 cups water
3 yellow onions, chopped
1 stalk celery, chopped
1 white potato, scrubbed and chopped
2 carrots, scrubbed and chopped
1 ear of corn, cut into pieces, or 1 cup corn kernels

¼ pound fresh green beans, cut into pieces
4 large, ripe tomatoes, chopped
½ small head cauliflower, chopped
1 zucchini, chopped
1 small bunch broccoli, chopped
6 ounces uncooked egg-free whole wheat pasta shells or elbows
low-sodium soy sauce
freshly ground black pepper

Place the beans and water in a large pot. Bring to a boil, reduce the heat, cover, and simmer until the beans are cooked but not mushy, about 2 to 2½ hours. Add more water if necessary. Meanwhile, prepare the vegetables. When the beans are tender, add the onions, celery, potato, carrots, corn, green beans, and tomatoes. Cook for 45 minutes, adding water if necessary. Add the remaining vegetables and cook an additional 20 minutes. When all the vegetables are tender, add the pasta and more water if necessary. Cook 20 minutes longer. Season with soy sauce and pepper to taste.

FRENCH MARKET SOUP

Store the dry bean mix in airtight containers for future use. It makes a nice gift packaged in a 2-cup container with a copy of this recipe. You can omit some of the types of beans if you like.

SERVINGS: 6–8
PREPARATION TIME: 10 MINUTES
(PLUS OVERNIGHT SOAKING TIME)
COOKING TIME: 2–4 HOURS

Bean Mix (makes about 26 cups):
1 pound each navy beans, pinto beans, Great Northern beans, green split peas, yellow split peas, black-eyed peas, barley pearls, lentils, baby limas, large limas, black beans, red beans, soybeans

Soup:
2 cups bean mix
2 quarts water
1 16 ounce can low-sodium stewed tomatoes
1 large yellow onion, chopped
1 clove garlic, minced
1 4 ounce can chopped green chilies
¼ cup lemon juice

To make the bean mix, combine the beans thoroughly in a large container. To make the soup, wash the 2 cups beans, place in a large pot, add water to cover 2 inches above the beans, and soak overnight. Drain. Add the 2 quarts water and the remaining ingredients, breaking the tomatoes up with a fork. Bring to a boil, reduce the heat, cover, and simmer 2 to 4 hours, depending on how "mushy" you like your beans.

GARDEN VEGETABLE SOUP

SERVINGS: 8
PREPARATION TIME: 20 MINUTES
COOKING TIME: 45 MINUTES

1 yellow onion, chopped
2 cloves garlic, crushed
2 white potatoes, scrubbed and
  chunked
2 carrots, scrubbed and sliced
½ cup water
1 leek, trimmed, cleaned, and
  sliced
1 zucchini, sliced
1 cup chopped fresh green beans
2 cups chopped broccoli
2 cups chopped kale

4 cups water
1 cup fresh or frozen lima beans
¼ cup low-sodium soy sauce
¼ cup red wine (optional)
2 teaspoons paprika
1 teaspoon dried marjoram
½ teaspoon cumin
¼ teaspoon cayenne
¼ cup uncooked egg-free whole
  wheat orzo, conchigliette,
  stelline, or other small pasta

In a large soup pot, sauté the onions, garlic, potatoes, and carrots in the ½ cup water for about 10 to 15 minutes, adding more water if necessary. Add the leek, zucchini, beans, broccoli, and kale and continue to cook for a few minutes. Then add the 4 cups water and the lima beans. Mix well, then add the seasonings and cook over low heat about 10 minutes. Add the pasta and cook an additional 10 to 15 minutes.

DINNERS

(Main Dishes)

SWEET AND SOUR VEGETABLES

SERVINGS: 6-8
PREPARATION TIME: 20 MINUTES
COOKING TIME: 30 MINUTES

2 yellow onions, coarsely chopped
2 carrots, scrubbed and sliced
2 medium white potatoes, peeled
and chopped
1 teaspoon grated fresh ginger root
2 cups broccoli pieces
2 cups cauliflower pieces

1 cup snowpeas
3 cups sliced Chinese cabbage
⅓ cup Oriental plum sauce
3 tablespoons low-sodium soy sauce
⅛ teaspoon dry horseradish powder
1 tablespoon cornstarch, dissolved
in 3 tablespoons cold water

Sauté the onions, carrots, potatoes, and ginger root in a 6-quart saucepan in a small amount of water for 10 minutes. Add the remaining ingredients except the cornstarch and cook until tender, about 15 to 20 minutes. Thicken with the cornstarch. Add to the vegetable mixture and cook and stir until the mixture boils and thickens.

PASTA E FAGIOL

Quick and easy!

SERVINGS: 6
PREPARATION TIME: 10 MINUTES
COOKING TIME: 40 MINUTES

2 15–16 ounce cans low-sodium
stewed tomatoes
1 cup low-sodium tomato sauce
1 clove garlic, minced
½ teaspoon dried oregano
1 8 ounce can mushroom pieces
1 bay leaf
½ teaspoon dried basil

2 15 ounce cans low-sodium,
water-packed red kidney beans,
drained and rinsed
1 teaspoon chopped dried parsley
1 teaspoon onion powder
8 ounces uncooked egg-free whole
wheat or spinach pasta

Place all the ingredients except the pasta in a large pot, bring to a boil, and simmer 20 minutes. Cook the pasta separately according to package directions and drain. Remove the bay leaf from the sauce mixture. Combine the sauce with the pasta in a 3-quart casserole dish and bake at 350° for 20 minutes.

VARIATION: The bean sauce may be served over cooked brown rice instead of pasta.

CAJUN SAUCE

Serve on brown rice or grain mix.*

SERVINGS: 4–6
PREPARATION TIME: 10 MINUTES
COOKING TIME: 30 MINUTES
(COOKED BLACK-EYED PEAS NEEDED)

1 small yellow onion, chopped
½ green pepper, chopped
1 cup frozen chopped okra
1 15–16 ounce can low-sodium
  stewed tomatoes
1 8 ounce can low-sodium tomato
  sauce
½ tablespoon parsley flakes
½ teaspoon dried basil

½ teaspoon Cajun spice mix (see
  page 194)
1 teaspoon chili powder
dash cayenne (optional)
1 cup cooked and drained black-
  eyed peas, or 1 15 ounce can
  low-sodium, water-packed black-
  eyed peas, drained and rinsed

* Prepare one of the mixes given on page 249 and cook as you would plain brown rice.

Sauté the onion and green pepper in a small amount of water for 5 minutes. Add the okra, tomatoes, tomato sauce, and seasonings. Cover and cook over medium-low heat for 15 minutes. Add the black-eyed peas and cook for 10 minutes more.

LENTIL STEW

This stew is good served over potatoes or whole grains, or just in a bowl by itself.

SERVINGS: 6–8
PREPARATION TIME: 15 MINUTES
COOKING TIME: 1–1¼ HOURS

1 yellow onion, chopped
2 stalks celery, sliced
2 cloves garlic, minced
1 green pepper, chopped
6 cups water
1 cup barley
1 cup dry lentils

1 carrot, scrubbed and shredded
2 cups low-sodium tomato sauce
2 tablespoons cider vinegar
2 tablespoons low-sodium soy sauce
1 teaspoon dried basil
½ teaspoon dried marjoram
freshly ground black pepper

Sauté the onion, celery, garlic, and green pepper in a small amount of water until softened. Add the 6 cups water and the barley and lentils. Bring to a boil, reduce heat, stir, cover, and cook for 30 minutes. Add the remaining ingredients, stir, cover, and cook for 30 to 40 minutes. If serving over potatoes or rice, serve immediately. If serving by itself, let it sit 10 minutes; the stew will thicken as it sits.

CURRIED VEGETABLES

Delicious served over brown rice or baked potatoes, or rolled up in a whole wheat tortilla.

SERVINGS: 6–8
PREPARATION TIME: 20 MINUTES
COOKING TIME: 50 MINUTES

1 yellow onion, chopped
2 cloves garlic, crushed
1 cup water
2 carrots, scrubbed and sliced
1 green pepper, chopped
1 stalk celery, sliced
1 tablespoon curry powder
1 teaspoon ground coriander
1 teaspoon turmeric
1 teaspoon ground cumin

¼ teaspoon dry mustard
¼ teaspoon crushed red pepper
2 white potatoes, peeled and chunked
3 cups water
2 cups cauliflower pieces
6–8 fresh mushrooms, cleaned and sliced
½ cup frozen peas

Sauté the onion and garlic in the 1 cup water until translucent. Add the carrots, green pepper, and celery. Add the seasonings and cook and stir about 10 minutes, adding more water if necessary to keep from sticking. Add the potatoes and the 3 cups water. Cover and cook for 15 minutes. Add the cauliflower and cook 15 minutes more. Add the mushrooms and peas and cook 10 minutes longer.

SPECIAL STUFFED PEPPERS

There may be some leftover filling. Either freeze it for future use or mix it with 4 ounces salsa and pour it over the peppers before serving.

SERVINGS: 6
PREPARATION TIME: 15 MINUTES
COOKING TIME: 45 MINUTES

6 large green peppers, tops cut off,
  cored, and seeded
1 cup uncooked quinoa
2 cups water
1 yellow onion, chopped
1/2 pound fresh mushrooms,
  cleaned and sliced

2 cloves garlic, crushed
1/4 cup water
8 ounces low-sodium, oil-free
  Mexican salsa

Preheat the oven to 325°. Steam the peppers until soft but not limp, about 5 minutes. Set aside. Rinse the quinoa well, place it in a saucepan, add the 2 cups water, cover, and cook until all the water is absorbed (10 to 15 minutes). Sauté the onion, mushrooms, and garlic in the 1/4 cup water until soft. Add the salsa and mix well. Cook for 10 minutes. Stir in the cooked quinoa. Place the peppers in a nonstick baking dish and stuff them with the quinoa mixture. Bake for 30 to 35 minutes. Serve with extra salsa to spoon over the baked peppers, if desired.

VARIATION: *After you have completed the twelve-day diet*, for a special treat you may sprinkle some grated mozzarella soy cheese over the stuffed peppers just before baking.

SPINACH PESTO SAUCE FOR SPAGHETTI

MAKES 2 CUPS
PREPARATION TIME: 10 MINUTES
COOKING TIME: 5 MINUTES

2 bunches spinach, washed
2 cloves garlic, crushed
1/4 cup chopped fresh parsley

2 teaspoons chopped fresh basil, or
  1/2 teaspoon dried basil

Wash the spinach and place in a small amount of water in a saucepan. Cover and bring to a boil. Reduce the heat and simmer 5 minutes, stirring occasionally. Drain, reserving the liquid. Put the spinach in the blender with the crushed garlic, parsley and basil. Blend until smooth, adding a little cooking liquid if necessary. Serve over egg-free whole wheat spaghetti.

LENTIL—POTATO BURGERS

MAKES 10 BURGERS
PREPARATION TIME: 10 MINUTES
COOKING TIME: 40 MINUTES
(COOKED LENTILS AND POTATOES NEEDED)

½ *cup chopped yellow onion*
½ *cup chopped celery*
¼ *cup water*
2 *cups cooked and drained lentils,*
  mashed
2 *cups mashed potatoes*
1 *cup whole wheat bread crumbs*
  (see page 211)

1 *teaspoon dried parsley*
1½ *teaspoons dried sage*
1 *teaspoon dried thyme*
½ *teaspoon dried marjoram*
¼ *teaspoon dried rosemary*
⅛ *teaspoon ground black pepper*

Preheat the oven to 350°. Sauté the onion and celery in the water about 10 minutes. Combine in a bowl with the remaining ingredients and mix well. Form into patties and place on a nonstick baking sheet. Bake for 20 minutes, then turn and bake for an additional 20 minutes. Serve hot on toasted whole wheat burger buns.

SWEET AND SOUR STUFFED CABBAGE

SERVINGS: 4–6
PREPARATION TIME: 30 MINUTES
COOKING TIME: 30 MINUTES
(COOKED BEANS NEEDED)

12 large cabbage leaves

Filling:
1 cup boiling water
¾ cup cracked wheat
⅓ cup minced yellow onion
½ cup peeled and shredded carrots
2 tablespoons low-sodium soy sauce

1½ cups minced or ground cooked
and drained beans, or 1
15-ounce can low-sodium,
water-packed beans, drained
and rinsed

Sauce:
2½ cups low-sodium tomato juice
3 tablespoons lemon juice
2 tablespoons molasses

2 tablespoons raisins
1 inch cinnamon stick

To prepare the cabbage leaves, steam a whole cabbage over boiling water for a few minutes until the leaves peel off easily. To prepare the filling, pour the boiling water over the cracked wheat in a bowl and let stand about 10 minutes to absorb the liquid. Meanwhile, prepare the remaining filling ingredients.

Stir these into the swollen grain.

Combine all the sauce ingredients in a heavy 15-inch skillet. Place 2 rounded tablespoons of filling onto each cabbage leaf and roll into a neat bundle. Place in the sauce in the skillet. Bring the sauce and cabbage to a boil, cover, and simmer over low heat for 30 minutes, spooning some sauce over the cabbage rolls occasionally. If the sauce becomes too thick, which may happen if it cooks too vigorously, stir in a little water to thin it. Serve the rolls on individual plates, and spoon sauce over the top.

VARIATIONS: If you are particularly fond of raisins, increase the amount to ¼ cup. *For Sweet and Sour Stuffed Lettuce*, replace the cabbage with about 20 Boston lettuce leaves. While these are a bit harder to handle and must be secured with a toothpick to keep them intact, their flavor is extremely delicate.

BREADED VEGETABLES

This breading method also works well with other vegetables, such as sliced yellow onions and whole mushrooms. Breaded Vegetables are good for snacks and also freeze well.

SERVINGS: 8
PREPARATION TIME: 10 MINUTES
COOKING TIME: 20 MINUTES

2 15 ounce cans low-sodium tomato
    sauce
2 teaspoons dried basil or 1½
    teaspoons dried oregano
1 1.3 ounce package Hain onion
    soup mix

1 cup cornmeal
½ cup unprocessed bran
½ cup brown rice flour
2 large eggplants, sliced in ½-inch
    rounds, or 4 large zucchini,
    sliced

Preheat the oven to 400°. Combine the tomato sauce, basil, and soup mix in a bowl and mix well. In another bowl, combine the cornmeal, bran, and rice flour for breading. Using tongs, dip a slice of vegetable in the tomato sauce mixture until coated. Then bread the vegetable by holding it above the breading bowl and spooning the breading mixture quickly over both sides. Place the breaded vegetables on a nonstick baking sheet and bake for 20 minutes, or until the vegetables are tender and brown.

CALIFORNIA STEW

Serve over brown rice or other whole grains.

SERVINGS: 4
PREPARATION TIME: 15 MINUTES
COOKING TIME: 30 MINUTES

1 yellow onion, chopped
1 clove garlic, crushed
1 white potato, peeled and chunked
1 carrot, scrubbed and sliced
1 stalk celery, sliced
1 zucchini, cut in chunks
1/4 pound fresh mushrooms,
   cleaned and cut in half
2 cups low-sodium tomato sauce

1 tablespoon parsley flakes
1/2 teaspoon paprika
1/2 teaspoon dried basil
1/2 teaspoon chili powder
1/4 teaspoon dry mustard
1/4 teaspoon cumin
dash ground black pepper

Sauté the onion, garlic, potato, carrot, and celery in a small amount of water for 10 minutes. Add the remaining ingredients and cook until all the vegetables are tender, about 20 minutes.

HEARTY STEW

Canned beans do not work in this dish. The cooking liquid from the dry beans makes a rich, flavorful stock which makes the base for the stew.

SERVINGS: 6
PREPARATION TIME: 30 MINUTES
(PLUS OVERNIGHT OR 1 HOUR SOAKING TIME)
COOKING TIME: 3–4 HOURS

1/2 cup dry garbanzo beans
1/2 cup dry kidney beans
2 quarts water
1 yellow onion, sliced
2 cloves garlic, crushed
2 tablespoons low-sodium soy sauce
2 teaspoons curry powder
2 parsnips, scrubbed and sliced

2 carrots, scrubbed and sliced
1 zucchini, cut in chunks
1/2 cup uncooked egg-free, whole
   wheat macaroni or shells
1/4 cup uncooked bulgur
1 tablespoon lemon juice
2 cups fresh spinach

Place the beans in a large pot with the water. Soak overnight, or bring to a boil, cook for 2 minutes, turn off heat, and let rest for 1 hour. Then add the onion, garlic, soy sauce, and curry powder. Bring to a boil, reduce heat, and cook for 2 hours. Meanwhile, prepare the rest of the vegetables and set aside.

Place the parsnips in a small amount of water in a small saucepan. Cook until soft, about 15 minutes. Cool. Place in a blender or food processor and process until smooth. When beans are almost tender, add the pureed parsnips and the carrots and zucchini. Cook for 30 minutes, then add the pasta and bulgur. Cook an additional 15 minutes. Stir in the lemon juice and spinach and cook about 5 minutes. Serve at once.

SWEET AND SPICY GARBANZO STEW

Serve over potatoes or brown rice or other whole grains, on top of whole wheat bread, or by itself in deep bowl.

SERVINGS: 8
PREPARATION TIME: 20 MINUTES
(PLUS OVERNIGHT SOAKING TIME)
COOKING TIME: 4 HOURS

1 cup dry garbanzo beans
7 cups water
1 yellow onion, coarsely chopped
2 yams or sweet potatoes, peeled
*   and cut in chunks*
1 carrot, scrubbed and sliced
1 stalk celery, sliced
1 leek, trimmed, cleaned, and
*   sliced*
2 cups broccoli pieces

1 tablespoon lemon juice
1 tablespoon low-sodium soy sauce
1 teaspoon ground coriander
½ teaspoon ground cumin
2 teaspoons pure prepared
*   horseradish*
⅛ teaspoon Tabasco sauce
dash or two cayenne (optional)

Place the beans and enough water to cover them in a large pot and soak overnight. Drain. Add the 7 cups water, bring to a boil, cover, reduce heat, and cook until tender, about 2 to 3 hours. Add the onion, potatoes, carrot, celery, and leek and cook for 30 minutes. Add the broccoli and seasonings and cook an additional 30 minutes.

HINT: This can easily be made in a slow cooker. Add all the ingredients at once and cook on the high heat setting for 8 to 10 hours. Be sure to soak the beans overnight before you begin.

PASTA STEW
SERVINGS: 6-8
PREPARATION TIME: 15 MINUTES
COOKING TIME: 30 MINUTES (COOKED BEANS NEEDED)
---

1 yellow onion, cut in chunks
2 cloves garlic, crushed
2 15–16 ounce cans low-sodium
  stewed tomatoes
1 15 ounce can low-sodium tomato
  sauce
1 cup chopped zucchini
1 cup corn kernels
1½ cups cooked and drained
  garbanzo beans, or 1 15–16
  ounce can low-sodium, water-
  packed garbanzo beans, drained
  and rinsed

1 teaspoon dried basil
1 teaspoon dried oregano
1 tablespoon low-sodium soy sauce
freshly ground pepper to taste
¼ pound uncooked egg-free, whole
  wheat spaghetti, broken in half
2 cups chopped romaine or spinach

In a large pot, sauté the onion and garlic in a small amount of water until soft. Add the tomatoes, tomato sauce, zucchini, corn, beans, and seasonings and cook for about 15 minutes. Add the spaghetti and cook until tender, about 10 minutes. Add the greens and stir until wilted. Serve at once.

APRICOT–VEGETABLE SAUCE FOR WHOLE GRAINS OR PASTA
SERVINGS: 6
PREPARATION TIME: 15 MINUTES
COOKING TIME: 30 MINUTES (COOKED BEANS NEEDED)

⅔ cup quartered dried apricots
3 tablespoons raisins
2 yellow onions, chopped
3 medium zucchini, chopped
1½ cups cooked and drained
  garbanzo beans (reserve cooking
  liquid), or 1 15–16 ounce can
  low-sodium, water-packed
  garbanzo beans, drained and
  rinsed

1½ cups water from soaking the
  fruit, plus some bean-cooking
  liquid (or water)
¾ teaspoon cinnamon

Soak the apricots and raisins in hot water to cover for 10 to 15 minutes. In a large pot, sauté the onion in small amount of water until soft. Add the zucchini and mix well. Drain the fruit, reserving the liquid, and add the fruit to the pot along with the garbanzo beans and cinnamon. Measure the reserved liquid and add enough bean-cooking liquid to make 1½ cups. Add to the pot, bring to a boil, cover, and simmer over low heat about 30 minutes, until zucchini is just tender.

SPLIT PEA AND VEGETABLE STEW

Serve over potatoes, pasta, brown rice, or whole wheat toast.

SERVINGS: 6
PREPARATION TIME: 15 MINUTES
COOKING TIME: 1 HOUR

2 cups dry green split peas
6 cups water
½ pound fresh green beans, cut into 1-inch lengths
½ pound zucchini, chopped
½ pound fresh mushrooms, cleaned and sliced

2 green peppers, chopped
2 tablespoons low-sodium soy sauce
2 teaspoons prepared mustard

Combine the split peas and water in a large pot. Bring to a boil, reduce the heat, cover, and let simmer for 1 hour. Meanwhile, place the vegetables in a pot with a small amount of water and steam for 20 minutes. Combine the cooked split peas with the vegetables. Season with the soy sauce and mustard and serve immediately.

VARIATION: *After you have completed the twelve-day diet*, you may add 4 tablespoons miso (fermented soybean paste) instead of soy sauce for a flavorful treat.

EGGPLANT SCALOPPINI

Serve over pasta or brown rice.

SERVINGS: 4
PREPARATION TIME: 15 MINUTES
COOKING TIME: 35–40 MINUTES

*1 medium yellow onion, cut in half
  and thinly sliced
2 cloves garlic, minced
½ cup water
1 large eggplant, sliced into
  4" × ¼" strips
1 bay leaf
½ pound fresh mushrooms,
  cleaned and sliced*

*2 tomatoes, chopped
1 6 ounce can low-sodium tomato
  paste
1 green pepper, chopped
1 teaspoon dried basil
1 tablespoon parsley flakes
½ cup dry Marsala wine or apple
  juice*

Sauté the onion and garlic in the water for 5 minutes. Add the eggplant and bay leaf and cook, covered, for 10 minutes, stirring often. Add the mushrooms, tomatoes, tomato paste, green pepper, herbs, and Marsala and mix well. Simmer over low heat, covered, about 20 minutes (or longer).

LIMA BEAN CURRY

Serve over brown rice.

SERVINGS: 6
PREPARATION TIME: 30 MINUTES
COOKING TIME: 3–4 HOURS

*2⅓ cups dry lima beans
7 cups water
1 cup bean-cooking liquid
½ cup water
2 teaspoons ground coriander
2 teaspoons ground cumin
1 teaspoon black mustard seeds
2 large yellow onions, chopped
6 cloves garlic, crushed
2 teaspoons grated ginger root*

*3 fresh hot chilies or canned
  jalapenos, seeded and chopped
2 cups chopped tomatoes, or 1 16
  ounce can low-sodium stewed
  tomatoes
2 tablespoons low-sodium soy sauce
2 tablespoons lemon juice
1 bunch fresh cilantro or parsley,
  chopped*

Cook the lima beans in the 7 cups water until tender (about 1½ hours). Drain, reserving 1 cup bean liquid. In the ½ cup water, sauté the coriander, cumin, and mustard seeds for 1 minute. Add the onions, garlic, ginger root, and chilies and continue cooking until the onions are soft. Add the tomatoes and cook until most of the liquid has been absorbed. Combine this mixture with the soy sauce, lemon juice, beans, and bean liquid. Stir in the fresh cilantro or parsley.

MEXICAN VEGETABLE SAUCE

This can be served over brown rice or potatoes, or used to fill a burrito shell and garnished with chopped tomatoes, chopped green onions, shredded lettuce, alfalfa sprouts, and your favorite salsa.

SERVINGS: 6–8
PREPARATION TIME: 15 MINUTES
COOKING TIME: 30 MINUTES (COOKED BEANS NEEDED)

1 yellow onion, chopped
1 carrot, scrubbed, cut in half, then sliced
1 stalk celery, chopped
1 green pepper, chopped
6 scallions, chopped (use green part too)
1 clove garlic, crushed
½ cup water
2 cups cooked and drained pinto beans, or 1 16 ounce can low-sodium, water-packed pinto beans, drained and rinsed

1 zucchini, chopped
1½ cups frozen corn kernels
¼ cup chopped canned green chilies
1 tablespoon chili powder
1 teaspoon ground cumin
1 teaspoon dried oregano
⅛ teaspoon cayenne
¼ cup water

Sauté the first six ingredients in the ½ cup water for 10 minutes. Add the remaining ingredients, with the additional ¼ cup water, and mix carefully. Bring to a boil, cover, reduce heat, and cook over medium-low heat for 20 minutes, stirring occasionally.

SLOPPY MEXICAN CASSEROLE
SERVINGS: 6
PREPARATION TIME: 20 MINUTES
COOKING TIME: 1½ HOURS

1 cup dry lentils
1 yellow onion, chopped
1 carrot, scrubbed and chopped
1 small green pepper, chopped
2 cups water
2 cups low-sodium tomato sauce
1 tablespoon parsley flakes
¼ teaspoon dried basil

¼ teaspoon garlic powder
1 tablespoon low-sodium soy sauce
¼–½ teaspoon ground cumin
½ cup uncooked egg-free, whole wheat elbow macaroni
4 soft corn tortillas, torn into bite-sized pieces

Preheat the oven to 350°. Cook the lentils, onion, carrot, and green pepper in the water for 30 minutes. Add the tomato sauce and seasonings to the pot and cook for 30 minutes longer. Stir in the elbow macaroni and torn-up tortillas. Spoon into a casserole dish and bake for 30 minutes.

DOUBLE RICE AND GREENS
SERVINGS: 4
PREPARATION TIME: 15 MINUTES
COOKING TIME: 60 MINUTES

3 cups water
1 cup long-grain brown rice
½ cup wild rice
1 bunch scallions, chopped
½ pound fresh mushrooms, cleaned and sliced

1 pound spinach, washed and chopped
1½ cups fresh mung bean sprouts
2 tablespoons low-sodium soy sauce

Bring the water to a boil, add both kinds of rice, bring to a boil again, cover, reduce heat, and simmer for about 45 minutes. While the rice is cooking, sauté the scallions in a large skillet in a small amount of water for a few minutes. Add the mushrooms and cook until both are tender. Stir in the spinach and bean sprouts. Cover the pan and cook over low heat 3 to 4 minutes. Stir in the soy sauce and cooked rice, mix well, and serve at once.

VARIATION: For a little more zip, try adding a few dashes of Tabasco and a dash of crushed red pepper when you add the soy sauce.

BAKED WINTER SQUASH WITH FIVE-GRAIN, BROWN, AND WILD RICE HOLIDAY STUFFING

If you plan to have the whole family over for a special Thanksgiving dinner, this recipe can easily be doubled and baked in an extra-large pumpkin. If there is extra stuffing mixture, it may be frozen after the initial cooking time (30 minutes) and then used as a stuffing at a later date.

SERVINGS: 6–8
PREPARATION TIME: 20 MINUTES
COOKING TIME: 1½ HOURS

*1 large winter squash or pumpkin
(about 6–7 pounds)*

Stuffing:
1 small yellow onion, diced
*¼ pound fresh mushrooms,
cleaned and sliced*
1 stalk celery, diced
⅛ cup low-sodium soy sauce
¼ teaspoon garlic powder
1 tablespoon parsley flakes
1 teaspoon ground sage

1 teaspoon ground thyme
*1½ teaspoons Italian seasoning
blend, Spice Islands Bouquet
Garni, or poultry seasoning*
¼ teaspoon dried rosemary
4 cups water
*5 roasted chestnuts, shelled and
chopped (optional)*

Grain Mix (choose one):
*1½ cups 5-grain rice plus ½ cup
brown rice plus 1 tablespoon
wild rice or 1½ cups brown rice
plus ⅛ cup each wheat berries,
rye berries, millet, barley, and
wild rice*

Place a small amount of water in a large saucepan. Add the onion, mushrooms, and celery and sauté for several minutes. Add the soy sauce and the remaining seasonings (these may easily be cut down or added to depending on your taste) and stir. Add the water and bring to a boil. Slowly add the chestnuts (if desired) and grains. Set the lid to let a small amount of steam escape and cook on low for 30 minutes. Meanwhile, cut off the top of the squash and save for a cover, then clean out the seeds and stringy portion. Stuff the squash with the grain mixture and replace the top. Place in a large roasting pan with 1 inch of water in the bottom and bake at 350° for 1 hour, or until the squash "meat" is tender.

VARIATION: *This may also be prepared in several small winter squashes.* Just cut the squash in half, remove the seeds and stringy portion, fill each half with stuffing, and bake in a *covered* baking dish as directed above.

SAVORY BAKED BEANS

SERVINGS: 8
PREPARATION TIME: 15 MINUTES
COOKING TIME: 3 HOURS

2 cups dry Great Northern beans
2 quarts water
1 yellow onion, chopped
2 stalks celery, chopped
1 green pepper, chopped
2 cloves garlic, crushed
½ cup water

1½ cups bean-cooking liquid
1½ teaspoons curry powder
2 tablespoons parsley flakes
2 tablespoons lemon juice
1 tablespoon low-sodium soy sauce
ground black pepper to taste

Cook the beans in the 2 quarts water until tender, about 2 hours. Drain, reserving the liquid. Preheat the oven to 350°. Sauté the onion, celery, green pepper, and garlic in the ½ cup water for 10 minutes. Remove from heat and add the cooked beans, 1½ cups bean-cooking liquid, and seasonings. Pour into a casserole dish and bake for 1 hour.

HINT: Mash or grind up the leftovers for a delicious cold sandwich spread.

PICANTE BLACK BEANS

SERVINGS: 8
PREPARATION TIME: 10 MINUTES
COOKING TIME: 3–4 HOURS

2 cups dry black beans
2 quarts water
1 16 ounce can low-sodium tomato paste
2 cloves garlic, minced

¼ cup chopped fresh cilantro or parsley
2 cups low-sodium, oil-free Mexican salsa

Cook the beans in the water until tender, about 3 hours. Preheat the oven to 350°. Drain the beans and place in a large casserole. Add the remaining ingredients, mix well, and bake 30 minutes.

HINT: Mash the leftovers and use as a sandwich spread.

DESSERTS

CARROT CAKE

MAKES 1 SQUARE CAKE (8'' × 8'' × 2'')
PREPARATION TIME: 20 MINUTES
COOKING TIME: 45 MINUTES

½ cup grated carrot
1¼ cups chopped dates
1 cup raisins
1⅓ cups water
¼ cup unsweetened applesauce
1 teaspoon cinnamon

1 teaspoon ground cloves
1 teaspoon nutmeg
2 cups whole wheat flour
1 teaspoon baking powder
1 teaspoon baking soda

Preheat the oven to 350°. Place the first eight ingredients in a saucepan, bring to a boil, reduce the heat, and simmer for 5 minutes. Cool. Stir the dry ingredients together. Combine the wet and dry mixtures and stir until well blended. Spoon the batter into an 8'' × 8'' nonstick cake pan and bake for 45 to 50 minutes.

VARIATION: *After you have completed the twelve-day diet*, for a treat you may add ½ cup chopped nuts to the wet ingredients before combining with the dry.

BAKED APPLES

Many different kinds of apples, such as Mackintosh, Rome Beauty, Gravenstein, etc., can be used in this recipe. Store leftover baked apples in the refrigerator for an easy snack or quick breakfast.

SERVINGS: 4
PREPARATION TIME: 10 MINUTES
COOKING TIME: 1–1½ HOURS

4 large apples
1 teaspoon cinnamon
4 whole cloves
nutmeg
8 teaspoons frozen apple juice
  concentrate

1 cup water
1 teaspoon cinnamon
2 whole cloves

Preheat the oven to 350°. Core the apples, leaving a ½-inch base, and set in a baking dish. Place ¼ teaspoon of the cinnamon, 1 whole clove, a dash of nutmeg, and 2 teaspoons apple juice concentrate into each apple. Pour the water around the apples. Add the remaining spices to the water and bake for 1 to 1½ hours, until the apples are soft. Serve warm or cold.

A P P L E   C R I S P

The Fruit Crisp Topping on this dish can be used in making other baked fruit desserts. Crumble over partially baked fruit and bake at 375° for 18 minutes or until golden.

MAKES 1 SQUARE PAN (8'' × 8'' × 2'')
PREPARATION TIME: 30 MINUTES
COOKING TIME: 40 MINUTES

3 tablespoons tapioca
1 cup pineapple juice
8 cups apples, peeled and sliced

2 tablespoons honey
½ teaspoon cinnamon

Fruit Crisp Topping:
⅔ cup quick-cooking oatmeal
⅔ cup regular rolled oats
½ cup whole wheat flour
scant ¼ cup oat flour*

2 tablespoons honey
¼ cup orange juice
½ teaspoon vanilla extract

Preheat the oven to 375°. Soften the tapioca in the pineapple juice in a measuring cup for 5 minutes. Combine with the remaining ingredients in a baking dish and bake for 20 minutes. Meanwhile, make the topping. Combine the dry ingredients and liquid ingredients separately. Pour the liquid ingredients over the dry and toss lightly to mix. Stir the apple mixture and crumble the topping over it. Bake for 18 to 20 minutes, until the topping is golden.

* *To make oat flour*, process regular rolled oats in a blender until they are a flourlike consistency.

12

TRANSITION TREATS:

Old Favorites,

McDougall Style

Many of you may be having a rough time giving up meat, dairy products, and eggs in any form. I can understand your difficulty, because I went through all this myself, long ago. I can sympathize with your longings for forbidden foods, but I cannot relax the rules of this life-saving program just to allow you to eat yourself into the grave a bit more slowly. Instead of giving you a dispensation from the rules, let me suggest some very tasty and at the same time still healthy substitutes for the meat, dairy, and egg dishes we were all brought up on. This chapter is filled with "transition" recipes to help you gradually adjust your hungers to both the Program's principles and your body's needs.

These recipes are made from richer ingredients than the McDougall diet usually allows—tofu and peanut butter, for example—to create satisfying dishes that suggest the forbidden foods yet are still relatively low in fat and salt and entirely free of cholesterol. If after you have completed the twelve days you still need help adjusting to the diet or you want a treat for special occasions, you can use these dishes. But use them sparingly, for they will not give you the marvelous benefits promised by the stricter McDougall Program dishes.

SOYFOODS

Soybeans and foods made from them, such as tofu, tempeh, and soy milk, are popular substitutes for meat and dairy products in vegetarian diets, but as I explained in Chapter 3, they are too high in vegetable fat to be standard fare on the McDougall Program. They work well as transition treats, however, because they are low in sodium, low in saturated fat, and contain no cholesterol. Tofu is particularly useful because it can take on the texture of some meats and cheeses and be combined with a wide variety of flavors so that it can be used in soups and sauces, entrées and desserts.

Buying and Storing Tofu

Most supermarket and natural food stores carry tofu either in packages or in bulk. You will find it in the refrigerated section—kept cold for freshness. Some packaged tofu will have a recommended purchase date. The package should list as ingredients: soybeans, water, and a coagulant (calcium chloride, magnesium chloride, or nigari) only. After purchase you should store the tofu in the refrigerator until use. As a general rule, use within a week. If that is not possible, then freeze the tofu in the packages it is sold in (including the liquid) for later use. Freezing changes the tofu from a soft cheesy texture to a chewy meatlike one.

You will find soft and firm varieties of tofu. Firm tofu is used for dishes where the tofu must retain its shape, or a firmer consistency is desired. Soft tofu is used where it will be blended or creamed.

NUTS AND SEEDS

Nuts and seeds are also popular staples in many vegetarian diets, but they too are too high in vegetable fat for regular use on the McDougall Program. As a treat, a small amount of nuts or seeds can be added to a dish for flavor and texture, but be sure to avoid those roasted in oils and salted.

Butters made from ground nuts, such as peanut butter, and ground seeds, such as tahini (sesame butter), are useful as spreads and as components of sauces. However, many commercial peanut butters contain added salt, sugar, preservatives and are hydrogenated to keep the spread in a more solid consistency at room temperature. You should choose one that lists peanuts only, or one with a little salt added. Some health food stores will grind fresh nuts into natural nut butters for you. In this case there will be no added salt—only ground nuts.

All nuts, seeds, nut butters, and seed spreads keep best in the refrigerator. You can dilute nut butters and seed spreads with water in order to lower the intake of fat and calories (blend equal amounts of water and nut or seed butter in a food processor or blender). On the other hand, children, pregnant women, athletes, and others needing easy-to-obtain energy may choose nuts and seeds—whole or ground—for more calories.

Acceptable High-Fat Treats

Soy Milks
Make these high-fat, nondairy milks healthier, and at the same time more palatable, by diluting 1 cup soy milk with 2 to 3 cups water. Avoid soy milks with added oils.

Manufacturer/Distributor	*Variety*
Ener-G Foods	Pure Soyquick
Health Valley Foods	Soy Moo
Eden Foods	Edensoy
Mitoku Co. Ltd.	Supersoy

Soy Cheeses
High in fat, but dairy-free.

Soyco Foods	Grated Parmesan Style
	Cheddar Style
	Monterey Jack Style
	Mozzarella Style
White Wave	soy a melt (Cheddar Style, Mozzarella Style)
Soya Kaas	American Cheddar Style
	Cream Cheese Style
Cemac Foods	Nu Tofu

Tofu "Ice Cream"

Tofutti Brands	Lite lite Tofutti (Vanilla)

Help us update this list. Please send packages and labels that identify packaged products that make healthful eating easier. This list was compiled in September 1989.

For an updated package list send with SASE to:
McDougalls
P.O. Box 14039
Santa Rosa, CA 95402

OTHER HIGH-FAT PLANT FOODS

Avocados and olives are naturally very high in fat, but may be used sparingly as treats. Olives are usually high in salt also, so those on a sodium-restricted diet should avoid them altogether.

MAKING TRADITIONAL RECIPES ACCEPTABLE

You probably have many favorite recipes you have been using for years that can be modified with healthier ingredients and still retain the same taste appeal. Choose recipes that already use large amounts of starches, vegetables, and/or fruits. Even baked goods and desserts can often be modified to be perfectly acceptable, or at least be considered as transitional recipes.

Butter, shortening, and oils can be easily eliminated in most recipes: Just omit them. When moisture is wanted in a cake, use unsweetened applesauce instead of oil in the mix. Mashed bananas also serve well for adding moisture to cakes and breads. So will portions of mashed squashes, zucchini, tubers, and other watery starches. Nut butters or seed spreads might be a better choice than animal fats and vegetable oils in some recipes, because of their lower concentration of fat and the rich tastes they provide. As a last resort, when you feel you simply cannot completely eliminate the oil, use only a fraction of the amount called for in most recipes. As a first step toward discovery, try making your favorite recipe with half the amount of fat called for.

Eliminate or greatly reduce the amount of *nuts and seeds* called for in your recipes. Replace them with waterchestnuts, which are actually a low-fat starchy vegetable rather than a true nut, and are almost oil-free.

Replace *eggs* in recipes with a product called Egg Replacer, made by Ener-G Foods. This mixture of flours acts as a binding agent. (Egg Replacer will not make scrambled eggs or omelets, but works nicely to hold together the ingredients in baked goods, muffins, waffles, pancakes, and cookies.)

Use tofu in place of *sour cream and mayonnaise*. Tofu is quite neutral in flavor and takes on the flavors of seasonings added to it. It can be blended easily into a smooth base which can be used in most recipes. But, don't forget that tofu is 54 percent fat—so use it sparingly. Tofu's saving virtue is that it is mostly water.

Soy milk works well in most recipes calling for *cow's milk*. Use low-fat soy milk (see page 57) for everyday, and richer (high-fat) soy milk as a treat.

Soy cheeses can be used to replace the *cheese* in most recipes. But they are high in vegetable fat and shouldn't be used too often. The advantage for some allergic people is that they are free of dairy protein. Tofu and nut butters can be used to replace cheese in some recipes.

Substitutes for *meat* are the starches you've learned about in this book. Now when you ask "What's for dinner?" you hear spaghetti, beans, rice, or potatoes rather than veal, chicken, or fish. Tofu simulates many characteristics of meat (even the undesirable qualities of being both low in fiber and high in fat).

BREAKFASTS

SCRAMBLED RED-GREEN TOFU

This dish resembles scrambled eggs in color and texture. The vegetables used may be varied or eliminated entirely as you choose.

SERVINGS: 6
PREPARATION TIME: 10 MINUTES
COOKING TIME: 10 MINUTES

---

1 small yellow onion, chopped
½ green pepper, chopped (optional)
½ red pepper, chopped, or 1–2
tablespoons diced pimiento
⅛ cup diced green chilies
(optional)
4 ounces sliced fresh mushrooms
(optional)

¼ cup water
2 cups firm tofu, drained and
crumbled
1 tablespoon low-sodium soy sauce
1 teaspoon parsley flakes
¼ to ½ teaspoon turmeric
dash ground black pepper

Sauté the vegetables in the water until soft. Add the remaining ingredients. Cook and stir over medium heat about 5 minutes.

VARIATION: *This may be used as a base for an interesting salad.* Allow to cool, then add 2 chopped tomatoes, 1 chopped green pepper, and ¼ cup chopped green onions.

BACO-YUBA

Use baco-yuba as you would use bacon. It is excellent with tomato and lettuce on a sandwich, crumbled over a salad, or plain for breakfast or a snack. It may be kept in Ziploc bags in the pantry and crisped before using by placing in a toaster oven, microwave or conventional oven for a very short time. I usually make lots at one time because it is quite time-consuming to make, but it keeps very well and it's nice to have on hand. Any soaking liquid that is left over may be saved in a glass jar in the refrigerator and used the next time you make baco-yuba.

If you are on a severely salt-restricted diet, you should avoid this recipe because so much soy sauce is used.

MAKES ABOUT 40 STRIPS
PREPARATION TIME: 30 MINUTES IF USING
HALF-DRIED YUBA, 45 MINUTES IF DRIED
COOKING TIME: 30 MINUTES

flat yuba sheets (see Note)
¾ cup low-sodium soy sauce
¼ cup water

1 tablespoon liquid smoke flavoring
(optional)

Cut the yuba sheets into strips about 4 to 5 inches by 2 inches. Combine the soy sauce, water, and smoke flavoring (if desired) in a shallow pan or tray. Soak strips of yuba in this mixture for 5 minutes, putting in at one time only as many as can be covered by the liquid. Remove the strips from the liquid and lay them on a broiler pan—do not overlap. Broil about 6 inches from the heat until the tops begin to bubble slightly, about 35 to 45 seconds. Watch them carefully—they burn easily! Turn over with tongs and broil on the other side about 30 seconds. (The whole broiling process will only take about 2 to 3 minutes.) Remove from the pan and place on paper towels to cool. Repeat with the remaining yuba strips.

NOTE: Yuba, also called dried bean curd, is a by-product of soy milk. It is generally sold in Oriental markets, or occasionally in progressive natural food stores, and is available in thin sheets or rolls either half dried (fresh) or completely dried. If you use the half-dried yuba, proceed as directed in the recipe above. *If you are using dried yuba sheets, you must soften them before using in this recipe.* Soak them in water until soft (about 15 minutes), then separate the softened sheets, cut into strips about 4 inches by 2 inches, and dry slightly on paper towels. Then proceed as directed.

CINNAMON BUNS

MAKES 12–15 BUNS
PREPARATION TIME: 1 HOUR
(PLUS 1½ HOURS RISING TIME)
COOKING TIME: 20–25 MINUTES

Dough:
1⅓ cups lukewarm water
1 teaspoon honey

1 tablespoon active dry yeast
2–3 cups whole wheat flour

Filling:
½ cup smooth natural peanut
  butter
¼ cup honey
½ cup unsweetened applesauce

2 tablespoons ground cinnamon
2 tablespoons water
⅔ cup raisins

Combine the water, honey, and yeast in a large bowl. Let sit for 5 minutes until foamy. Add the flour 1 cup at a time, beating well after each addition. When the dough becomes too stiff to mix, turn it out onto a floured board and knead for 5 to 10 minutes until smooth and elastic. Put it in a *very lightly* oiled bowl, cover, and allow to rise for 1 hour. (If a very light dough is desired, you may punch it down, cover, and allow to rise another 40 to 45 minutes.)

While the dough is rising, combine the peanut butter and honey in a saucepan and mix over low heat until easily blended (or warm in a microwave until easily blended). Beat in all the remaining ingredients except the raisins.

Remove the risen dough from the bowl and knead about ten times on a clean board. Roll out into a large rectangle about 15″ × 14″. Spread with filling to ½ inch of the edge. Sprinkle raisins evenly over the filling. Roll the rectangle into a log, starting at the 15-inch side, pinch the edges to seal, and slice into one-inch-thick rounds. (They will be *very* gooey.) Place on a *nonstick* baking sheet, cover, and allow to rise for about 20 minutes, or until light. Bake in a preheated 350° oven for 20 to 25 minutes, until golden brown on top.

LUNCHES

Dips and Sauces

CURRIED TOFU DIP

This is excellent as a dip for raw vegetables, as a sauce for cooked artichokes or asparagus, or as a topping for baked potatoes. Or dilute with a little water for a creamy curry salad dressing.

MAKES 1 CUP
PREPARATION TIME: 10 MINUTES
(PLUS 1 HOUR CHILLING TIME)
COOKING TIME: NONE

8 ounces firm tofu, drained and
  crumbled
1 teaspoon curry powder
1/4 teaspoon ground cumin

1/2 tablespoon parsley flakes
1 teaspoon low-sodium soy sauce
1/8 cup water

Place all the ingredients in a blender or food processor and process until smooth. Add more water if necessary to make processing easier. Refrigerate until serving time, at least 1 hour.

SPICY TOFU DIP

Use as a substitute for sour cream dips. It also makes a delicious topping for baked potatoes and keeps well in the refrigerator.

MAKES 1 CUP
PREPARATION TIME: 10 MINUTES
(PLUS 1 HOUR CHILLING TIME)
COOKING TIME: NONE

8 ounces firm tofu, drained and
  crumbled
1 tablespoon low-sodium soy sauce
2 teaspoons Dijon mustard
1 teaspoon pure prepared
  horseradish

1/2 teaspoon dried dill
1 clove garlic, crushed
2 tablespoons chopped fresh
  cilantro or parsley (optional)

Combine all the ingredients in a blender or food processor and process until smooth. Add a little water if necessary for ease in preparation. Chill at least an hour before serving.

TOFU DIP

Use as a substitute for sour cream dips or as a sandwich spread, or dilute with a little water to make a creamy salad dressing.

MAKES 1 CUP
PREPARATION TIME: 10 MINUTES
(PLUS 1 HOUR CHILLING TIME)
COOKING TIME: NONE

*8 ounces firm tofu, drained and
  crumbled*
1 tablespoon low-sodium soy sauce
½ tablespoon Worcestershire sauce

½ tablespoon lemon juice
1½ teaspoons parsley flakes
1½ teaspoons dried dill
dash or two ground white pepper

Process the tofu in a blender until smooth, adding a little water if necessary to make blending easier. Add the remaining ingredients and process until well blended. Chill at least an hour to blend flavors before serving.

TAHINI SPREAD

Use this delicious spread on sandwiches, as a dip, or as a sauce for cooked vegetables.

MAKES ABOUT 2 CUPS
PREPARATION TIME: 5 MINUTES
COOKING TIME: NONE

1 cup tahini (sesame butter)
⅔ cup water

¼ cup fresh lemon juice
2–3 cloves garlic (optional)

Place all the ingredients into a blender or food processor and process until smooth.

TOFU MAYONNAISE OR SOUR CREAM

Use in place of mayonnaise in salads, dips, or dressings. Substitute for sour cream in dips and toppings. (Do not use in cooked recipes.)

MAKES ABOUT 2 CUPS
PREPARATION TIME: 10 MINUTES
COOKING TIME: NONE

---

*1 pound firm tofu, drained and
  crumbled
1 tablespoon cider vinegar*

*1 tablespoon lemon juice
1 teaspoon low-sodium soy sauce*

Put all the ingredients into the blender and process until smooth.

VARIATIONS:
1. Instead of vinegar and lemon juice, use all vinegar or all lemon juice, 2 tablespoons of each.
2. Add 2 tablespoons minced onion and 1 tablespoon parsley flakes.
3. Add ¼ teaspoon dried dill and 1 clove garlic, crushed.
4. Add 1 teaspoon fresh ginger root.
5. Add ½ teaspoon Italian herb seasoning.

SPECIAL GREEN BEAN PÂTÉ

This versatile and delicious pâté can be used as a sandwich filling, cracker spread, dip, or topping for baked potatoes.

MAKES 2 CUPS
PREPARATION TIME: 15 MINUTES
(PLUS 2 HOURS CHILLING TIME)
COOKING TIME: 5 MINUTES

---

*½ cup walnuts
1 medium yellow onion, chopped
¼ cup water
¼ cup dry white wine or water
2 cups cooked green beans*

*½ pound firm tofu, drained and
  crumbled (about 1 cup)
1 tablespoon low-sodium soy sauce
dash ground black pepper
dash nutmeg*

Toast the walnuts in a dry skillet for 3 to 5 minutes, stirring or shaking the pan frequently. Sauté the onion in the water for 5 minutes. Combine the walnuts and onions with the remaining ingredients and process into a smooth paste in a food processor or blender. (If you use a blender, you may need to add a little more liquid.) Chill at least 2 hours before serving.

CARROT BUTTER

Use as a substitute for butter on cooked vegetables and potatoes or as a spread for muffins. It keeps well in the refrigerator.

MAKES ABOUT 1 CUP
PREPARATION TIME: 15 MINUTES
(PLUS 1 HOUR CHILLING TIME)
COOKING TIME: 30 MINUTES

---

4 medium-size carrots, scrubbed and finely chopped or grated
½ cup water
1½ tablespoons carrot-cooking liquid

2 tablespoons natural peanut butter
1 tablespoon frozen orange juice concentrate

Put the carrots and water in a small saucepan and bring to a boil. Cover, lower the heat, and simmer for ½ hour, stirring occasionally. Drain the carrots and reserve the liquid. Place the carrots, 1½ tablespoons cooking liquid, peanut butter, and orange juice concentrate in the blender and process until very smooth, stopping blender and stirring contents as needed. Add more liquid *only if* absolutely necessary, as the mixture should be thick. Chill thoroughly (at least 1 hour) before using.

MELTY CHEESE

This "cheese" is great as a dip for chips or raw vegetables, or as a sauce for cooked veggies. It can also be drizzled on pizza. If made with potatoes instead of cashews, it is acceptable for use on the twelve-day diet and can be used as often as you like.

MAKES ABOUT 2 CUPS
PREPARATION TIME: 10 MINUTES
COOKING TIME: NONE

¼ cup raw cashews or cooked peeled and chopped potato
2 cups water
1 4 ounce jar pimientos
1 teaspoon salt (optional)

½ teaspoon onion powder
¼ cup brewer's yeast flakes
3 tablespoons cornstarch
2 tablespoons lemon juice

Place the cashews (or potatoes) in the blender and add just enough water to cover. Blend at low speed until smooth. Add the remaining ingredients and blend again until smooth. Pour into a heavy saucepan and cook at medium-high heat, stirring constantly, about 7 to 8 minutes. The mixture will thicken to the consistency of nacho cheese. Serve immediately, for the "cheese" will set upon cooling.

MILLET "CHEESE"

Use this soft, sliceable cheese on sandwiches or on crackers or bagels. Store in the refrigerator.

MAKES 1 BRICK (4'' × 2'')
PREPARATION TIME: 15 MINUTES
COOKING TIME: 45 MINUTES

½ cup millet
1½ cups water
3 tablespoons Emes unflavored
  gelatin (see Note)
½ cup cold water
¼ cup raw cashews

1 tablespoon lemon juice
3 tablespoons brewer's yeast flakes
1½ teaspoons onion powder
½ teaspoon garlic powder
½–1 tablespoon pimiento (for
  color)

Cook the millet in the 1½ cups water about 45 minutes, until soft. Set aside. Place the Emes unflavored gelatin and the ½ cup cold water in a blender. Let stand for a few minutes, then add 1 cup hot cooked millet and the remaining ingredients. Process until smooth. Pour into a plastic-wrap-lined 4" × 2" loaf pan and chill until set.

NOTE: Emes unflavored gelatin is a non-animal-based gelatin. If you cannot find it in your natural food store, it can be ordered from the company at the following address: Emes Kosher Products, 4138-42 West Roosevelt Road, Chicago, IL 60624.

VARIATION: For more flavor, fold in some diced chilies before pouring into the loaf pan.

CASHEW–PIMIENTO CHEESE SAUCE

Use any time you want a melted cheese sauce—on lasagna, pizza, burritos, vegetables, potatoes, etc. It will keep four or five days in the refrigerator.

MAKES 2 CUPS
PREPARATION TIME: 5 MINUTES
COOKING TIME: NONE

1 cup raw cashews
2–3 tablespoons lemon juice
2 teaspoons onion powder
2½ cups water

1 4 ounce jar pimientos
1 teaspoon salt (optional)
⅛ teaspoon garlic powder

Mix all the ingredients in a blender and process until smooth.

Salads

EGGLESS SALAD WITH TORTILLA CHIPS

This eggless "egg salad" is great served as a dip with the chips at a party. It's also good in sandwiches.

MAKES 2½ CUPS
PREPARATION TIME: 10 MINUTES
(PLUS 1 HOUR CHILLING TIME)
COOKING TIME: 15 MINUTES

1 pound firm tofu, drained and
  crumbled
½ teaspoon no-salt seasoning blend
1 tablespoon prepared mustard
1 teaspoon crushed garlic

1 stalk celery, minced
3 scallions, minced
1 tablespoon low-sodium soy sauce
2 ounces green chilies, diced
1 tablespoon chili powder

Chips:
12 soft corn tortillas

Chili powder

Mash the tofu with a potato masher. Mix in the remaining ingredients and chill at least 1 hour before serving. To make the "chips," cut the soft tortillas into wedges, sprinkle with chili powder, place on a nonstick baking sheet, and bake at 350° for 15 to 20 minutes, until crisp.

POTATO SALAD

The spicy mayonnaise in this salad can be used whenever mayonnaise is called for.

SERVINGS: 12
PREPARATION TIME: 40 MINUTES
(PLUS 2 HOURS CHILLING TIME)
COOKING TIME: 30–40 MINUTES

8 large red potatoes, scrubbed and
  cut into pieces
3 tomatoes, diced
1 green or red pepper, chopped
½ Bermuda onion, or 5 scallions,
  chopped

1 cucumber, chopped
handful fresh parsley, chopped
handful alfalfa sprouts
2 celery stalks, chopped
6 or 7 radishes, chopped
2 or 3 carrots, grated

Mayonnaise:
1 pound regular tofu, drained and
  crumbled
1 lemon, squeezed
1½ teaspoons ground coriander
3 garlic cloves, crushed
½ cup cider vinegar

2–3 teaspoons dry mustard
2 teaspoons tarragon
1 teaspoon garlic powder

lemon wedges (optional)
chives (optional)

Cook the potatoes until tender but still firm. Cut into pieces. Place all the vegetables into a large bowl. Combine all the mayonnaise ingredients and mix in a blender or food processor. Add to the potato salad and mix well. Chill at least 2 hours and serve with lemon wedges or chives.

DINNERS

Main Dishes

NOODLES, NOODLES, NOODLES

SERVINGS: 8-10
PREPARATION TIME: 45 MINUTES
COOKING TIME: 60 MINUTES

---

1 cup each, three different kinds of uncooked egg-free, whole wheat pasta (shells, spirals, elbows, bows, etc.)
2 sliced yellow onions

3 sliced zucchini
1 teaspoon paprika
2 tablespoons low-sodium soy sauce
freshly ground black pepper to taste
2 sliced tomatoes

Sauce:
2 cups regular soy milk
3 cups water
2 tablespoons low-sodium soy sauce
1 teaspoon dried basil

½ teaspoon dried dill
dash or two ground white pepper
6 tablespoons arrowroot or cornstarch

Combine all the sauce ingredients in a medium saucepan. Heat until it has boiled and thickened, stirring constantly. Remove from heat and set aside. Cook each kind of pasta separately. Undercook slightly, drain, and set aside. Sauté the onions in a small amount of water for 15 minutes. Add the zucchini, paprika, soy sauce, and pepper. Cook for about 10 minutes, until the zucchini is almost tender. Remove from heat.

To assemble, spread a small amount of the sauce in the bottom of a casserole dish. Spread one kind of noodle over the sauce. Spread some zucchini mixture over the noodles, then a layer of sliced tomatoes. Repeat sauce, noodles, zucchini mixture, and tomatoes twice, ending with a layer of sauce. Cover and bake at 350° for 35 minutes. Let rest a short time before serving.

EASY BARBECUED TOFU

This dish can also be cooked on a grill. The tofu must be frozen for at least a day and then thawed before using.

SERVINGS: 8–10
PREPARATION TIME: 15 MINUTES
(NOT COUNTING FREEZING AND THAWING THE TOFU)
COOKING TIME: 40 MINUTES

2 14 ounce packages firm tofu, frozen and thawed (see Note page 270)

1 18 ounce bottle low-sodium, oil-free barbecue sauce

Preheat the oven to 350°. Squeeze the excess water from the thawed tofu and cut into ¼-inch-thick strips. Lay the strips in a single layer in the bottom of two 9″ × 13″ baking dishes that have been lightly coated with oil. Spoon about half of the barbecue sauce over the tofu strips and spread until all are evenly coated. Bake for 20 minutes. Remove from the oven, turn the strips over, spread with the remaining barbecue sauce, and bake for another 20 minutes.

"MEAT" LOAF

The leftovers make excellent sandwich fillings.

MAKES 1 LOAF, SERVING 6–8
PREPARATION TIME: 20 MINUTES
COOKING TIME: 1 HOUR

28 ounces firm tofu, drained and mashed
1⅔ cups rolled oats
¾ cup whole wheat bread crumbs (see page 211)
⅓ cup low-sodium ketchup or low-sodium, oil-free barbecue sauce

¼ cup low-sodium soy sauce
2 tablespoons Dijon mustard
2 tablespoons Worcestershire sauce
¼ teaspoon garlic powder (optional)
¼ teaspoon ground black pepper (optional)

Preheat the oven to 350°. Combine all the ingredients in a large bowl and mix well. Press the mixture into an 8″ × 4″ × 3″ nonstick loaf pan.* Bake for 1 hour, then remove from the oven. Let rest for 15 minutes, then loosen the sides gently with a spatula and invert over a serving platter to remove.

* If you do not have a nonstick pan, you will need to lightly oil the bottom of your loaf pan before pressing in the tofu mixture.

BARBECUED SPARE RIBS
(WITHOUT BONES)

For this recipe, the tofu must be frozen for at least a day and then thawed. You can use the marinade whenever you want tofu to have a spicy, meaty flavor. The barbecue sauce can also be used on hash-browns, baked potatoes, or "burgers" (see recipes later in chapter) or wherever barbecue sauce is called for.

SERVINGS: 8–10
PREPARATION TIME: 45 MINUTES
(NOT COUNTING FREEZING AND THAWING THE TOFU)
COOKING TIME: 1 HOUR FOR SAUCE,
50 MINUTES FOR "RIBS"

*2 14 ounce packages firm tofu,
frozen and thawed (see Note)*

Marinade:
3 tablespoons natural peanut butter   *1/4 teaspoon ground black pepper*
1/3 cup hot water   *1/2 teaspoon garlic powder*
1 tablespoon paprika   *2 tablespoons low-sodium soy sauce*

Barbecue Sauce:
1 yellow onion, chopped   *1/3 cup prepared mustard*
2 cloves garlic, crushed   *1 teaspoon allspice*
3 8 ounce cans low-sodium tomato   *1 1/4 teaspoons crushed red pepper*
* sauce*   *2 teaspoons parsley flakes*
1/4 cup water   *1/4 cup water*
1/4–1/2 cup honey   *1/4 cup lemon juice*
1 tablespoon molasses   *2 teaspoons low-sodium soy sauce*

Squeeze the water out of the thawed tofu and cut into 1/4-inch-thick strips. Lay the strips in a single layer in the bottom of two 9" × 13" baking dishes that have been lightly coated with oil. Mix all the marinade ingredients together and whisk until smooth. Spoon over tofu strips and let marinate at room temperature for 1 hour. Sauté the onion and garlic in a small amount of water until soft. Add the tomato sauce, 1/4 cup water, honey, molasses, mustard, allspice, crushed red pepper, and parsley. Bring to a boil, reduce heat, and cook uncovered for 1 hour. Add the remaining ingredients and heat through. Remove from heat and set aside.

After the tofu strips have marinated, bake them in the remaining marinade in a 350° oven for 25 minutes. Turn the strips, pour the barbecue sauce over them, and bake for another 25 minutes.

NOTE: Freeze the tofu in the packages that it is sold in, including the liquid. Just place the unopened package in the freezer and freeze for at least a day before using. (Or if you prefer, remove the tofu from the package, drain, and freeze it in a plastic freezer container or bag.) To thaw the tofu, remove from freezer and let stand at room temperature for 6 to 8 hours. To quick-thaw, remove the tofu from the package it was frozen in, place in a large bowl, and cover with boiling water. This will thaw the tofu in about 1 hour. Drain the tofu before using.

CHILI ENCHILADAS

SERVINGS: 10–12
PREPARATION TIME: 60 MINUTES
(NOT COUNTING FREEZING AND THAWING THE TOFU)
COOKING TIME: 30 MINUTES

3 14 ounce packages firm tofu, frozen and thawed (see Note pages 270–271)

20 whole wheat burrito shells or corn tortillas

Marinade:
⅓ cup low-sodium soy sauce
3 tablespoons low-sodium tomato sauce

3 tablespoons natural peanut butter
3 teaspoons onion powder
2 teaspoons chili powder

Enchilada Sauce:
1 yellow onion, chopped
2 cloves garlic, crushed
3 8-ounce cans low-sodium tomato sauce

3 cups water
3 tablespoons chili powder
2 tablespoons cornstarch
¼ cup cold water

Squeeze the excess water from the thawed tofu and tear the tofu into pieces. Mix the next five ingredients together, pour over the tofu, and mix well. Cook and stir in a large saucepan over medium to high heat until slightly browned, stirring constantly. Set aside.

To make the sauce, sauté the onion and garlic in a small amount of water until translucent, add the remaining ingredients, and simmer over low heat for 30 minutes. Dissolve the cornstarch in the cold water and gradually add to the sauce while stirring. Cook and stir until sauce boils and thickens. Preheat the oven to 350°.

Pour about 1 cup of the sauce into the bottom of a 15″ × 10″ baking dish or two smaller baking dishes. Place ⅓ cup of the tofu mixture down the center of each burrito shell, roll up, and place in baking dish. Repeat until all burritos are filled and rolled. Pour the remaining enchilada sauce over the filled burritos and bake for 30 minutes.

VARIATION: For added richness, sprinkle with some grated soy cheese and sliced olives before baking.

PINTO ENCHILADAS

SERVINGS: 6–8
PREPARATION TIME: 30 MINUTES
COOKING TIME: 30 MINUTES
(COOKED BEANS AND RICE NEEDED)

2 yellow onions, chopped
1 stalk celery, finely chopped
1 carrot, scrubbed and finely grated
1 cup cooked brown rice
3 cups cooked and drained pinto
   beans, or 2 15–16 ounce cans
   low-sodium, water-packed pinto
   beans, drained and rinsed
1 cup bean-cooking liquid (or
   water)

1 teaspoon garlic powder
1 teaspoon cumin (optional)
15–18 corn tortillas
1 recipe Tomato Sauce (below),
   heated until hot
1 recipe Cashew–Pimiento Cheese
   Sauce (page 266)

Sauté the onions, celery, and carrots in a small amount of water until soft. Add the cooked rice, pinto beans, bean liquid, garlic powder, and cumin (if desired) and heat thoroughly. Preheat the oven to 350°. Place a small amount of the Tomato Sauce in the bottom of a 13″ by 9″ baking dish.

Dip each tortilla in hot Tomato Sauce to soften and fill with 3 tablespoons of the rice-bean mixture. Roll up and put into the baking dish. Repeat until all tortillas are filled and rolled. Cover with Tomato Sauce and top with Cashew–Pimiento Cheese Sauce. Bake for 30 minutes. Baste occasionally during baking or cover with a lid to prevent the enchiladas from drying out.

TOMATO SAUCE

This sauce can also be used on pizza or lasagna.

MAKES 2 ½ CUPS
PREPARATION TIME: 5 MINUTES
COOKING TIME: 5 MINUTES

8 ounces low-sodium tomato sauce
6 ounces low-sodium tomato paste
1 cup water
⅛ teaspoon dried oregano

⅛ teaspoon dried basil
¼ teaspoon onion powder
¼ teaspoon garlic powder

Combine all the ingredients in a saucepan and heat thoroughly.

INTERNATIONAL TOFU STUFFING FOR TORTILLAS OR VEGETABLES

This stuffing can be made with a variety of seasonings and may be used to stuff many different foods. Try it in corn tortillas, pita, or burritos with a variety of toppings or sauces. You may also use it to stuff various vegetables, such as green peppers, eggplants, zucchini, or tomatoes (see Note below). The tofu must be frozen for at least a day and then thawed before using.

SERVINGS: 8–10
PREPARATION TIME: 15 MINUTES
(NOT COUNTING FREEZING AND THAWING THE TOFU)
COOKING TIME: 30 MINUTES (COOKED BEANS NEEDED)

1 large yellow onion, chopped
½ cup chopped celery
⅓ cup water
3 cups frozen and thawed firm tofu
(see Note page 270)
½ cup currants (optional)

½ cup cooked and drained beans
(garbanzo, white, pinto, or
kidney), or 1 8 ounce can low-
sodium, water-packed beans,
drained and rinsed
2 cups low-sodium tomato sauce

Seasoning options:

Mexican:
2½ tablespoons chili powder
¼ cup chopped black olives
(optional)

Italian:
1 teaspoon dried basil
1 teaspoon dried oregano
1 tablespoon parsley flakes

French:
½ teaspoon dried thyme
½ teaspoon dried rosemary
½ teaspoon dried marjoram
1 tablespoon red wine (optional)

Oriental:
½ teaspoon powdered ginger
½ teaspoon dry mustard
1 tablespoon low-sodium soy sauce
1 tablespoon sherry (optional)

Greek:
½ teaspoon cinnamon
½ teaspoon ground cumin
1 tablespoon lemon juice
dash ground black pepper

Indian:
1 teaspoon turmeric
1 teaspoon ground coriander
1 teaspoon ground cumin
dash ground black pepper

Squeeze the excess water from the thawed tofu and crumble it. Sauté the onion and celery in the water until translucent. Stir in the tofu and cook a few minutes. Add the currants, beans, and tomato sauce. Mix well. Add your choice of seasonings from the options list and simmer over low heat about 20 to 25 minutes.

NOTE: *To prepare stuffed vegetables*, cut off their tops, scoop out the insides (reserve for other uses), fill with the stuffing, place in a baking dish, add ½ inch water to the dish, and bake at 350° for 30 to 45 minutes.

POLYNESIAN TOFU STEW

The tofu must be frozen for at least a day and then thawed before using.

SERVINGS: 8
PREPARATION TIME: 20 MINUTES
(NOT COUNTING FREEZING AND THAWING THE TOFU)
COOKING TIME: 45 MINUTES

*1 pound firm tofu, frozen and
  thawed (see Note page 270)*
2 cloves garlic, crushed
½ cup water
1 large yellow onion, chopped
1 green pepper, chopped
2 tomatoes, chopped
1 tablespoon low-sodium soy sauce
*3 white potatoes, scrubbed and
  cubed (large chunks)*

2½ cups vegetable stock or water
*1 medium butternut squash, or 2
  Japanese pumpkin, acorn
  squash, or other winter squash,
  cubed*
2 cups fresh or frozen corn kernels
*2–3 tablespoons cornstarch,
  dissolved in ¼ cup cold water
  (optional)*
2 bananas, cubed

Squeeze the excess water from the thawed tofu and crumble. Sauté the garlic in the water for a minute or two. Add the onion and pepper; sauté for 5 minutes. Add the tomatoes, tofu, and soy sauce; sauté for 10 minutes. Add potatoes and stock or water, cover and cook for 10 minutes. Add the cubed squash and corn. Stir well and cook, covered, for 10 to 15 minutes, until squash and potatoes are tender. If desired, the stew can be thickened with the cornstarch at this point. Then add the bananas and stir well.

MACARONI AND "CHEESE"

SERVINGS: 6–8
PREPARATION TIME: 20 MINUTES
COOKING TIME: 45 MINUTES

*2 cups uncooked egg-free whole
  wheat or spinach macaroni*
2 quarts boiling water
*1 recipe Cashew–Pimiento Cheese
  Sauce (page 266)*

*½ cup soft bread crumbs (see page
  211) or cubes*

Preheat the oven to 350°. Add the macaroni to the boiling water and cook until tender (about 10 minutes). Drain and rinse the macaroni and place in a flat 7½″ × 11¾″ baking dish. Pour the Cashew–Pimiento Cheese Sauce over the top and bake, covered, for 30 minutes. Uncover and top with soft bread crumbs or cubes; then bake for 15 additional minutes.

STUFFED MANICOTTI
SERVINGS: 6–8
PREPARATION TIME: 40 MINUTES
COOKING TIME: 40 MINUTES

16 manicotti shells

Filling:
1 yellow onion, chopped (optional)
2 cups drained and mashed firm
  tofu
2 tablespoons low-sodium soy sauce
¼ cup whole wheat flour
1 teaspoon dried oregano

8 cups Marinara Spaghetti Sauce
(recipe page 183)

½ teaspoon dried basil
½ teaspoon dried dill
freshly ground pepper to taste
1 10 ounce package frozen chopped
  spinach, thawed, drained, and
  well squeezed

Sauté the onion in a small amount of water for 5 minutes. Remove from heat, add all the remaining filling ingredients, but the spinach, and mix well. Crumble the spinach and add to the filling mixture, stirring well.

Preheat the oven to 350°. Place about 2 cups of spaghetti sauce in the bottom of a 9″ × 13″ baking dish. Stuff each manicotti with some filling mixture (pack rather tightly for the manicotti expand when cooked). Place them side by side in the baking dish and cover with the remaining spaghetti sauce. Cover and bake for 35 to 40 minutes. Let rest a short time before serving.

ZUCCHINI–SPINACH LASAGNA
SERVINGS: 8–10
PREPARATION TIME: 45 MINUTES
COOKING TIME: 45 MINUTES

12 uncooked egg-free whole wheat
  or spinach lasagna noodles
1 cup chopped yellow onion
½ cup chopped green pepper
2 medium zucchini, sliced
1 16 ounce can low-sodium stewed
  tomatoes (including juice)

1 8 ounce can low-sodium tomato
  sauce
¼ teaspoon dried basil
¼ teaspoon dried oregano
1 bunch spinach
1 recipe Cashew–Pimiento Cheese
  Sauce (page 266)

Cook the noodles as directed on the package. Sauté the onion and green pepper in a small amount of water until tender. Add the zucchini, tomatoes, tomato sauce, basil, and oregano and simmer slowly for 20 minutes.

Preheat the oven to 350°. Clean the spinach, chop, and steam until softened. Drain and rinse the noodles. In a 9″ × 13″ baking dish, make layers beginning with the tomato-vegetable mixture, followed by the noodles, the spinach, and topped with the Cashew–Pimiento Cheese Sauce. Cover and bake for 45 minutes. Let rest for 15 minutes before serving.

EASY BAKED TEMPEH

Tempeh is a compact patty made by fermenting cooked hulled soybeans with a beneficial mold that binds the beans together. Other legumes, such as peas and lentils, and also grains, such as rice, wheat, and barley—alone or in various combinations—are sometimes added. Because it has a dense, solid consistency, it is often used to replace meat in various dishes and on sandwiches. Like tofu, it is high in fat and protein. You will find tempeh in the refrigerated or frozen food sections of your local natural food store. Refrigerated, it lasts a week, and frozen, it lasts indefinitely. Freezing does not change its texture appreciably.

SERVINGS: 4
PREPARATION TIME: 20 MINUTES
COOKING TIME: 20–30 MINUTES

1 pound tempeh
1 15–16 ounce can low-sodium
  tomato sauce
¼ cup finely chopped onion

¼ cup cider vinegar
¼ cup low-sodium soy sauce
½ teaspoon curry powder
¼ teaspoon ground ginger

Cut the tempeh into bite-sized pieces and set aside. Preheat the oven to 350°. Combine the remaining ingredients in a small saucepan and simmer over low heat until the sauce thickens slightly, about 10 minutes. Spoon a thin layer of sauce on the bottom of a 2-quart baking dish. Add the tempeh pieces and cover with the remaining sauce. Bake for 20 to 30 minutes.

Burger Fixings

SLOPPY JOE MIX

This makes a large amount, but it freezes well so it's easy to divide into small portions to use for other meals.

SERVINGS: 16
PREPARATION TIME: 30 MINUTES
COOKING TIME: 30 MINUTES

2 tablespoons low-sodium soy sauce
1 tablespoon low-sodium tomato
  paste
1 tablespoon natural peanut butter
1 teaspoon onion powder
⅛ teaspoon garlic powder
¼ cup water
3 cups drained and crumbled firm
  tofu

1 yellow onion, chopped
1 green pepper, chopped
1–2 cloves garlic, crushed
½ cup water
1 10 ounce package Nature's
  Burger Mix
4 cups low-sodium, oil-free
  barbecue sauce
whole wheat buns or bread

Mix the soy sauce, tomato paste, peanut butter, onion powder, and garlic powder together until they are smooth. Add the water and mix well. Pour over the crumbled tofu and stir until the tofu is coated with the mixture.

Sauté the onion, green pepper, and garlic in the water until soft. Add the tofu mixture and continue to cook and stir about 5 minutes to absorb some of the liquid. Add the Nature's Burger Mix and the barbecue sauce and mix well. Cook over low heat for 20 minutes, stirring occasionally. Serve on whole wheat buns or whole wheat bread.

SLOPPY JOES TOO

The tofu must be frozen for at least a day and then thawed before using.

SERVINGS: 8
PREPARATION TIME: 15 MINUTES
(NOT COUNTING FREEZING AND THAWING THE TOFU)
COOKING TIME: 20 MINUTES

1 yellow onion, chopped
1 green pepper, chopped
1 pound (2 cups) frozen and
  thawed tofu (see Note page 270)
½ cup low-sodium ketchup
1 tablespoon prepared mustard

2 tablespoons cider vinegar
2 tablespoons low-sodium soy sauce
2 tablespoons honey
1 teaspoon chili powder
whole wheat buns

Garnish options:
chopped onion
sliced tomato

shredded lettuce

Squeeze the excess water from the thawed tofu and crumble. Sauté the onion and green pepper in a small amount of water until softened. Add the tofu and the remaining ingredients and mix well. Cook about 10 to 15 minutes, stirring occasionally. Serve on whole wheat buns with your choice of garnishes.

VARIATION: For added richness, top with grated soy cheese.

TOFU BURGERS

This recipe makes a lot of burgers. The burgers freeze well (after cooking) and are great to have on hand for a fast, easy meal when you are rushed. Just thaw in a microwave for 1 minute or a toaster oven for 4 to 5 minutes, and they're ready to eat. They are a favorite with children as well as adults, and may be cooked on a grill at a cookout. Serve with your favorite burger toppings: ketchup, mustard, Worcestershire sauce, lettuce, sliced tomato, pickles, etc. Or top with a slice of soy cheese to make a "cheese" burger.

MAKES 16–18 BURGERS
PREPARATION TIME: 15 MINUTES
COOKING TIME: 30 MINUTES

2 pounds firm tofu, drained
3 cups rolled oats
2 tablespoons low-sodium ketchup
2 tablespoons Dijon mustard

2 tablespoons low-sodium soy sauce
2 tablespoons Worcestershire sauce
whole wheat buns

Preheat the oven to 350°. Place the tofu in a large pan and mash with a potato masher. Add the oats and mix well. Add the remaining ingredients and stir until well combined. Shape into patties and place on a nonstick baking sheet. Bake for 20 minutes on the first side, then turn over and bake an additional 10 minutes. Cool on racks. Reheat by placing under the broiler or in the microwave for a few minutes. Serve on whole wheat buns.

MARINATED TEMPEH BURGERS

SERVINGS: 4
PREPARATION TIME: 15 MINUTES
(PLUS 4 HOURS OR OVERNIGHT FOR MARINATION)
COOKING TIME: 10 MINUTES

½ pound tempeh, cut into
  4 squares
1 15–16 ounce can low-sodium
  tomato sauce
3 tablespoons honey

2 tablespoons prepared mustard
2 tablespoons Worcestershire sauce
2 cloves garlic, crushed
1 teaspoon dried oregano
¼ teaspoon ground black pepper

Mix all the ingredients except the tempeh in a medium-sized bowl. Add the tempeh squares and toss gently to coat with marinade. Marinate at least 4 hours, or overnight, tossing occasionally. Broil or grill the tempeh, using the marinade as a basting sauce, until it is browned on both sides. Serve with some of the remaining sauce on top, or in a whole wheat bun with your favorite fixings.

BIG MCBURGERS

This recipe makes a large amount of burgers. Freeze and thaw any extras as directed in the previous recipe and they're ready to eat. (If you like, you can brown them on a grill or in a broiler or skillet before serving.) Serve with your favorite burger toppings, or open-face-style with barbecue sauce, Tahini Spread (page 262), guacamole, or salsa.

MAKES 20–22 BURGERS
PREPARATION TIME: 30 MINUTES
COOKING TIME: 30 MINUTES

2 yellow onions, chopped
½ pound fresh mushrooms,
  cleaned and chopped
3 cloves garlic, crushed
2 pounds firm tofu, drained
3 cups rolled oats
1 10 ounce package frozen chopped
  spinach, thawed and squeezed

2 tablespoons low-sodium soy sauce
4 tablespoons Worcestershire sauce
½ teaspoon ground black pepper
1 teaspoon paprika
1 teaspoon lemon juice
whole wheat buns

Preheat the oven to 350°. Sauté the onions, mushrooms, and garlic in a small amount of water until softened and all water is absorbed. Mash the tofu in a large bowl.

Add the oats, spinach (be sure all excess water is squeezed out), and seasonings to the tofu and mix well. Add the onion-mushroom mixture and mix again. Shape into patties and place on a nonstick baking sheet. Bake for 20 minutes, turn over, and bake an additional 10 minutes. Serve on whole wheat buns.

DESSERTS

CAROB HERMITS

SERVINGS: MAKES 34 COOKIES
PREPARATION TIME: 15 MINUTES
COOKING TIME: 10 MINUTES

1½ cups whole wheat flour
2 tablespoons unsweetened carob
* powder*
½ teaspoon baking soda

½ cup unsweetened applesauce
½ cup honey
1 teaspoon vanilla extract
⅔ cup raisins

Preheat the oven to 350°. Mix together the flour, carob powder, and baking soda in a large bowl. In a separate bowl, mix the applesauce, honey, and vanilla. Add the liquid ingredients to the dry and mix very well. Stir in the raisins. Drop by rounded teaspoonfuls onto nonstick cookie sheets, then flatten slightly with a fork. Bake for 10 minutes. Cool about 10 minutes before removing from cookie sheet.

TOFU CHEESECAKE

The longer the cheesecake chills, the richer it will taste and the firmer it will be.

SERVINGS: 8–10
PREPARATION TIME: 45 MINUTES
(PLUS AT LEAST 1 HOUR CHILLING TIME)
COOKING TIME: NONE

Crust:
2 cups Grape-nuts cereal or oil-free
* granola*

⅓ cup frozen apple juice
* concentrate, thawed*

Filling:
2 16 ounce tubs firm tofu
¾ cup honey

1 teaspoon vanilla extract
¼ teaspoon cinnamon (optional)

Topping:
fresh or frozen fruit of your choice,
* sliced*
or 1 10 ounce jar no-sugar pure
* fruit preserves*

Process the Grape-nuts or granola in a blender briefly to crush. Place in a bowl. Add the apple juice concentrate and mix well. Press into a 9-inch pie plate and set aside. Combine the tofu and honey and mix well. Add the vanilla and cinnamon and beat until fluffy with an electric beater. Spoon into the crust and smooth out the top. Cover loosely with plastic wrap and refrigerate until serving time. Just before serving, arrange the fruit over the top of the cheesecake.

TOFU FRUIT PUDDING

A beautiful pink creamy pudding.

SERVINGS: 4
PREPARATION TIME: 10 MINUTES
(PLUS AT LEAST 1 HOUR CHILLING TIME)
COOKING TIME: NONE

½ pound firm tofu
3 tablespoons honey

1 cup frozen fruit (raspberries,
strawberries, blueberries, etc.)

Combine all ingredients in a food processor or blender and process until smooth and creamy. Pour into a serving dish, cover with plastic wrap, and chill at least 1 hour before serving.

CAROB PUDDING

SERVINGS: 6 – 8
PREPARATION TIME: 10 MINUTES
(PLUS AT LEAST 1 HOUR CHILLING TIME)
COOKING TIME: NONE

1 pound firm tofu
1 large banana, peeled
⅓ cup honey
2 tablespoons unsweetened carob
 powder

½ teaspoon vanilla extract
dash cinnamon
dash nutmeg

Break the tofu into small pieces and set aside. Break up the banana and place into a blender or food processor. Add the honey and process briefly. Add the tofu, piece by piece, processing in between. If the mixture is too thick, add water a tablespoon at a time until the mixture is of pudding consistency. Add the remaining ingredients and process until smooth. Pour into a serving dish, cover with plastic wrap, and chill at least 1 hour before serving.

13

THE PLEASURES

OF EATING OUT

If you're one of the many people who don't have either the time or the inclination to do much cooking at home, then finding healthful foods to eat away from home will be important to you. Remember that every commercial eating establishment, ranging from your neighborhood family-run twelve-seat lunch counter to the largest fast-food chain in town, is operated for profit. You can bet that as soon as its customers express a wish to eat healthful foods, such selections will appear very soon on the restaurant's menu. A trend toward change has already begun. Look at the salad bars that have sprung up almost everywhere, even in supermarkets, and notice that most restaurants will serve you whole wheat bread if you ask for it.

Finding healthful places to eat shouldn't be difficult. One or two restaurants where you can be served a few dishes that you like will keep you going for weeks or months while you look for others. Healthy places to eat in are all around you waiting to be noticed. In all probability, you can find a health food restaurant or sandwich bar closer to your workplace than you think. Look in your local telephone directory's Yellow Pages. Phone or visit any likely candidates and ask if they serve a vegetarian vegetable soup made without oil or dairy products. Ask the same questions about their bread. What kinds of sandwiches do they make? Do they serve brown rice? Learn as much as you can about their policies and attitudes, and decide whether or not you feel like trusting yourself to them in the future.

Next, look around for Chinese, Japanese, Thai, and Indian restaurants. Ask if they can make oil-free, pure vegetarian dishes for you. After a little searching, especially if you live in or near a metropolitan area, you'll work up a list of many places to which you can go for safe and healthy meals.

Don't hesitate to make special requests. Restaurants know that, in the end, they have a lot to gain from your patronage. Talk to the manager or the chef. Explain that you've read the 1988 Surgeon General's Report on *Nutrition and Health*, and that now you're on the diet for the new-age American. Or just say that your doctor has put you on a special diet. You might start the conversation with a diplomat's ploy: "I understand you have an outstanding chef. Could he make me a dish from grains and fresh vegetables, nicely seasoned, but without any oil in it?"

Let the manager know that you have to eat out a lot and therefore would like to give some of your business to his establishment. You can also imply that you'll introduce your health-conscious friends and family to the place if it serves sensible and tasty meals. Soon the waiters or waitresses will recognize you at sight, and all the restaurant's employees will anticipate your requests. In a short time you'll be able to bring business associates who are not aware of the importance you attach to safe foods and order your "usual" fare without causing the slightest disturbance even though your meal is not a standard part of the menu. If you eat at the same restaurant often enough, the chef may order special ingredients for you. Eventually, you may even find your favorite vegetarian dish listed on the menu for other diners to enjoy.

If you're too shy to ask questions and make requests, then you'll have to settle for a more limited range of dishes to choose among. However, at the very least, you must discover (preferably not by trial and error) whether your food will be swimming in oil, and whether or not it will contain any meat or dairy products.

Restaurant Flavorings

To be sure your food will be seasoned both healthily and to your liking, you may want to bring along some acceptable flavorings from home (see the Survival Kit on pages 115–117). However, you can usually find some healthful possibilities at a restaurant if you ask. Restaurant salad dressings are almost always unacceptably laden with oils and/or dairy products, but in any restaurant you should be able to get a wedge of lemon or a dash of vinegar for your salad. Salt and black pepper are present on every table. Most of you can use these ingredients sparingly without adverse results. The ketchup most restaurants serve is likely to have lots of sugar in it, and possibly too much salt, but at least it has no fats, so it may be acceptable if you use it sparingly.

Many restaurants will provide soy sauce to which monosodium glutamate (MSG) has been added. As we have seen, not only is this ingredient high in sodium, but some people have reactions to the glutamate portion of it. Read the label on the bottle, or ask what the soy sauce contains before using it.

Beverages

Order water—it is the ideal beverage. Nothing quenches thirst better, or serves you more faithfully. For a little more sparkle, order seltzer or soda water (preferably without sodium). Non-caffeinated (herbal) teas are available in most restaurants, or can be brought from home in individual packets—every restaurant can supply you with hot water.

Practical Breakfast Suggestions

Hot Cereals

Order oatmeal without butter, cream, or milk. If sweeteners do not affect your health adversely, then add a small amount of apple juice, orange juice, honey, pure maple syrup, or sugar. Cream of wheat, a cornmeal porridge called polenta, and corn grits appear on some breakfast menus.

Cold Cereals

Most restaurants have Shredded Wheat. Top it with hot water or cold apple or orange juice, or bring along low-fat soy milk. Some restaurants offer Nutri-Grain cold cereals, Grape-nuts, or Skinner's raisin bran. (Check the list of acceptable cold cereals, pages 100–101.)

Fruits and Fruit Juices

Everywhere you eat you will find a selection of fruits and fruit juices.

Hash-brown and Home-Fried Potatoes

Home-fried potatoes are cooked white potatoes cut in about one-inch chunks. Hash-browns are grated boiled potatoes, often frozen in rectangular cubes. Ask if you can get these fried in a little water or on a dry skillet, instead of oil. Both home-fries and hash-browns turn nicely brown, even without oil.

Whole Wheat Toast, Dry

Tell the waiter that you want the toast without butter. If your health can tolerate simple sugar, then spread a thin layer of honey, jelly, or jam on your toast. Or bring along your own no-sugar, pure fruit jam.

Bagels

Make sure they're oil-free. Bagels are wonderfully tasty, but they are not lacking in calories. Therefore, if you're trying to lose weight rapidly I'd suggest you eat them sparingly, and avoid them during your first twelve days on the program.

Pancakes and Waffles?

Sure, why not? If you're lucky enough to find a restaurant willing to make them with healthful ingredients. See recipes on pages 223 and 224 of Chapter 11.

Practical Lunch Suggestions

Baked Potatoes

Let's start easy with a baked potato—no, make that two baked potatoes. At less than 150 calories each, you can afford to eat two. They're best eaten plain, or sprinkled with chives, onions, vegetable seasoning, lemon juice, and/or vinegar. Or dust them with a light shake of table salt, soy sauce (without MSG), or Tabasco. Or if you prefer, bring along a spice bottle of your favorite seasoning blend or acceptable salad dressing, barbecue sauce, or hot pepper sauce (see Survival Kit, pages 115–117). As a variation, break the potatoes with a fork into small pieces and mix thoroughly with your choice of spices, sauce, and/or dressing.

Salad Bars

From fast-food joints to supermarkets to fine restaurants, salad bars are growing in popularity. Make sure the establishment does not use sulfites to keep the food fresh—see page 97. Even without this preservative, not every ingredient on display is for you—too many are laced with gobs of oils, salt, and mayonnaise. Look closely and you'll be able to identify the vegetables covered with sauces and shining with oil. Use lemon juice, vinegar, or your own bottled, low-sodium, oil-free dressing over the vegetables you collect. Sprinkle some no-salt seasoning blend over your salad. Most salad bars allow "all you can eat," so don't hesitate to take seconds.

Vegetable Sandwiches or Soups

Ask a sandwich shop for a sandwich with healthy ingredients such as whole grain bread (no-oil, no dairy), lettuce, bean sprouts, tomatoes, onions, green peppers, and any other low-fat vegetables. I have found some restaurants that serve an excellent oil-free vegetable soup, the only ingredients vegetables, spices, and a little salt.

Eating Out of Supermarkets

Take a sharp knife and a fork to work with you so you can make your own sandwich from ingredients you buy at your local grocery. Find an acceptable whole wheat bread and pick any combination of low-fat vegetables you like. Then find a comfortable location (your office, or a bench in the park) where after washing the ingredients you can slice them and build a sandwich. Top with various dressings or condiments (see Survival Kit, pages 115–117). Or for a quick lunch on the run, buy a round of whole pita bread and a fruit or two. If that's too simple, then fill the pita bread with lettuce, tomato, sprouts, and onions. Add some drained and mashed low-sodium, water-packed canned pinto beans and you'll have a hearty sandwich that with a little imagination tastes like it's made with meat.

With a bit more work you can make your own "bean burrito" or a "chapati roll-up." Chapati disks made of whole wheat flour (and little or no oil) and soft corn tortillas can often be found in the refrigerated or frozen foods section. Get some low-sodium, water-packed canned kidney beans, some acceptable salsa or salad dressing, and some tomatoes, onions, lettuce, and/or sprouts. Drain and mash the beans, spread the beans over the chapati, or tortilla, and cover with chopped vegetables. Top with salsa or salad dressing and roll closed. You can heat all of this in a microwave oven if you like, but it's tasty enough to eat at room temperature or cold. As a variation, you might try different ethnic seasoning sauces, such as Indian, Chinese, or Indonesian. But be sure to check the ingredients.

Practical Dinner Suggestions

Royally Seasoned Steamed Vegetables

Call several of the better restaurants in your area and ask if they serve a steamed vegetable platter, and if they will make yours without butter and cheese. The more expensive and fancier restaurants often list a vegetable dish on the menu, at a reasonable price. Usually the chef will add his own special blend of spices and herbs to the dish before it reaches your table. If you feel that more zest is needed to make the vegetables to your liking, then sprinkle them with lemon juice, vinegar, or a favorite salad dressing or seasoning blend from your Survival Kit (pages 115–117). If, after that, you're still hungry, order another serving.

A Steak House

Try a steak house. You can get a tasty meal at the salad bar (check for sulfites—see page 97) while your unconverted friends stuff themselves with slabs of steak and oily fried shrimp. Bring along your own salad dressing or ask for vinegar and/or lemon juice. My favorite place now provides ingredients for making burritos and tacos at its salad bar. Ask if the refried beans contain lard or vegetable oil. I cover a soft wheat tortilla shell with rice, tomatoes, onions, lettuce, bean sprouts, and salsa. (I don't touch the high-fat olives or the avocado dip.) This same salad bar also serves eggless spaghetti noodles with a tangy red marinara sauce and a vegetarian minestrone soup. If I'm really hungry, I can order a baked potato and a platter of steamed vegetables on the side.

Mexican Foods

Most Mexican foods are full of lard! But, by telephoning around, you can find a Mexican restaurant that does not use lard or vegetable oil in its beans, or at least that is willing to make your beans without them. This should be a simple request because of the way many Mexican chefs cook. They start preparing the beans the night before by boiling them with water only. Then they refrigerate or freeze the cooked beans, and, as they need them, take small portions to be pan-fried with vegetable oil or lard, salt, and seasonings. Simply ask if you can have your serving heated before the lard, oil, and salt are added. With these low-fat beans the cook can make you a bean tostada on a soft cornmeal shell (just cornmeal and lime, not fried), or a bean burrito from a soft whole wheat tortilla shell (more than likely the burrito shell will contain refined flour and a little oil). Add to the bean foundation a mix of lettuce, onions, and tomatoes and a bit of Mexican salsa (which is hot and salty, but oil-free). Remember to tell the waiter that you want no cheese, no sour cream, no olives, and no avocado (or guacamole) on your bean burrito. Once you have established your wishes at a good Mexican restaurant, think of the delicious dinners that await you there for the rest of your life.

Italian Foods

Seek an Italian restaurant that uses egg-free noodles and ask if they can serve you an oil-free marinara sauce. Some may even have an oil-free vegetarian minestrone soup.

A Pizza Night Out

Surprisingly, you can do pretty well with a pizza, especially if salt restriction is not important to you. Find a place that uses whole wheat flour and little or no oil in the crust and an oil-free tomato sauce. Be specific in your order of toppings. You want generous amounts of oil-less tomato sauce followed by onions, green pepper, mushrooms, and/or tomatoes. No cheese or pepperoni.

My best experiences have been with the "we make, you bake" shops. Usually you can watch them prepare your pizza and therefore know exactly what goes on it. Then you cook it yourself in a dry pizza pan. It's not bad for a (fairly) healthy meal.

Chinese Foods

Remember, no fat Chinese live in China, a good indication that Chinese food has many healthy qualities. If possible, find a place that serves brown rice. (Sometimes when you ask for brown rice they think you mean white rice coated with soy sauce, so ask for whole grain rice.) Along with your rice (whether white or brown), ask for vegetables cooked in a "light" sauce that contains no oil or MSG (monosodium glutamate). Beware of the hot mustard found on the table—it contains oil from the mustard seeds (and it can incinerate your tonsils). And watch for the MSG in the soy sauce. Many Chinese restaurants now advertise in the telephone directory that they use no MSG.

Japanese Foods

Do you have a Japanese restaurant or two nearby? I hope so, because they can serve you some excellent meals. Ask the waitress about the cooked dishes the chef can make for you from vegetables but without oil; one of these treats is rice topped with finely sliced vegetables that have been slightly cooked in a light ginger sauce. If they have a sushi bar, you're definitely in luck. You can always order the makisushi, which is rice rolled up in seaweed with a central core of raw cucumber and other vegetables (kappamaki) or with pickled daikon (oshinkomaki). The rice in the roll is white, but for all but the most sensitive eater, this occasional mild insult to your system need not be harmful. The hot green horseradish, called Wasabi, does add a little oil to your meal, but not much because you'll use so little of it (it's *very* hot). A mixture of soy sauce (no MSG) and hot green Wasabi is traditional for Japanese sushi, and gives the dominant accent regardless of what vegetables are inside the roll of rice. You can order pickled salads too. Look in the Tsukemono section of the menu for a whole variety of salads featuring assorted pickled vegetables. A cucumber and carrot salad is especially delectable. If you have finished the twelve-day diet and regained your health, you might also order miso soup, made from miso, tofu, vegetables, and soy sauce.

Thai Foods

Try green papaya and cabbage salad, or sweet and sour vegetables over brown rice. Be careful, Thai food can be very hot, especially if you use the pepper sauce placed on every table. Ask the chef to fix you "mild" or "cool" dishes if you don't want them to be too hot.

Indian Foods

Indians from India are quite stratified in their culture and therefore in their eating habits. Less affluent Indians eat plenty of rice and vegetables. In general, the more affluent classes may be vegetarian by religious conviction and up-bringing but most likely will reveal their affluence by the rotund shapes that good living encourages. Their diet is rich in dairy products and makes much use of a "purified butter" called ghee (ghi). Even though most Indian restaurants advertise vegetarian meals, all they usually mean is that no meat is present in the so-called vegetarian dishes. Ask if the chef can prepare your vegetarian meal without oil and dairy products.

A Vegetarian or Health Food Restaurant

You should be able to find whole grain (brown) rice and steamed vegetables even on your first visit. Ask about dishes made without oil, eggs, and dairy products. Such a restaurant should consider your dietary requests a challenge—if not a matter of fact—for them. After all, they do advertise, directly or indirectly, the health benefits of vegetarian foods.

Eating with Members of the Radical Fringe

Do you want to do something unusual and fascinating, but possibly very much out of character for you? Most large cities will have a food service, often a nice restaurant, operated by the Hari Krishnas or by a macrobiotics group. I mention them in the same sentence not because they are associated philosophically but because both are observers of strict vegetarian diets. (Commonly, a Hari Krishna restaurant is called Govinda's.) Don't worry, you are not likely to be confronted with people who will try to impose their philosophy on you. However, you will have gained a glimpse of different sub-cultures and had a good meal. Be sure to ask about their use of dairy products, eggs, salt, and oils in preparing the meals they serve.

EATING OUT
IN SOMEONE'S HOME

Being a considerate guest can be mildly challenging. Therefore, being honest about your intentions and needs will help everyone involved. If for the sake of convenience or courtesy you decide to eat what the hostess is serving, then consider this as one of those infrequent "special occasions" that probably will not cause you any lasting harm (as long as you don't eat too much). However, if you decide to stay with your diet (and I believe that most of my disciples should take such a stand), then explain clearly to your hostess that you are on a special diet, and tell her what you can eat and what you must avoid. Say that you are "simply following the doctor's orders" and can eat only whole grains, vegetables and fruits. (After you have revealed all this, be sure to obey your self-imposed rule at the dinner table, even if what used to be your favorite meat dish, veal scaloppini, is served to the other guests. Nothing is worse than a twice-double-crossing hypocrite!)

If you're dining with close friends, then your new style of eating should be no inconvenience to them. Just ask that they prepare some extra vegetables without salt and free of oil. Or offer to bring along a special vegetable dish you yourself have fixed for the oc-casion. (You'll discover that the other guests will pounce upon your low-fat, no-cholesterol contribution with sounds of approval.) If you think that the party will not feed you well enough, or that you may not be able to resist temptation, then eat at home, just before you go out. It will be much easier to be strong when your stomach is already nicely full.

If the people you're supposed to meet at the party are not close acquaintances, and you're not sure what everyone will be eating and talking about during the dinner, then ask the hostess if you can join the group after dinner for tea (herbal! even if you have to bring it yourself) and conversation.

AIRPLANE FOOD

Traveling by air is no excuse to drop your diet, even when you fly first class and are plied with all those extravagant "treats." In the past few years, requests for vegetarian meals have been doubling almost annually on major airlines. Interesting and healthy meals can be obtained, but you must call the airline twenty-four hours ahead of time if you want to order a special meal. Any travel agent can include your preferences in meals in your computerized reservation file, so that they are automatically ordered every time you schedule a flight. Ask for "pure-vegetarian, no-oil" meals. If you also need to restrict sodium and or/protein intake, you'd better order a fruit plate. If on a domestic flight you are traveling on a smaller airline that cannot take care of your needs, carry your own food from home.

P·A·R·T
3

A MEDICAL GUIDE TO HEALTHFUL LIVING

DIETARY AND LIFESTYLE

TREATMENT OF

MEDICAL CONDITIONS*

Your conscientious and well-informed personal physician should tell you the advantages and disadvantages of whatever treatments he has recommended for easing your condition—and in addition, he should tell you about all reasonable options that are available to you. Unfortunately, in the real world of today this seldom happens. I'm especially concerned about this deficiency because simple, sensible, safe, self-help approaches based upon a healthy diet and an equally healthy lifestyle are almost never mentioned by doctors. Instead, almost routinely, life-threatening drugs and dangerous surgeries are prescribed as if no other avenue of treatment were available or even imaginable.

I don't consider that the standard medical practice of today is stunningly effective for most of the diseases from which the American people suffer. Nevertheless, you must do your best to evaluate each kind of therapy that's recommended to you, including the approaches I use, according to its own merits. If you are considering being treated by surgery, medications, or by any other method, then weigh these factors:

1. The potential benefits from the treatment;
2. The possible risks, the side effects, and the aftereffects of the treatment;
3. The consequences—or the merits—of doing nothing;
4. The alternatives to the recommended therapy;
5. The comparable costs in effort, time, and money of each approach.

Go through the same checklist when different laboratory tests are recommended. You should certainly take advantage of all the great advances that modern medicine has to offer—but only if the benefits of them clearly outweigh their risks and costs. Remember, the burden of proof for a treatment's effectiveness and safety rests upon the one who is making the recommendation—and most often this person is your doctor. Don't get

* References to the scientific literature supporting many of the issues discussed in this section are found on pages 387–405.

involved in treatments that are still considered to be experimental, or in those that have already been shown to be of questionable effectiveness.

How can you know the value of a treatment? You could place blind faith in your doctor, or you could do some research. Start by asking probing questions of your doctor. Then get second and even third opinions from other doctors. Ask for material you can read about the proposed therapy and any alternatives to it. If you want to make a thorough study of the subject, go to a good library for textbooks and research articles. Computer searches of the pertinent literature are inexpensive and will provide quickly the most useful clues for finding volumes of information that will help to answer your questions.

Opinions about the cause, prevention, and treatment of many different diseases that affect human beings vary widely among medical professionals. Generally speaking, no single approach to treatment has proved to be ideal, so further opinions are always arising and more scientific study is needed. Most physicians are genuinely convinced about the merits of the therapies they offer, just as I myself have no hesitation in enthusiastically telling you what many sensible patients can accomplish by choosing to make changes in their diet and lifestyle.

How can you find a doctor who recognizes the value of a healthy diet and lifestyle? I give some suggestions in Chapter 4. Don't try to make do on your own. This book gives you a lot of basic information, but you should have a doctor who will evaluate your health and be available if problems arise. If you have a health problem and/or are on medication, you must not make changes in your therapy or diet unless you are under a doctor's supervision.

In this guide I have not attempted to present exhaustive discussions of the illnesses listed. Rather, I have set forth points of interest for your serious consideration that should promote a useful dialogue between you and your doctor. Each of the health problems mentioned in this section is examined twice. First, I discuss briefly the current medical treatment and some of the advantages and shortcomings of that approach. Then, I describe the benefits that a change in diet and lifestyle can bring to people who are affected by that condition. At the very least, the changes I recommend will be helpful supplements to the other kinds of treatment a patient is receiving. But, in many cases the changes I recommend will solve the medical problem within a short time and therefore make those other therapeutic approaches unnecessary.

If you're a person who is suffering from one or more of the illnesses discussed in this book, then I hope that the day will come soon when you can give to your doctor the message I've heard over and over again with great satisfaction. "Well, doc, I guess I'll not need to come and see you for a long while. I'm not sick anymore!"

MEDICAL CONDITIONS COVERED

I suggest that in this section of the book you read *only* those pages concerning conditions that interest you.

ACNE
ALLERGIC DISEASES
ALZHEIMER'S DISEASE
ANEMIA
ARTHRITIS
ATHEROSCLEROSIS
CANCER
CHOLESTEROL, HIGH
COLITIS, MILD (Spastic Colon)
COLITIS, SEVERE (Inflamma-
  tory Bowel Disease)
  Crohn's Disease
  Ulcerative Colitis
COLON POLYPS and COLON
  CANCER
CONSTIPATION
  Varicose Veins
  Hemorrhoids
DEPRESSION and ANXIETY
DIABETES
  Childhood-Onset
  Adult-Onset
DIVERTICULAR DISEASE
FATIGUE
GALLBLADDER DISEASE
HEADACHES
HEART DISEASE, PREVENTION
HEART DISEASE, TREATMENT

HIATAL HERNIA
HORMONE-DEPENDENT
  DISEASES
  Abnormal Uterine Bleeding
  Early Menarche
  Fibrocystic Breast Disease
  Fibroids of Uterus
  Late Menopause
  Ovarian Cysts
  Premenstrual Syndrome (PMS)
  Prostate Disease
  Baldness (Male-Pattern)
HYPERTENSION (High Blood Pressure)
HYPOGLYCEMIA
KIDNEY DISEASE
  Kidney Failure
  Glomerulonephritis
KIDNEY STONES
LIVER DISEASE
MULTIPLE SCLEROSIS
OBESITY
OSTEOPOROSIS
UPPER INTESTINAL
  DISTRESS
  Acid Indigestion
  Esophagitis
  Gastritis
  Ulcers

ACNE

STANDARD PRACTICE

Pimples (the medical name is acne vulgaris) are an inflammatory reaction that is produced by bacteria (*Propionibacterium acnes*) living in and on the skin. These bacteria feed upon the fats in the skin, splitting them into fatty acids. These fatty acids irritate the surrounding cells, causing the reactions that end as pimples. Fats and oils on the skin can come from internal sources introduced in your foods, and from external sources such as machine grease or cosmetics and skin-care preparations.

A reputable textbook, *Harrison's Principles of Internal Medicine* (10th Edition, 1983) says, "There is no evidence suggesting that diet has any effect on the course or severity of acne vulgaris."

Current Treatment: Many common "pimple therapies" are directed at removing the oil, or sebum, from the skin, and at lowering the number of bacteria present on the skin and in its pores. Washing with soap and water is a simple "degreasing" method. Washing is more effective when supplemented with an abrasive pad, called a buff pad, which increases the cleansing effect. Benzoyl Peroxide is an "anti-acne" medication that dries the skin and keeps the bacterial content lower. Antibiotics can be applied to the skin and taken internally (as pills) to decrease the number of pimple-causing bacteria on the skin. Also a vitamin A derivative, Accutane (isotretinoin), is a very powerful acne medication which among other things reduces the body's production of sebum.

Drawbacks: Drug therapy is effective only as long as the lotions are applied or the pills are taken, because one major cause of the problem, the oily skin, continues. An exception to this temporary kind of action is Accutane, which has effects that continue after therapy is stopped. Then, too, most drugs have side effects and are costly. The most effective drug, Accutane, also has the most terrible side effects (liver damage and serious birth defects).

The McDougall Program (Dietary and Lifestyle Implications)

Eighty-five percent of all teen-agers have acne at some time, and for many people the skin trouble continues into adult life. Nevertheless, acne is a preventable disease, not a normal condition. Certainly, the hormone surges that accompany puberty are related to increased sebum production and therefore to acne. Some scientists have considered acne to be an inherited disease, while others believe that environmental factors such as diet are more important. In a society like ours, where most people eat foods rich in fats, genetic factors do play an important role in determining individual susceptibilities. To learn if diet is a primary factor in acne cases, we would have to demonstrate absence of the disease in populations of people whose diet differs considerably from that of Americans.

Unfortunately, population studies on relationships between diet and acne are limited. But recent surveys in Kenya and Zambia report far less acne in their native populations than among black people in the United States. Some evidence exists, too, that acne becomes a problem for black Africans who move from the villages to the cities and there adopt a diet with a higher fat content that is more similar to the richer American diet.*

---

* Because everyone eats a similar diet, studies within our society find few differences and yield few clues about the origin of common diseases. In Western societies nearly everyone exceeds the thresholds for dietary substances that cause common illnesses. Scientists must compare people with dissimilar diets to find clues to disease origins. Try contrasting the health of rural Chinese with their rice diet to Americans—the most casual observer would be struck by the influence of diet on health.

Current Treatment: Some debate exists in the American medical profession as to whether or not diet has an influence on the course of acne, but most doctors are convinced that diet has nothing to do with causing it. This opinion is based mostly on hearsay, rather than on scientific fact. From medical school to retirement, that's what doctors have always been taught. The evidence for this antidiet position is based primarily on one study published long ago in a medical journal, which declared that no relation had been found between the number of pimples teen-agers developed and the amount of chocolate they ate. However, the diet used for the "chocolate-free" comparison group was just as loaded with fats as was the diet for the group given chocolate. Adequate scientific studies have not actually been done to determine to what extent acne is affected by diet. These studies are not likely to be done, for the usual reason: No money can be made from evaluating the effects of diet on acne. You can't package the results of your research in a tube or a capsule and sell the product to suffering teen-agers.

On the other hand, some reliable evidence does indicate that people with acne who adopt a low-fat diet can improve their condition and reduce the amount of sebum their skin cells secrete. In my experience, a marked reduction of fats in the diet causes a phenomenal reduction in the production of sebum by skin glands. Why would you expect otherwise? The fats we eat are distributed throughout the body, including the skin. We easily accept the idea of dietary fats being transferred to the skin and hair of animals. When we ask veterinarians how to make our dog's coat glossy, we are told to add oil, eggs, or lard to its food. In order to decrease the shine of your own coat, you should follow the opposite of this advice.

Once the oiliness of the skin is decreased, the pimples will soon disappear. The reason that other doctors may not have had a similar positive experience with their disfigured patients lies in the simple fact that few patients ever remove *all* the fats that can be possibly eliminated from their diet. The skin is very sensitive to even small amounts of fats in the diet: One pepperoni pizza can mean a crop of pimples on your face that will last a week.

My Recommendations: Follow a very low-fat diet; keep your skin free of dirt, oils, and oil-based cosmetics; wash several times a day with a mild soap and a "buff pad." A person with acne must be very strict for at least a month before evaluating the effects of the diet. Don't cheat!

If you have taken full advantage of the new diet, following it for at least two months, and your problem persists, then consider lotions, gels, and creams (Benzoyl Peroxide, Retin-A, tetracyclines and other antibiotics). Next, try antibiotic pills. As a last resort, a few of the very worst cases, after careful medical counseling (especially concerning the risk of birth defects), may find value in Accutane.

ALLERGIC DISEASES

STANDARD PRACTICE

The substances that cause allergic reactions are known as allergens. They include most of the natural components in foods and beverages, and particles breathed in with the air, such as house dust, pollens, mold spores, and insect parts. Chemicals added to natural and manufactured products

---

Common Allergic Reactions

Gastrointestinal: canker sores in mouth (aphthous stomatitis), vomiting, colic, stomach cramps, abdominal distention, intestinal obstruction, bloody stools, colitis, malabsorption of foods, loss of appetite, growth retardation, diarrhea, constipation, painful defecation, irritation of tongue, lips, and mouth.

Respiratory: nasal stuffiness, runny nose, chronic cough, hoarseness, middle ear trouble (otitis media), sinusitis, asthma (bronchitis), pulmonary infiltrates, tonsil and adenoid enlargement.

Skin: rashes, atopic dermatitis, eczema, seborrhea, hives, hair loss.

Behavioral: irritability, restlessness, hyperactivity, lethargy, fatigue, allergic tension-fatigue syndrome, muscle pain, mental depression, enuresis (bed-wetting).

Blood: abnormal blood clotting, iron-deficiency anemia, low levels of serum proteins, low platelet count (thrombocytopenia), allergy-related white blood cells (eosinophilia).

Miscellaneous: arrhythmias (of the heart), arthritis, eye inflammation (conjunctivitis), generalized headaches, migraine headaches, sudden infant death syndrome (SIDS, crib death).

Immune Complex Diseases: rheumatoid arthritis, lupus erythematosus, periarteritis nodosa, polymyositis, scleroderma vasculitis, Henoch-Schonlein purpura, arteritis, milk-induced gross intestinal bleeding in infants, occult intestinal bleeding, gastroenteropathy, pulmonary hemosiderosis, glomerulonephritis (see KIDNEY DISEASE), nephrotic syndrome (orthostatic albuminuria nephrosis).

Allergies to gluten (gluten is found in high concentrations in wheat, barley, and rye): schizophrenia (a mental disorder benefited in a few cases by avoiding gluten and dairy proteins), celiac disease (a bowel disorder), dermatitis herpetiformis (a skin disorder).

can also cause allergic reactions in sensitive people. And, of course, the very medications that doctors prescribe for our well-being can betray some people by becoming allergenic to them. Most allergy-prone people will react to several different kinds of allergens. The reactions they display range from a runny nose to a burning bladder, as well as afflictions of any of the body's other parts and systems, from head to soles. Heredity and emotional stress are regarded as important contributory factors in the development of allergic responses.

Current Treatment: Symptom-relieving drugs such as antihistamines, stimulants of the sympathetic nervous system, smooth muscle relaxants, and steroids. "Allergy shots" (using extracts of the implicated allergens).

Many different kinds of tests are used to identify the substances that cause allergic reactions to make a person sick. They include skin tests, provocation tests, and blood tests. Their accuracy at identifying what you are actually allergic to ranges from useless to fair. Some tests are uncomfortable, all are costly.

Drawbacks: Drugs are effective for relief of symptoms only, and side effects to the medications are significant. The destruction of tissues that is caused by the allergic reaction continues unchecked. Tests may never pinpoint the source of the problem.

The McDougall Program (Dietary and Lifestyle Implications)

Allergies are responses to the harmful interaction of our immune systems with agents from the world around us. You can take two broad approaches to improve your condition. First, you can try to find and eliminate the substance that is causing the reaction. Second, you can make your immune system stronger and therefore more resistant to the harmful substance that is at fault.

Why some people are allergic and others are not is still a grand puzzle. Most scientists think that susceptibility to allergens may be due to an inherited predisposition. However, considerable evidence indicates that introducing certain foods (including cow's milk) too soon into an infant's diet, at the time when its intestinal tract and immune systems are still immature, may provoke responses in its tissues that will lead to symptoms of allergy later in life. Similarly, respiratory allergies and skin problems may be started at that tender age, when the infant's immune responses are unable to cope properly with the alien allergens.

The ultimate and best test for identifying the substance suspected of causing an allergy is to *eliminate the substance* (whether it is a food, or a pollen, or a chemical compound), and then to note if the symptoms disappear and the patient's health is improved. Confirmation of the diagnosis is made by adding the offending substance back into the patient's diet or environment and observing if the illness returns. Don't overlook the obvious truth that elimination of the villainous allergen is also the ultimate—and only—treatment for "curing" the allergy.

Although countless substances can cause allergies, the foods he eats should be the first suspects that an allergic person should investigate. This is true for two reasons. First, whatever we eat is 100 percent within our control. Therefore, once the cause of a food allergy is identified, you can decide to remove that item from your diet. Second, suspecting your food is a good bet: Foods represent one of our most frequent, intimate, and diversified contacts with our environment. Molecule for molecule, we interact with the components in our foods more than with air or water, and, obviously, the complexity of the substances we contact through our foods is many times greater than that of compounds found in air or water.

Even allergic problems that on first impression seem to be due to agents other than those present in foods (pollens, for instance) can often be helped by a change in diet. The immune system has a limited capacity to handle allergens from many sources. If your immune system is overwhelmed and you can lighten its burden in any way (for example, by eliminating all dairy products), then you will be helped to tolerate the pollen grains swirling about you from the tree outside your bedroom window.

Current Treatment: Eliminate entirely, or reduce significantly, the allergens in your environment, whether in air, or drinks, or foods. Most people will resolve their food allergies by simply adopting a starch-based diet as taught in the McDougall Program, for the simple reason that six of the leading causes of food allergies are eliminated immediately when this change is made: Gone are the dairy products, eggs, chocolate, nuts, shellfish, and fish. If your problems persist after four weeks on a starch-based diet, then the next suspects to eliminate are wheat, corn, citrus fruits, tomatoes, and strawberries—the most frequent causes of allergy among the foods in the vegetable kingdom.

The next step in identifying a food that might be the cause of your allergy is to follow an elimination diet. This diet allows you to eat only the foods that are least likely to cause your allergic reaction (see the box below). When you begin this diet, allow about one week in order to completely clear your body of foods that were eaten before starting the diet. By the end of this week, if their trouble was indeed due to these foods, most people will be relieved of symptoms. During the elimination period, all foods should be thoroughly cooked, because cooking alters the proteins in them, making them less likely to provoke allergic responses.

The Only Foods to Eat on an Elimination Diet:

Starches (all cooked):

brown rice	taro (or poi)
sweet potatoes	tapioca
winter squash	puffed rice and rice flour

Most Green, Yellow, or Orange Vegetables (all cooked):

beets	celery
beet greens	string beans
chard	asparagus
summer squash	spinach
artichokes	lettuce

Most Non-citrus Fruits (all cooked):

peaches	plums
cranberries	prunes
apricots	cherries
papaya	

Condiments:
salt only, if not restricted for other health reasons (This means *no* salad dressings, mustard, lemon juice, vinegar, herbs and spices, or other flavorings.)

Beverages:
water only

After a week on this kind of fare, your food allergies should have ended and you should be feeling well. If this is the case, then you should begin to add other foods to the diet, but only *one at a time*, to determine if any of them cause your allergic reactions. For testing purposes, each "new" food should be eaten in large amounts three times a day for two days. If the food does not cause a reaction, you can conclude that it is nonallergenic. Most reactions occur within a few hours, but rarely a reaction may not show up for several days. Each food must be tested individually; *do not introduce two new foods at once.* When you do have an allergic reaction to a specific food, you must wait four to seven days before testing the next item. This interval gives you the time you need to clear your system of that allergy-causing food.

My Recommendations: In general, if you cannot identify a definite organic cause for your health problem, then suspect that it might be due to an allergy, especially to one caused by something you're eating, and search for the culprit. A dietary approach to managing food allergies is the safest and most sensible step you can take for testing *and* for treatment. Take symptom-controlling drugs only as a last resort.

ALZHEIMER'S DISEASE

STANDARD PRACTICE

Alzheimer's disease is considered to be a degenerative disease of the nervous system. It is an insidious, gradual, progressive, generalized wasting away of brain cells and other nervous tissues, and a reduction of their functions. Even though the onset of the disease may appear to be sudden in some cases, careful questioning of family members will reveal a history of a gradually developing deterioration leading to the condition called senility. Emotional disturbances, depression, anxiety, and odd quirks of behavior may be seen in the early stages. Lapses of memory and, at later stages, inability to speak are common. The intellectual function progressively deteriorates, often over a ten-year period.

Alois Alzheimer provided the classical description of this condition in 1906; since then this form of loss of mental function has been referred to by his name. Although the disease can appear in any age period, it occurs more frequently among older people and has become the most common form of generalized loss of brain function. Alzheimer's disease affects at least 3 percent of the American population over the age of sixty-five and is clearly distinguishable from other problems with the brain that are common among the elderly, such as damage from strokes, atherosclerosis, and "normal aging."

The cause of Alzheimer's is unknown, according to many authorities.

Current Treatment: None. Custodial care is usually required.

Drawback: No hope for prevention of the condition in people as yet unaffected or for treatment of those affected.

The McDougall Program (Dietary and Lifestyle Implications)

In patients having Alzheimer's disease the brain is somewhat shrunken and, on postmortem examination, a definite loss of nervous tissue is noted. Examination of the brain tissues under a microscope reveals small bundles of material called senile plaques, scattered throughout the tissues. The more plaques that are present, the worse is the mental condition of the patient. Chemical analysis reveals the presence of the metal aluminum at the core of each plaque and within many of the cells found in the plaques. Evidence is accumulating to indicate that aluminum may be involved in the formation of the plaques, and it is therefore a prime suspect as the initial cause of the disease.

Five population studies now link Alzheimer's disease to aluminum in drinking water. As early as 1885, aluminum was shown to be toxic to the nervous tissues of animals. Aluminum can also produce a degeneration of the nervous tissues in cats and rabbits that resembles in some ways that seen in the brains of human patients with Alzheimer's disease. Patients with diseased kidneys accumulate large amounts of aluminum in their bodies from medications and from kidney-machine solutions that have been used until recently. This accumulation results in a severe mental deterioration.

Aluminum is the third most common element in the earth's crust. "Normal" dietary intake of aluminum is about 3 to 5 mg per day, of which only a very small amount is absorbed by the body's tissues. The aluminum to which we are exposed comes from many sources, and most of these are under our control. Dust, water, and even unprocessed foods contain aluminum that may be difficult to avoid. But aluminum in cosmetics, many medicines, food additives (for example, some brands of baking powders; and highly absorbable aluminum maltol used in instant chocolate mixes), cans, kitchenware, and utensils can easily be avoided. A popular antacid, Amphojel, consists of aluminum hydroxide and should be avoided.

Most of this daily aluminum intake is eliminated by healthy kidneys. However, some individuals seem to absorb aluminum more readily, or are less able to eliminate it; these people, who cannot be identified before symptoms begin, are most likely to suffer from Alzheimer's disease. Certainly not every one of the multitudes of us who have been fed for a lifetime on foods cooked in aluminum pots and pans will end our days in this world as severely mentally deficient patients. Aluminum is only one strongly suspected culprit. Scientists believe that other factors, yet to be identified, are involved in the interactions that allow the body to suffer this form of degeneration.

Some scientists are particularly worried about inhaled aluminum because autopsy studies have shown a high proportion of senile plaques in the olfactory (smelling) lobes of the brain. Spray antiperspirants would be a likely product for this concern.

Your choice of cookware is important. Glass and porcelain are relatively nonreactive with foods. Metal cookware does react with the acids in foods and the metal ions thereby released gain access to your body. In the case of copper, iron, and stainless steel cookware the metals are actually essential trace elements, and therefore make a valuable nutritional contribution if they are not absorbed in excess. Aluminum, on the other hand, not only has no recognized function in the body, but is toxic.

Current Treatment: The available evidence offers hope for preventing the beginning of Alzheimer's disease and for a possible slowing of its progress by avoiding ingestion of aluminum. Some attempts have been made to treat Alzheimer's disease patients with approaches that decrease the amount of aluminum already in the body by use of metal chelators, called deferoxamine and transferrin. Results suggest that indeed the progression of the disease may be slowed. I know of no treatment that will return lost mental function, nor do I expect that one will be found. The brain cannot replace its destroyed cells, and the scar tissue left behind in damaged parts is permanent.

My Recommendations: Based on present information, prudent action would be to avoid all sources of ingestable and inhaled aluminum. Those who fail to heed this advice will serve as "guinea pigs" for the human experiments that may eventually prove the presence or absence of serious health effects of aluminum.

ANEMIA

STANDARD PRACTICE

Anemia means a reduction in the number of red blood cells below a level determined according to the values commonly found in the general population. It is actually a sign of an underlying condition producing blood loss, such as from bleeding (intestinal, menstruation, trauma), a deficiency of iron or B vitamins, excessive blood cell destruction, or a defect in the production of blood cells. The latter can either be from hereditary causes, such as sickle cell anemia, or from acquired diseases such as kidney failure, rheumatoid arthritis, and leukemia. The most commonly seen type is iron-deficiency anemia in women, which is believed to be due to loss of blood during menstrual periods and/or to a deficiency of iron in the diet.

Current Treatment: One of the first steps usually is to determine if there has been any blood loss and if so to find the reason and stop the bleeding. Clues gained from the clinical and laboratory investigation of the patient will usually direct the physician toward a diagnosis, and also a worthwhile treatment. Iron supplements, injections of vitamin B_{12}, and blood transfusions are a few of the common treatments with benefits. The search for toxins that can cause anemia and their removal may also be rewarding.

Drawbacks: Many people with anemia are treated inappropriately. In the routine practice of medicine, iron supplements and/or vitamin B_{12} shots are often given without searching for the primary cause of the anemia. (This is poor medicine by any good doctor's standards.) Sometimes blood transfusions are given "as a last resort," and sometimes they're given without careful consideration of the patient's actual need for them or the possible consequences—the laboratory test rather than the patient is treated. Those patients with anemia due to a chronic disease may be given iron pills, but they will not respond to such therapy.

Iron also has side effects such as indigestion and black stools. Blood transfusions introduce possibilities for the spread of disease, and for life-threatening incompatibility reactions, and they decrease survival rates in cancer patients. During my years in surgical and hospital care, I saw patients being given blood as indiscriminately as if it were sterile saline water. Finding the underlying cause of the anemia and correcting it is the proper therapy, and it is too often overlooked.

The McDougall Program (Dietary and Lifestyle Implications)

Anemia from Blood Loss: Diseases of the gastrointestinal tract that lead to loss of blood must be sought. The foods you choose to eat can provoke visible blood loss in the intestinal tract by causing diseases such as ulcers, colitis, diverticulosis, and hemorrhoids. Loss of blood undetectable by the eye can be caused by subtle injury from ingesting the wrong foods. Even though the amount of blood lost at any one time may be small, if this flow continues over a long period it can still result in significant anemia. One more common source of blood loss in women is heavy menstrual flow.

Iron-deficiency Anemia is associated with low levels of the mineral iron in the body. People obtain iron from eating plants or animals that have been fed on plants, and absorb it into their bodies through the upper gastrointestinal tract. The amount of iron absorbed depends mostly upon the body's needs. Absorption of iron (as well as of other minerals) is *active*, not passive. When the stores of iron in the body's tissues are adequate, then approximately 5 percent of the iron present in the food is absorbed. If a person is iron-deficient and, accordingly, his needs are high, then the amount absorbed from the foods he eats increases to as much as 20 percent. This absorption normally represents 1 to 2 mg per day, and up to 6 mg per day in iron-deficient conditions.

Secondary factors also influence the absorption of iron from ingested foods. Absorption depends upon the acidity of the stomach, the amount of ascorbic acid (vitamin C) in the foods, the kinds of amino acids present, the amount of fiber in the diet, and the form in which the iron is presented (whether heme or nonheme). Ascorbic acid is one of the main enhancers of iron absorption, and fruits and vegetables provide plentiful amounts of this vitamin, whereas all red meats, poultry, and fish are deficient in ascorbic acid and dairy products are not only deficient in ascorbic acid, they are also very low in iron content, and actually inhibit the absorption of iron present in other foods (calcium and phosphates in milk form insoluble complexes with iron). Coffee and the tannic acid in tea will also decrease absorption of iron from foods.

Recent concern has focused on the effect of the fibers in plant foods on mineral absorption. Fibers will bind minerals and decrease absorption. However, to date the concern is merely theoretical, since actual cases of mineral deficiency attributed to presence of fibers are rare to nonexistent. Furthermore, long-term studies show that vegetarians develop no deficiency in iron from their high-fiber foods.*

Iron-deficiency anemia can also be caused by blood loss. In the United States, about 20 percent of the women of childbearing age are iron-deficient. Women who eat the high-fat American foods have abnormally increased levels of estrogens in their bodies that cause a thicker buildup of endometrial tissues, the inside lining of the uterus. When this lining is shed at the end of each monthly cycle, bleeding from this overgrown endometrium is heavier and longer, and therefore more iron is lost than would be shed in periods of lighter menstruation. In men the most common cause of iron-deficiency anemia is blood loss through ulcers, hemorrhoids, etc, in the gastrointestinal tract.

Another common source of iron loss is microscopic bleeding in the intestine. Dairy products are the most likely causes of this bleeding. The problem has been thoroughly studied in young children, and milk products have been found to be the cause of more than half the cases of juvenile iron-deficiency anemia. The problem has not been thoroughly studied in adults, yet some population groups and individuals have been identified as having iron-deficiency anemia associated with the intake of dairy products. High-fat foods—dairy products being a primary example—also increase menstrual blood loss by elevating estrogen levels in women (see HORMONE-DEPENDENT DISEASES). I believe that someday dairy products will be recognized as the main cause of iron-deficiency anemia in adult women.

Chronic Systemic Diseases That Produce Anemia. The degree of anemia follows the course of the disease and the only effective treatment is elimination of the disease. Some, such as rheumatoid arthritis and kidney disease, can be caused by faulty diet and treated with correct diet.

Runner's Anemia. More than 10 million long-distance runners live in the United States today and many of them are developing iron-deficiency anemia from no obvious organic cause. Several possible reasons for the loss of iron have been suggested: the destruction of blood cells when the feet hit the hard ground so frequently for so long a time, loss of blood through

* In terms of vegetarianism, the important question to answer is this: "Is the amount of iron in vegetable foods (and the absorption characteristics of iron) adequate to meet the needs of people eating little or no meat?" Many studies have looked at this question and consistently the answer is yes. Hemoglobin levels in vegetarians, which reflect the amount of iron in the blood, are comparable to those in people who eat flesh as a large part of their diet; and anemia has actually been found less commonly among people who eat vegetable-based diets.

the kidneys, iron lost in the sweat, reduced absorption of iron from the gut, and decreased production of blood cells in the bone marrow.

Recent studies have found blood in the stools of runners after a race that was not present before the long run. Vigorous exercise shifts a great amount of the circulating blood to the muscles in order to help them do all that hard work, thereby depriving the intestines of 80 percent of their rich supply of blood. The poorly nourished, oxygen-deprived inner lining of the intestines may suffer subtle injury in consequence, and bleed.

This type of anemia will not be corrected by taking iron supplements. A runner committed to this demanding sport must decide with his or her physician how serious a health problem the anemia represents. The evidence from only slightly abnormal laboratory tests may not call for giving up a favorite sport. Even so, this runner certainly should be checked periodically by a physician, with blood tests, if not more. A less vigorous form of exercise may be the only recommendation for many marathoners with iron-deficiency anemia.

Current Treatment: Depends upon the cause of loss of iron. Certainly, a healthy diet, without coffee, tea, or dairy products, is a sensible step toward any long-term prevention and treatment of anemia.

My Recommendations: Look for the cause and correct it. If you have iron-deficiency anemia of unknown cause (especially if you are a menstruating woman), change to a low-fat diet free of dairy products. Try to detect and correct any chronic disease processes. Iron supplements may offer additional benefit early in treatment. If your anemia is caused by distance running, find another sport.

ARTHRITIS

STANDARD PRACTICE

Arthritis is an inflammation of the joints. The cause is unknown, except for the type known as gout which, in susceptible people, is caused by foods rich in purines (present in foods commonly thought of as high in proteins, such as meats and organ meats). For other forms of arthritis, if you consult most doctors you will be told, "We don't know the cause, but diet has nothing to do with it," and "High-tech, powerful drugs will relieve your pains (if you are able to tolerate them)."

Current Treatment: Many kinds of drugs to suppress inflammation and reduce pain and swelling.

Drawbacks: A recent paper reported the data from a long-term study of the treatment of rheumatoid arthritis patients with the most powerful drugs currently available (gold salts, penicillamine, chloroquine, prednisone, and certain cytotoxic drugs). The investigators found that after twenty years of study, half the patients were either dead or severely disabled. The idea that drugs induce remissions was described as "fallacious." Modern drug therapy often contributes to the misery and early death of the arthritis patient. Many serious side effects and high costs are associated with drug therapy. Some medications will reduce pain and swelling but, over the long haul, most drugs are simply failures for victims of arthritis.

Another recent study has shown that popular nonsteroidal, anti-inflammatory arthritis drugs which inhibit the activity of the hormones called prostaglandins can actually cause osteoarthritis to progress more quickly—destroying more joint tissue than would be lost without the medication. Examples of prostaglandin-inhibiting drugs include aspirin, Indocin, Meclomen, Motrin, Nalfon, Naprosyn, Rufen, and Tolectin.

I have often been told (by other physicians) that patients seeking a dietary approach such as mine are harmed because they are deprived of the benefits of "sound medical therapy." On the contrary—arthritis is one of the many conditions in which the standard practice of medicine may best be avoided or at least accepted with great caution and understanding of its limitations. It is important that you understand what current therapies have to offer you—and how they can fail you.

The McDougall Program (Dietary and Lifestyle Implications)

Many aggressive and crippling forms of severe arthritis, including rheumatoid arthritis, ankylosing spondylitis, psoriatic arthritis, and systemic lupus, are grouped together as "inflammatory arthritis." Their cause is generally held to be unknown. *But*, consider these facts: Inflammatory arthritis is much more common among people of countries where rich foods are eaten, such as the United States, Canada, Western Europe, Australia, and New Zealand. In parts of the world (including most of Asia and Africa) where people eat little meat and few dairy products, where grains, vegetables, and fruits make up most of the diet, rheumatoid arthritis, ankylosing spondylitis, psoriatic arthritis, and lupus arthritis are very rare. In the few individuals in whom an arthritis does occur, the disease is mild and not crippling.

This difference is not explained by genetics, or heredity. When people migrate from Asia and Africa to the United States—and subsequently learn to eat the rich American foods—arthritis becomes common and severe among them and their offspring. In third-world countries where industrialization has brought wealth to some people along with "foods fit for kings," arthritis has become common and debilitating among the privileged folk who indulge in those rich delectables.

One way in which things we eat can cause arthritis is by contributing to the formation of persistent "immune complexes," in which animal proteins, especially those from dairy sources, enter the bloodstream and combine there with specific antibodies *produced against them*. In most people these complexes would be "eaten up" by "scavenger cells" found in the liver, the spleen, and along the lining of blood vessels, and would quickly be removed from the bloodstream. However, in the unfortunate victims of arthritis these complexes persist, and are not removed by scavenger cells. Eventually, they are filtered out of the bloodstream by the capillaries traversing the tissues of the joints. There, imbedded in the tiny blood vessels of the joint tissues, these complexes act much like slivers of wood stuck under the skin, causing severe inflammation of the joints.

One reason these immune complexes persist may be that the activity of the scavenger cells has been inhibited by a high-fat, high-cholesterol diet. Another explanation is that the influx of animal proteins into the bloodstream from the gut may be so great that the guarding mechanisms of the immune system are overwhelmed. (In a few people, some plant proteins can also be the source of these complexes.)

Osteoarthritis, or degenerative arthritis, is described as a normal part of aging—"wear and tear arthritis," it is called. By the age of fifty-five, essentially everyone in developed countries, where rich foods are part of the daily fare, has this form of arthritis to some degree. But in underdeveloped Asian and African countries, even though people work hard throughout life, their joints remain flexible and pain-free, and osteoarthritis is a much less common problem. Osteoarthritis is reversible to a certain extent. People can become pain-free by changing their diet, but any deformity that has been created will last forever unless surgery can help to correct it.

Current Treatment: The medical literature contains many documented cases of people dramatically improved and even cured of severe, progressive inflammatory arthritis after they changed their diet. The actual percentage of people who would be benefited by a better diet is not known, because such studies have not been done. It's sad to say and hard to admit, but proper studies will be a long time in coming, because there is no profit in healing people with advice about changing the kinds of foods they eat. However, from my experience, I would estimate that the majority of those patients who are suffering with inflammatory arthritis will unquestionably be benefited in a few short weeks. Many are undeniably *cured*. Loss of weight in the obese arthritic patient has the obvious benefit of reducing wear and tear on the body's weight-bearing joints. But the health benefits of a change in diet are far more than those related to simple weight loss.

My Recommendations: The diet that supports the health of the joints and dramatically reduces the destructive activity of inflammatory arthritis offers no animal products and almost no kinds of fats and oils. (Such a diet will also prevent arthritis from developing.) In some people, eliminating certain highly allergenic plant foods, such as wheat, corn, and citrus fruits, is also important. Benefits are usually seen within a few days. If such benefits are not clearly evident within three weeks, then I start my patients on an elimination diet (see ALLERGIC DISEASES).

(For more information on arthritis, see my book *McDougall's Medicine—A Challenging Second Opinion*. New Century Publishers Inc., Piscataway, N.J., 1985.)

ATHEROSCLEROSIS

STANDARD PRACTICE

Atherosclerosis, the clogging of the arteries with an accumulation of fatty deposits, is the leading—in fact, almost the exclusive—cause of heart attacks and strokes in the United States. It also causes hearing loss, kidney failure, impotency, and gangrene of the lower extremities. Atherosclerosis itself is caused by a combination of heredity, diet, lack of exercise, psychological stresses, and smoking. The diet believed to cause this disease of arteries is high in fats and cholesterol. The medical profession is divided on the identity of the most important culprit—heredity or diet. A few doctors say that smoking is the real villain.

Current Treatment: Three forms of surgery: bypass surgery, to detour around the severely diseased segments in the arteries supplying the heart; balloon angioplasty, to fragment and push aside partial blockages of arteries due to atherosclerotic plaques; and endarterectomy, to remove the inside lining in a diseased segment of an artery. Lowering the cholesterol level with diet and drugs is a therapy being used more frequently, but many physicians still do not know that atherosclerosis is a reversible disease.

Drawbacks: Although the *surgical procedures* do relieve symptoms such as chest pain, they result in little or no improvement in survival rates for the patients and they are also dangerous: Some patients die during surgery or soon afterward. Drugs given to relieve symptoms of heart pain do only that—and fail to prolong lives. Cholesterol-lowering drugs have been partially effective in reversal of atherosclerosis, and in prolonging lives, but they must be taken for a long time, are costly, and produce some unwanted side effects.

The McDougall Program (Dietary and Lifestyle Implications)

Heredity may play a role in the development of atherosclerosis and associated complications (heart attacks and strokes), but little attention should be given to this factor when planning therapy. First of all, heredity is obviously not an overriding factor, since whole populations of people in the non-American world (as in most Asian and African countries) show no clinical evidence of atherosclerosis and do not suffer heart attacks or strokes. Their genes are *not* protecting them—if they change to an American diet, they soon develop this disease in epidemic proportions, just as Americans do. The second reason heredity should be given little or no attention is the obvious one: You can't do a thing about it. However, you *can* control the amount of cholesterol and fats you eat, the buildup of which forms the plaques that clog the arteries.

Current Treatment: An atherosclerotic plaque is not made of concrete; it can be removed. When you start controlling your knife and fork, keeping them from scooping up gobs of grease and clumps of cholesterol-filled fats, you stop promoting the disease. Soon, with such restraint on your part, more cholesterol leaves your arteries than enters them. The plaques shrink and the artery walls strengthen. The risk of tragedy to you from a ruptured blood vessel or a blocked artery is diminished almost overnight.

To reduce the risk to your health and to hasten the progress of your recovery, focus your attention on the amount of cholesterol you eat each day and the cholesterol level in your circulating blood. Estimates by respected doctors say that when a person's cholesterol level has fallen by 65 mg/dl, then reversal of his atherosclerosis has probably begun. (People on the McDougall Program drop an average 28 mg/dl in only twelve days, and some individuals drop 100 mg/dl or more in this short time.) And consider this optimistic prediction: When elevated cholesterol levels fall to 150 mg/dl or less, almost everyone will have turned the tide on blood vessel closure and be reversing atherosclerosis. (Many people on the McDougall Program attain this ideal easily with diet alone; a few need the additional help of cholesterol-lowering drugs.)

It is never too late to start. During World War II, when rich foods almost disappeared from civilian markets in Western Europe, people there had no choice but to eat simpler fare, lower in fats and cholesterol, and their rates of death from heart disease began to decrease very quickly. This rapid fall occurred for people in every decade of life, including elders over the age of eighty, who were undoubtedly already suffering from advanced atherosclerosis acquired in the well-fed years before the war.

My Recommendations: A low-fat, no-cholesterol diet. Monitor your progress by how you feel, by your improved physical activity and reduced chest pains, and by laboratory tests to measure your blood cholesterol values (ideally 150 mg/dl or less). Take time for regular moderate exercise. Use surgery and drugs to control symptoms only as a last resort. (For a more detailed discussion, see my book *McDougall's Medicine—A Challenging Second Opinion.* New Century Publishers, Piscataway, N.J., 1985.)

CANCER

STANDARD PRACTICE

Cancer can be caused by smoking, alcohol, diet, carcinogenic chemicals, radiation, certain viruses, and heredity. A very few scientists still doubt the primary role of diet in causing cancer.

Current Treatment: Chemotherapy, radiation, and surgery.

Drawbacks: In the United States, almost 450,000 people each year die from cancer, making it the second leading cause of death. During the last twenty years the death rate from cancer has increased by nearly 9 percent. More than 60 percent of all such deaths are from cancers of the lung, colon, breast, prostate, pancreas, and ovary. The death rates from these six kinds of cancer have either increased or stayed the same during the past fifty-five years, a grim testimony to the undeniable failure of the drug/radiation/surgical therapies that are prescribed currently for combating most cancers.

Only a few of the less common forms of cancer, many of these limited to children have been cured by therapy. Most forms, unfortunately, are largely beyond the reach of any kind of effective treatment. Moreover, the treatments are often debilitating and mutilating, with little or no benefit toward survival or greater comfort of body. And the financial burden for a cancer victim's family is usually devastating, with total national costs amounting to more than 35 billion dollars annually.

The McDougall Program (Diet and Lifestyle Implications)

Advice about a practical way of preventing cancer by controlling diet was presented by the Senate Select Committee on Nutrition and Human Needs in 1977, the National Cancer Institute in 1979, the National Academy of Sciences in 1982, the American Cancer Society in 1984, and the Surgeon General of the United States in 1988. These reports agree that we should cut down our intake of meats, dairy products, and fats from all sources (including vegetable oils), and that we should increase the amount of grains, fresh fruits, and vegetables in our diets. The amount by which we should reduce the meats, dairy products, and oils and increase the grains, vegetables, and fruits is the only point of confusion. For me, telling people to cut their daily fat intake from 40 percent to 30 percent in order to reduce their risk of getting colon, breast, and prostate cancer makes as little sense as telling smokers to cut down from thirty cigarettes to twenty per day in order to reduce their risk of developing lung cancer. *All* of the excess fats should be eliminated for best results—and the best results come from being content with just the fats that are present naturally in starches, vegetables, and fruits. The fats from these sources amount to less than 10 percent of the diet's total calorie count—and are more than adequate to meet the body's needs without being a cancer-causing burden.

Knowing how a typical cancer grows will help you to understand why early detection and treatment are so difficult and thus why attention to prevention is so important. Normal healthy cells of the body live in a neighborly manner. Cells are created in an orderly way, next to each other, and divide only when adjacent cells die. A cancer cell, however, loses this kind of self-control: It divides without any regard at all for the cells that surround it, pushing them aside to form the swelling lump that is the tumor, as it grows, and grows, and grows.

The transformation of a normal cell to a cancer cell is caused by some kind of injury—from harmful agents in cigarette smoke perhaps, or from radiation or toxic chemicals. The receiver of this injury, the single initial cancer cell, divides into two cells, after about a hundred days (on the average). The next division, about a hundred days later, produces four cells. After a year or so, as few as twelve maverick cells can make up an entire cancer. This nest of microscopic cells would take even a dedicated pathologist a lifetime to find, hiding somewhere in your body's organs and tissues. The doubling of cells continues until, after about six years, the cancerous lump contains about one million cells. Now the cancer is a little larger than the size of a period on this page, about a millimeter in diameter. Neither X-rays, specialized mammography, radioactive scans, nor careful palpation can find a tumor this small.

By this time—after six years of existence, a tumor consisting of a million cells, the whole a millimeter in size—cancer cells growing in the tissues of colon, breast, prostate, or lung (as well as in most other solid tumors) have broken out of the initial lump, entered the neighboring blood vessels, and traveled through the bloodstream to other parts of the body. This kind of breaking out happens in more than 90 percent of cases. Some of these migrating cells then establish themselves in normal tissues, and start new tumors wherever they lodge. This process of spreading throughout the body is called *metastasis*, and metastatic cancers grow at about the same rate as did the original tumor, doubling in size and number of cells about every hundred days, on the average.

After about ten years of growth, the first tumor reaches a size that is detectable by present-day techniques—the cancerous lump is now the size of a small marble, consisting of at least a billion cells. Then, in wild alarm on the part of everyone involved, the patient is rushed off to the operating room to save his or her life "by getting it all in time." The unfortunate patient has been host to his cancer for ten years, and only heaven knows how many metastases have been spun off during that decade. But he's given not even a minute to think about and choose among the options of therapy that are available to him.

Current Treatment: Knowing these facts relating to cancer, and the odds against ever being able to eradicate it successfully, allows you to understand the importance of preventing the disease from beginning in the first place. Only prevention can reduce the incidence of cancer in our population, just as prevention (not treatment) has been the prime factor that finally controlled so many other deadly diseases, such as tuberculosis, malaria, scurvy, and cholera.

Most knowledgeable people now believe that our rich American diet is an important factor in causing cancers of the breast, colon, prostate, and other organs. (Even the incidence of lung cancer, connected as closely as it is with smoking cigarettes, is influenced by the amount of fats in a smoker's diet.) It seems probable, therefore, that in individuals who are already stricken with cancer, the further growth of the tumor could be slowed and life could be prolonged if they switched to the opposite of a cancer-provoking diet. There's no sense in "throwing gasoline on the fire," you will agree.

Proper changes in diet and lifestyle definitely offer improvements in the quality of a cancer victim's life and, I believe, will also add to the quantity of life for such a person. Could five years' expected survival time (the usual common statistical expectation for victims of many of the major cancers who receive treatment of one kind or another) be lengthened to ten or fifteen years by improving the health of the patient?

Understanding the natural growth processes of cancers will help you to avoid unnecessary treatments that can disfigure and otherwise harm you. In most cases, because the disease has been present for more than ten years by the time of its discovery, all that can be justified scientifically is the removal of the obvious cancer—all of it. This means a lumpectomy for breast cancer, destruction by electrical "burning" for cancers of the lower bowel, and other limited procedures for other kinds of cancers, so as to leave the patient's appearance and functioning as normal as possible.

My Recommendations: Prevention is the only approach possible today to "win the war on cancer." Choose minimal therapy to control obvious disease (unless you have one of those rare cancers that does offer a chance to gain dramatic benefits from therapy). Limited surgery is almost always best (such as a lumpectomy). Chemotherapy for most cancers is still either experimental or has *proved* to be of limited or no benefit. Furthermore, it has serious adverse side effects, and such toxic therapy is best avoided unless proof of benefit is well established. I believe that breast cancer patients benefit from an anti-estrogen drug (Tamoxifen). In all kinds of cancers, you should change to a healthier diet, if for no other reason than to keep yourself as healthy as possible—both to fight against the cancer and to withstand the debilitating side effects of any proposed treatments.

You should make an effort to be well informed about any and all treatments your doctor may propose. Cancer treatment is a big business, run by doctors presiding in a world of hopes and dreams. You need to know the facts in order to protect yourself and your family from potentially harmful therapies. Of course, you must locate valuable therapy if it is available. Ask to see the scientific studies of any suggested treatment. Then go to the nearest big library or call a medical research service and arrange for a computer-generated search for information about your specific cancer and the treatment proposed (cost for this service ranges from nothing to $50). As a general rule, the burden of proof rests upon those physicians who recommend mutilating, debilitating, painful, and expensive therapies. Make your doctor prove the advantage of his proposed treatment over simpler treatments or no treatment at all. (For more help, read my book *McDougall's Medicine—A Challenging Second Opinion*. New Century Publishers Inc., Piscataway, N.J., 1985.)

CHOLESTEROL, HIGH

STANDARD PRACTICE

Cholesterol is a fatlike substance our bodies use in the manufacture of cell walls, bile acids, sex hormones, and vitamin D. Our bodies make plenty of cholesterol for our needs. However, we get additional cholesterol in the animal foods (eggs, meats, poultry, fish, milk) we consume, and this cholesterol is readily absorbed from the intestinal tract. Our problems develop because our bodies can excrete only limited amounts of this substance. The amounts in excess of what our bodies need are accumulated in certain body tissues, such as the linings of arteries, the skin, abdominal organs, and deposits of body fat. The degree of accumulation is reflected in the level of cholesterol present in our circulating blood.

A high level of cholesterol in the blood is not a disease in itself, but it is a condition that leads to atherosclerosis and heart disease. The majority of doctors today believe that an inherited predisposition and a high-fat, high-cholesterol diet are the causes of this condition, but there is disagreement about what a "normal" cholesterol level should be. Most hospital laboratories until 1985 reported "normal" as 150 mg/dl to 350 mg/dl. More recent recommendations are calling for levels at the lower end of this range. I'm bewildered about what the health profession's *true* feelings about and understanding of the importance of cholesterol really are, because the dietary departments in every major hospital in the country still serve high-cholesterol foods to their ailing patients.

A high cholesterol level is sometimes a genetic fault, found in about one person in 500. People with this condition often die of heart attacks while in their twenties, thirties, or early forties.

Current Treatment: Switch to chicken and fish from beef and pork; change to low-fat milk; take oat bran or niacin, and cholesterol-lowering medications such as cholestyramine and lovastatin.

Drawbacks: Switching from beef and pork to chicken and fish will do very little to lower cholesterol levels because all these meats contain about the same amount of cholesterol. Studies on people who have made this switch consistently show that the resulting change in blood cholesterol levels is insignificant. You should also know that saturated fats tend to raise cholesterol levels. Saturated fats are found in animal products like meats, milk, and cheeses and also in coconut, chocolate, and hydrogenated oils (in shortening and margarines). People trying to avoid cholesterol are often fooled by "hidden" quantities of lard and butter put into breads, pastries, refried beans, and many other prepared foods that they assume are "vegetarian."

Switching from saturated fats (animal fats) to polyunsaturated fats (vegetable fats) will lower blood cholesterol and decrease your risk from heart disease, but there is a price to be paid. The polyunsaturated oils cause the liver to excrete more cholesterol with the bile into the gallbladder and then out into the intestinal tract. These fats cause a change in the consistency of the bile which may account for an increase in incidence of gallbladder disease that has been found when people are switched from animal fats to vegetable fats. Higher rates of cancer, especially colon cancer, may result from a change to a diet that is predominantly polyunsaturated fats. The cholesterol and bile acids excreted in the colon in larger amounts because of the polyunsaturated fats in the diet may be turned into cancer-causing substances (carcinogens) by bowel bacteria, or act as substances that enhance the cancer-promoting properties of other chemicals (co-carcinogens).

Drugs given to lower cholesterol levels are useful in this respect, but they have side effects and are costly, and if you stop taking them your cholesterol level rises again.

The McDougall Program (Dietary and Lifestyle Implications)

The American diet is the real culprit. A cholesterol level of 210 mg/dl is the average for people living in industrialized countries; this level predicts a 50 percent chance of premature death from strokes or heart attacks due to atherosclerosis. A rise in cholesterol level from 200 mg/dl to 260 mg/dl increases the risk of death fivefold. People with levels below 180 mg/dl during their lifetime rarely have heart disease; and in the famous Framingham study on the relationship between heart disease and cholesterol levels, *coronary heart disease was not observed in those whose cholesterol* *level was below 150 mg/dl.** Each 1 percent decrease in cholesterol is represented by a 2 to 3 percent decrease in the risk of dying from heart disease. Based on all I know, I would set a goal for you of less than 150 mg/dl.

Cholesterol Predicts Risk of Death from Heart Disease:

Blood Level of Cholesterol (mg/dl)	*Risk of Atherosclerosis*
150	Virtually None
210	Average (for Americans)
265	Very High

Some studies show that coffee, even decaf, will increase the cholesterol level by an average of 10 percent. More sensitive individuals will show even greater rises in response to these beverages.

Current Treatment: I treat my patients by a two-step approach. My goal is to get cholesterol levels down below 150 mg/dl safely, and as soon as possible.

Step 1 is a no-cholesterol, low-fat, starch-based diet. A low-fat, no-cholesterol diet will reduce cholesterol levels by an average of 12 percent (28 mg/dl) in twelve days and a total 25 to 37 percent in four to six weeks. There are several components of this healthier diet that lower blood cholesterol. Cholesterol intake is reduced from 400 to 600 mg or more a day to none. Saturated fat, which raises blood cholesterol, is dramatically reduced from 30 to 40 percent of the total calories to less than 2 percent. Dietary fiber, which binds and removes cholesterol, is increased from 10 grams daily on the typical American diet to 60 grams.

Step 2 is cholesterol-lowering drugs. I have been prescribing cholesterol-lowering medications for those people who are not able to reach the ideal of 150 mg/dl or less by diet alone. If the person has a history of artery disease (past heart attack, bypass surgery, angioplasty, TIA, stroke, etc.), then I am even more devoted to lowering their cholesterol quickly in an effort to reduce the risk of a tragedy. The decision boils down to this question: *Does the risk of death and disability due to artery disease exceed the side effects, costs, and inconvenience of taking cholesterol-lowering medication?* There is no clear-cut answer—incomplete studies and research information, judgment, and guesswork lead to a course of action.

---

* Researchers have observed 5,209 people living in Framingham, Massachusetts, for nearly forty years.

Summary of Effects and Costs:

	Percent cholesterol-lowering after 6 weeks of therapy	Cost / day
Cholestyramine	5–20	$2.96 (4 scoops)
Colestipol	5–20	$2.40 (4 scoops)
Gemfibrozil	5–15	$1.90 (1200 mg)
Lovastatin	20–32	$3.20 (40 mg)
Niacin	15–30	$0.60 (3000 mg)
Oat Bran*	10–20	$0.42 (1 cup)
Psyllium	5–10	$0.75 (3 teaspoons)
Probucol	10–15	$2.00 (1000 mg)

* Based on consumption of ⅔ to 1½ cup dry weight oat bran / day.

CHOLESTEROL-LOWERING AGENTS

Cholestyramine (Questran) combines with bile acids and cholesterol in the intestine to form an insoluble complex which is excreted with the feces. The total and LDL ("bad") cholesterol are lowered.
Side Effects: Constipation is common (⅓ of patients), followed by abdominal discomfort, gas, and nausea. Rarely, a bleeding tendency from vitamin K deficiency.
Dosage: Two to six scoops (or packages) a day, based on tolerance of side effects.
Cost: Powder in cans is much cheaper than packages—Can 378 g (42 scoops) for $31; 60 (4 g) packages for $66; Cholebars 25 (4 g) for $36. Prescription required.
Colestipol (Colestid) works like cholestyramine, and has similar side effects.
Dosage: Three to six packages a day.
Cost: Can (500 g) for $60; 30 (5 g) packages for $29. Prescription required.
Gemfibrozil (Lopid) lowers serum lipids (fats), primarily by lowering triglycerides with variable reduction in cholesterol. HDL ("good") cholesterol may be increased. Action may be by decreasing breakdown of fats, and by slight increase in cholesterol excretion.
Side Effects: Mostly intestinal disturbances such as abdominal pain, diarrhea, and nausea. Also fatigue, joint pains, abnormal liver tests.
Dosage: 600 mg twice a day.
Cost: 100 (300 mg) for $48; 60 (600 mg) for $55. Prescription required.
Lovastatin (Mevacor) causes a decrease in production and an increase in the breakdown of cholesterol, especially LDL cholesterol. HDL cholesterol is increased.

Side Effects: Lovastatin is generally well tolerated, with only 1 to 2 percent of people stopping medication due to side effects. Mild abdominal distress occurs in about 5 percent of people; headaches in 9 percent. About 2 percent of people suffer an elevation of liver function tests greater than three times normal levels (the medicine must be stopped, then the tests return to normal). Liver enzymes should be checked before therapy and every six weeks for the first fifteen months of therapy. Should not be combined with niacin, gemfibrozil, or immunosuppressive drugs because of the potential for serious adverse effects.

Dosage: 20 mg to 80 mg / day in a single or divided dose.

Cost: 60 (20 mg) for $95; 60 (40 mg) for $183. Prescription required.

Niacin (vitamin B₃) lowers cholesterol and triglycerides. It works by causing a decrease in release of fatty acids into the bloodstream from fat stores, and it reduces the liver synthesis of triglycerides and cholesterol. Niacin can be bought in health food stores, drugstores, and supermarkets without a prescription. Niacinamide (another form of niacin) will not lower cholesterol or triglycerides.

Side Effects: Flushing, GI distress, malaise, and fatigue. May worsen diabetes by increasing blood sugar, raise uric acid levels and aggravate peptic ulcers. It can cause drug-induced hepatitis, middle ear disease and eye problems (macular edema.) Liver function tests should be checked periodically while on niacin. Symptoms of flushing are reduced by taking "time-release" capsule, taking niacin with meals, and taking aspirin ½ hour before dose. You should be under doctor's supervision if you're treating cholesterol with this drug.

Dosage: Begin with low dosage of 250-mg time-release capsules twice a day and build dosage to 3000 mg / day based upon tolerance of side effects. Some people take 6000 mg / day.

Cost: 100 (500 mg) time-release capsules for $9.

Oat Bran is a natural water-soluble fiber which combines with bile acids and cholesterol in the intestine, causing them to leave with the feces rather than be reabsorbed. Soluble fibers are found in all plant foods, but are abundant in oats and beans. Oat bran requires no prescription. Purchase in grocery store.

Side Effects: Abdominal discomfort and gas due to the fiber.

Dosage: ½ to 2 cups dry weight / day divided dosages.

Cost: In bulk $1.69 / pound; packaged $1.84 / pound.

Psyllium (Metamucil and generic brands) works like oat bran, and has similar side effects. Purchase in drugstore without prescription.

Dosage: Three rounded teaspoons / day; 1 teaspoon mixed in 8 oz. of water three times a day.

Cost: 7 oz. (28 teaspoons) for $7 (Metamucil), and 14 oz. (54 teaspoons) for $7 (generic).

Probucol (Lorelco) lowers cholesterol without lowering triglycerides. Lowers HDL cholesterol. Acts by increasing the breakdown of cholesterol and also slightly inhibits synthesis and absorption of cholesterol.

Side Effects: Diarrhea, gas, heart (EKG) changes, headaches, rash, etc.
Dosage: 500 mg twice a day.
Cost: 120 (250 mg) for $60; 100 (500 mg) for $90. Prescription required.

My Recommendations: A no-cholesterol, low-fat, starch-based diet is the foundation of your care. I also suggest oat bran for everyone in need of lower cholesterol who can tolerate it, because it is cheap, safe, over-the-counter, and effective. Check your cholesterol every three weeks; if after three to six months your cholesterol level has not decreased sufficiently, and especially if your risk is high, I often recommend adding drugs (if you have carefully considered the possible risks and benefits of drug therapy).

For those people looking for a more natural and also inexpensive approach, niacin (vitamin B₃) is effective. But you must remember that niacin is a powerful drug with lots of side effects. For those people able to afford and willing to take prescription drugs, I like lovastatin and cholestyramine. With many patients, especially those with serious artery disease and high cholesterol levels, I use lovastatin (which lowers cholesterol synthesis) along with cholestyramine or colestipol (which remove cholesterol). This combined therapy is even more effective than either alone. Patients given lovastatin 20 mg and colestipol 10 g (both) twice a day had a 36 percent decrease in cholesterol (48 percent decrease in LDL cholesterol) in two months.

Once you find a mediction schedule that will lower your cholesterol to the ideal of 150 mg/dl (without significant side effects), then I recommend you stay on this dosage for six months. After six months you should try reducing one medication at a time and see if your cholesterol remains ideal. (Be careful. You can lower cholesterol too much—less than 100 mg/dl—*with drugs* and this may cause problems with the metabolic processes that use cholesterol.) Your goal is to take as little medication as possible to achieve the desired effects.

COLITIS, MILD (SPASTIC COLITIS)

STANDARD PRACTICE

Colitis is a nonspecific term used to characterize irritation and inflammation of the large intestine, and is usually accompanied by lower abdominal pain, loose stools, and sometimes blood and mucus in the stools. The condition can be minor and of short duration, or it can be a severe and prolonged life-threatening condition. Severe colitis is discussed separately, below.

Mild, nonspecific colitis involves the superficial inner lining of the large intestine and may be simply the result of temporary irritation from spicy foods, such as hot chili peppers. A chronic form of mild colitis is spastic colitis, also known as spastic colon and irritable bowel syndrome. This is the most common bowel disorder seen by clinicians in the general practice of medicine. Stools are small in caliber, often frequent, and accompanied by mucus. Lower abdominal pain is common, and intermittent diarrhea and constipation may occur. The medical education system teaches young physicians that usually the cause of this bowel disorder is emotional distress such as is common among middle-aged women. The wrong diet is rarely mentioned.

Current Treatment: The treatment that most doctors give most patients with spastic colitis is to reassure them that the condition will not lead to anything more serious, along with the disheartening conclusion that more than likely it will stay with them forever because it cannot be cured. Treatment with medication is recommended, depending upon which symptoms happen to need relief at the time of consultation. Laxatives, bulking agents, antispasmodics, tranquilizers, sedatives, and antidiarrheal compounds are commonly prescribed. The motto "When all else fails, send the patient to the psychiatrist," is often invoked with frustrating bowel problems that persist.

Drawbacks: Drug treatment at best only quiets the symptoms; it never cures the patient of this troublesome disorder. Side effects and costs of drugs are significant. Most often, even with all those medications, the patient suffers continued bowel distress, and suffers side effects from the drugs as well.

The McDougall Program (Diet and Lifestyle Implications)

The contents of the bowel are the primary determinant of the health and function of the intestine, and a spastic colon is no exception to this rule. Few physicians have even an elementary understanding of the influence that foods can have on the body; they are unprepared to deal with health and disease from this fundamental perspective.

Possibly it is too simple and obvious a fact that the contents of the large intestine will determine whether or not the stool will be large or small, hard or soft, and if defecation will be painful or not, and whether or not blood and mucus will accompany passage of the stool. (This is a clear case of not seeing the forest for the trees.) Could the fear that the very foods the physicians and dietitians themselves eat and feed to their families can also be the cause of their patient's illness be too personal a threat for most health professionals? The high-tech drug solution seems to be much more easy to accept for most men and women of science.

The correct stool contents that make a healthy colon are what remains after the digestive processes have acted upon foods high in fibers and low in fats, and devoid of all animal components (especially dairy products). Fibers will actually soothe the irritated bowel. They resist normal digestion by enzymes in the human small intestine, and therefore end up more or less intact in the large bowel. The intestinal bacteria in the colon do have the capacity to break down some of the linkages in those fibers, and the microscopic remnants are soft, not irritating to the intestinal lining, and will absorb water to help form a soft stool that still has considerable bulk.

Most people with irritable bowel syndrome improve almost as soon as they begin to eat a starch-based diet that provides all types of fresh or fresh-frozen plant foods.

My Recommendations: Don't you take the blame for having this disease. The cause is not stress or "tranquilizer deficiency." Your bowel problems are not due to your emotional make-up (although unending bowel pains and diarrhea can drive even the strongest person to emotional collapse). Rather, you should focus your attention on the contents of your intestine. A starch-centered diet brings almost overnight relief for this "psychological" disease.

In the beginning, you should eat a large amount of these good foods in order to fill up the lower intestine with the right stuff quickly. However, an occasional sufferer will need to avoid the specific plant foods that may be causing an allergic reaction. Plant foods notorious for inducing "allergic-type" reactions are wheat and citrus fruits, and they should be avoided initially when trying to end bowel distress. As a final step toward resolving a difficult case of irritable bowel syndrome, an elimination diet should be followed (see ALLERGIC DISEASES). Some patients may need medication to control symptoms when first starting the elimination diet.

If your colitis is triggered by "hot spices" such as Mexican salsa or Indian curries, then the solution is obvious—eliminate these irritants.

COLITIS, SEVERE
(INFLAMMATORY BOWEL DISEASE)

STANDARD PRACTICE

Colitis is a nonspecific term used to characterize irritation and inflammation of the large intestine. Mild colitis, which involves the superficial lining of the large intestine, is discussed separately above. More severe colitis conditions, called inflammatory bowel disease, involve the deeper layers of the colon and can adversely affect the entire body. *Crohn's disease* (also known as regional enteritis) and *ulcerative colitis* are inflammatory diseases of the bowel that have many similarities. Symptoms are characterized primarily by severe abdominal pain and frequent diarrhea with blood and mucus. Usually these bowel diseases are accompanied by generalized ailments involving the entire body, followed by skin changes, liver disease, and arthritis—especially as the basic condition progresses to become more severe. The cause is unknown; possibly genetic, infectious, or immunologic, with psychological overtones.

Current Treatment: Drugs, including steroids, corticosteroid enemas, Azulfidine (sulfasalazine), psychotherapy, and surgery. Psychotherapy is recommended because many physicians are convinced that emotional-mental disturbances can be internalized to affect the bowel adversely, thereby creating the inflammatory disease. Meanwhile, the likelihood of curing severe colitis through psychotherapy varies from zero to slight. Unfortunately, the standard diet that physicians recommend, essentially one low in fiber with lots of milk, is not much different from the usual menu the patient is already following.

Drawbacks: Even with the best of current medical care, 75 percent of patients experience relapses, and the prognosis may be so poor that as some studies show, victims have less than a 50 percent chance of surviving fifteen years after the onset of the disease. Furthermore, 25 percent of patients with ulcerative colitis require removal of the colon (a colectomy) and attachment of the small intestine to an orifice opened in the abdominal wall (an ileostomy). The decision to remove the colon usually is made because the disease is so severe that it does not respond to any kind of therapy or else requires dangerous amounts of steroid medication in order to keep it under reasonable control. In 10 percent of patients the colon is removed because of the occurrence of precancerous changes or the actual development of colon cancer.

The McDougall Program (Dietary and Lifestyle Implications)

Inflammatory bowel diseases occur almost exclusively in parts of the world where the diet is high in meat and dairy foods, and are rare in countries where people still consume starch-based, almost entirely vegetarian meals. Severe "allergic-type" reactions to some of those rich foods have been suspected as being the causes of these conditions.

Some clustering of cases in a family occurs, which is consistent with the fact that we learn our food preferences from our parents. Wealthy people in many parts of the world are noted for their high susceptibility to diseases that are common in affluent societies, and they rank at the top in incidence for both types of inflammatory bowel disease, probably because of the rich foods that affluent people eat.

Current Treatment: Bowel contents must be changed continually in order to get long-lasting significant improvement. The simple increase of the fiber content in the foods eaten has been shown to reduce the frequency of attacks and to improve symptoms in many patients. A starch-based diet, which is inherently high in fiber, is highly effective at alleviating the distress from this condition.

One step further in effective therapy is to avoid the foods that most often cause allergies—dairy products, eggs, chocolate, wheat, and citrus fruits, as well as fats of all kinds. If this approach is not successful, the final step toward treatment is to use an elimination diet (see ALLERGIC DISEASES).

An important study was performed with Crohn's disease patients who had been suffering from severe diarrhea for many years, with twenty stools or more per day. The subjects were changed from a high-fat diet to one low in fats and this gave relief from the frequent watery stools within two to three days. Most patients continued to form solid bowel movements as long as they kept the animal and vegetable fats out of their diet.

A person with a functioning healthy small intestine reabsorbs the bile secreted from the liver in the last part of the small intestine, called the ileum. In patients with Crohn's disease, this portion of the ileum often is damaged and unable to absorb the bile. Bile continues to flow along the ileum into the large intestine, where it causes irritation and discharge of mucus and water. In these patients the immediate benefit from a change in diet is the decrease in bile acids produced by the liver as a response to lowering the fat content of the foods eaten. In addition, the fibers introduced in a plant-based diet bind and neutralize many of the bile acids and absorb free water present in the stool.

The benefits of a dietary approach for ulcerative colitis patients are equally dramatic. A large series of patients improved, and many were actually cured of this serious condition simply by removing milk (dairy proteins) from their diet. Other investigators have approached this problem with the broader therapy of eliminating many sources of common food allergens, and have shown great success with their patients—and no side effects.

Another strong reason to change the diet of someone suffering from inflammatory bowel disease is that the high-fat, high-cholesterol, low-fiber American diet increases the risk of developing cancer of the colon. People with inflammatory bowel diseases are at greater risk than is the average American lucky enough to have a healthy intestinal tract.

For a person with Crohn's disease or ulcerative colitis, who must endure pain and diarrhea every day, the option of choosing a simple meal plan is not a difficult one, especially when the penalty for making the occasional mistake of submitting to temptation from a rich repast is so immediately evident.

My Recommendations : Patients who are very ill may need to be put on very simple diets, supplemented with some drugs until the bowel quiets down. As soon as the patient can eat regular foods comfortably, he should be started on a starch-centered diet without wheat or citrus fruits initially (later, these two kinds of plant foods may be tried). The elimination diet is the next approach for stubborn cases (see ALLERGIC DISEASES).

COLON POLYPS and COLON CANCER

STANDARD PRACTICE

Approximately 5 to 10 percent of our population more than forty years old has intestinal polyps of various kinds. By age seventy-five the figure reaches 50 percent. The noncancerous, hyperplastic type consists of an overgrowth of normal colon cells into a visible lump. Many investigators, but not all, believe that these are precancerous growths which in time turn into cancers. Adenomatous polyps are the kind most likely to develop into cancers. The cells making up these polyps no longer resemble normal colon cells. Approximately 5 percent of the adenomatous polyps contain cancer cells. The longer these polyps grow in the colon, the bigger they get, and the longer they are subjected to the influences that cause cancer in the first place. Therefore, the larger the polyp the greater is the chance of finding that it will be cancerous. Polyps less than 5 mm in diameter are not usually cancerous, but of those 10 mm in size, 1 percent are cancerous, and at 20 mm, 17 percent show cancerous changes. Estimates suggest that a polyp will develop into a cancer in from fifteen to twenty years.

Cancer of the colon will be found in about 138,000 Americans in any one year, and 60,000 will die from it during this year. This killer affects between 20 and 30 percent of the families in the United States and is our country's second leading cause of death from cancer. Eventually, 6 percent of our population—10 million Americans alive today—will die of colon cancer. The cause is unknown—possibly dietary.

Current Treatment: Early detection and removal of polyps is believed by many doctors to decrease the risk of future colon cancer. However, there is some disagreement on this point: Definitive studies have not yet been done to prove the benefits of removing polyps, especially when the risks and costs of surgical intervention are considered.

Drawbacks: Until the diet is changed, the cancer-causing substances (carcinogens) remain at high levels in the colon and continue to injure the colon lining. After removal of the first polyps, as many as 48 percent of the people so treated will develop new polyps, and 2.7 percent go on to develop colon cancer during the next decade. Even one year after the first removal, on reexamination approximately 30 percent of patients are found to have new polyps or older ones not detected on the first round.

Efforts to prolong a patient's survival by detecting colon cancer as early as is medically possible by searching for minute quantities of blood in stool specimens have been largely disappointing. Furthermore, the processes involved in looking for colon cancer create potential causes for serious harm: The discovery of blood in the feces leads to invasive and complex medical investigations (particularly colonoscopy), which are now recommended for all patients showing a positive blood test. These investigations are costly, and complications from injuries sustained during the examinations can harm otherwise healthy patients.

After the first cell in a polyp becomes cancerous, an average of ten years must pass before the cancer grows to a barely detectable size of about ½ inch. In almost all cases the disease is far advanced by the time the cancerous growth is discovered. This means that in a significant percentage of cases the cancer cells have already spread by way of the bloodstream to other parts of the body. When a cancer metastasizes in this manner, the probability that it will eventually kill its victim is vastly increased.

The McDougall Program (Dietary and Lifestyle Implications)

Worldwide, polyps in the colon are found commonly in populations with a high incidence of colon cancer. Both are believed to have the same cause—the diet. Common sense would suggest that the contents of the colon—the remnants of foods a person has eaten—would be highest on the suspect list. Colon cancer is found most frequently in wealthy countries, where people eat rich foods consisting predominantly of meats, poultry, fish, dairy products, vegetable oils, white bread and other refined grains, and highly processed foods. On the other hand, people following diets providing plentiful amounts of whole grains, vegetables, and fruits and with very little in the way of meats and dairy products develop few cases of colon cancer. When people move from a country of low incidence to a country of high incidence, their risk of developing colon cancer increases as they adopt the richer foods. This correlation shows the importance of environment, rather than of genetics, in the epidemiology of colon cancer.

In animal studies, cancer-causing chemicals, known as carcinogens, produce adenomatous polyps and colon cancers that seem to be identical to those present in human beings. Many kinds of carcinogens found in the intestinal contents result from eating the foods found in the American diet. Fats, especially beef fats, are degraded to yield cancer-causing substances in the colon. Other components of a diet that is high in animal proteins, cholesterol, polyunsaturated vegetable fats, and sugar while being low in vegetables and fibers also adversely affect the colon lining and contribute to development and growth of polyps and cancers.

Current Treatment: The key to preventing recurrences of polyps is to improve the contents of the colon by making a change in diet. Changing to a low-fat, no-cholesterol diet rapidly and dramatically reduces the total amount of carcinogens released in the colon; an increase in fibers dilutes the few dangerous substances that do remain and shields the colon from their harmful effects; and an increase in vegetables—especially broccoli, cauliflower, Brussels sprouts, turnips, and leafy greens—causes the colon's cells to secrete enzymes that inactivate many carcinogens.

Surgical operations that divert the flow of feces away from the segment of the colon where polyps have formed have resulted in regression of the polyps. This finding clearly shows that polyps are reversible, and suggests that a stage in the transition of polyps toward the development of cancerous cells can be prevented. Studies should be made to determine if a low-fat, high-fiber diet—which is opposite to the one believed to be the cause of colon polyps and cancer—would result in similar regression. (A study in the 1989 *Journal of the National Cancer Institute* has demonstrated the benefits of diet on colon polyps.)

Patients who already have colon cancer should seriously consider a change in diet as a major part of therapy. Animal experiments show that diets high in fat and cholesterol promote the growth of several kinds of cancers and they further demonstrate that low-fat, no-cholesterol diets retard the growth of cancers and prolong the animal's life.

My Recommendations: Prevent polyps and colon cancer with a starch-based diet. If large polyps do form, then of course have them removed. If a cancerous polyp or actual tumor is found, surgery should be limited to removal of the obvious cancer. (Avoid blood transfusions, because they impair the immune system and dramatically decrease chances of survival.) After polyps or cancer of the colon have developed, a health-promoting diet is very important: It may check or slow further progress of either condition, and, in doing so, prolong your survival.

CONSTIPATION

STANDARD PRACTICE

Emotional, psychological, and developmental disorders are often blamed for constipation. These scapegoat excuses take such fancy explanations as "repressing the urge to defecate" and "poor toilet training as a child." Fatherly physicians advise such unyielding patients to "respond to the call of nature" and "to defecate at the same time each day," as ways to end constipation.

Current Treatment: Laxatives, stool softeners, and bulking agents, such as bran, Metamucil, and Fiber-al, in assorted combinations, are both self-administered and medically prescribed.

Drawbacks: Increasing dependency upon laxatives. Not only does laxative dependency repress the colon's natural ability to contract, but laxatives suppress important warning signs—constipation and the pain of defecation. Without those warnings, people continue to eat foods that really can cause serious health problems. The most effective solution, removing the cause of constipation by making a sensible change in diet, is rarely given adequate attention by practicing physicians and dietitians. Blatant evidence for this neglect is shown by the routine prescription for laxatives and stool softeners that is written on the admission orders for patients being hospitalized. This is the doctor's attempt to anticipate and compensate for the constipating hospital food.

The McDougall Program (Dietary and Lifestyle Implications)

More kinds of painful sufferings are located in the eight-foot segment of writhing tubing that constitutes the lower bowel than emanate from any other part of the body. Some of the problems are merely nuisances, while others are life-threatening, but the one thing that can be said for certain is that none of them need be tolerated as a "normal part of life."

Constipation means different things to different people. I have met people who tell me that they move their bowels only once in every six to twelve days, and then only with the help of a strong laxative, and they accept this pattern as normal because they know nothing else. Bowel activity associated with good health does vary considerably among "normal people." For some, a movement once every two days may be normal, and others may have three or more stools a day and be in perfect health. The criterion I use for deciding what is normal is that *the stool should be moderately soft and easy to pass without pain or strain.* The accumulation of feces between movements should not reach the point where severe bloating of the intestine and discomfort occur.

Constipation happens when the stool is hard, small (or "pelletized," so to speak), and requires physical effort before it is passed. Under such demands, the abdominal muscles must contract and a deep breath must be held as the diaphragm is forced downward. This creates strong internal abdominal pressures to help force the contents out of the colon. The additional force from straining is necessary because the pressure from the contraction of the colon walls is inadequate to evacuate the compacted fecal mass.

One unmistakable sign of this physical effort is that the muscles of the neck and face tense up as you strain to evacuate. If you could see it, you'd notice that your face turns red too. But most people don't realize that permanent and destructive changes result from these powerful muscle forces, even if they don't persist for very long.

Veins in your legs are damaged by the straining created by the muscular activity needed for a difficult bowel movement. Valves are located at frequent intervals along the course of the leg veins; they help the blood to rise to the heart, in a stepladder fashion, against the forces of gravity. These valves are stretched and damaged by the high pressures that are required to move small hard, dry stools. The valves soon become incapable of holding up the blood. Without valves in good working order, a four-foot column of blood presses on the lower veins all day long. One result of this unrelieved pressure is *varicose veins*, the torturous blue "worms" which detract so much from the appearance of a person's legs, often causing pain and sometimes ulcers.

Similar to varicose veins in cause if not location are *hemorrhoids*. All kinds of myths are associated with these painful nuisances. You may have heard people say they got theirs from sitting on cold toilet seats or from having babies. The veins that become hemorrhoids are located in the very last parts of the intestinal tract, called the rectum and the anus. The veins at this terminus of the gut perform the important function of making a tight seal there, by means of blood-filled cushions, to prevent feces and gas from leaking out of the intestine. The seal is actually a double one, and consists of two rows of veins. The higher row at the end of the rectum is called the internal hemorrhoidal veins, and the lower row, those in the anus, are covered by skin and are called external hemorrhoidal veins. Underlying these veins is a powerful muscle which acts as the primary regulator in the passage of feces, and is therefore of great social, as well as physical, importance.

The hemorrhoid veins in the rectum suffer a fate similar to the veins in the legs. After years of straining at stool, when each time veins are filled beyond their normal capacity, stretching them like overinflated balloons, they become permanently dilated and hang out of the rectum. Now they are persistent and painful bulges, with the further troublesome symptoms of bleeding and itching. This same straining causes the anal muscles to be pushed outward. Eventually they become displaced from their normal internal position, and contribute this painful part to hemorrhoidal problems.

Pregnancy can increase hemorrhoidal complications, since the uterus may lie on the veins in the pelvis and cause hemorrhoids to be enlarged. However, this temporary situation does not cause the permanent ruination that results from chronic constipation. The best example of the overwhelming influence of a starch-based diet in preventing anal problems, even in pregnancy, is presented by African women, who often have as many as ten babies and yet remain free of troublesome hemorrhoids throughout life. These women never have to strain at stool, because of their diet of grains, beans, and vegetables. (They do not have varicose veins, either.)

Yet another potentially serious problem can be caused by constipation. The natural opening in the diaphragm, through which the esophagus passes, stretches as the stomach is pushed up against it while a person strains to move the bowels. Eventually tears in the muscular diaphragm happen, and a portion of the stomach sits forever above the diaphragm, part way up into the chest, in the condition that is called a hiatal hernia (see HIATAL HERNIA).

Constipation is not a consequence of an emotional disorder, at least not initially. However, a lifetime of bowel problems could make anyone question his sanity and lose his stability. If you eat mostly fiber-free foods, such as animal products (e.g., fish, pork, beef, chicken, lobster, cheese, milk, etc.), visible fats (e.g., butter and corn oil), alcohol, and grains that are highly refined (e.g., white bread and white rice), then little will be left to make feces with adequate bulk. Your BM will resemble hard rabbit pellets.

Fibers are the prime requirement for healthy bowel function. Plant foods contain fibers, a variety of nondigestible complex carbohydrates. After all the soluble components derived from digested fats, proteins, and carbohydrates, along with the vitamins and minerals, are absorbed from the small intestine, then nondigestible fibers remain (along with a huge number of friendly microorganisms) to form the bulk of the remnant stool. These fibers have the capacity to hold water, thereby increasing the stool volume further. Also, the more foods and beverages that are consumed, the greater will be the intestinal content, and therefore the frequency and amount of the bowel movement.

Current Treatment: A starch-based diet along with vegetables and fruits is a sure cure for constipation. Certain foods, like fruits, contain generous amounts of water and fibers, and therefore contribute to a bulkier, softer stool. Prunes are famous for their beneficial effect on constipation, due to the helpful changes they promote in the lower bowel. Grains contain many kinds of fibers, two of which—cellulose and hemicellulose—are very water-absorbent. African natives living on a grain-based diet have, on the average, three large, unformed bowel movements a day. So might you, too, with a healthier vegetarian diet.

Avoiding proteins from milk and milk products is very important. I have seen some people who have made nearly a complete change to a health-supporting diet but were unable to give up the little bit of skimmed milk in the morning on their dry cereal—and their bowels didn't work very well. A little dairy protein can literally jam up the works for most people who are sensitive to it.

People who have had intestinal troubles for years, and are labeled as laxative abusers, may have stretched out their colons to twice the normal length and have developed redundant coils of bowel tubing that sort of loop back and forth in the abdominal cavity like a roller coaster. These people need a little extra help. First of all, the colon of a chronic laxative user is accustomed to receiving from a drug the message to contract. The colon has not recently responded to the body's natural message to contract that should be provided by the stretching of the colon wall as the segment fills with remnants of yesterday's meals. A person with such a laxative dependency must be encouraged first to renounce his laxatives, and then to wait patiently while the elongated colon fills enough to provide the natural stimulation to evacuate. Initially, several days may be needed to fill a very large, stretched-out colon, but eventually the muscles in the bowel wall will contract as they should and a movement will follow. Once a natural cycle of filling and emptying is started with high-fiber foods, the process continues unaided by anything except the correct choice of foods.

My Recommendations: A starch-based diet, frequent meals, a little extra water (ten glasses per day instead of the usual four or five), and fruits. Prunes should be eaten as the next step, and following this, for extra help, add bran and flax seeds. (Add 2 to 4 tablespoons of flax seeds to each cup of a grain, such as rice, before cooking.)

As a last resort, I will recommend a nonabsorbable sugar called lactulose (Chronulac); this draws water into the colon and helps to end constipation in even the toughest cases. Lactulose is available only with a doctor's prescription.

DEPRESSION and ANXIETY

STANDARD PRACTICE

Often our emotions are difficult to explain, much less control. Depression and anxiety are commonly seen together in the same person, though not always. Frequently, there is no apparent reason for unhappiness or depression.

The cause of chronic depression and anxiety is unknown. It could run in families. Situation-related depression commonly occurs after a tragic event, such as loss of a spouse or a child, financial ruin, or other kinds of devastations. But when no such situation has occurred and the person is otherwise healthy, depression is not easily explained. Possibly a neuro-chemical imbalance is at fault.

Current Treatment: Antidepressant drugs, tranquilizers, antipsychotic drugs, psychotherapy, electroconvulsive shock therapy, and what some psychologists are calling the "tincture of time"—that is to say, just waiting long enough for the condition to go away, all by itself.

Drawbacks: Medications may reduce the symptoms or change neuro-chemical imbalances, but such therapy must be followed for a long term and the side effects are significant. (And, in the first place, can anyone believe that depression is caused by a lack of drugs, or by a shortage of electrical shocks?) As for psychotherapy, it may be safe to receive, but the benefits are questionable and may simply be those evolving from the passage of time and the accompanying changes in all the agencies that affect a body and its psyche.

The McDougall Program (Dietary and Lifestyle Implications)

Some of the substances we eat and drink can affect our behavior. Familiar examples of the dramatic behavioral changes resulting from our drinking habits are the effects of alcohol and caffeine. Alcohol is a depressant, even though the first evidences of intoxication may be an elevation in mood. Caffeine for most people is a mood elevator, but this can soon lead to an uncomfortable anxiety.

Withdrawal from caffeine can be a problem, characterized by headaches and depression for those who are trying to quit. Although the uncomfortable symptoms last for only a few days, their victims consider themselves to be severely tested (and, alas, not always heroically triumphant).

Many other substances can affect our tendency to be anxious or depressed, including some foods we eat. Probably the best studied example of a specific "behavior modifying" substance in our foods is the essential amino acid tryptophan. This amino acid is converted in the brain into serotonin, a powerful agent in a variety of responses made by the brain. Serotonin regulates *overreactiveness* to different stimuli from smell, taste, vision, and social relationships. Accordingly, sleep patterns, sexual behavior, aggressiveness, physical activity, perceptions (including pain), and moods are affected. Tryptophan pills have been used to reverse insomnia, prevent muscle spasms, and in some cases to relieve depression.

The amount of tryptophan in the foods that are eaten has only a small influence upon the amount of tryptophan that enters the brain. The most important factor determining the total amount of tryptophan that does enter the brain is the concentration of other large-molecule amino acids concurrently present in the blood. Large-molecule amino acids, among them tryptophan, compete with each other to enter "gates" between the circulating bloodstream and the relatively confined brain fluids. A high-protein meal (full of meats, dairy foods, and eggs) provides many other amino acids that compete with tryptophan for entry into the brain; the end result is less tryptophan passing into the brain and a decrease in the synthesis of serotonin. Conversely, a low-protein, carbohydrate-rich diet (full of starches, vegetables, and fruits) results in the highest levels of serotonin in the brain, because fewer large-molecule amino acids are competing with tryptophan to enter the brain. For you, this means less hyperactivity, anxiety, depression, and insomnia—provided you eat that healthier diet.

In some people, anxiety, depression, and fatigue are caused by allergic reactions to foods. The most common causes of food allergies are dairy products, followed by eggs. Other common culprits are wheat, corn, and citrus fruits, but almost any foodstuff finds somewhere an individual who is allergic to it. These reactions are often subtle and difficult to recognize until the offending food has been eliminated, either by accident or by intention, and then, later, when the body is challenged with the suspect food, a recognizably adverse reaction occurs.

A serious psychological disease caused by foods in some people is schizophrenia. In hospital-based studies, some patients have been identified who react with dramatic behavioral changes to milk products and high-gluten foods (like wheat, barley, and rye). Some people with schizophrenia have actually been cured of their disease by changing their diet to eliminate the trouble-making foodstuff.

Current Treatment: When I see a patient who says he is depressed, I usually begin my course of treatment by paying close attention to some general principles of medicine and health. First, of course, I examine him for the presence of any serious organic disease and always check for adequacy of thyroid function. I consider the amounts of coffee and alcohol that he drinks, and the foods he chooses to eat. I also check to see if any medications may be causing changes in his behavior. High blood pressure medications (beta-blockers), birth control pills, tranquilizers, and, indeed, almost any other medication should be suspected. If all organ systems seem to be well medically, then I suggest that the patient change to a starch-based diet, and I remind him that daily exercise—something as simple as walking—helps to relieve minor depression and anxiety.

My Recommendations: Stop taking any drugs (under a doctor's supervision) that might be causing anxiety or depression. Stop drinking alcohol (this too may need to be done under a doctor's supervision) and caffeinated beverages. Change to a starch-based diet. Exercise daily. Look for a professional person (minister, counselor, psychologist, psychiatrist) who is a good listener, with whom to talk over your problems. Only as a last resort consider taking doctor-prescribed psychoactive drugs.

DIABETES

STANDARD PRACTICE

Diabetes (more correctly, diabetes mellitus) is a metabolic disorder in which the ability to utilize carbohydrates is more or less lost as a result of disturbance of the body's insulin activities. The blood sugar rises and sugar is found in the urine. Early symptoms include frequent urination, thirst, hunger, loss of weight, and weakness. Later on, labored breathing and finally coma can develop in some seriously ill diabetics. Diabetes is classified as two separate diseases, each having similar symptoms in response to differing mechanisms: childhood-onset (insulin-dependent) diabetes and adult-onset (non-insulin-dependent) diabetes. The childhood diabetic produces too little insulin or none at all, whereas the adult-type diabetic produces plenty of his own insulin (often in more than normal amounts) but the activity of this hormone that is supposed to control blood sugar levels is impaired.

The cause of childhood-onset diabetes is unknown; possibly genetic or the result of injury to the pancreas by one or more viruses or by harmful immune reactions or chemical agents. The cause of adult-onset diabetes is also unknown, but is thought to be related to obesity and to "run in families."

Current Treatment: Following an "exchange diet" that is designed to keep the daily calorie intake constant. Very recently the American Diabetic Association has liberalized the carbohydrate intake to 65 percent (from 45 percent) of the calories allowed, restricted the fat content to less than 30 percent and cholesterol to less than 300 mg. and limited protein intake to protect the diabetic's kidneys.

Oral medication to reduce sugar levels and insulin by injection (a required treatment for childhood diabetes) are used to adjust blood sugar to levels near normal.

Drawbacks: Insulin and pills control one sign of the disease—an elevated sugar level caused either by an absolute lack of insulin or by inadequate activity of the hormone if it is produced. However, both forms of diabetes involve the entire body, affecting many metabolic systems. Most diabetics, even those who are receiving traditional treatment, suffer blindness, heart attacks, or kidney failure within seventeen years after diagnosis of their disease. Treatment with insulin or drugs does little or nothing to change this disastrous outcome. The final report of the University Group Diabetes Program (UGDP) reiterated its earlier findings that neither insulin nor any other drug that lowers blood sugar levels can succeed in altering the course of blood vessel complications (atherosclerosis, heart attacks, strokes) in cases of adult-onset diabetes.

What is worse, taking hypoglycemic pills regularly has been found to increase the risk of dying from heart disease by 2½ times more than that among diabetics treated by diet alone. Insulin and diabetic pills have serious side effects that include life-threatening episodes of hypoglycemia; they also make most diabetics obese by causing them to store excess calories in their fat cells.

The McDougall Program (Dietary and Lifestyle Implications)

Both forms of diabetes are rare in parts of the world where meals are based on starches. This rarity is easy to understand as far as adult-type diabetes is concerned, since the primary cause of that illness is the rich Western diet. Fat inhibits action of the body's insulin, and the lack of fibers allows rapid passage of glucose from the gut into the blood, at which point the blood sugar content rises rapidly. Carbohydrates surprisingly stimulate insulin activity, thereby lowering blood sugar levels and making the diabetic feel better.

However, for cases of childhood diabetes no explanation has been formed to account for the fact that it is so much more common in places where people eat foods high in fats. Possibly the burden of the diet weakens the body's defenses to such a degree that a predatory virus is able to devastate the pancreatic cells in the young person which are responsible for synthesizing the insulin he needs.

Many of the complications that occur in both forms of the disease are the consequences of a rich diet burdening a weakened system. A diabetic person cannot defend himself from the harmful American diet or repair the damages it causes as well as can someone who does not have diabetes. Consider how a small infection in a diabetic's toe can soon extend to the point where amputation of the foot or of the leg will be necessary. The various manifestations of atherosclerosis can progress much more rapidly in a diabetic. Even mild variations in blood sugar control are associated with an increased rate of heart attacks in Americans.

Atherosclerosis is remarkably uncommon in the few cases of diabetes found in countries in Africa and Asia where the diet is largely starch-based. These few diabetics live almost free of heart disease, strokes, and gangrene, which are too common among diabetics indulging in the unending American feast.

Current Treatment for Childhood-Onset Diabetes: On a starch-based diet, these patients will usually drop their insulin needs by 30 percent and their blood sugar levels will be more stable (less "brittle"). Most important, their risk of complications is markedly decreased with a low-fat, no-cholesterol diet. Insulin adjustments are made as usual, with the aid of urine-sugar and blood-sugar tests, under a doctor's supervision.

Current Treatment for Adult-Onset Diabetes: Change in diet will allow 75 percent of these patients to stop taking all insulin, and more than 95 percent to stop taking all diabetic pills. (The few who continue to need medication should be treated with small doses of insulin.) Insulin adjustments are made as usual, with the aid of urine-sugar and blood-sugar tests, under a doctor's supervision.

My Recommendations: Never take oral hypoglycemic drugs, because they increase your chances of dying sooner. Change to a low-fat, high-complex-carbohydrate diet (starches, vegetables, and about three fruits a day). If you're obese, lose weight, for added health and blood-sugar control. You should also be physically active. Exercise, in addition to helping you lose weight, has independent benefits that increase the activity of insulin and improves your diabetic condition.

Childhood-onset diabetics will continue to need insulin! If a childhood diabetic stopped all insulin he would likely develop ketoacidosis, slip into a coma, and soon die. Insulin in this disease is lifesaving, because childhood-onset diabetics make little or none of their own.

Adult-onset diabetics will need insulin if they suffer from the most obvious symptoms of their disease—such as too much weight loss too soon, too much thirst, and too frequent urination. The question of better control, meaning fewer complications, has not been settled. I believe the closer to normal the blood sugar level is kept, the better. But blood sugar levels should not be under such "good" control that the patient runs the increased risk of suffering damaging hypoglycemia from overzealous use of insulin. More specifically, damage to the eyes is more severe and more common when blood sugar levels are too low. Fasting blood sugar levels, if you are taking insulin, should be controlled at 150 mg/dl to 200 mg/dl. The advantages of tighter control than this must be weighed against the risks and effort.

People with diabetes are usually experts at adjusting their own medication and rarely have trouble making necessary changes. I usually stop adult-onset diabetics' pills the very day they start the Program. *Adult diabetics on insulin should cut their dosage at least in half upon starting the Program.* They will find themselves lowering (rarely raising) their intake of insulin, depending on what level their blood and/or urine sugars are each day. If your urine sugars were 0 and +1 all day long, a 5 unit drop will probably be suggested by your doctor for tomorrow. If you had a hypoglycemic reaction, then as an adult-type diabetic you will be told by your doctor to lower your dosage even more (10 to 20 units) and possibly to stop the insulin altogether. Blood sugar levels can also be used to regulate insulin dosage. You will want to keep your sugar between 150 mg/dl and 350 mg/dl while you are changing your diet these days (higher levels are safer than lower levels). I have seen adult diabetics come off of 75 to 180 units of NPH insulin within three days of a change in diet and exercise. Be careful to lower the dosage quickly enough. Have sugar (hard candy) around for all-too-likely hypoglycemic reactions.

Childhood diabetics should reduce their insulin dosage by 30 percent when beginning the Program, then make further adjustments as indicated by blood-sugar or urine-sugar readings. As a general posture, it is safer to be undermedicated with a slightly higher blood sugar than overmedicated with hypoglycemia that causes sweating, confusion, and finally coma.

(For more details on diabetes, see my book *McDougall's Medicine—A Challenging Second Opinion*. New Century Publishers Inc., Piscataway, N.J., 1985.)

DIVERTICULAR DISEASE

STANDARD PRACTICE

A diverticulum (plural, diverticula) is a sac created by the herniation of the inner lining of mucous membrane through a defect in the muscular wall of a tubular organ. Diverticulosis describes a condition where diverticula are present in the colon. These saclike protrusions occur at the weakest places along the colon wall. Such a point of weakness is the site where a blood vessel passes from the colon's outside surface, through the wall, to the interior of the gut wall.

Usually the diverticula themselves cause no symptoms. Most often they are discovered incidentally when a person is given a barium enema X-ray in an attempt to diagnose some other condition. However, problems of pain and sporadic or chronic bleeding can occur in some people with diverticula. These sacs can be closed off at the entrance, whereupon inflammation and infection may set in. This infected condition is termed diverticulitis. Because the symptoms are so similar to those of appendicitis, diverticulitis is sometimes referred to as left-sided appendicitis (usually the appendix is found in the lower right part of the abdomen).

Since these sacs develop next to an artery that enters the bowel wall, leaks commonly arise in the adjacent blood vessel. Bleeding can be slow and long lasting, but occasionally is rapid and life-threatening. Sometimes the patient's life can be saved only by removing all or part of the bleeding colon.

The cause of diverticular disease is unknown; it is possibly due to a low-fiber diet, which could cause increase in pressures within the colon, but the exact role of dietary fiber still must be determined, they say. Diverticular disease is found in as many as 50 percent of the people in modern technologically developed societies over the age of sixty-five. With passing years the condition becomes more common.

Current Treatment: The immediate symptoms of inflammation and pain associated with diverticulitis must be treated, usually with antibiotics and a liquid diet. Most mild bleeding and pain will end in a short time. Sometimes surgery is necessary for more intense involvements. For long-term care, many doctors now realize the value of fiber and recommend a change in diet and/or the addition of fiber supplements like Metamucil, bran, and Fiber-al.

Drawbacks: Until recently the long-term dietary management of diverticular disease used a "low-residue" (low-fiber) diet. Patients were warned to stay away from fruits containing small seeds, and from all dried seeds and nuts, for fear that particles of these might get stuck in the opening of the diverticula and cause diverticulitis. However, there is no reliable evidence that bits of seeds or of other plant parts stick in the opening of a diverticulum. Moreover, real harm comes from this advice because many people interpret it to mean they should avoid all plant foods. Be careful! Some doctors still keep this idea of a low-fiber diet in their bag of outdated tricks.

Diverticular disease progresses, as the years pass, and the condition of the colon worsens, unless the causative agents are removed—unless, in other words, the diet is changed.

The McDougall Program (Dietary and Lifestyle Implications)

Herniation through the muscle wall is caused by increased pressures upon the colon that are necessary to move the small hard fecal mass that is the usual consequence of the American low-fiber diet. Laws of physics explain that constricting pressures in a hollow organ are higher when the diameter of the organ is small. The few hard fecal pellets left in your gut by hamburgers and fiber-less white bread fail to fill the colon to a capacity that allows for easy, low-pressure flow of the residue.

Development of diverticular disease is not an inevitable part of growing older. The colons of people living in underdeveloped countries show a virtual absence of diverticular disease. Healthy low pressures in the colon happen when the diet is high in starches, vegetables, and fruits, with their generous content of fiber.

Current Treatment: Contrary to what was once popular opinion, the addition of fibers in the form of brans or high-fiber foods has relieved symptoms in 90 percent of cases of severe colon disease, even with recurrent pain and bleeding. A high-fiber diet will also decrease the likelihood of developing new diverticula. The diverticula already formed are permanent herniations of the colon, and will not disappear except by surgical removal, which is rarely indicated.

My Recommendations: A starch-based, high-fiber diet for the relief of chronic diverticular problems. There is no reason to avoid seeds or any other natural plant foods, as particles from these will not get stuck in your diverticula and cause inflammation.

FATIGUE

STANDARD PRACTICE

Are you always tired, weak, rundown, worn out, lacking energy, weary, and exhausted? In one other word, fatigued? Although not exactly synonymous, these descriptive words shade into one another, and do sum up the feelings of millions of people. More than half of all patients entering a hospital for treatment of other conditions complain of fatigue. This condition is expected after prolonged physical and mental labor, but too many people are tired for no clear reason.

Some people do have less obvious reasons to be fatigued. Fatigue can be evidence of a serious illness, such as an infection, anemia, thyroid disease, adrenal insufficiency, diabetes, or other physical impairments. It can also be a sign of emotional depression and chronic tension.

Diet is believed by many to be a cause of fatigue only when not enough food is eaten: Starvation makes people weak and tired.

Current Treatment: Find the cause and apply appropriate treatment. For example, in cases of anemia, find the reason for blood loss; in conditions where thyroid levels are low, prescribe thyroid medication; and with infections, give antibiotics and other appropriate therapy.

Drawbacks: Most often the cause of a person's fatigue is not easily linked to a specific cause, and therefore not easily treatable. In desperation, some doctors will give patients thyroid tablets, iron pills, vitamin B_{12} shots, and all kinds of stimulants to pep them up. Many times this sort of treatment is inappropriate, and usually it is ineffective. Little attention is given to diet and lifestyle.

The McDougall Program (Dietary and Lifestyle Implications)

Many people who after thorough examination show no detectable cause for their fatigue are suffering the ill effects of an unhealthy diet and lifestyle. The rich American diet can wear you down in several ways. The primary fuel for our bodies is carbohydrates. Meats contain almost no carbohydrate. The primary carbohydrate in cow's milk is lactose, but many people cannot digest and utilize it. In the preparation of cheeses, bacteria will ferment almost all the lactose in milk. Thus, many Americans, even those who eat dairy products, are on a diet that does not provide enough carbohydrates to generate sufficient high-quality energy. You may have some idea of how important carbohydrates are if you are involved in sports. Before a race, long-distance runners "carbohydrate-load" (often on spaghetti and other forms of pasta) to provide their body with almost immediately available fuel, filling their muscles and liver cells with long-chain sugars that will be converted to the simple sugar glucose for use during the marathon race. Athletes who do not have this store of fuel can be heard complaining about "hitting the wall," a term that describes exactly how they feel when they've run out of energy. Winning a race may not be one of your goals, but getting through the day full of energy is possible if you will "carbohydrate-load" three or more times during the day.

Another cause of fatigue is the sludging of blood that follows a meal high in fats. Do you recall going without lunch when you have an important meeting in the afternoon, because experience tells you that soon after a meal you'll be sleepy and sluggish? Molecules of assorted fats from your meal enter the bloodstream from the gut and immediately coat the circulating red blood cells. Uncoated blood cells bounce off each other naturally and are flexible enough to bend and twist through the smallest capillaries in their zeal to take blood to all the cells in all the tissues. Once coated with fat, however, they lose that essential elasticity: They stick together in clumps and become relatively rigid. The overall effect is a lowered oxygen content in the blood and worsened circulation to your tissues, which you experience as muscular weakness and lassitude.

Some people also suffer from food allergies that result in a condition known to the medical profession as "tension-fatigue syndrome." The most common cause of a food allergy is milk; egg, chocolate, wheat, corn, and citrus fruits are other common sources of allergens (see ALLERGIC DISEASES).

Current Treatment: When I see patients who complain of persistent fatigue, I follow a series of steps to bring them relief. First, I rule out any physical illness by taking a careful history and making a thorough physical examination along with appropriate laboratory tests. Then I look at their drug history. Do they use depressant drugs, alcohol, or other "recreational" drugs? Are they taking doctor-prescribed or over-the-counter drugs that might easily cause fatigue, such as tranquilizers, sedatives, or beta-blocker pills (for lowering blood pressure)? (The list is endless. If they are taking any medication at all, they should consider it from the very first as a possible cause of fatigue or of any other discomfort they may be suffering.)

Once I'm sure they are free of any treatable physical illness and from the effects of drugs, I look into their diet and lifestyle. Are they eating a high-carbohydrate, low-fat diet? Do they get daily exercise, which is known to relieve depression and anxiety, and which contributes to a feeling of energetic well-being?

Lastly, I consider emotional factors, such as depression (which can range from mild to severe). The emotional problem that is causing the fatigue may be as commonplace as family strains, job dissatisfaction, or money worries. Often people are simply bored—life is no longer enjoyable for them. I encourage people who are enduring situations that are detracting from their health and happiness to resolve them, and, when necessary, to get help in doing so. Life is too short (and too wonderful) to waste another day on being miserable in body and unhappy in spirit.

My Recommendations: See your doctor to rule out physical health problems. Change to a health-supporting diet and lifestyle. Consider the possibility of a food allergy. Take steps to make every day an enjoyable and productive day.

GALLBLADDER DISEASE

STANDARD PRACTICE

The gallbladder is an elongated sack connected to the underside of the liver, and its primary function is to store the bile that is produced by the liver. After a meal, especially one high in fats, the gallbladder contracts periodically, squirting its stored bile into the first part of the small intestine. Thereafter, if all goes as nature intends, foodstuffs are rapidly degraded by the action of the bile and other intestinal enzymes, and proper digestion proceeds.

Formation of stones in the bladder (cholelithiasis) and chronic inflammation of the sack itself (cholecystitis) are the most common forms of gallbladder disease. Twenty percent of the American adult population have gallstones that do not trouble them, a condition referred to as "asymptomatic gallstones." After retirement age (about sixty-five), 40 percent of people have these gallstones, which generally remain undiscovered unless an X-ray or ultrasound study or surgery of the abdomen is made for some reason.

The cause of gallbladder disease is unknown, but it is frequently related to being female, fat, and forty, although males of similar attributes also can be affected. Heredity is possibly involved.

When symptoms of gallstones occur, they are due to inflammation of the gallbladder and obstruction of the outlet duct. Pain and jaundice (yellow skin) result from obstruction of the sack's outlet duct with a stone.

Current Treatment: Surgery is the treatment of choice for an inflamed gallbladder (cholecystitis). Removal of gallstones, even those that cause no symptoms, is usually done by surgery soon after they are discovered.

Recently, media attention has focused on the dissolving of gallstones by drinking daily a drug made from one component of bile. The drug is called chenodeoxycholic acid (CDCA); a derivative of it, called ursodeoxycholic acid (UDCA), is also available. The treatment continues for one to three years, and the success rate shows a 50 percent chance for partial or complete disappearance of the stones. But many doctors hesitate to use these drugs because they are toxic to the liver and cause diarrhea.

At some medical centers, sonic shock waves are used to break up gallstones. The fragments can pass through the duct into the bowels and leave the body by that route.

Drawbacks: Risks of death and disability from the surgery and the anesthesia are all too real. Moreover, half of the people who are operated on still feel distress in the upper intestinal tract. Many people develop diarrhea after removal of the gallbladder, because the steady flow of bile from the liver irritates the colon. (This constant irritation may also increase chances of developing colon cancer.) Painful irritation of the stomach, a form of gastritis, is common after removal of the gallbladder, because of the upward flow of strongly alkaline bile components into the stomach from the small intestine.

The McDougall Program (Dietary and Lifestyle Implications)

Understanding the cause of gallbladder disease will help you in preventing or treating it. More than 90 percent of gallstones found in people living in affluent nations are composed primarily of cholesterol. When the bile fluids in the gallbladder become oversaturated with cholesterol, precipitation of the cholesterol into solid crystals begins, and then gradually accumulates to form stones of variable sizes. A diet high in cholesterol-containing foods—red meats, poultry, fish, and dairy products—is the primary culprit for the development of the supersaturated levels of cholesterol in the bile. Polyunsaturated oils (vegetable oils), too, will cause the liver to excrete larger quantities of cholesterol that pass into the fluids in the gallbladder, and thereby favor stone formation.

Current Treatment: Avoid surgery whenever possible. Several recent studies have addressed the issue of whether or not asymptomatic gallstones should be removed. The findings consistently show that your risk of dying and/or developing complications is much greater if you choose to have surgery than if you decide to leave the stones alone (even in diabetic patients).

People suffering pain from gallbladder disease are most likely to visit hospital operating suites. If, however, they are not too ill, they still have a very good chance of avoiding the surgeon's knife by making the sensible decision to stop eating the high-fat, high-cholesterol foods that provoke the formation of gallstones. A low-fat diet is the time-honored approach for relieving gallbladder pain and preventing further attacks. However, changing the diet does not cause the gallstones to dissolve; and *the disappearance of stones should not be your goal.*

Well-meaning doctors will sometimes frighten patients into accepting surgery by emphasizing the possibility of developing cancer of the gallbladder from the constant irritation produced by the gallstones. Actually, the risk of cancer from this cause is insignificant. Don't be fooled into submitting to the surgeon's knife for the removal of asymptomatic gallstones because of a doctor-induced cancer phobia.

The idea that gallstones will slip into the duct and get caught there is another excuse given to patients to justify the need to operate on their "silent" asymptomatic gallstones. Actually, very rarely do small stones, even those that are being dissolved away through the use of drugs, become trapped in the duct to block it.

If you have gallstones, then alter your diet today. If this approach for one reason or another is not successful, you will have no trouble in finding an experienced surgeon to take out your gallbladder. Each year an estimated 515,000 patients in the United States have this operation, at an average cost of $10,000 per operation.

My Recommendations: A no-cholesterol, low-fat diet (excluding all vegetable fats too), for preventing gallbladder disease and gallstones. If you develop pain, see your doctor. If the attack subsides and your situation is not a surgical emergency, then eat a very low-fat diet to avoid further attacks. Do not agree to an operation to remove gallstones that do not cause you trouble.

HEADACHES

STANDARD PRACTICE

The term *headache* encompasses all aches and pains in and about the head, and sometimes in the neck. It refers to one of the most common of human discomforts and has acquired a list of causes that vary as much as does a headache's location, intensity, and quality. You've probably heard that headaches, especially migraines, "run in the family." Foods are rarely considered as possible causes.

Current Treatment: After appropriate examination to rule out serious correctable causes such as leaking blood vessels and brain tumors, the standard treatment turns to pain killers, tranquilizers, antidepressants, steroids, blood vessel relaxants, beta-blockers, and other medications, depending on the suspected cause and the complaining subject. On very rare occasions, surgery is attempted.

Drawbacks: Drug therapy is symptomatic therapy, because it does not deal with the basic cause. Such treatment goes on and on, and rarely is sufficient to gain complete relief. Side effects of treatment themselves can be "disease-producing."

The McDougall Program (Dietary and Lifestyle Implications)

One common cause of headaches is drugs, such as alcohol and caffeine. The toxic effects of alcohol cause the head to hurt. One version of the condition is commonly known as a "hangover." People who drink coffee and tea may get a headache as a direct result of the drinks, or more commonly, as a result of withdrawal from the caffeine in them. This withdrawal may come at the end of the day or on weekends, when less coffee than usual is drunk. Headaches stop with complete abstinence from any drug (usually within less than five days). Don't forget that recreational, doctor-prescribed, and over-the-counter drugs can be likely causes of your headaches; even medications apparently as innocent as birth control pills and cold tablets can provoke headaches.

Foods, I believe, are the most common causes of headaches. Some "food" headaches develop as a result of allergic reactions to components in your diet. These components may be as natural as the proteins in your milk or as foreign as the chemical additives that are sprinkled about so liberally by food technologists. Since 1913, migraine headaches have been suspected to be caused by allergic reactions, and many scientific articles have established a definite cause-and-effect relationship between migraines and common foods. Most encouraging is the finding that between 70 percent and 90 percent of long-term migraine patients can be freed of their headaches in less than two weeks once they identify and eliminate the offending foods.

The benefits of a change in diet are not limited only to migraine patients. I usually see complete relief of headaches from an unidentified cause within days after a change in diet. (This statement of miraculous benefits does not apply to people who have head and neck pains from known causes, such as injury, tension, infections, cancer, or degenerative arthritis.)

Because one common source of headaches is sinus trouble, we can easily see why dietary change is so beneficial. The membranes lining the sinuses produce mucus, and the tissues become swollen and inflamed as a direct result of allergic reactions to foods consumed or to things breathed into the nose and lungs. Pain is a part of the inflammation process and from the pressure of fluids that accumulate in poorly draining sinuses. The foods that most commonly provoke sinus trouble are dairy products. I think you're unfortunate if you miss this opportunity to relieve your aching head by simply eliminating milk, cheese, and ice cream from your diet. But other foods too can be causes of sinus trouble.

Current Treatment: The direction of change most beneficial to sufferers from migraine and unclassified generalized headaches is, as you might expect, one toward healthier foods. I find that the most important foods to eliminate are the dairy products (yes, even skimmed milk, yogurt, and cottage cheese). The next most likely culprits are eggs and chocolate, then citrus fruits, corn, and wheat. However, the possibilities for being harmed by offending foods are limitless. Some people must resort to an elimination diet to identify the foods to which they are sensitive. (See ALLERGIC DISEASES for an effective elimination diet.)

My Recommendations: First, see a qualified specialist to identify any condition that can be corrected by medical treatment. If that doesn't help, then change to a low-fat, non-dairy, starch-based diet; also consider the possibility that you may be allergic to other kinds of foods. Stop taking alcohol, caffeine, and any other drugs that *may* be causing your headache, including doctor-prescribed drugs (but do so only with proper medical supervision).

HEART DISEASE, PREVENTION

STANDARD PRACTICE

Heart disease is recognized as the number-one epidemic among affluent people. In the United States, approximately 1.25 million heart attacks occur each year. Half the victims of such attacks die before they reach a hospital. These scary statistics deserve your very serious attention. The disease process that leads to heart attacks and strokes begins with eating too much fat and cholesterol. Over the course of many years, this devotion to gluttony does damage to the arteries, causing atherosclerosis, in which fats and cholesterol are deposited along the inside lining of the arteries and form swellings called plaques. Eventually, the atherosclerosis becomes so extensive that the plaques are like dispersed time bombs simply waiting to detonate. In physical terms, each bomb is a plaque, overstuffed with fat. During the final moments of apparent "good" health in a person so endangered, a small crack appears in the surface of the plaque. Through this opening a stream of fat spurts into the blood flowing through the artery, like a pimple rupturing on a teen-ager's face. The globule of fat causes the blood to suddenly form a clot, or thrombosis, closing off the vessel. The disastrous effect is death of the tissues once nourished by this artery—in familiar terms, a heart attack, or a stroke, and, half the time, a dead victim.

A healthy diet and lifestyle are essential for preventing the underlying atherosclerosis as well as the blood clotting that accompanies the final events. Blood clotting involves certain of the body's proteins called clotting factors and fibrin, and billions of specialized blood elements called platelets. These components are all present all the time in the circulating blood, ready to perform successful "clot-making" when the body is hurt. This is valuable help when you cut a finger, for example, or bite your cheek, but unfortunately, this mechanism interprets the globule of fat rupturing from the plaque into the bloodstream as a reason to form a clot.

You might guess from this description that suppressing the clotting of the blood would help prevent some of these tragedies from happening. Drugs such as Coumadin that interfere with the clotting proteins have been given to patients for years in attempts to prevent future heart attacks and strokes. Unfortunately, use of this drug requires careful monitoring and brings with it unacceptable risk of fatal hemorrhaging.

Safer ways to inhibit the tendency to form clots have recently become popular. These approaches affect the clot-forming system by decreasing the activity of the blood platelets. (Even when the platelets are completely inactivated, bleeding eventually stops because of the actions of the protein components of the clotting system. However, without fully active platelets the process is slower and less effective.) Substances that affect the activity of the platelets include familiar medications like common aspirin and food-stuffs like vegetable oils and fish oil.

Current Treatment: **Diet and Lifestyle.** A reduction in dietary cholesterol and saturated fat intake to lower blood cholesterol levels and future risk of heart disease. This usually means switching from beef and pork to chicken and fish, and using only dairy products made with skimmed milk. Attention is also given to weight reduction, quitting cigarette smoking, stress reduction, and daily exercise.

Aspirin. More than twenty years ago, aspirin was shown to inhibit the action of platelets, and thereby thin the blood. However, you should know the facts before starting aspirin treatment.

When thirty-one randomized trials using drugs that inhibit the action of platelets, such as aspirin, were analyzed, benefits certainly were found. Overall, the risk of dying was reduced by 15 percent, and the risk of suffering a nonfatal heart attack or stroke was reduced by 30 percent. These trials involved 29,000 patients with a history of TIAs (transient ischemic attacks, or small temporary strokes), more severe strokes, heart attacks, or chest pain (unstable angina). Thus, the use of aspirin (and other drugs that inhibit platelets) can reduce the risk of suffering a serious artery event in people *with a previous history of severe atherosclerosis.* However, in people who have *no* history of serious atherosclerosis—who, in other words, have *not* suffered from TIAs, strokes, chest pains, or heart attacks—the benefits of taking aspirin have *not* been shown to outweigh the risks of being harmed by the drug.

Fish and Fish Oil. For many years, investigators have wondered why the Eskimos, who live on a diet so rich in meats (whale, walrus, and fish), rarely suffer from heart disease. Some scientists thought that their short lifespan never allowed them time to develop clogged arteries. Others suggested that during periods of food scarcity, any atherosclerotic plaques that had built up were burnt off to yield energy. More than a decade ago, another theory explaining the rarity of heart disease among meat-eating Eskimos appeared in the medical literature when scientists discovered a high concentration of a biologically active fat known as eicosapentaenoic acid (EPA, or omega-3 fat) in the blood of the Eskimos. Researchers traced this fat to some of the Eskimos' most important foods, the cold water marine (ocean) fish. One of the biological activities of this fat is to prevent the blood platelets from sticking together and forming clots.

The original source of eicosapentaenoic fat is plants. This fat is located in the plants' chloroplast membranes; it is not derived from seeds, as are many vegetable oils that are processed commercially to be used as foods. Fish do not synthesize this biologically active fat (nor does any animal).

However, marine algae and other sea plants that these fish live on, do synthesize the fat. This plant fat is stored in the fish's fatty tissues, and is consumed later by people. Eicosapentaenoic acid is present in high concentrations only in cold-water marine fish, which are by nature high in fat, including cod, herring, menhaden, and salmon. (Recall that a few years ago we were told to eat only low-fat white fish.)

In addition to inhibiting platelet activity, this fish fat has been shown to lower blood levels of cholesterol and triglycerides, and to decrease the inflammation of arthritis. Fish oil is commonly sold in capsules in drugstores, supermarkets, and health food stores. When used in this manner, fish fat must be thought of as a drug. As with all drugs, we must beware of side effects and costs.

Drawbacks: **Diet and Lifestyle.** The changes recommended are too little, too late—see CHOLESTEROL, HIGH. As a result, the small dietary improvements that are made show very little if any benefit for lowering cholesterol, preventing heart disease, or improving health when studied.

Aspirin therapy can have *serious side effects* for many people. The aspirin itself irritates the stomach lining, causing pain (indigestion) and bleeding, and in rare cases the amount of blood lost can be life-threatening. The increased tendency to bleed caused by the aspirin's ability to inhibit clotting can turn a minor injury into fatal bleeding. Hemorrhagic strokes are increased in those who take aspirin. (In hemorrhagic strokes, bleeding occurs into the brain due to leakage from a weakened blood vessel, rather than due to formation of a clot, as in the more common form of stroke.) Finally, some people are allergic to aspirin.

Fish oil, like all other oils, is loaded with calories. Fats provide approximately twenty times more calories than do equal weights of fresh vegetables and fruits. Eating these fish fats every day can contribute to making you obese.

The studies showing that fish oil lowers blood cholesterol levels have fed 2½ to 3 ounces (75 to 100 grams) of fish oil a day to patients. This would amount to an additional 675 to 900 calories a day from pure concentrated oil alone. When investigators used more commonly prescribed doses of fish oil, such as four 1-gram capsules a day, blood cholesterol levels did not significantly decrease. And, most disturbing has been the discovery that this dosage of fish oil actually raised the level of LDL cholesterol, which damages the arteries and promotes atherosclerosis. Thus, this drawback negates some of the benefits that are expected from "thinning the blood" with EPA in the hope of preventing heart disease.

Moreover, most commercial fish oils are loaded with cholesterol, though some brands have been specially processed to remove it. Cod liver oil contains 570 mg cholesterol, herring oil 766 mg, menhaden oil 521 mg, salmon oil 485 mg, and Max EPA (a commercial concentrated fish oil) 600 mg per 100 g (3½ ounces).*

Cod liver oil contains significant amounts of two potentially toxic vitamins, A and D. Some cod liver oil products actually recommend levels of intake that can result in hypervitaminosis A and D. Hain Norwegian High Potency Cod-Liver Oil, for example, lists its content of vitamin A at 35,000 units (the toxic level is 10,000 units daily), and of vitamin D at 3500 units (the toxic level is 1000 units daily).

Fish oil also interferes with the body's mechanisms for controlling diabetes. It makes the blood sugars rise to higher levels by inhibiting insulin, whether this is produced by the pancreas or injected. Oils of all kinds promote development of cancers, contribute to gallbladder disease, and cause oily hair and skin with associated acne. Studies on the effects of fish fat on the enhancement of tumor growth in animals are conflicting; however, some studies have shown that fish fats, even in small amounts, do promote cancer growth.

Furthermore, fish oils may increase the length of normal pregnancy in human mothers, and thereby increase birth weight and risk to the newborn baby. Changes in hormones and body functions that give some of the benefits mentioned above (such as the anti-inflammatory action), also appear to delay the onset of delivery of a baby. A 1986 study published in *Lancet* showed that in the Faroe Islands, where half of the total caloric intake of the main meals is based upon fish, birth weights are among the highest in the world, averaging about 7 ounces higher than in babies born to women in Denmark, where the intake of fish fat is much lower. The health of an infant is related to its birth weight—being bigger is not necessarily better. Death rates among fetuses during late pregnancy are almost twice as high in the Faroe Islands as in Denmark. The fat in the fish is suspected as being the reason for these differences.

The McDougall Program (Dietary and Lifestyle Implications)

The wisest way to prevent tragedies from a defective blood vessel system is to deal with the cause. Heart disease and strokes are not due to any deficiency in aspirin or fish oil; they are due in large part to atherosclerosis, which in turn is due to a high level of cholesterol in the blood (see ATHEROSCLEROSIS and CHOLESTEROL, HIGH). Your first-line therapy, therefore, should be a low-fat, no-cholesterol diet.

* Don't forget! Fish flesh itself is also high in cholesterol, with bass at 68 mg, cod at 55 mg, haddock at 74 mg, halibut at 41 mg, herring at 76 mg, mackerel at 75 mg, perch at 115 mg, pike at 86 mg, salmon at 49 mg, smelt at 89 mg, and tuna at 49 mg per 3½ ounce serving, compared to beef at 85 mg and white meat (skinned) chicken at 85 mg per 3½ ounce serving.

Current Treatment: *Thinning the blood with aspirin or fish oil should be second-line therapy,* as is true of any medication, used only if you are at high risk for a heart attack or stroke. *If you do decide to take aspirin,* you should know that small doses are just as effective as larger doses, and cause fewer side effects. As little as 50 mg of aspirin a day will inactivate every platelet in your body. New platelets must be made before any blood-clotting activity attributable to them can occur. A tablet of aspirin for adults contains 300 mg. A tablet intended for children holds only 90 mg. Studies have been done only with doses as small as one 300 mg tablet, but one "baby aspirin" or one quarter of an "adult aspirin" a day should be enough. Coated aspirin (such as Ecotrin) dissolves in the small intestine, thereby avoiding irritation of the stomach's membranes.

If you decide to take blood thinning oils you should know that other generous sources of platelet-inactivating omega-3 fats are available besides marine fish, and all are plants or derived from plants, and therefore are cholesterol-free: purslane, walnut oil and walnuts, wheat germ oil, rapeseed oil, soybean lecithin, soybeans and tofu, common beans, butternuts, and certain edible seaweeds. (Purslane, a vegetable eaten extensively in Greece, where the incidence of both heart disease and cancer is low, is the richest source of these beneficial omega-3 fats of any plant yet studied. Because of this happy fact, you may find this leafy vegetable becoming a popular food item in the United States.) But don't forget the adverse effects of oil derived from plants.

Diet is your first-line therapy. Life-saving benefits provided by a healthy diet are gained in a matter of hours. Shortly after a change to a low-fat, no-cholesterol diet the dominant flow of cholesterol and fat changes from *into* the artery walls to *out of* the walls. This quickly reduces the pressure on the inside of the atherosclerotic plaque, reducing the risk of rupture.

In addition to the profound cholesterol-lowering effects of a low-fat, no-cholesterol diet, there are many other benefits of a healthy diet that reduce the risks of heart attacks and strokes almost overnight. Animal (saturated) fats are the strongest promoters of blood clotting that we contact daily. The day you stop eating animal fats is the day your blood "thins out," and in the event one of your plaques does rupture the blood is less likely to clot and the blood vessel remains open. Animal fats also increase the production of prostaglandin hormones that cause the blood vessels to constrict, which may slow the flow of blood and increase the chance of the blood's clotting. Another factor is the sludging of blood cells that follows meals high in any kind of fat. Fat from the food enters the bloodstream and coats the blood cells causing them to stick together. The clumped blood moves slowly and clots easily. Thus, because of the multiple benefits of healthy food, *diet is the foundation* of any therapy intended to keep you alive and functioning fully.

My Recommendations: Follow the McDougall Program. A low-fat, no-cholesterol, starch-based diet will lower your cholesterol level and reduce atherosclerosis. Daily exercise will also reduce your risk of heart attacks and premature death by increasing HDL cholesterol, enlarging the caliber of the existing heart arteries, and possibly developing new (collateral) circulation for the heart muscle. Don't smoke or drink alcohol. (Alcohol in small amounts may lower your risk of heart disease, but may increase risk of accidents and liver disease; alcohol is not "health food.")

Second-line therapy might include a baby aspirin a day for those people at high risk. If taken in the form of leafy green vegetables and common beans, omega-3 fat would have few, if any, drawbacks. I don't recommend fish oil because of its many side effects and costs.

HEART DISEASE, TREATMENT

STANDARD PRACTICE

The underlying cause of heart disease is atherosclerosis, a condition in which fatty plaques are formed along the internal walls of the arteries, and the fundamental cause of that is the high-fat, high-cholesterol diet preferred by affluent people living in Western nations, and the resulting high blood cholesterol levels in people who eat these rich foods. Other factors, too, play their parts, including heredity, cigarette smoking, physical inactivity, obesity, high blood pressure, and stress. The importance given to each factor varies greatly among "experts" in the medical community.

Current Treatment: A low-fat, low-cholesterol diet, which generally means a switch from beef and pork to chicken, fish, and dairy products made with skimmed milk to lower the blood cholesterol level. Aspirin and fish oils in the hope of preventing future heart attacks. Many different kinds of drugs to lower cholesterol levels and relieve chest pains. Bypass surgery and angioplasty, a procedure in which a balloon-tipped catheter is inserted into an area of atherosclerosis and the balloon expanded with fluid, which fractures the plaque, opening the artery lumen in many cases.

Drawbacks: The commonly prescribed changes in diet are too minimal to help such very sick people. The cholesterol levels in chicken and fish are equivalent to those in beef and pork. Aspirin and fish oil "thin the blood" by preventing the activity of platelets, but the side effects of both are significant—see HEART DISEASE, PREVENTION. Cholesterol-lowering drugs reduce the risk of future events, but costs and side effects are considerable—see CHOLESTEROL, HIGH. Pain-relieving drugs for angina relieve the pain, but they do not reduce the chance of a heart attack or sudden death.

Bypass surgery and angioplasty relieve chest pain also, but their role in saving lives is seriously in question. Most doctors these days, when among themselves at medical meetings, talk only about the advantages of less pain; few suggest that either of these kinds of surgery will save lives. However, often the story they will tell a patient is quite different. For example, I've heard doctors say, "Without this surgery you won't live to make it to the hospital door." Too often patients are not told the truth.

Actually, a patient suffering for a period of time with heart artery disease serious enough to deprive his heart muscle of blood—a condition usually causing serious chest pain (angina)—is at much less risk of dying than you might suspect. During the time the heart muscle has suffered poor circulation, extra (collateral) circulation has grown to supply the compromised muscle tissue. If the diseased artery does clot off, then this additional circulation takes over and prevents sudden death. People who have a minimal to moderate amount of artery closure are really the ones that are at the highest risk of sudden death if one of their heart arteries closes off from a blood clot—they have not had the previous long-term stimulus of poor circulation to develop protective collateral circulation.

The only clear-cut exception to the doctors' carefully hidden belief that "bypass surgery fails to save lives" happens when a blockage involves a large artery providing blood to an area of the heart that is large enough to be essential to life. This is the left main coronary artery, and only 4 to 11 percent of the people who submit to having angiograms and bypass surgery show significant blockage of this artery. Otherwise, surgery has no survival benefit over nonsurgical therapy for almost all other patients. Few patients understand the real limitations of bypass surgery, or attempt in any way to defend themselves and their families from knife-happy surgeons. In one recent report, published in the *Journal of the American Medical Association*, an expert panel of doctors judged that 44 percent of bypass surgeries were performed for inappropriate or equivocal reasons. In the same journal, other doctors reported a number of cases that had asked for a second opinion and these second physicians decided not to recommend bypass surgery. The decision was found to be safe (leading to no deaths), and, moreover, the authors concluded that need for surgery can be reduced by 50 percent. Only extraordinarily determined patients (or well-informed ones) will take a stand against their doctor's recommendations, or even ask for a second opinion. But, obviously, such an effort would be well worth making.

Bypass surgery is also often sold to patients as being "safe." They are told that they have less than a 2 percent chance of dying as a result of the surgery. These glorious figures are dreamed up for ideal patients in ideal settings. Over all, mortality rates across the country average between 5 and 10 percent. Recent data show that, nationwide, 10.5 percent of the Medicare patients who have bypass surgery die before they can be sent home from the hospital—and many are inconsiderate enough to die on the operating table. If they do live through the operation and its aftermath, then the death rate is about 2 to 4 percent per year thereafter. These figures make it pretty hard to claim benefits from surgery, when only 2 to 4 percent of patients who show comparable levels of heart disease die each year *without* surgery.

Bypass surgery is associated with a postoperative complication rate of 13 percent: these complications include heart attacks, strokes, serious bleeding, infections, kidney failure, and death. Brain injury from the time spent on the "heart-lung machine" happens in almost every heart bypass patient. Nearly two thirds show physical signs of brain damage one week after operation. Subsequently, permanent brain damage is recognized by loss of memory, personality changes, sleep disturbances, and physical impairments in a third of post bypass patients. (The actual incidence of permanent brain dysfunction is probably much more common than the 15 to 44 percent reported in scientific studies. Tests are not sensitive enough to detect all the subtle but important deficits.) Physical fitness, i.e., freedom from disabling chest pain and/or shortness of breath, appears to be restored in fewer than one half of the patients who undergo bypass surgery.

Current Treatment: A low-fat, no-cholesterol, starch-based diet begun after the development of heart disease heralded by onset of chest pain (angina) improves the circulation to the heart muscle almost overnight by allowing the blood supply to flow more freely. When people eat rich foods, fats enter the bloodstream from the gut and coat the blood cells, causing them to stick together in clumps. The sludging that results decreases the flow of oxygen and nutrients to the tissues in the heart muscle. Within hours of a change to a starch-based diet, when fats are no longer present to enter the bloodstream, the oxygen content of the blood increases, blood flow improves, and the chest pain diminishes or disappears. Keep in mind that the prime reason for bypass surgery and angioplasty is the relief of the chest pain, since neither intervention, in the long run, can really save the lives of most patients. When the pain is gone (or at least tolerable), the need for these surgeries is removed. By no strained coincidence, the low-fat diet that relieves the chest pain is the same no-cholesterol, low-fat diet that allows the sick arteries to heal by reversing the processes of atherosclerosis.

Following the dietary change, drugs that were intended to reduce chest pain should be decreased gradually in dosage and then discontinued entirely as soon as possible.

My Recommendations: Believe what your chest pain is trying to tell you: "You are on the verge of dying of a dietary disease. Help!" Your heart is pleading with every twinge of pain for relief from the lard you're shoveling into your belly three or more times a day. Have you noticed how the chest pains become worse after you've gulped down a fat-filled meal? Or chomped upon a thick juicy steak?

Change to a starch-based diet *at once*! In the few cases where diet is not enough, use drugs to relieve the chest pain. If all these fail, only then should you agree to allow surgery for the sake of relieving that terrible pain so that once again you can function at the level of activity you consider best for you. Heart disease demands that you use all the cautions and skills that you have ever learned, or even heard about, as a sensible and thinking person trying to be in charge of your health. When you consult members of the medical profession for help with your diseased heart, remember that on occasion you are dealing with a big business whose enthusiastic employees, especially some cardiologists and bypass surgeons, are overly enthusiastic about the benefits of many of the testing procedures, like angiograms, as well as heart disease surgery such as angioplasty and bypass operations.

If you are on medication for chest pain already and you are about to start or have started the McDougall Program, ask yourself, "Do I need less angina medication?" If you have had no chest pain recently, then your doctor may reduce the dosage of pills and patches you will need, especially if you have felt weak or dizzy and your blood pressure has been low. I usually treat my angina patients with short-acting nitroglycerin (under the tongue) tablets (NTG 1 / 150), and discontinue the swallowed pills (Isordil, Cardizem) and patches (nitroglycerin) shortly after the start of the Program. This way, they only take medication when they need it. Beta-blockers (e.g., Inderal, Lopressor) must be stopped slowly because sudden withdrawal can provoke chest pain and possibly a heart attack. As a general rule, I cut the dosage in half every three days, until the pill size is so small the next sensible option is to quit altogether.

(For further information on the treatment of heart disease, see my book *McDougall's Medicine—A Challenging Second Opinion*. New Century Publishers Inc. Piscataway, NJ, 1985.)

HIATAL HERNIA

STANDARD PRACTICE

A hiatal hernia (also known as a diaphragmatic hernia) is a condition in which the stomach protrudes into the chest cavity through an opening in the diaphragm. The cause is unknown, possibly genetic.

Current Treatment: Antacids, and antacids combined with simethicone (Gelusil, Mylanta), have been the basis of initial therapy designed to reduce pains caused by this condition. Medications that suppress the flow of acid from the stomach walls, such as Tagamet, have been used recently with some success. Raising the head of the bed about six inches in order to keep the stomach acid from flowing into the esophagus during sleep is usually recommended, and helps some people. A variety of surgical procedures have been designed to close the opening in the diaphragm, or otherwise keep the stomach in its proper location within the abdominal cavity.

Drawbacks: The patient must take medications several times a day in order to keep the stomach quiet. Drugs have side effects and are expensive, and unfortunately, fail all too frequently. Surgical repair is a serious operation, incurring all the expenses and risks that accompany any major surgery, and should be chosen only as a last resort. Furthermore, the success rate of surgical intervention is low; the patients still have symptoms of stomach distress.

The McDougall Program (Dietary and Lifestyle Implications)

The esophagus passes along the midline of the chest to enter the stomach, which lies in the abdomen. En route, the hollow esophageal tube reaches the stomach through a hole in the muscular "breathing" diaphragm that separates the chest from the abdominal cavity. Straining to pass the hard and pebbly feces that the well-fed American produces causes an upward pressure in the abdominal cavity that forces the stomach and lower esophagus up into the chest cavity with each and every desperate push. In the process, the natural tight opening in the diaphragm muscle is widened, inviting the hernia—the protrusion of the stomach into the chest cavity (see CONSTIPATION). When the stomach is up there in the chest, it is subjected to negative pressures as the chest cavity expands in the act of breathing. This negative pressure draws stomach acid up into the esophagus, causing erosion of the esophageal lining and pain. Half the people over age fifty living in America have permanently stretched their diaphragm muscle to acquire a hiatal hernia.

Current Treatment: As with other intestinal disorders, primary attention must be focused on the cause—your foods and beverages. Relief of the pain is evident within only a few days of dietary change, sometimes within hours. The hernia does not go away, but the irritation and resulting discomfort almost always disappear after a victim makes more careful choices of starches, fruits, vegetables, condiments, and beverages. (See UPPER INTESTINAL DISTRESS for a discussion of irritating fruit juices and other beverages, vegetables, and condiments.)

My Recommendations: Eat a starch-based diet and take care to avoid irritating fatty foods, alcohol, decaffeinated as well as caffeinated coffee, hot peppers, Mexican salsas, raw onions, cucumbers, green peppers, radishes, and fruit juices.

Antacids, and in difficult cases more powerful acid-reducing drugs such as Tagamet (cimetidine) and Zantac (ranitidine), may be helpful. Raise the head of your bed on six-inch blocks in order to keep stomach acid out of the esophagus while you're sleeping. (Avoid aluminum-containing antacids.)

HORMONE-DEPENDENT DISEASES

STANDARD PRACTICE

In women, these diseases include abnormal uterine bleeding, early menarche (first period), fibrocystic breast disease, fibroids (tumors) of the uterus, late menopause (last periods), ovarian cysts, and premenstrual syndrome (PMS). In men, they include prostate enlargement and male-pattern baldness. These hormone-dependent diseases are clearly caused by imbalances in the levels of the sex hormones. However, the reason for elevated or depressed hormone levels is unknown. Possibly the problems are genetic; this is especially likely with male-pattern baldness.

Sex hormones, known as estrogens, progesterones, and testosterones, influence the growth and activity of hormone-sensitive organs—the breasts, ovaries, and uterus in women, and the prostate and testicles in men. If the amount of hormone circulating in the blood is too high or too low, disease problems can result. We're not talking about rare diseases, either. One in four women will develop fibroid tumors in her uterus. At least half of all women suffer from lumpy-tender breasts, known as fibrocystic breast disease, and almost all women experience one or more episodes of abnormal uterine bleeding between menarche (the first menstrual period) and menopause. The premenstrual syndrome (PMS), which is characterized by emotional crisis, swelling, abdominal bloating, and tiredness a few days prior to the start of a menstrual period, is a common complaint of many women. Prostate enlargement is an almost universal phenomenon in aging men, and businesses selling hair replacement gimmicks thrive on men living in Western societies.

When women's ovaries shut down production of hormones after menopause, their hormone-related problems diminish or disappear; even the fibroid tumors shrink away. The hormone-related changes in men are much less correctable.

Current Treatment: Drugs, including male and female hormones, and vitamin pills. Surgery for breast and uterine lumps, and for uterine bleeding. Some women resort to a total hysterectomy to end PMS and painful periods, and to bilateral mastectomies for fibrocystic breast disease. Enlargement of the prostate is temporarily relieved by surgery (TURP, trans-urethral resection of the prostate). But in many men the remaining parts of the prostate continue to enlarge, and relief is not permanent. Little help is available as yet for male-pattern baldness. Hair transplants and Minoxidil may give partial relief to the ego as well as the appearance.

Drawbacks: The problems are only temporarily and partially relieved by drug therapy, and the side effects of medication are ever-present. Surgical interventions, with all their associated costs and risks, should be considered as last resorts—a desperate, "patch-up" approach.

The McDougall Program (Dietary and Lifestyle Implications)

Women are supposed to be healthy and their female organs and functions should not be "a curse," as many women have referred to menstrual troubles for centuries. But in fact, most women do suffer considerably. You should not look for defects in the "female design" to explain the reasons for these epidemics of female troubles, but look rather to factors within your own control. Men seem to have less frequent and less severe hormonal problems, in part because their sexual nature is more hidden.

Blood levels of hormones that influence the female reproductive tissues (breasts, ovaries, and uterus) including estrogens, progesterones, and pro-lactin, a pituitary hormone, are dependent upon your diet. A high-fat diet will increase the levels of these hormones in a woman's body through a variety of mechanisms. Certain kinds of bacteria living normally in the colon of people who eat fatty foods are able to convert bile acids into other substances that have hormone activity.

Another important dietary mechanism involves recirculation of hormones. For example, estrogens, made in the ovaries and the adrenal glands, are secreted into the bloodstream and then pass through the liver into the intestine. To prevent reabsorption by the intestine, these estrogens are combined in the liver with a nonabsorbable substance. A high-fat diet encourages growth of the bacteria in the colon that produce enzymes that uncouple those unabsorbable estrogen complexes formed in the liver. Then the uncoupled "free" estrogen is absorbed back into the bloodstream, resulting in higher total levels of estrogen in the woman's body. Fats, especially meat fats, will encourage the growth of these colon bacteria that are capable of splitting these complexes. Obviously, this means of making free estrogens available for reabsorption can contribute to a situation that favors development of breast cancer.

Fortunately, fibers present in vegetable foods also help to block the absorption of "free" estrogens found in the bowel. Vegetarian women excrete two to three times more estrogen in their feces than do those who eat meats. Furthermore, the blood levels of certain powerful estrogens are 50 percent lower than are those in meat eaters.

Obesity, too, causes a body to produce more estrogens. Male hormones, called androgens, naturally present in small amounts in women, are converted to estrogens by their body fat. The more obese a woman is, the more of this conversion occurs, and the higher will be the levels of estrogen hormones from this source. The same process occurs in obese men, which is why they so often take on certain characteristics of women.

Abnormal Uterine Bleeding. The amount of bleeding and the severity of pain during menses are a direct consequence of the quantity of endometrial tissue (the cells lining the inside of the uterus) that is built up each month and must be shed at the time of menstrual flow. The amount of tissue that is formed is a consequence of estrogen stimulation. A diet higher in fats means more estrogens, which means more endometrial buildup. Passage of large clots through the neck of the uterus during menstrual flow causes pain. Normally, menstrual blood contains factors that prevent clotting. But animal fats of the saturated type introduced in the diet cause blood to clot more readily, adding more pain to the menses.

Early Menarche. Growing girls become women capable of reproduction at a younger age when they are raised on a high-fat diet. In most women, their first period (the menarche) begins at about age twelve. On a low-fat diet the first menstrual period starts around age sixteen. A similar early maturation occurs in boys, but the effects are less dramatic. Consider the impact on girls and boys in junior and senior high school when they start expressing sexual desires four years before their mental maturity can help them to deal with adult matters. Social disharmony stirs them up, to say the least! Here's something else for the girls to worry about; earlier onset of menstruation, not surprisingly, is associated with greater risk of developing uterus and breast cancer later on in life, a result of the longer stimulation of the vulnerable tissues by cancer-promoting estrogens.

Fibrocystic Breast Disease. For most women, breasts become tender just before the onset of their menstrual periods, when estrogen hormones reach their highest monthly levels. In approximately 10 percent of women the pain is described as severe. Overstimulation of the mammary tissues by higher than normal levels of estrogens causes the breasts to swell and become tender. Eventually, after repeated bouts of inflammation, the breasts develop scar tissue in many places, and some of the milk ducts become plugged, forming cysts. Fibrocystic breast disease, again not surprisingly, is associated with a higher risk of breast cancer.

Fibroids of the Uterus. Overstimulation of the muscle cells that make up the body of the uterus by estrogens results in the unregulated proliferation of some of these cells. The noncancerous growth becomes a lump in the uterus. Such lumps vary in dimensions—some rare ones have grown to the size of a basketball! These tumors do not become cancerous; the best reason for removing them is the discomfort they cause. However, for many doctors, just their presence, whether small or middle-sized, is reason enough for recommending that they be removed. After menopause, when hormone production decreases due to natural "ovary shut-down," these fibroids soon shrink, making their owner safe both from them and from the surgeon's knife.

Late Menopause. Elevated levels of estrogen cause women to menstruate approximately four years longer than they would if they kept to a low-fat diet. The average age of menopause should be about forty-six years, rather than fifty. A prolonged menstrual life is associated with a much higher risk of breast cancer and cancer of the body of the uterus for an obvious reason: the longer stimulation of vulnerable cells by cancer-promoting estrogens.

Ovarian Cysts. Researchers have discovered a simple alternative to fertility drugs and surgery for treating polycystic ovary disease in overweight women. Just losing weight can correct the abnormalities in the functioning of the sex hormones that are responsible for the lack of ovulation, infertility, excessive hair growth, and acne that often accompany polycystic ovaries. (Need I add that the most effective way to lose weight, and at the same time to dramatically improve the hormone balance in the body, is to adopt a low-fat, starch-based diet?)

Premenstrual Syndrome (PMS). The cause, for obvious reasons, has been considered hormonal since the condition was first described in 1931. An estrogen-progesterone imbalance is considered to be the underlying mechanism. Because of this theory, many treatments have focused on the use of female hormone pills, especially the progesterones, for relief of the disturbance. The reason progesterone pills work probably lies in their anti-estrogen effect. However, taking progesterone is not without undesirable side effects; it causes changes in the cholesterol in the blood, which will increase the risk of atherosclerosis and its complications, such as heart attacks and strokes. Recent concern has been raised because of the findings that women who take progesterone for years have four times the risk of breast cancer as women who took none.

The symptoms of PMS coincide with the highest levels of female hormones in the body during the time of the menstrual cycle. Preventing high levels of estrogens (and correcting any other hormone imbalances that may be present) is the key to dealing with PMS. A low-fat starch-based diet brings hormones into balance within a couple of menstrual cycles and relieves PMS for most women. (And it never hurts for a woman to *look* better as she manages the complexities of *feeling* better all over.)

Prostate Enlargement. The prostate gland is located deep inside the pubic region and surrounds the urethra, the hollow tube in the penis through which the urine passes out of the bladder. In most men, beginning in about the fifth decade of life the prostate gland will gradually enlarge. When this growth presses on the urethra, then problems with urination develop. Feeling the need for frequent urination, they need to wake up to urinate during the night (and experience the attendant difficulties of going back to sleep again). Difficulty getting the stream started and dribbling during and after urination are common symptoms. Many men have enlarged prostates, and the size of the gland alone is not reason enough to submit to surgery. Only when the patient feels that these symptoms are so troublesome that his enjoyment of life is significantly affected should surgery be performed. A very rare exception to this general statement happens when the kidneys are being damaged by back pressure of the urine accumulating in the bladder. This degree of damage seldom occurs without symptoms to warn the man and his physician. Simple blood tests and X-rays will help to identify the condition in its early stages.

Sometimes, the gland enlarges in parts that do not affect the flow of urine. However, in more unfortunate men, the enlargement will be a sign of cancer. Even so, the mere suspicion of cancer should not be used to force a patient into accepting surgery to remove the prostate gland. Usually the presence of suspected cancer is first noticed by the physician's probing finger. And, when appropriate, the suspicion can be confirmed (or dismissed) by taking specimens at biopsy.

Long-term overstimulation of the prostate gland with male hormones such as testosterone is believed to be the cause of benign prostate enlargement. Higher testosterone levels are found in men who eat foods rich in fats. Malignant enlargement, caused by cancerous cells, is believed to be provoked by the same agencies.

Male-Pattern Baldness. You're probably thinking right now that if I blame your diet for the loss of your hair, I've gone too far. I wouldn't risk losing your trust if I weren't supported by a review of a Japanese book that appeared in the *Journal of Dermatology, Surgery, and Oncology* titled, of all things, "Can Hair Grow Again?". The author of this book proposes that the loss of hair is the result of increased activity of sebaceous glands in the scalp that is caused by overstimulation of these glands by the male hormone testosterone in men susceptible by genetic predisposition. He points out an undisputed observation: a direct correlation among increased levels of animal fats (saturated fats) that are eaten by males in Japan, increased levels of sebaceous gland activity in the scalps of those men, and an increased incidence of male-pattern baldness in Japanese during the past forty years. Before World War II almost every Japanese man in Japan had a full head of hair. When they move to Hawaii or California, or change their diet in Japan, as many have recently done, a number of Japanese men have become bald just as white and black American males do.

The author of this book, Dr. Masumi Inaba, recommends treatment of male-pattern baldness with a diet low in animal sources of fats and calories, accompanied by regular shampooing and treatment of the scalp with a lotion containing an oxidizing agent to deactivate the testosterone found in the surface cells of the scalp (Minoxidil may act as an oxidizing agent). Dr. Inaba reports mild to moderate regrowth of hair in 30 to 50 percent of his cases.

Current Treatment for Women: There is a better way to deal with hormone imbalance than giving hormone pills or removing the ovaries. The kinds of foods that people eat have a tremendous influence upon the hormones produced in their bodies. Therefore, a sensible change in eating habits will lower the estrogen levels within days, and will improve all aspects of your life that are affected by your monthly cycle. Marked benefits can be expected as soon as two months after the change in diet.

Exercise and reduction in weight in obese women can also lower their levels of estrogens. The net result from reducing the exaggerated amounts of hormones found in too many American women down to healthier levels will be better general well-being all the time and relief from troublesome signs and symptoms during menstruation. For example, painful periods and copious bleeding become lighter and less painful. I have seen the pain from a large fibroid uterus stop completely after the recommended change in diet was adopted. I would also expect that the lower hormone levels would cause the tumors to shrink, just as they do after menopause. (Studies on the relationship between fibroids and diet still must be done.) Women near menopause (the mid-forties) very often stop menstrual bleeding soon after they change their diet and start to exercise, because of the decrease in estrogens. The change to a low-fat diet has caused a reduction in breast tenderness and swelling in 60 to 100 percent of women afflicted with breast pains during the menstrual period.

Current Therapy for Men: Prostate enlargement, like prostate cancer, is related to the levels of the sex hormones in a man's body throughout his life. These levels are a direct consequence of the foods he chooses to eat. More specifically, a diet high in fat results in elevated blood levels of these hormones, and is the primary factor in the cause of both conditions. In general, factors that cause a disease also promote the progress of that disease. Therefore, any man with prostate cancer or simple enlargement of the gland should change his choice of foods to those that provide very little fat, in hope of gaining some benefit from the reduction of hormone levels. Certainly, no harm can be done by following this recommendation.

Recently, hormones that interfere with the production of testosterone have been found effective in treating prostate cancer and prostatic enlargement. You should look into these investigational approaches.

Symptoms relating to frequent urination can be helped by decreasing fluid intake, especially after the evening meal. Also, stop drinking caffeinated beverages, which irritate the bladder and increase the urge to urinate.

My Recommendations: Change to a low-fat, starch-based diet. Lose excess weight (easily accomplished on this type of diet) and take moderate exercise. Avoid surgery and drugs, whenever possible.

HYPERTENSION (High Blood Pressure)

STANDARD PRACTICE

Estimates are that between one half to one fourth of the people in the United States have an elevated blood pressure, and therefore run an increased risk of suffering from a stroke, a heart attack, or sudden death. In 98 percent of cases the disease is termed "essential," which implies that the cause is unknown. Heredity is blamed (you've heard this bit of folklore: "it runs in the family"). High intake of table salt may be an important contributory factor for some people.

Current Treatment: Lower the blood pressure with a variety of drugs. Beta-blockers (such as Inderal and Lopressor) act by blocking the action of adrenalin, thus weakening the strength of the heart muscle. Diuretics remove sodium ions from body fluids, and in doing so lower the volume of the circulating blood. Vasodilators relax healthy segments of blood vessels, and so decrease "peripheral resistance."

Drawbacks: The first thing to point out is that this approach simply doesn't work: The risk of strokes, heart attacks, and sudden death is not decreased for the vast majority of people with high blood pressure who take medications hoping to lower it. Moreover, the side effects of these therapeutic drugs are significant and include an increased risk of death from the medications themselves. (Studies have shown that hypertensive patients being treated with diuretics run double the risk of sudden death.)

An important medical review concerned with the treatment of blood pressure with drugs came to the following conclusions:

- There will be no appreciable benefit to an individual patient from treating a diastolic pressure of less than 100 mm Hg.
- There is no evidence that any particular level of systolic pressure should be treated, and thus there is no reason to treat patients with isolated systolic hypertension, however that might be defined.
- Blood pressure varies . . . It is prudent to check the pressure on several occasions before deciding whether to treat. . . .
- It is probably more important to stop a patient smoking than to treat his mildly raised blood pressure.

Overzealous treatment of high blood pressure with medications results in an increased risk of heart attacks and death, especially when with those drugs the diastolic pressure is lowered below 85 to 90 mm Hg. Some investigators even declare that lowering blood pressure below 105 mm Hg with drugs is associated with an increased risk of heart attack. Possibly this ill effect of reaching too low a blood pressure by treatment with drugs is the result of a sudden critical decrease in the flow of blood to the heart muscle. (This relationship is true only for lower blood pressures in people *on medication*—a low pressure of 110/70 with *no medication* is a sign of good health.)

The McDougall Program (Dietary and Lifestyle Implications)

Elevated blood pressure is not a disease but, rather, high blood pressure is the *sign* of a life-threatening sickness of the blood vessel system itself. The blood vessels are made nonelastic and are clogged with the plaques of atherosclerosis; the fats in our diet cause the blood to sludge and the vessels to spasm. All this leads to a serious resistance to the easy flow of the blood. This resistance causes the pressure to rise, just as the pressure in a garden hose goes up when you press a finger over the nozzle.

Treating just the major sign of this unhealthy blood vessel system—elevated blood pressure—cannot be expected to be any more effective than treating only the signs of other diseases. What happens to the person with pneumonia when only a major sign of the disease, the fever, is treated with aspirin, rather than the infected lungs with antibiotics? You soon have a dead patient, albeit with a normal body temperature. Similarly, in cases of high blood pressure, the actual disease is the sickened blood vessels and the sludged blood in them, and that underlying disease must be corrected or the patient's life will end in tragedy. For the typical patient, treating hypertension with blood pressure-lowering medications results in a heart attack victim with little more to applaud than a normal blood pressure. Remember, people with high blood pressure die of strokes and heart attacks—complications of arteries weakened by years of atherosclerosis.

When a physician evaluates the risk of stroke, heart attack, or death for a patient, elevated blood pressure is only one sign of the extent of disease in the blood vessels. Other indicators of risk include blood levels of cholesterol and triglycerides, obesity, family history, and age.

The main cause for the development of high blood pressure is a few short years of living too luxuriously, gobbling down all those rich tempting foods, full of fats and salt, that you simply haven't the strength, or the sense, to refuse. It doesn't take long to change the dynamics of flow in the blood vessels—one in eight high school students in the United States already has an elevated blood pressure. The blood vessels in a person who does not watch his diet eventually become so diseased that one day a vessel is blocked by a clot or bursts open, killing parts of the heart muscle, or of the brain, leaving him an invalid for the rest of his life—or often killing the whole body, in a matter of seconds.

Current Treatment: The blood vessels must be made healthier and stronger as soon as possible so they don't burst toward either the inside or the outside. They begin to heal as soon as the causative processes are corrected. Changing to a low-fat, no-cholesterol, low-sodium, high-potassium diet (in other words, to a starch-based diet) allows the blood to flow more easily within a few hours (in short, as soon as fats stop coating the blood cells and making them stick together). Spasms in the blood vessels also stop within hours. With such relief of sludging and spasms, the blood pressure often drops to normal in less than forty-eight hours.

Dosages of blood pressure medications must be lowered quickly, after the changeover diet is begun, in order to avoid *hypotension* (low blood pressure), weakness, and dizziness. On the day the diet is started, I generally stop all blood pressure medications if the patient is taking less than four mild pills a day. I make exceptions to this rapid discontinuation of medication when a blood pressure condition is more severe than usual or if the patient is taking beta-blockers.

If the patient is on very strong dosages of medication, this is itself an indication of a serious health problem. With powerful medication I generally cut dosages in half every three days (based on an improving blood pressure), until the amount of medication taken is insignificant; then I have them stop. Beta-blockers should be stopped slowly to prevent the onset of chest pain and rapid heartbeat associated with withdrawal. *You must have the help of your physician in reducing your medication.*

Step-down on Blood Pressure Medications:

Step 1. Minoxidil, guanethidine.
Step 2. Hydralazine, captopril, clonidine, prazosin, methyldopa, reserpine.
Step 3. Beta-blockers (reduce dosage slowly, usually cut in half every three days). Calcium channel blockers.
Step 4. Diuretics.
Step 5. Off all medications.
Reduction in medications is started with those in Step 1. Once these medications are stopped and the blood pressure is found acceptable, then the Step 2 medications are stopped—and so on.

After you start the diet, your blood pressure should be measured at least once a day. Your goal is a pressure of 110/70 or less *without* medication. Medication to lower pressure may be given when the pressure is found by many readings to be greater than 100 mm Hg diastolic (lower number). When taking medication, the goal is to lower the pressure to about 85 to 90 mm Hg diastolic. You should not make it lower, since too low a pressure, when produced by drugs, results in more heart attacks and death. (Low blood pressure without medication is, of course, healthy.)

My Recommendations: Change to a starch-based, low-salt diet. Exercise daily; physical activity has been shown to lower blood pressure. Stop your medications quickly, under your doctor's supervision. Pay attention to all controllable health-risk factors—cholesterol, triglycerides, weight, and such personal habits as smoking and caffeine and alcohol consumption.

HYPOGLYCEMIA

STANDARD PRACTICE

Hypoglycemia is an abnormally low level of sugar in the blood. The cause of the common form that is called postprandial (after-meals), or reactive, hypoglycemia is unknown. Rare cases of hypoglycemia occur with liver disease, post-stomach surgery, insulin-producing tumors of the pancreas, certain enzyme defects, hormone disturbances, drugs, and other serious illnesses. Diabetics frequently suffer hypoglycemia as a consequence of too much medication. Furthermore, symptoms suggesting those of hypoglycemia may actually be due to stress and anxiety, and other unrelated conditions.

Some doctors doubt the existence of a specific disease that can be called hypoglycemia. Those who do recognize the problem, consider it rare, and insist that certain criteria must be met in order to make a correct diagnosis: dropping of blood sugar levels to less than 50 mg/dl during a glucose tolerance test, as is usually seen in true hypoglycemia. (Normal blood sugar levels are 70–120 mg/dl.) However, these low levels of blood sugar must also be accompanied by symptoms consistent with hypoglycemia before a firm diagnosis can be established. These symptoms are the dizziness, weakness, headaches, sweating, and sometimes mental confusion that develop when the body's tissues are deprived of an adequate supply of glucose as the blood sugar level falls. Hypoglycemic symptoms can be very disturbing and can trouble a person throughout much of the day, but they are especially pronounced about one to four hours after eating.

Current Treatment: The traditional medical treatment of reactive hypoglycemia, until very recently, has been a low-carbohydrate, high-protein diet, offering plentiful amounts of meats and cheese.

Drawbacks: High-protein diets characteristically are also high in fats and cholesterol, and low in fiber and carbohydrates. They are composed largely of dairy products, red meats, poultry, and fish, all of which can, in time, lead to heart attacks and cancer, to name just the two most alarming effects of such a diet. Furthermore, few patients have been helped by this type of diet—they're still sick! And now they're constipated as well.

The McDougall Program (Dietary and Lifestyle Implications)

Two basic physiologic mechanisms are now recognized as being involved in lowering the blood sugar to symptom-producing levels. Eating plant foods in which the fiber has been disrupted or removed by food processing can cause the blood sugars to drop low enough to cause symptoms. For a simple example, your pancreas will produce more insulin in response to your eating applesauce than it would if you ate the whole apple. This greater quantity of insulin can lower your blood sugar to the levels of hypoglycemia within a couple of hours. This response is further exaggerated if the disrupted apple fibers have been removed from the applesauce to make apple juice. The grinding of whole grains, such as brown rice, into flour will cause a similar increase in insulin response with exaggerated falls in blood sugar levels. Thus, it is important not only to eat vegetable foods, but, for a few very sensitive individuals, to eat those foods only as nature provided them—unprocessed, complete with all their fibers.

Secondly, the many kinds of fat in the American diet can inhibit insulin function, causing "insulin resistance." With poorly functioning insulin, the blood sugar levels rise too high. As a consequence of the high sugar, more insulin is produced, finally catching up to and surpassing the body's needs. This excess insulin soon drives the sugar to hypoglycemic levels. (This paralysis of insulin function is also seen with adult-onset diabetes.)

Hypoglycemia has been blamed for a multitude of complaints, ranging from frequent headaches to chronic fatigue. Actually, most of the people I have seen who complain of hypoglycemia simply had no better way to explain to me that they feel miserable all the time. Rarely have they had a glucose tolerance test that might confirm or rule out hypoglycemia. For the most part, the complaints of these people are vague expressions of continuous ill health. They don't know this, but their troubles come from eating the wrong foods, hypoglycemia or no hypoglycemia.

Current Treatment: Recommendations, even from apparently well qualified dietary and medical professionals, to eat a high-protein diet are outdated and should be disregarded, not only because they have very little chance of relieving symptoms, but because of the dangerous amounts of the damaging components in the recommended foods—cholesterol, fats, and excess proteins.

A starch-based diet will quickly relieve the disorder and its symptoms. In fact, this disease is so closely tied to the wrong diet (excessive fats, fiber deficiency, the presence of excess simple sugar and refined foods) that if the change to the proper foods does not result in quick relief, the diagnosis of hypoglycemia should be questioned.

People with hypoglycemia have often suffered for years, and as a result of so much physical misery they sometimes become injured emotionally, having an overpowering preoccupation with their feelings and well-being. Even after the hypoglycemia is relieved, such a person may not immediately regain confidence in his health, or accept the fact that he or she is well again, feeling well again, every day, all day.

If a "magic pill" came on the market today that offered a cure for adult-type diabetics, and improved the health of all diabetics by reducing the risk of life-threatening complications, and if this same pill also cured almost every case of hypoglycemia, a medical miracle would be proclaimed, equal in value to penicillin. For those people who are willing to put in the necessary effort, this "magic pill" is available today—in the starch-based diet. Unfortunately, this pill takes some effort to swallow. For me, the earnest hope is that some day soon every person with a blood-sugar disorder will at last be informed of the healing potential that is offered by sensible changes in diet.

My Recommendations: Change to a starch-based diet, with *no* refined foods. Limit fruits initially, because of their high content of simple sugars. Eat frequently, maybe six or more times a day when beginning. Eat plenty of food at each meal, and don't be concerned about gaining weight (because starches make you thin). Keep in mind also that your symptoms may be due to a problem other than low blood sugar levels, such as a food allergy (see ALLERGIC DISEASES).

KIDNEY DISEASE

STANDARD PRACTICE

The primary function of the kidneys is to excrete a variety of substances, including water, consumed in the diet and also waste products of our body's metabolism. The kidneys also produce hormones that control blood pressure and red blood cell production. There are many causes of kidney disease and resulting kidney failure, including high blood pressure, diabetes, and atherosclerosis. Toxic chemicals too can destroy kidney tissues. Furthermore, common inflammatory diseases of the kidney, known as glomerulonephritis (either chronic or acute) result in damage to the tissues and in the nephrotic syndrome, a condition characterized by edema, or accumulation of fluids in the tissues, and release of proteins in the urine. The cause of the inflammatory diseases is unknown. In addition, serious generalized diseases, such as several kinds of bacterial infections, autoimmune responses (lupus), and genetic predisposition (polycystic kidneys), can underlie kidney failure.

Current Treatment: Drugs to control symptoms of itching and fatigue and signs of edema and hyptertension that accompany failing kidneys. Eventually, toward the final stages of the kidney failure, dialysis while attached to an artificial kidney machine is prescribed. Kidney transplant is a route taken by many end-stage kidney patients. Little or no attention is given to the patient's diet. Many are told that what they eat doesn't matter—that, in effect, the kidney machine will compensate for their mistreatment of themselves at mealtimes.

Drawbacks: Life without healthy kidneys is the pits. If you have any doubts about the value of the effort you should devote to preserving the good health of your kidneys, take a trip to your local hospital's dialysis unit and see how those unfortunate patients look and how they are obliged to live. This kind of therapy is so expensive that Great Britain will not allow anyone over the age of fifty to receive help from the dialysis because of limited funds available through national health insurance—they simply die. Moreover, people who are dependent on dialysis have very high rates of infections, heart attacks, strokes, and other life-threatening complications because they are weakened people, limited in their ability to defend themselves and to repair damaged tissues. As for kidney transplantation, although the life of a person with a transplant is much improved over life tied to a kidney machine, there are side effects from the powerful medications taken to prevent rejection of the new kidney, and even with the medication there is still a very real possibility of losing the new kidney.

The McDougall Program (Dietary and Lifestyle Implications)

There are many causes of kidney damage; you must pay attention to those you can control. Fats and cholesterol in the diet promote atherosclerosis in the kidney arteries, which is one of the leading causes for failing kidneys. Add to this diabetes or high blood pressure and you invite almost certain kidney trouble by eating too well, but not at all wisely.

Among the most subtle and important of the many toxic threats to the kidneys are the excess amounts of protein that are consumed by the average person. Daily intake of more proteins than the body really needs means that the excess must be eliminated through the kidneys (usually as urea). We're equipped with no storage depots for proteins, as we are for fats and carbohydrates.

The proteins not used for body repair and growth float around in the bloodstream until they are metabolized by the liver and their remnants are removed by the kidneys. The filtering units in the kidneys are called nephrons. Destruction of these nephrons occurs directly from years of increased flows and pressures created by exposure to those proteins or to the products of their degradation. The damage from excessive intake of proteins is so common that in an otherwise healthy person, 25 to 50 percent of the functional capacity of the kidneys will be destroyed after eight decades of high living, American style. Even so, we're lucky to have much reserve tissue to rely on: With only 25 percent of kidney function remaining, plenty of tissue cells still survive to handle the waste products of body metabolism, and the damaged and failing kidneys go unnoticed. Our bodies are very forgiving!

But not forever. This damaging effect from a high-protein diet becomes a life-and-death matter with someone who has already lost kidney tissue from one or more other causes. For example, a person with diabetes, high blood pressure, atherosclerosis, physical injury, or surgical loss will be under a great disadvantage. Unfortunately, serious instruction about the value of a low-protein diet is an important part of essential education that is missing from the medical care given most patients who have lost part of their kidney function.

Glomerulonephritis. Twelve children aged four to sixteen were studied, who suffered from nephrotic syndrome due to glomerulonephritis (the condition where the kidneys become inflamed and pass large amounts of proteins and blood into the urine, while the body's tissues swell with accumulating fluid). All of the children had failed to respond to treatment with powerful anti-inflammatory drugs called steroids, and many also failed on anticancer drugs called cyclophosphamides. During the study, they were started on a diet that excluded common causes of food allergies—dairy products, eggs, pork products, tomatoes, etc. (see ALLERGIC DISEASES). In four of the children the nephrotic syndrome improved in less than a month. Within four to six months, remission was seen in six children. Then three were challenged with milk and all three had an immediate recurrence of glomerulonephritis.

Thus, a debilitating, often fatal kidney disease was cured in half the patients by simply excluding from their diets some common causes of food allergies, especially dairy products. Apparently the proteins in milk (or in other foods) succeed in entering the body through the walls of the intestinal tract. Once in the bloodstream, these proteins are attacked by antibodies (proteins synthesized by our own immune system in order to attack foreign invaders, such as bacteria, viruses, and food proteins). The milk proteins and antibodies form complexes that are filtered out of the circulating blood in the small capillaries of the kidneys.

Once stuck in the kidney tissues, these complexes act like a sliver of wood stuck in the skin, causing inflammation. The inflamed cells in the kidneys leak blood and protein into the urine. Soon the injured kidney tissues are permanently damaged, and the kidneys begin to fail. Many other investigators have reported the "cure" of nephrotic syndrome by the elimination of milk and other animal proteins, such as pork. Presumably, the cause of the condition is present in the foodstuffs that were eliminated.

Current Treatment: People with kidney disease often lose proteins in their urine, and because of this some doctors mistakenly recommend a high-protein diet in an attempt to compensate for the loss. The effort is foolish. All natural diets, whether based on plants or on animal foods, provide plenty of proteins. The strategy of adding even more protein in the diet not only does not help to affect the body's protein balance, but actually worsens the kidney disease.

The best treatment for someone having kidney trouble is a low-protein, low-fat, low-sodium, low-phosphate, and cholesterol-free diet. Potassium (which is high in fruits and vegetables) needs to be limited as the kidney disease progresses. Someone with a serious degree of the disease should unquestionably be under the care of a competent specialist.

My Recommendations: Try to identify the spiral cause of the condition, such as the specific animal protein that is responsible for many cases of glomerulonephritis. Eliminate these damaging meats and dairy products from all meals, thereby protecting and preserving the kidney functions that remain.

To begin with, in order to prevent development of any kidney destruction at all, follow a low-fat, no-cholesterol diet with limited and reasonable amounts of proteins. If damage has already occurred, then the amount of proteins must be restricted much further. To lower the protein intake while on a starch-based diet, consumption of beans, peas, and lentils must be restricted even more (indeed, often eliminated entirely). If kidney failure is far advanced, then simple sugars, even refined white sugar, should be added to your diet in order to increase the number of calories without relying upon more proteins. (Low-protein pasta products are available through dietetic specialty stores.) The goal is about 20 to 30 grams of protein a day. (Consider that a diet of white rice alone—2000 to 3000 calories—provides 40 to 60 grams of protein a day.)

Medications may be needed to control symptoms of kidney failure. Kidney dialysis may be your last resort, short of a kidney transplant. (For further details, see my book *McDougall's Medicine—A Challenging Second Opinion.* New Century Publishers Inc., Piscataway, N.J., 1985.)

KIDNEY STONES

STANDARD PRACTICE

Kidney stones are solid conglomerates of minerals that resemble gravel or stones that can form in the upper portion of the system of collecting tubules that drain the kidneys. When the stones break loose from that upper drainage system, they become lodged in the narrow stretches of the ureter, where they can cause indescribable pain in the abdomen and back. At least microscopic amounts of blood will be present in the urine when this occurs.

Most often kidney stones occur in men over thirty years of age, but women can have them too. Statistics indicate that stones will form in about 12 percent of our population. The two most common types of stones seen in the United States, calcium stones and uric acid stones, are named for the dominant ingredient in each kind of stone. Calcium oxalate and calcium phosphate stones comprise 75 to 85 percent of the total, and uric acid stones account for 5 to 8 percent. Other types of stones are rare and can be the result of metabolic defects or infections. The cause of kidney stones is unknown. Uric acid stones may be due to a diet high in purines (the basic building blocks of our genetic material, RNA and DNA, and present in certain foods rich in protein).

Current Treatment: To reduce the chance of recurrence of calcium stones, thiazide diuretics are sometimes prescribed. Sometimes a low-calcium diet is recommended. Allopurinal (a drug to reduce uric acid production) and a low-purine diet are offered as the best ways to prevent uric acid stones.

Painful kidney stones that fail to pass naturally through the ureter are removed by surgical procedures or by a new ultrasonic technique called lithotripsy, which uses high-frequency sound waves to fragment a stone into bits that easily pass through the ureter. Generally, from 500 to 1500 shock waves over a period of thirty to sixty minutes are administered to a completely or partially anesthetized patient partly submerged in water.

Drawbacks: Side effects and costs of drugs for preventing formation of kidney stones are significant. The ultrasound technique, first used in 1980, is both dramatic and expensive, but it has spared many people from surgery. A loud noise resounds through the operating room each time a shock wave is fired off, and both the patient and attending personnel must wear protective ear plugs. The cost of one machine and its specialized operating room is about 2 million dollars. About 85 percent of all stones can be fragmented by this ultrasonic technique. The side effects are minimal and most patients can leave the hospital in three to four days. On very rare occasions, tissues surrounding the stone are seriously injured and restorative surgery is required.

The McDougall Program (Dietary and Lifestyle Implications)

Throughout the world, the incidence of kidney stones can be correlated with the wealth of a country, especially as it is defined by expenditures for foods. The dietary component that is most strongly related to the formation of kidney stones is animal proteins. After World War I, when expensive foods became more abundant again after several years of austerity, near epidemics of kidney stones occurred in many populations in Europe. Since many Japanese people have changed toward an American-type diet after World War II, the incidence of kidney stone formation among them has been rising. Formation of stones in the kidneys and the upper ureters is almost unknown in underdeveloped societies whose people follow a starch-based diet that is low in animal products. In the United States, vegetarians have about half the incidence of stones that the general population experiences. (Of course, the term *vegetarian* can mean a wide variety of diets—some high in protein, purines, and calcium.)

Proteins, especially animal proteins, increase the excretion of calcium—from the foods eaten and from the stores of it in the eater's bones—through the kidneys into the urine. If a person is on a high-protein diet, his urine carries calcium in high concentrations. As the urine becomes saturated with calcium and other minerals, microscopic crystals form, and around these core crystals the stones will eventually grow to a visible and very troublesome size.

Some people who form kidney stones are told repeatedly that they suffer from *idiopathic hypercalcuria*, high levels of calcium excreted in the urine. The word *idiopathic* refers to an illness of unknown cause, that is peculiar to an individual. Idiopathic is an incorrect term for this problem, because in most cases the cause is known. However, since all too often the subject of nutrition is a neglected part of a physician's medical education, he seldom gives any thought to the probability that the large amounts of proteins eaten by a patient have contributed to the elevated levels of calcium in his urine. Until physicians and dietitians give up the mistaken notion that the "well-balanced American diet" offers correct nutrition to every one at all times, the medical profession will be handicapped both in its attempts at diagnosis of even some common diseases and in its ability to provide effective treatments for patients.

Current Treatment: In almost every case the presence of calcium in high levels in the urine is corrected by lowering the protein content of the patient's diet. Reducing the intake of proteins from *animal* sources is especially important. Meat proteins consist of large amounts of sulfur-containing amino acids, which have a very powerful calcium-leaching effect on the kidneys. Reducing the intake of meats will also reduce other components in the urine that favor stone formation, such as uric acid.

A low-protein, low-purine diet is an accepted therapy prescribed by some physicians and dietitians for the prevention of uric acid stones. However, the dietary programs now recommended most often would be more effective if they were changed to eliminate animal products altogether.

Doctors are just starting to investigate use of proper foods as a means of treating patients who have already produced actual kidney stones. Uric acid stones can be dissolved in place by making the patient's urine more alkaline. This is accomplished by decreasing the intake of animal proteins, increasing the amount of potassium contributed by vegetable foods, and drinking more water. A medication called Allopurinol is recommended, in addition to potassium salts. In one small study this approach was 100 percent effective in dissolving uric acid stones. Future studies will determine how effective dietary control will be in dissolving all other types of stones.

My Recommendations: A low-protein diet to prevent the initial formation of stones and/or to prevent recurrence. Ultrasound treatment for troublesome stones that won't pass naturally; surgery only as a last resort.

LIVER DISEASE

STANDARD PRACTICE

The primary function of the liver is to detoxify and excrete the waste products of our body's metabolism and excrete excess proteins, cholesterol, fats, and additives consumed in the diet. The liver also produces proteins necessary for the clotting of the blood and a protein called albumin that serves to keep fluid in the blood vessels. A failing liver results in the accumulation of breakdown products of metabolism, edema, and finally coma and death.

There are many causes of liver disease; the most common are infections with viruses and consumption of alcohol. Continuous injury by either of these agents results in permanent loss of liver tissue. One of the changes in the liver that occurs during injury is the accumulation of fat within the liver cells. This condition, known as fatty infiltration, commonly occurs in alcoholism, diabetes, and obesity, and is in part due to a high-fat diet. With severe liver damage, liver cells are replaced by extensive scar tissue—the condition is known as cirrhosis of the liver.

Current Treatment: Liver damage is first treated, whenever possible, by stopping drinking alcohol, especially when alcohol is the primary cause. The recommended diet for anyone suffering from liver disease is high in carbohydrate and low in protein, fat, and sodium.

Drugs are used to help control some of the complications of the ailing liver. Diuretics are often given to help relieve the edema. Drugs such as lactulose decrease the absorption of protein from the intestine and thereby further reduce the protein load to be handled by the liver. Steroids are sometimes used to decrease inflammation.

Drawbacks: Medications deal primarily with symptoms and fail to prolong the patient's life in most cases. Survival is not improved with the use of steroids and other anti-inflammatory drugs. Unfortunately, strict adherence to a healthy diet is rarely encouraged by the physician until liver disease is far advanced. By this time, there is too little liver left to make much of a difference.

The McDougall Program (Dietary and Lifestyle Implications)

The primary treatment of liver disease is a low-fat, low-protein, high-complex-carbohydrate, starch-based diet *started early*—long before liver failure is advanced. A healthier diet will relieve much of the burden on the diseased liver, since it will not have to metabolize excess proteins, cholesterol, fats, and additives. Vegetable proteins are much easier for the diseased liver to metabolize than similar amounts of animal-derived proteins, probably because vegetable proteins contain lower amounts of certain amino acids and other burdensome materials. The low-fat quality of the McDougall diet helps relieve the fatty infiltration stage of the liver disease; there is a gradual disappearance of fat from the liver in four to eight weeks along with the improvement in diabetes and weight loss following the introduction of the diet. Progress can often be measured by reduction in the liver enzymes SGOT and SGPT seen in blood tests.

Current Therapy: A person with liver failure must be as kind to his body as possible, primarily by avoiding toxic substances and making food choices that are not excessive in fats and proteins. Low sodium may be important in advanced liver failure to reduce fluid accumulation. Because all foods are naturally plentiful in protein, it is often necessary to make up as much as half the diet from "empty calorie" foods, such as honey, white sugar, high-sugar fruit juices, and protein-free pasta in order to dilute the protein content of the starches, vegetables, and fruits to a tolerable level.

My Recommendations: Primary prevention of liver disease means avoiding injury to the liver. In terms of alcohol, this means don't drink excessively. In the case of hepatitis virus infections, this means "safe sex," clean hypodermic needles, hygienic living, and avoiding blood transfusions. There are also effective vaccines for people at high risk of contracting viral hepatitis. Benefits from dietary treatment are real, but limited—you only have one liver, so *prevention should be your goal.*

MULTIPLE SCLEROSIS

STANDARD PRACTICE

Multiple sclerosis is a chronic neurologic disease which develops between the ages of twenty and fifty and is characterized by recurrent attacks that can leave the patient with impaired vision, loss of feeling, loss of balance, spasticity, bladder problems, weakness, and/or paralysis. The cause is unknown; possibly genetic, an autoimmune response, or infectious.

Current Treatment: Watchful waiting, steroids, immunosuppressive therapy (Imuran), and treatment of symptoms with drugs.

Drawbacks: The present approach to multiple sclerosis is a disheartening failure. No effective treatment has been accepted as yet by the general medical profession. The drugs used often have serious side effects, contributing to the suffering and early death of patients, and the treatments are costly. In most cases the disease is progressive, and unaltered by any therapy. Within ten years, more than half the afflicted people will be disabled or dead. These frightening statistics should make us all eager to examine any approach with the slightest possibility of improving the health of multiple sclerosis patients.

The McDougall Program (Dietary and Lifestyle Implications)

When the subjects of multiple sclerosis and diet are mentioned in the same sentence, the reaction from most health professionals is to dismiss the connection as being absolutely ridiculous. How could something as simple as what we eat be involved with such a mysterious disease as multiple sclerosis? Most professionals are expecting that the answer will be found, someday, by some "high-tech," high-profit research in viral or immunological investigations.

However, when I have asked doctors and dietitians who are supposed experts in the field of multiple sclerosis to support their contention that diet has nothing to do with the cause or cure of the disease, they have consistently been unable to give me a scientifically supported answer. In my research, I have yet to see a study which says that a sensible diet will not help victims of multiple sclerosis. In fact, the scientific evidence published to date provides evidence supporting the remarkable benefit of diet for victims of this debilitating disease.

Multiple sclerosis is common in Canada, the United States, Northern Europe; it is rare in Japan, elsewhere in Asia, and in Africa. When people migrate from a country of low incidence of multiple sclerosis to a country of high incidence, their chance of getting this disease increases as they learn new ways to live and to eat. Many investigators have looked into the environmental factors that would account for the differences in disease incidence among different populations.

The culprit appears to be the strongest contact we have with our environment—the foods we eat each day. Does this surprise you? After all, "we are what we eat." One general observation that can be made is that countries with lots of cases of multiple sclerosis are also wealthy countries. An exception has been the wealthy country of Japan. But there is an explanation for this: Even though the Japanese have money, stress, pollution, and the smoking habits characteristic of people in other industrialized nations, their traditional rice-based diet is more characteristic of the foods consumed in poorer nations. When the Japanese change their diet by moving to a Western country or as the diet of younger generations of Japanese becomes more Westernized, the disease becomes more prevalent.

A diet filled with rich foods assails us with many different substances that may be related to diseases that trouble us, but the animal fats, especially those from dairy products, have been most closely linked to the development of multiple sclerosis. One important theory proposes that cow's milk consumed in infancy lays the foundation for injuries to the nervous system that appear later in life. Cow's milk contains one fifth as much of the essential unsaturated fat, linoleic acid, as does human mother's milk. This essential dietary-derived substance helps to make up some of the chemical components in nervous tissues. Children raised on a linoleic-acid-deficient, high-animal-fat diet, as are most kids in our modern affluent society, are quite possibly starting life with a damaged nervous system, susceptible to insults and injuries in later life. Analysis has shown that persons with multiple sclerosis have a higher content of saturated fats (less unsaturated fats) in brain tissue than do people who do not have this disease.

The factors that can precipitate the attacks of multiple sclerosis in midlife are suspected to be viruses, allergic reactions, and/or disturbances of the flow of blood to the brain. Most likely, whatever factor may be involved, there is a close tie to the circulatory system, because the areas of injury sustained by the nerve cells surround blood vessels.

One theory holds that the primary injury to a person with multiple sclerosis is caused by a decrease in the supply of blood to tissues in certain parts of the brain. Dietary fats in the amounts consumed by Americans can and do cause a decrease in flow of blood to many kinds of tissues, including those in the brain. Fats from the gut enter the bloodstream, coat the red blood cells, and thereby inhibit the normal property of their membranes that keep the cells from sticking together. Therefore, blood cells coated with fats do stick together, forming clumps that slow the flow of blood to vital tissues. In many blood vessels the clumping and sludging become so severe that the flow of blood stops entirely, and the overall oxygen content of the blood falls. Tissues deprived of nutrients and oxygen for even short periods of time will die. Could something as basic as this be a factor in the attacks that destroy nerve cells in victims of multiple sclerosis?

Current Treatment: *A low-fat diet reduces frequency of attacks.* During World War II, civilians in Western Europe were under tremendous stress, as their countries were occupied by one enemy or another, yet doctors observed that patients with multiple sclerosis needed two to two and a half times fewer hospitalizations during this war period. At that time, all kinds of foods were scarce, and the civilian populations could no longer afford to eat their meat-producing animals. Instead, they ate the grains and vegetables that earlier had nourished their cows, chickens, and pigs. The overall result was a significant reduction in the amounts of animal products they ate, and, therefore, in the amounts of animal fats they consumed.

Following publication of these observations about improvement in the well-being of multiple sclerosis patients (as well as of patients suffering from other diseases, such as atherosclerosis), Dr. Roy Swank, former head of the University of Oregon's Department of Neurology and presently a practicing physician at the Health Science Center of the University of Oregon, began treating his patients with a low-fat diet. Dr. Swank can now draw upon more than thirty-five years of experience in the use of a low-fat diet for more than 3000 multiple sclerosis patients. His results are unchallenged by other studies, and unmatched in effectiveness by any other treatment for this crippling disease.

The course of this disease usually leads to a progressive decline in the patient, reducing him to existence in a wheelchair (or worse) likely by the end of ten years. However, according to his landmark research published in the *Archives of Neurology*, Dr. Swank reports that if this disease is detected early, and if attacks have been few and the patient adopts a low-fat diet, then he has a 95 percent chance of remaining in the same condition or even for improvement over the next twenty years. Even people who have had multiple sclerosis for a long time, and have already suffered severe nervous system damage, will slow the progress of the disease with a change to the low-fat diet.

The healthiest diet is based on low-fat vegetable foods. In recently published research in the December 1988 issue of the *American Journal of Clinical Nutrition*, Dr. Swank presented data from patients studied for more than thirty-four years, showing the importance of strict dietary practices for multiple sclerosis patients. First, he and his colleagues found that every incremental increase in intake of saturated fats (that is, animal fat) is associated with a corresponding increase in frequency of attacks. Second, to arrest the disease the diet must contain as little fat as possible, or approximately 7 percent fat. Those on a low-fat (17 grams of animal fat) diet lived almost three times as long as patients on a high-fat diet and generally improved their level of function. On a higher fat diet (42 grams of animal fat) the average patient went from active to wheelchair and bedridden (or dead) over the three and a half decades of study. Thus, the threshold of safety can be reached with the diet taught by the McDougall Program. A diet consisting of starches, vegetables, and fruits contains only 5 to 10 precent total fats, and less than half of this amount is represented by the saturated fats. Obviously, this is the ideal diet for patients suffering from multiple sclerosis. And it is a practicable diet, as well as a palatable one.

Dr. Swank has added a small amount of vegetable oil (polyunsaturated) to his diet, hoping that the polyunsaturated fats may make the diet more palatable, if not more helpful. However, studies that simply added oils high in essential fats, such as linoleic acid, to the diet have shown conflicting results concerning any benefit. Therefore, I believe the low-fat content of his diet (not the added vegetable oil) is the explanation for his successful treatment of people with multiple sclerosis. Dr. Swank himself also inclines toward the view that the lowest level of saturated (animal) fats is the critical issue. Furthermore, other health reasons prevent me from adding vegetable oils to a person's diet. At the very least, these oils contribute calories that may lead to obesity, and, at worst, they may promote cancer and gall-bladder disease.

My Recommendation: Follow the McDougall diet. The results of this sensible dietary treatment have been very gratifying for my patients (and for me), not only because the progress of the multiple sclerosis has been halted in most cases, but also because their health is unquestionably improved. And no one will deny that these unfortunate people need every bit of help they can get.

OBESITY

STANDARD PRACTICE

It was estimated in 1987 that 34 million people in the United States between the ages of twenty and seventy-five were overweight. A sizable percentage of these people go on one weight-loss diet after another in an attempt to reduce. The cause of their excess pounds is said to be overeating, stress, depression, and/or genetics.

Current Treatment: Low-calorie diets, low-carbohydrate diets, liquid-protein diets, diet pills, stomach balloons, stomach stapling, intestinal by-pass, jaw-wiring, psychotherapy, and hypnosis.

Drawbacks: Ninety-five percent of the people who go on a series of different weight-loss diets gain most or all of their weight back within a year. Dieters of that giddy sort are appropriately called failures.

Attempts to improve the failure rates of diet programs that tell you to eat less food have caused many different kinds of problems. Some diets cause you to develop ketosis (a condition that also occurs with several common illnesses, and suppresses your appetite); these are the low-carbohydrate diets—and they can and do make you sick. Cans of protein powders are convenient variations upon the low-carbohydrate "make-yourself-sick" diets. Diet pills suppress the hunger drive a little, and only a little weight loss is accomplished as long as you're on the pills. Meanwhile, side effects and expenses are considerable.

The desperately obese go for exotic surgery—jaws wired together, stomach stapled to make it "smaller," balloon inserted in stomach to make it feel fuller, intestines bypassed. However, many patients find a way to foil these weight-loss gimmicks. For example, they eat small meals more frequently or liquefy their foods so they will pass easily through the wired teeth. The latest approach to quick weight loss is liposuction, by which your unsightly deposits of body fat are sucked out through a small-bore metal tube. The physical shapes that emerge are less than human in too many cases, when the procedure is used for general weight reduction.

The McDougall Program (Dietary and Lifestyle Implications)

The most obvious and prevalent signs of malnutrition in our affluent country are the layers of blubber worn by most people—usually to the despair of themselves and often to the disgust of their associates. I hear many people say that their obesity is due to a design problem: They're genetically defective, so they declare, almost proudly. They tell me things like this:

"I was born fat."
"I have too many fat cells."
"My set-point is set too high."
"I'm overweight because my mother was overweight."
"I inherited big bones."
"My stomach is too large."
"Through years of overeating my stomach has stretched out. Now
    I need more food to fill it than a normal person does."

When I hear these excuses for being vastly overweight, I sigh, roll my eyes and lift eyebrows, and deliver myself of an expletive: "Nonsense!"

If you had the opportunities to see the basic human anatomy that I've had, you'd know that all people are built according to pretty much the same plan. Those of the same height have bones of about the same size. The extra fat they carry around is what enlarges those awkward, corpulent bodies. As for the stomach, I've participated in hundreds of surgeries on it, and I've never seen even one that had been stretched out to unnatural dimensions.

I'm not entirely ruling out a genetic predisposition to be fat. There may be some truth to that for some people, but even they will find that they'll slim down considerably if they eat the proper diet. What you're far more likely to have acquired from a parent is not "bad genes" but the bad habit of eating all those heaped-up platters of rich foods that your mother, in innocent kindness, set on the table for her family to dig into.

People are always being told by their physicians, dietitians, and know-it-all friends that they're fat because they "eat too much." Generally, the fat ones respond with a cringe and a guilty nod. However, 99.9 percent of the time that explanation is also unmitigated nonsense.

The human body has a mechanism that regulates the drive for food, known as hunger. Do you really think that your hunger drive was designed awry? Think about your basic drives. The three that keep us alive are the drives for air, for water, and for food. Have you ever met anyone who overbreathed air? And how many people do you know who have to consciously regulate the number of glasses of water they drink each day? Apparently these two basic drives are correctly designed and never fail us.

So what's the story? Did our Creator have a bad day when He designed the hunger drive? I don't think so. I'm a firm believer in all the wonders of the human body. It's not our appetite, but our range of choices that gets us into trouble. When we eat the foods we should be eating, not only do we not feel the need to eat too much, but we cannot eat too much because heathful foods are safe to eat in unlimited amounts.

We have a wide range of choices among the foods available to us. We get our calories from three different kinds of sources: carbohydrates, fats, and proteins. In working out the combinations of foods we prefer, we choose from thousands of different edible things, ranging from avocados to zucchinis.

The concentration of calories in these foods varies greatly, so that at one extreme we have those that yield the maximum of 9 calories per gram (a gram is about $\frac{1}{30}$ of an ounce). Familiar examples are lard and vegetable oils such as corn, olive, and safflower. At the other extreme we have tubers, such as potatoes, at half a calorie per gram, and assorted fruits and yellow-green vegetables at less than one third of a calorie per gram. You'll find a twentyfold difference in calorie yields between the olive oil and the carrots in your salad. So you see, by your *choice* of the foods you eat, you can control your weight. But what do most people do? Just look about you, and see how much they *overdo*.

You must satisfy your hunger drive, of course, or else you'll be miserable all the time with hunger pangs. These never stop (unlike the cravings for alcohol or tobacco, which subside as time passes). You're not likely to beat your hunger drive, but you can easily learn to like delicious foods that satisfy your hunger drive with just the right amount of calories to let you lose weight effortlessly and keep trim—and yet feel full.

One more fact about obesity is just coming to light. All calories are not created equal. Extra carbohydrate calories released from starches, vegetables, and fruits are stored in the muscles and liver as glycogen, for use at a later time. The storage of glycogen is not reflected in our appearance. The body seldom converts these carbohydrates to derivatives that are stored as body fats. However, calories derived from both animal and vegetable fats are easily and quickly shifted to storage as body fats. One obvious result is that roll of fat we laughingly call "a spare tire"—foolishly ignoring the ugly truth about it.

People who switch to a starch-based diet lose six to fifteen pounds a month effortlessly—and that while eating as much as they want of the good foods the diet offers. Generally, very obese people lose faster, men lose easier than women, and those who actively exercise lose the most, the fastest.

In plain and simple terms, the causes of obesity are:

1. Eating too much of foods that are too concentrated in calories, especially the fats and oils that are present naturally in foods or are added to foods being prepared for the table.
2. Not eating enough starches, because of the mistaken notion that "starches make you fat."
3. Not enough exercise.

Current Treatment: Switch to foods that provide fewer calories and more fibers. A change to a diet of starches, vegetables, and fruits will allow you to eat twice as much, as measured by volume, and yet take in only half as many calories as you did while stuffing yourself with the dishes offered by the rich American diet. As an added bonus, you're eating helpful, healthful foods that contain no cholesterol and no additives, and are all low in fats and sodium.

My Recommendations: Switch immediately to a starch-based diet. Eat, eat, and eat, all that you can hold of low-fat, no-cholesterol foods. In fact, the more you eat the healthier and trimmer you will be. Why? When your stomach's full, you will be less tempted to cheat with treacherous goodies that hold too many calories. To lose weight faster, eliminate bread at first, and keep fruits to less than three per day. Instead, eat more squash, white potatoes, corn, and rice. Green and yellow vegetables, like carrots, wax beans, broccoli, asparagus, lettuce, zucchini, and onions are ideal for weight loss because of their very low calorie concentrations, so enjoy them liberally. And don't forget to excercise, daily.

OSTEOPOROSIS

STANDARD PRACTICE

Osteoporosis is a generalized disorder of the skeleton characterized by a reduction in bone mass below that required for adequate mechanical support. It is the commonest of the metabolic bone diseases and an important cause of disability and death in the elderly. The bones become so weak that they fracture under physical stresses expected in daily life: ribs fracture from a friendly hug, the backbone collapses while riding over a bumpy road, and a normal step fractures the hip and Grandma falls to the floor. Repeated fractures of the backbone can reduce height and cause a forward curvature of the spine called a "dowager's" or "widow's" hump. After age forty to fifty the skeleton loses bone, at a faster rate in women than men. Over the next three or four decades the skeletal mass may be reduced by 30 to 50 percent of that of a young adult. The cause is unknown; however, nutritional factors such as lack of calcium, fluorides, and vitamin D are believed to be involved. Lack of estrogens, for example due to menopausal changes, results in loss of calcium from bones. Phosphates from sodas and caffeine also cause calcium losses.

Current Treatment: Estrogens, progesterones, calcium. Sometimes fluorides, vitamin D, and calcitonin (a hormone given by injection).

Drawbacks: Estrogens slow bone loss, but at a price. Risk of cancer of the uterus is increased by five to fourteen times over that for women not taking estrogens; risk of breast cancer is doubled with estrogens and may be quadrupled with the combination of estrogens and progesterones. Gallbladder disease is four times more common in women receiving estrogens. Progesterones are added to reduce the cancer-causing effects of estrogens, but, unfortunately, progesterones lower the levels of "good" HDL cholesterol and raise those of triglycerides; these are risk factors for more heart disease. Women on estrogen/progesterone combination therapy experience lifelong menstrual periods. Biannual biopsies of the uterus, which are bothersome and painful, are required to check for cancer while on hormone therapy.

Calcium supplements have little or no positive effects on the condition of bones. The gut absorbs only the amount of calcium the body needs. Higher intakes do not promote greater absorption—the intestine is not a porous sieve. Evidence so far fails to show that added calcium enters the bones or strengthens them. The effectiveness of vitamin D and fluorides is highly questionable, and the side effects of fluorides are serious and troublesome for many people.

The McDougall Program (Dietary and Lifestyle Implications)

Excess amounts of proteins (especially of animal proteins) cause changes in kidney activity, resulting in large losses of calcium from the body. Experimental studies show that protein levels commonly consumed by Americans (90 grams and more—15 percent of the calories) will cause more calcium to be lost from the body than can be absorbed from the gut, even when the person is consuming very high levels of calcium. This is why populations around the world that eat rich diets loaded with animal proteins (as in the United States, England, Israel, Finland, Sweden, etc.) have high rates of osteoporosis, while people in countries that consume small amounts of animal proteins (including dairy foods), such as those living in Asian and African countries, have strong bones and little osteoporosis.

An African woman can have ten babies, nurse each of them for ten months, and still be expected to have good solid bones when she reaches the age of seventy, bones which are comparable to those of a twenty-year-old woman in America. Eskimos, who daily consume 250 to 400 grams of proteins per day in fish, walrus, or whale meats and 2200 mg of calcium from fish bone, have the highest incidence of osteoporosis of any population in the world. Proof of the Eskimos' affliction with "thin bones" can be found in bodies that are centuries old. Recently the well-preserved frozen bodies of two women who were buried in an ice floe in the Arctic more than 500 years ago were discovered and autopsied. The examination showed that both women, about twenty and forty years old when they died, had suffered from extensive osteoporosis (and significant atherosclerosis).

Current Treatment: The only way to have more calcium entering the body than is leaving it is to eat foods low in protein content (especially those low in animal proteins). Exercise of all kinds has also been shown to strengthen bones. Evidence indicates that osteoporosis is a reversible disease when factors causing the bone loss are corrected. (Obviously, already acquired deformities are not corrected, but bones are remineralized.)

My Recommendations: Adopt a low-protein diet, avoid caffeine and phosphate-containing sodas, and exercise daily. (For more details, see my book *McDougall's Medicine—A Challenging Second Opinion.* New Century Publishers Inc., Piscataway, N.J., 1985.)

UPPER INTESTINAL DISTRESS

STANDARD PRACTICE

Acid indigestion is a term frequently used to describe the burning distress from an inflamed esophagus (esophagitis), an inflamed stomach (gastritis), and the pain associated with ulcers (loss of intestinal lining tissue). Some health professionals and lay persons attribute these conditions to emotional stress. The most obvious explanation for these conditions, the foods and beverages we swallow, is rarely considered important enough to mention to the patient. However, for a long time most health professionals have recognized the harmful effects of alcohol, tobacco, and caffeinated beverages on the upper gastrointestinal tract.

Current Treatment: Avoiding alcohol, coffee, and spicy foods. Some doctors still recommend drinking milk to soothe the pains, and many tell their patients to switch to decaffeinated coffee. Drugs are prescribed, such as over-the-counter antacids in liquid and tablet forms, prescription medications for inhibiting acid production, such as cimetidine (Tagamet) and ranitidine (Zantac), and sucralfate (Carafate—contains aluminum), a drug that coats ulcers to speed healing. Surgery, these days, is a last resort.

Drawbacks: A diet offering lots of milk has long been recommended to patients with ulcers, even though physicians should have known since 1958 that milk fails to favor healing of ulcers. Scientific studies demonstrate that production of stomach acid actually increases when milk is fed to people either with or without ulcers. The proteins and calcium in the milk directly stimulate the stomach's cells to synthesize more gastric acid.

A 1986 article in the *British Medical Journal*, "Effect of milk on patients with duodenal ulcers," reported that sixty-five patients suffering with these ulcers were placed for a month either on a routine hospital diet or on one consisting almost entirely of milk. Patients in both groups were also given an antacid drug (Tagamet) that inhibits acid secretion. Examination at the end of the month showed that healing occurred in 78 percent of those who ate the routine hospital foods and in only 53 percent of those maintained on the milk diet. The authors concluded that the milk has an adverse effect on ulcer healing.

To improve the health of the stomach and of the body in general, people are switching to decaffeinated coffee. This therapeutic change is wholeheartedly accepted by health professionals, dietitians, and the general population. However, studies on the production of stomach acid show that decaffeinated coffee stimulates the release of nearly as much gastric acid as does regular coffee, and about three times as much acid as does an equivalent amount of pure caffeine.

The McDougall Program (Dietary and Lifestyle Implications)

Fatty foods with low fiber content, alcohol, caffeinated beverages, and irritating foods, such as peppers, raw onions, cucumbers, green peppers, radishes, and fruit juices, are the primary causes of upper gastrointestinal distress.

Current Treatment: Avoiding the wrong foods and beverages, and eating foods that are not irritating will bring quick and long-lasting relief.

High-fat, low-fiber foods have been associated with an increased incidence of ulcers worldwide. Coffee, decaffeinated coffee, caffeinated colas, sometimes strong tea (black and green teas), and alcoholic beverages are the most common substances that can inflame the lining of the esophagus, stomach, and the whole intestinal tract. Use of alcohol and tobacco have been associated with esophageal cancer. Although raw onions, cucumbers, radishes, and green peppers are very irritating for many people, they cause less trouble when cooked. With onions, cooking boils off a toxic oil that provokes the distress. Fruit juices, especially citrus, pineapple, and apple, will cause distress, although the whole fruit rarely causes trouble. Tomato sauces, juice, and other canned tomato products are also troublesome for some sensitive stomachs. Hot peppers (chili, black, white, green, yellow, and red) and products containing peppers, such as kim chi and Mexican salsas, can "burn" the lining of the esophagus and cause almost immediate discomfort in many people.

Frequent meals focusing primarily on starches will bring quick relief to people with esophagitis, gastritis, and ulcers. For serious ulcer disease, therapy may be started with liquid antacids, and powerful drugs, such as Tagamet or Zantac, to speed the initial phases of healing.

Once the ulcer is healed by whatever method, the next most important issue is to prevent its recurrence. This return can affect as many as three fourths of the patients within six months. A low-fat, high-fiber diet will cut the recurrence rate by at least half that observed in people who remain on high-fat, low-fiber diets. Giving up smoking cigarettes will reduce the risk of recurrence in six months from 72 percent to 21 percent. Quitting alcohol and coffee (including decaffeinated coffee) will further decrease the risk of recurrence as well as restore and maintain health.

My Recommendations: Follow a starch-based diet, avoiding the irritating beverages and plant foods mentioned above. Antacids may offer additional symptomatic relief during the early stage of treatment, and some are relatively harmless medications. Liquid antacids are much more effective than are those in tablet form, especially in cases of esophagitis, because the liquid can coat the inflamed areas while tablets just slide past them (avoid aluminum-containing autacids; see ALZHEIMER'S DISEASE). In rare cases, a patient will need more powerful drugs at first to promote healing.

REFERENCES

(The following references apply to material discussed in Part 3.)

ACNE

Rosenberg, E. Acne diet reconsidered. *Arch. Dermatol.* 117:193, 1981.
Pochi, P. Sebum production, casual sebum levels, titratable acidity of sebum and urinary fractional 17-ketosteroid excretion in males with acne. *J. Invest. Dermatol.* 43:383, 1964.
Wilkinson, D. Psoriasis and dietary fat: the fatty acid composition of surface and scale (ether-soluble) lipids. *J. Invest. Dermatol.* 47:185, 1966.
Rasmussen, J. Diet and acne (review). *Int. J. Dermatol.* 16:488, 1977.
Fulton, J. Effect of chocolate on acne vulgaris. *JAMA* 210: 2071, 1969.

ALLERGIC DISEASES

Bahna, S. Allergies to milk. Grune & Stratton, NY, 1980.
Editorial—Food allergy. *Lancet* 1:249, 1979.
Heiner, D. Respiratory diseases and food allergy. *Ann. Allergy* 53:657, 1984.
Lindahl, O. Vegan regimen with reduced medication in the treatment of bronchial asthma. *J. Asthma* 22:45, 1985.
Boyles, J. Food allergy. Diagnosis and treatment. *Otolaryngol. Clin. North Am.* 18:775, 1985.
Cant, A. Food allergy in childhood (review). *Hum. Nutr. Appl. Nutr.* 39:277, 1985.
Jenkins, H. Food allergy: the major cause of infantile colitis. *Arch. Dis. Child.* 59:326, 1984.
Wright, A. Food allergy or intolerance in severe recurrent aphthous ulceration of the mouth. *Br. Med. J.* 292: 1237, 1986.
Settipane, G. The restaurant syndromes (review). *N. Engl. Reg. Allergy. Proc.* 8:39, 1987.

Barton, M. Controversial techniques in allergy treatment. *J. Nat. Med. Assn.* 75:831, 1983.

Sethi, T. How reliable are commercial allergy tests? *Lancet* 1:92, 1987.

VanArsdel, P. Diagnostic tests for patients with suspected allergic disease. Utility and limitations. *Ann. Intern. Med.* 110:304, 1989.

Saarinen, U. Prolonged breast-feeding as prophylaxis for atopic disease. *Lancet* 2:163, 1979.

ALZHEIMER'S DISEASE

Krishnan, S. Aluminum toxicity to the brain. *Sci. Total. Environ.* 71:59, 1988.

Bertholf, R. Aluminum and Alzheimer's disease: prospectives for a cytoskeletal mechanism. *CRC-Crit. Rev. Clin. Lab. Sci.* 25:195, 1987.

Candy, J. Aluminosilicates and senile plaque formation in Alzheimer's disease. *Lancet* 1:354, 1986.

Perl, D. Aluminum neurotoxicity—potential role in the pathogenesis of neurofibrillary tangle formation. *Can. J. Neurol. Sci.* 13 (4 suppl.) :441, 1986.

Edwardson, J. Aluminosilicates and the ageing brain: implications for the pathogenesis of Alzheimer's disease. *Ciba Found. Symp.* 121:160, 1986.

Martyn, C. Geographical relation between Alzheimer's disease and aluminum in drinking water. *Lancet* 1:59, 1989.

Birchall, J. Aluminum, chemical physiology, and Alzheimer's disease. *Lancet* 2:1008, 1988.

Shore, D. Aluminum and Alzheimer's disease. *J. Nervous and Mental Disease* 171:553, 1983.

Perl, D. Uptake of aluminum into the central nervous system along nasal-olfactory pathways (letter). *Lancet* 1:1028, 1987.

Cowburn, J. Aluminum chelator (transferrin) reverses biochemical deficiency in Alzheimer brain preparations (letter). *Lancet* 1:99, 1989.

Greger, J. Aluminum content of the American diet. *Food Technol.* 39:73, 1985.

ANEMIA

Hamblin, T. Blood transfusions and cancer: anomalies explained? *Br. Med. J.* 293:517, 1986.

Dallman, P. Iron deficiency in infancy and childhood. *Am. J. Clin. Nutr.* 33:86, 1980.

Morck, T. Inhibition of food iron absorption by coffee. *Am. J. Clin. Nutr.* 37:416, 1983.

Anderson, B. The iron and zinc status of long-term vegetarian women. *Am. J. Clin. Nutr.* 34:1042, 1981.

Abdulla, M. Nutrient intake and health status of vegans. Chemical analyses of diets using the duplicate portion sampling technique. *Am. J. Clin. Nutr.* 34:2464, 1981.

Wilson, J. Studies on iron metabolism. V. Further observations on milk-induced gastrointestinal bleeding in infants with iron-deficiency anemia. *J. Pediatr.* 84:335, 1974.

Murray, M. An ecological interdependence of diet and disease? A study of infection in one tribe consuming two different diets. *Am. J. Clin. Nutr.* 33:697, 1980.

Buckman, M. Gastrointestinal bleeding in long-distance runners. *Ann. Intern. Med.* 101:127, 1984.

ARTHRITIS

Scott, D. Long-term outcome of treating rheumatoid arthritis: results after 20 years. *Lancet* 1:1108, 1987.

Kushner, I. Does aggressive therapy of rheumatoid arthritis affect outcome? (editorial). *J. Rheumatol.* 16:1, 1989.

Rashad, S. Effect of non-steroidal anti-inflammatory drugs on the course of osteoarthritis. *Lancet* 2:519, 1989.

Hess, E. Cartilage metabolism and anti-inflammatory drugs in osteoarthritis. *Am. J. Med.* 81:36, 1986.

Taylor, H. Systemic lupus erythematosus in Zimbabwe. *Ann. Rheum. Dis.* 45:645, 1986.

Mets, T. Rheumatoid arthritis and tuberculosis in Africa (letter). *Lancet* 2:1344, 1986.

Solomon, L. Rheumatic disorders in the South African Negro. Part I. Rheumatoid arthritis and ankylosing spondylitis. *S. Afr. Med. J.* 49:1292, 1975.

Beighton, P. Rheumatoid arthritis in a rural South African population. *Ann. Rheum. Dis.* 34:136, 1975.

Beasley, R. Low prevalence of rheumatoid disease in Chinese. Prevalence survey in a rural community. *J. Rheumatol.* (suppl. 10) 10:11, 1983.

Solomon, L. Rheumatic disorders in the South African Negro. Part II. Osteo-arthrosis. *S. Afr. Med. J.* 49:1737, 1975.

Valkenburg, H. Osteoarthritis in some developing countries. *J. Rheumatol.* (suppl. 10) 10:20, 1983.

Corman, L. The role of diet in animal models of systemic lupus erythematosus: possible implications for human lupus. *Seminars Arthritis Rheum.* 15:61, 1985.

Welsh, C. Comparison of arthritogenic properties of dietary cow's milk, egg albumin and soya milk in experimental animals. *Int. Arch. Allergy Appl. Immunol.* 80:192, 1986.

Ratner, D. Does milk intolerance affect seronegative arthritis in lactase-deficient women? *Israel J. Med. Sci.* 21:532, 1985.

Beri, D. Effect of dietary restrictions on disease activity in rheumatoid arthritis. *Ann. Rheum. Dis.* 47:69, 1988.

Panush, R. Food-induced (allergic) arthritis. Inflammatory arthritis exacerbated by milk. *Arthritis Rheum.* 29:220, 1986.

Panush, R. Nutritional therapy for rheumatic diseases. *Ann. Intern. Med.* 106:619, 1987.

Parke, A. Rheumatoid arthritis and food: a case study. *Br. Med. J.* 282:2027, 1981.

Darlington, L. Placebo-controlled, blind study of dietary manipulation therapy in rheumatoid arthritis. *Lancet* 1:236, 1986.

Hafstrom, I. Effects of fasting on disease activity, neutrophil function, fatty acid composition, and leukotriene biosynthesis in patients with rheumatoid arthritis. *Arthritis Rheum.* 31:585, 1988.

Marshall, R. Food challenge effects on fasted rheumatoid arthritis patients: a multicenter study. *Clinical Ecology* 4:181, 1984.

ATHEROSCLEROSIS

Detre, K. Overview of coronary artery bypass graft surgery. *Prog. Cardiovasc. Dis.* 28:387, 1986.

Petch, M. Coronary angioplasty: time for reappraisal. *Br. Med. J.* 295:453, 1987.

Sandercock, P. Asymptomatic carotid stenosis: spare the knife. *Br. Med. J.* 294: 1368, 1987.

Inkeles, S. Hyperlipidemia and coronary atherosclerosis: a review. *Medicine* 60:110, 1981.

McGill, H. The pathogenesis of atherosclerosis. *Clin. Chem.* 34:B33, 1988.

Blankenhorn, D. Prevention or reversal of atherosclerosis: review of current evidence. *Am. J. Cardiol.* 63:38H, 1989.

Blankenhorn, D. Reversal of atherosis and sclerosis. The two components of atherosclerosis. *Circulation* 79:1, 1989.

Blankenhorn, D. Beneficial effects of combined colestipol-niacin therapy on coronary atherosclerosis and coronary venous bypass grafts. *JAMA* 257:3233, 1987.

Strom, A. Mortality from circulatory diseases in Norway 1940–1945. *Lancet* 1:126, 1951.

CANCER

Bailar, J. Progress against cancer? *N. Engl. J. Med.* 314:1226, 1986.

GAO Report. Cancer patient survival—What progress has been made? GAO / PEMD-87-13, 1987.

Cairns, J. The treatment of diseases and the war against cancer. *Scientific American* 253:51, 1985.

Cote, R. Monoclonal antibodies detect occult breast carcinoma metastases in the bone marrow of patients with early stage disease. *Am. J. Surg. Path.* 12:333, 1988.

Clinton, S. Growth of Dunning transplantable prostate adenocarcinomas in rats fed diets with various fat contents. *J. Nutr.* 118:908, 1988.

Haybittle, J. Postoperative radiotherapy and late mortality: evidence from the Cancer Research Campaign Trial for early breast cancer. *Br. Med. J.* 298:1611, 1989.

Hermann, R. The changing treatment of breast cancer (letter). *JAMA* 260:2834, 1988.

Marteau, T. Psychological costs of screening. *Br. Med. J.* 299:527, 1989.

Wynder, E. Association of dietary fat and lung cancer. *JNCI* 79:631, 1987.

Smith, G. Plasma cholesterol and primary brain tumors. *Br. Med. J.* 299:26, 1989.

CHOLESTEROL, HIGH

Sempos, C. The prevalence of high blood cholesterol levels among adults in the United States. *JAMA* 262:45, 1989.

Flynn, M. Serum lipids in humans fed diets containing beef or fish and poultry. *Am. J. Clin. Nutr.* 34:2734, 1981.

Flynn, M. Dietary "meats" and serum lipids. *Am. J. Clin. Nutr.* 35:935, 1982.

O'Brien, B. Human plasma lipid responses to red meat, poultry, fish, and eggs. *Am. J. Clin. Nutr.* 33:2573, 1980.

Betterridge, J. High density lipoprotein cholesterol and coronary heart disease. How it protects is still a mystery. *Br. Med. J.* 298:974, 1989.

Pearce, M. Incidence of cancer in men on a diet high in polyunsaturated fat. *Lancet* 1:464, 1971.

Birt, D. Fat and calorie effects on carcinogenesis at sites other than the mammary gland. *Am. J. Clin. Nutr.* 45:203, 1987.

Clement, I. Fat and essential fatty acid in mammary carcinogenesis. *Am. J. Clin. Nutr.* 45:218, 1987.

Sturdevant, R. Increased incidence of cholelithiasis in men ingesting a serum cholesterol lowering diet. *N. Engl. J. Med.* 288:24, 1973.

Illingworth, D. Drug therapy of hypercholesterolemia. *Clin. Chem.* 34:B123, 1988.

Schonfeld, G. Dietary treatment of hyperlipidemia. *Clin. Chem.* 34:B111, 1988.

Luria, M. Effect of low dose niacin on high density lipoprotein cholesterol and total cholesterol high-density lipoprotein cholesterol ratio. *Arch. Intern. Med.* 148:2493, 1988.

Jacobs, L. Effect of dietary fiber on colonic cell proliferation and its relationship to colon carcinogenesis. *Prev. Med.* 16:566, 1987.

Vega, G. Treatment of primary moderate hypercholesterolemia with lovastatin (Mevinolin) and Celistipol. *JAMA* 257:33, 1987.

Kannel, W. Cholesterol and risk of coronary heart disease and mortality in men. *Clin. Chem.* 34:B53, 1988.

Anderson, K. Cholesterol and mortality: 30 years of follow-up from the Framingham study. *JAMA* 257:2176, 1987.

Castelli, W. Epidemiology of coronary artery disease: the Framingham study. *Am. J. Med.* 76(2A):4, 1984.

Stamler, J. Is relationship between serum cholesterol and risk of premature death from coronary artery disease continuous and graded? Findings in 356,222 primary screenees of the Multiple Risk Factors Intervention Trial (MRFIT). *JAMA* 256:2823, 1986.

Lipids Research Clinics Program. The Lipid Research Clinics coronary primary prevention trial results. *JAMA* 251:351 & 365, 1984.

Pocock, S. Concentrations of high density lipoprotein cholesterol, triglycerides, and total cholesterol in ischaemic heart disease. *Br. Med. J.* 298:998, 1989.

Pocock, S. High density lipoprotein cholesterol is not a major risk factor for ischaemic heart disease in British men. *Br. Med. J.* 292:515, 1986.

Grundy, S. The place of HDL in cholesterol management. *Arch. Intern. Med.* 149:505, 1989.

McManus, B. Progress in lipid reporting practices and reliability of blood cholesterol measurement in clinical laboratories in Nebraska. *JAMA* 262:83, 1989.

COLITIS, MILD (SPASTIC COLITIS)

Danivat, D. Prevalence of irritable bowel syndrome in a non-Western population. *Br. Med. J.* 296:1710, 1988.

Harvey, R. Prognosis in the irritable bowel syndrome: a 5-year prospective study. *Lancet* 1:963, 1987.

Sullivan, S. Management of the irritable bowel syndrome: a personal view. *J. Clin. Gastroenterol.* 5:499, 1983.

Bentley, S. Food hypersensitivity in irritable bowel syndrome. *Lancet* 2:295, 1983.

Jones, V. Food intolerance: a major factor in the pathogenesis of irritable bowel syndrome. *Lancet* 2:1115, 1982.

Childs, P. A new look at diarrhoea, diverticulitis and "colitis" after 25 years of clinical study. *Practitioner* 215:757, 1975.

COLITIS, SEVERE
(INFLAMMATORY BOWEL DISEASE)

Spiller, G. Recent advances in dietary fiber and colorectal diseases. *Am. J. Clin. Nutr.* 34:1145, 1981.

Hutt, M. Epidemiology of chronic intestinal disease in Middle Africa. *Israel J. Med. Sci.* 15:314, 1979.

Segal, I. The rarity of ulcerative colitis in South African blacks. *Am. J. Gastroenterology* 74:332, 1980.

Jones, V. Crohn's disease: maintenance of remission by diet. *Lancet* 2:177, 1985.

Heaton, K. Treatment of Crohn's disease with an unrefined-carbohydrate, fibre-rich diet. *Br. Med. J.* 2:764, 1979.

Acheson, E. Early weaning in the aetiology of ulcerative colitis. *Br. Med. J.* 2:929, 1961.

Andersson, H. Fat-reduced diet in the symptomatic treatment of small bowel disease. Metabolic studies in patients with Crohn's disease and in other patients subjected to ileal resection. *Gut* 15:351, 1974.

Truelove, S. Ulcerative colitis provoked by milk. *Br. Med. J.* 1:154, 1961.

Wright, R. A controlled therapeutic trial of various diets in ulcerative colitis. *Br. Med. J.* 2:138, 1965.

COLON POLYPS AND COLON CANCER

Frank, J. Occult-blood screening for colorectal carcinoma: the yield and the costs. *Am. J. Prev. Med.* 1:18, 1985.

Chapuis, P. Predictive value of rectal bleeding in screening for rectal and sigmoid polyps. *Br. Med. J.* 290:1546, 1985.

Wegener, M. Colorectal adenomas. Distribution, incidence of malignant transformation, and rate of recurrence. *Dis. Colon Rectum* 29:383, 1986.

Correa, P. The epidemiology of colorectal polyps. *Cancer* 39:2258, 1977.

Editorial—Questions about occult-blood screening for cancer. *Lancet* 1:22, 1986.

Leffall, L. Surgical management of colorectal polyps. *Cancer* 34:940, 1974.

Tornberg, S. Risks of cancer of the colon and rectum in relation to serum cholesterol and beta-lipoprotein. *N. Engl. J. Med.* 315:1629, 1986.

Bristol, J. Sugar, fat, and the risk of colorectal cancer. *Br. Med. J.* 291:1467, 1985.

Nauss, K. Dietary fat and fiber: relationship to calorie intake, body growth, and colon tumorigenesis. *Am. J. Clin. Nutr.* 45:243, 1987.

Williams, R. Multiple polyposis, polyp regression, and carcinoma of the colon. *Am. J. Surg.* 112:846, 1966.

DeCosse, J. Effect of wheat fiber and vitamins C and E on rectal polyps in patients with familial adenomatous polyposis. *J. Natl. Cancer Inst.* 81:1290, 1989.

Gingold, B. Local treatment (electrocoagulation) for carcinoma of the rectum in the elderly. *J. Am. Geriatrics Society* 29:10, 1981.

Fielding, L. Red for danger: blood transfusion and colorectal cancer. *Br. Med. J.* 291:841, 1985.

CONSTIPATION

Council on Scientific Affairs. Dietary fiber and health. *JAMA* 262:542, 1989.

Dwyer, J. Health aspects of vegetarian diets (review). *Am. J. Clin. Nutr.* 48 (3 suppl.):712, 1988.

Dehn, T. Haemorrhoids and defaecatory habits (letter). *Lancet* 1:54, 1989.

Read, N. Haemorrhoids, constipation, and hypertensive anal cushions (letter). *Lancet* 1:610, 1989.

Burkitt, D. Dietary fiber and disease. *JAMA* 229:1068, 1974.

Burkitt, D. Varicose veins, deep vein thrombosis, and haemorrhoids: epidemiology and suggested aetiology. *Br. Med. J.* 2:556, 1972.

DEPRESSION AND ANXIETY

Ashkenazi, A. Gluten and autism (letter). *Lancet* 1:157, 1980.

Dohan, F. Schizophrenia and neuroactive peptides from food (letter). *Lancet* 1:1031, 1979.

Editorial—Gluten in schizophrenia. *Lancet* 1:744, 1983.

Gelenberg, A. Tyrosine for the treatment of depression. *Am. J. Psychiatry* 137:622, 1980.

Lieberman, H. The effects of dietary neurotransmitter precursors on human behavior. *Am. J. Clin. Nutr.* 42:366, 1985.

Wurtman, J. Behavioural effects of nutrients. *Lancet* 1:1145, 1983.

Glaeser, B. Changes in brain levels of acidic, basic, and neutral amino acids after consumption of single meals containing various proportions of protein. *J. Neurochem.* 41:1016, 1983.

Phillips, F. Isocaloric diet changes and electroencephalographic sleep. *Lancet* 2:723, 1975.

DIABETES

Knatterud, G. Effects of hypoglycemic agents on vascular complications in patients with adult-onset diabetes. VIII. Evaluation of insulin therapy: final report. *Diabetes* 31(suppl. 5):1, 1982.

Goldner, M. Effects of hypoglycemic agents on vascular complications in patients with adult-onset diabetes. III. Clinical implications of UGDP results. *JAMA* 218:1400, 1971.

Noth, R. Diabetic nephropathy: hemodynamic basis and implications for disease management. *Ann. Int. Med.* 110:795, 1989.

Editorial—Insulin dependent? *Lancet* 2:809, 1985.

Leslie, P. Effect of optimal glycaemic control with continuous subcutaneous insulin on energy expenditure in Type I diabetes mellitus. *Br. Med. J. (Clin. Res.)* 293:1121, 1986.

The DCCT Research Group. Weight gain associated with intensive therapy in the diabetes control and complications trial. *Diabetes Care* 11:567, 1988.

Fuller, J. Coronary-heart-disease risk and impaired glucose tolerance. *Lancet* 1:1373, 1980.

Teuscher, T. Absence of diabetes in a rural West African population with a high carbohydrate/cassava diet. *Lancet* 1:765, 1987.

Bodansky, H. Insulin dependent diabetes in Asians. *Arch. Dis. Child.* 62:227, 1987.

Snowdon, D. Does a vegetarian diet reduce the occurrence of diabetes? *Am. J. Public Health* 75:507, 1985.

Rolfe, M. Macrovascular disease in diabetics in Central Africa. *Br. Med. J.* 296:1522, 1988.

Stern, M. Lack of awareness and treatment of hyperlipidemia in type II diabetes in a community survey. *JAMA.* 262:360, 1989.

Steiner, G. From an excess of fat, diabetics die. *JAMA* 262:398, 1989.

The Kroc Collaborative Study Group. Diabetic retinopathy after two years of intensified insulin treatment. *JAMA* 260:37, 1988.

Mann, J. Diabetic dietary prescriptions. The cost of oral hypoglycemic agents could be cut by sensible dietary advice. *Br. Med. J.* 298:1535, 1989.

Barnard, R. Response of non-insulin-dependent diabetic patients to an intensive program of diet and exercise. *Diabetes Care* 5:370, 1982.

Kiehm, T. Beneficial effects of a high carbohydrate, high fiber diet on hyperglycemic diabetic men. *Am. J. Clin. Nutr.* 29:895, 1976.

Ney, D. Decreased insulin requirement and improved control of diabetes in pregnant women given a high-carbohydrate, high-fiber, low-fat diet. *Diabetes Care* 5:529, 1982.

Parillo, M. Metabolic consequences of feeding a high-carbohydrate, high-fiber diet to diabetic patients with chronic kidney failure. *Am. J. Clin. Nutr.* 48:255, 1988.

Anderson, J. Dietary fiber and diabetes: a comprehensive review and practical application. *J. Am. Diet Assoc.* 87:1189, 1987.

DIVERTICULAR DISEASE

Manousos, O. Diet and other factors in the aetiology of diverticulosis: an epidemiological study in Greece. *Gut* 26:544, 1985.

Gear, J. Symptomless diverticular disease and intake of dietary fibre. *Lancet* 1:511, 1979.

Segal, I. Diverticular disease in urban Africans in South Africa. *Digestion* 24:42, 1982.

Ohi, G. Changes in dietary fiber intake among Japanese in the 20th century: a relationship to the prevalence of diverticular disease. *Am. J. Clin. Nutr.* 38:115, 1983.

Hyland, J. Does a high fibre diet prevent the complications of diverticular disease? *Br. J. Surg.* 67:77, 1980.

Findlay, J. Effects of unprocessed bran on colon function in normal subjects and in diverticular disease. *Lancet* 1:146, 1974.

Leahy, A. High fibre diet in symptomatic diverticular disease of the colon. *Ann. R. Coll. Surg. Engl.* 67:173, 1985.

FATIGUE

Nieman, D. Vegetarian dietary practices and endurance performance. *Am. J. Clin. Nutr.* 48(3 suppl.):754, 1988.

Kirwan, J. Carbohydrate balance in competitive runners during successive days of intensive training. *J. Appl. Physiol.* 65:2601, 1988.

Editorial—Fatigue. *Lancet* 2:546, 1988.
Evans, W. Dietary carbohydrates and endurance exercise. *Am. J. Clin. Nutr.* 41:1146, 1985.
Editorial—Nutrition in sport. *Lancet* 1:1297, 1987.
Kuo, P. The effect of lipemia upon coronary and peripheral arterial circulation in patients with essential hyperlipemia. *Am. J. Med.* 26:68, 1959.
Freidman, M. Effect of unsaturated fats upon lipemia and conjunctival circulation. A study of coronary-prone (pattern A) men. *JAMA* 193:882, 1965.
Bahna, S. Allergies to milk. Grune & Stratton, NY, 1980, pages 67–69.
Shoenfeld, Y. Walking—a method for rapid improvement of physical fitness. *JAMA* 243:2062, 1980.

GALLBLADDER DISEASE

Finlayson, N. Cholecystectomy for gallstones. A good thing if they cause symptoms. *Br. Med. J.* 298:133, 1989.
Bateson, M. Gallstone disease—present and future. *Lancet*, 2:1265, 1986.
Editorial—Cholecystectomy: the dissatisfied customer. *Lancet* 1:339, 1988.
Bilhartz, L. Cholesterol gallstone disease: the current status of nonsurgical therapy. *Am. J. Med. Sci.* 296:45, 1988.
Thistle, J. The natural history of cholelithiasis: The National Cooperative Gallstone Study. *Ann. Intern. Med.* 101:171, 1984.
Pixley, F. Dietary factors in the aetiology of gall stones: a case control study. *Gut* 29:1511, 1988.
Pixley, F. Effect of vegetarianism on development of gall stones in women. *Br. Med. J.* 291:11, 1985.
Wechsler, J. Influence of increased fibre intake on biliary lipids. *Scand. J. Gastroenterol.* Suppl. 129:185, 1987.
DenBesten, L. The effect of dietary cholesterol on the composition of human bile. *Surgery* 73:266, 1973.
Hepner, G. Altered bile acid metabolism in vegetarians. *Dig. Dis.* 20:935, 1975.
Friedman, L. Management of asymptomatic gallstones in the diabetic patient. A decision analysis. *Ann. Intern. Med.* 109:913, 1988.
Ransohoff, D. Prophylactic cholecystectomy or expectant management for silent gallstones. A decision analysis to assess survival. *Ann. Intern. Med.* 99:199, 1983.
Maringhini, A. Gallstones, gallbladder cancer, and other gastrointestinal malignancies. *Ann. Intern. Med.* 107:30, 1987.
Linos, D. Cholecystectomy and carcinoma of the colon. *Lancet* 2:379, 1981.

HEADACHES

Smith, R. Caffeine withdrawal headache. *J. Clin. Pharm. Ther.* 12:53, 1987.

Lai, C. Clinical and electrophysiological responses to dietary challenge in migraineurs. *Headache* 29:180, 1989.

Mansfield, L. Food allergy and adult migraine: double-blind and mediator confirmation of an allergic etiology. *Ann. Allergy* 55:126, 1985.

Monro, J. Migraine is a food-allergic disease. *Lancet* 2:719, 1984.

Egger, J. Is migraine food allergy? A double-blind controlled trial of oligoantigenic diet treatment. *Lancet* 2:865, 1983.

Mansfield, L. Food allergy and headache. Whom to evaluate and how to treat. *Postgrad. Med.* 83:46, 1988.

HEART DISEASE, PREVENTION

DeWood, M. Prevalence of total coronary occlusion during the early hours of transmural myocardial infarction. *N. Engl. J. Med.* 303:897, 1980.

Antiplatelet Trialists' Collaboration. Secondary prevention of vascular disease by prolonged antiplatelet treatment. *Br. Med. J.* 296:320, 1988.

Orme, M. Aspirin all round? *Br. Med. J.* 296:307, 1988.

Yetiv, J. Clinical applications of fish oils. *JAMA* 260:665, 1988.

Glomset, J. Fish, fatty acids, and human health. *N. Engl. J. Med.* 312:1253, 1985.

Herold, P. Fish oil consumption and decreased risk of cardiovascular disease: a comparison of findings from animal and human feeding trials (review). *Am. J. Clin. Nutr.* 43:566, 1986.

Harris, W. Effects of a low saturated fat, low cholesterol fish oil supplement in hypertriglyceridemic patients—a placebo-controlled trial. *Ann. Intern. Med.* 109:465, 1988.

Glauber, H. Adverse metabolic effect of omega-3 fatty acids in non-insulin-dependent diabetes mellitus. *Ann. Intern. Med.* 108:663, 1988.

Weiner, M. Cholesterol in foods rich in omega-3 fatty acids (letter). *N. Engl. J. Med.* 315:833, 1986.

Simopoulos, A. Purslane: a terrestrial source of omega-3 fatty acids (letter). *N. Engl. J. Med.* 315:833, 1986.

Hopkins, G. Polyunsaturated fatty acids as promoters of mammary carcinogenesis induced in Sprague-Dawley rats by 7,12-Dimethylbenz[a]anthracene. *JNCI* 66:517, 1981.

Foran, J. Increased fish consumption may be risky (letter). *JAMA* 262:28, 1989.

Olsen, S. Intake of marine fat, rich in (n-3)-polyunsaturated fatty acids, may increase birthweight by prolonging gestation. *Lancet* 2:367, 1986.

Barnard, R. Effects of a low-fat, low-cholesterol diet on serum lipids, platelet aggregation and thrombaxane formation. *Prostaglandins Leukot. Med.* 26:241, 1987.

Saunders, T. Dietary fat and platelet function. *Clin. Sci.* 65:343, 1983.

Meade, T. Hypercoagulability and ischemic heart disease. *Blood Rev.* 1:2, 1987.

HEART DISEASE, TREATMENT

Epstein, S. Sudden cardiac death without warning. *N. Engl. J. Med.* 321:320, 1989.

Winslow, C. The appropriateness of performing coronary artery bypass surgery. *JAMA* 260:505, 1988.

Graboys, T. Results of a second-opinion program for coronary artery bypass graft surgery. *JAMA* 258:1611, 1987.

Hueb, W. Two- to eight-year survival rates in patients who refused coronary artery bypass grafting. *Am. J. Cardiol.* 63:155, 1989.

Shortell, S. The effects of regulation, competition, and ownership on mortality rates among hospital inpatients. *N. Engl. J. Med.* 318:1100, 1988.

Blauth, C. Retinal microembolism during cardiopulmonary bypass demonstrated by fluorescein angiography. *Lancet* 2:837, 1986.

Shaw, P. Neurological complications of coronary artery bypass graft surgery: six month follow-up study. *Br. Med. J.* 293:165, 1986.

Henriksen, L. Evidence suggestive of diffuse brain damage following cardiac operations. *Lancet* 1:816, 1984.

Ekestrom, S. Effort dyspnea after coronary artery bypass grafting. *Int. J. Cardiol.* 11:287, 1986.

Ornish, D. Effects of stress management training and dietary changes in treating ischemic heart disease. *JAMA* 249:54, 1983.

HIATAL HERNIA

Burkitt, D. Prevalence of diverticular disease, hiatus hernia, and pelvic phleboliths in black and white Americans. *Lancet* 2:880, 1985.

Burkitt, D. Hiatus hernia: is it preventable? *Am. J. Clin. Nutr.* 34:428, 1981.

Capron, J. Evidence for an association between cholelithiasis and hiatus hernia. *Lancet* 2:329, 1978.

HORMONE DEPENDENT DISEASES

Aldercreutz, H. Diet and plasma androgens in postmenopausal vegetarian and omnivorous women and postmenopausal women with breast cancer. *Am. J. Clinc. Nutr.* 49:433, 1989.

Woods, M. Low-fat, high-fiber diet and serum estrone sulfate in premenopausal women. *Am. J. Clin. Nutr.* 49:1179, 1989.

Rose, D. Effect of a low-fat diet on hormone levels in women with cystic breast disease. I. Serum steroids and gonadotropins. *J. Natl. Cancer Inst.* 78:623, 1987.

Rose, D. Effect of a low-fat diet on hormone levels in women with cystic breast disease. II. Serum radioimmunoassayable prolactin and growth hormone and bioactive lactogenic hormones. *J. Natl. Cancer Inst.* 78:627, 1987.

Howie, B. Dietary and hormonal interrelationships among vegetarian Seventh-Day Adventists and nonvegetarian men. *Am. J. Clin. Nutr.* 42:127, 1985.

Hill, P. Plasma hormones and lipids in men at different risk of coronary artery disease. *Am. J. Clin. Nutr.* 33:1010, 1980.

Hill, P. Diet, lifestyle and menstrual activity. *Am. J. Clin. Nutr.* 33:1192, 1980.

Hill, P. Diet and prolactin release. *Lancet* 2:806, 1976.

Hamalainen, E. Diet and serum sex hormones in healthy men. *J. Steroid Biochem.* 20:459, 1984.

Ingram, D. Effect of low-fat diet on female sex hormone levels. *J. Natl. Cancer Inst.* 79:1225, 1987.

Gorbach, S. Estrogens, breast cancer, and intestinal flora. *Rev. Infect. Dis.* 6(suppl. 1):S85, 1984.

Goldin, B. Estrogen excretion patterns and plasma levels in vegetarian and omnivorous women. *N. Engl. J. Med.* 307:1542, 1982.

Goldin, B. Effect of diet on excretion of estrogens in pre- and postmenopausal women. *Ca. Res.* 41:3771, 1981.

Boyd, N. Effect of a low-fat high-carbohydrate diet on symptoms of cyclical mastopathy. *Lancet* 2:128, 1988.

Aksel, S. Etiology and treatment of dysfunctional uterine bleeding. *Obstet. Gynecol.* 44:1, 1974.

Baird, D. Medical management of fibroids. *Br. Med. J.* 296:1684, 1988.

McKenna, T. Pathogenesis and treatment of polycystic ovary syndrome. *N. Engl. J. Med.* 318:558, 1988.

Polson, D. Polycystic ovaries—a common finding in normal women. *Lancet* 1:870, 1988.

Abraham, G. Nutritional factors in the etiology of the premenstrual tension syndromes. *J. Reprod. Med.* 28:446, 1983.

Prior, J. Conditioning exercise decreases premenstrual symptoms: a prospective, controlled 6-month trial. *Fertil. Steril.* 47:402, 1987.

Vaitukaitis, J. Premenstrual syndrome. *N. Engl. J. Med.* 311:1371, 1984.

Sanchez, A. A hypothesis on the etiological role of diet on the age of menarche. *Med. Hypotheses* 7:1339, 1981.

Schwartz, S. Dietary influences on the growth and sexual maturation in premenarchial rhesus monkeys. *Horm. Behav.* 22:231, 1988.

Inaba, M. Can human hair grow again? *J. Dermatol. Surg. Oncol.* 12:672, 1986.

Wilson, J. The pathogenesis of benign prostatic hypertrophy (review). *Am. J. Med.* 68:745, 1980.

Hill, P. Environmental factors and breast and prostate cancer. *Ca. Res.* 41:3817, 1981.

Johansson, J. Natural history of localized prostatic cancer. A population-based study in 223 untreated patients. *Lancet* 1:799, 1989.

Editorial—Obesity: the cancer connection. *Lancet* 1:1223, 1982.

Editorial—Running, jumping, and . . . amenorrhoea. *Lancet* 2:638, 1982.

Ding, J. High serum cortisol levels in exercise-associated amenorrhea. *Ann. Intern. Med.* 108:530, 1988.

HYPERTENSION: HIGH BLOOD PRESSURE

Wilcox, R. Treatment of high blood pressure: should clinical practice be based on results of clinical trials? *Br. Med. J.* 293:433, 1986.

Cruickshank, J. Benefits and potential harm of lowering blood pressure. *Lancet* 1:581, 1987.

Nelson, L. Effect of changing levels of physical activity on blood-pressure and haemodynamics in essential hypertension. *Lancet* 2:473, 1986.

Sanders, T. Blood pressure, plasma renin activity and aldosterone concentrations in vegans and omnivore controls. *Hum. Nutr. Appl. Nutr.* 41A:204, 1987.

Lindahl, O. A vegan regimen with reduced medication in the treatment of hypertension. *Br. J. Nutr.* 52:11, 1984.

Weinsier, R. Recent developments in the etiology and treatment of hypertension: dietary calcium, fat, and magnesium. *Am. J. Clin. Nutr.* 42:1331, 1985.

Rouse, I. Nutrient intake, blood pressure, serum and urinary prostaglandins and serum thrombaxane B2 in a controlled trial with a lacto-ovo-vegetarian diet. *J. Hypertens.* 4:241, 1986.

Stamler, R. Primary prevention of hypertension by nutritional-hygienic means. Final report of a randomized, controlled trial. *JAMA* 262:1801, 1989.

Pollare, T. A comparison of the effects of hydrochlorothiazide and captopril on glucose and lipid metabolism in patients with hypertension. *N. Engl. J. Med.* 321:868, 1989.

HYPOGLYCEMIA

Saunders, L. Refined carbohydrate as a contributing factor in reactive hypoglycemia. *South. Med. J.* 75:1072, 1982.

Haber, G. Depletion and disruption of dietary fibre, effects on satiety, plasma-glucose, and serum-insulin. *Lancet* 2:679, 1977.

Monnier, L. Restored synergistic entero-hormonal response after addition of dietary fiber to patients with impaired glucose tolerance and reactive hypoglycemia. *Diabet. Metab.* 8:217, 1982.

Olefsky, J. Reappraisal of the role of insulin in hypertriglyceridemia. *Am. J. Med.* 57:551, 1974.

KIDNEY DISEASE

Genova, R. Food allergy in steroid-resistant nephrotic syndrome (letter). *Lancet* 1:1315, 1987.

Lagrue, G. Food sensitivity and idiopathic nephrotic syndrome (letter). *Lancet* 2:777, 1985.

Lagrue, G. Food allergy in idiopathic nephrotic syndrome (letter). *Lancet* 2:277, 1987.

Howanietz, H. Idiopathic nephrotic syndrome, treated with steroids for five years, found to be allergic reaction to pork (letter), *Lancet* 2:450, 1985.

Sato, M. Estimation of circulating immune complexes following oral challenge with cow's milk in patients with IgA nephropathy. *Nephron.* 47:43, 1987.

Russell, M. IgA-associated renal disease: antibodies to environmental antigens in sera and deposition of immunoglobulins and antigens in glomeruli. *J. Clin. Immunol.* 6:74, 1986.

Brenner, B. Dietary protein intake and the progressive nature of kidney disease. *N. Engl. J. Med.* 307:652, 1982.

Bay, W. The living donor in kidney transplantation. *Ann. Intern. Med.* 106:719, 1987.

Giovannetti, S. Answers to ten questions on the dietary treatment of chronic renal failure. *Lancet* 2:1140, 1986.

Evanoff, G. Prolonged dietary protein restriction in diabetic nephropathy. *Arch. Intern. Med.* 149:1129, 1989.

KIDNEY STONES

Breslau, N. Relationship of animal protein-rich diet to kidney stone formation and calcium metabolism. *J. Clin. Endocrinol. Metab.* 66:140, 1988.

Rao, P. Dietary management of urinary risk factors in renal stone formers. *Br. J. Urol.* 54:578, 1982.

Fellstrom, B. The influence of a high dietary intake of purine-rich animal protein on urinary urate excretion and supersaturation in renal stone disease. *Clin. Sci.* 64:399, 1983.

Fellstrom, B. Effects of high intake of dietary animal protein on mineral metabolism and urinary supersaturation of calcium oxalate in renal stone formers. *Br. J. Urol.* 56:263, 1984.

LIVER DISEASE

Iturriaga, H. Overweight as a risk factor or a predictive sign of histological liver damage in alcoholics. *Am. J. Clin. Nutr.* 47:235, 1988.

Editorial—Towards prevention of alcoholic liver disease. *Lancet* 2:353, 1978.

Takada, A. Effects of dietary fat on alcohol-pyrazole hepatitis in rats: the pathogenic role of nonalcohol dehydrogenase pathway in alcohol-induced hepatic cell injury. *Alcoholism* 10:403, 1986.

Walker, A. Anomalies in the prediction of nutritional disease. *Nutrition Reviews* 19:257, 1961.

Greenberger, N. Effect of vegetable and animal protein diets in chronic hepatic encephalopathy. *Dig. Dis.* 22:845, 1977.

MULTIPLE SCLEROSIS

Agranoff, B. Diet and the geographical distribution of multiple sclerosis. *Lancet* 2:1061, 1974.

Alter, M. Multiple sclerosis and nutrition. *Arch. Neurol.* 31:267, 1974.

Swank, R. Multiple sclerosis: twenty years on low fat diet. *Arch. Neurol.* 23:460, 1970.

Swank, R. Multiple sclerosis: the lipid relationship. *Am. J. Clin. Nutr.* 48:1387, 1988.

Elian, M. Multiple sclerosis among the United Kingdom-born children of immigrants from the West Indies. *J. Neurol. Neurosurg. Psychiatry* 50:327, 1987.

Swank, R. Multiple sclerosis: a correlation of its incidence with dietary fat. *Am. J. Med. Sci.* 220:421, 1950.

Bates, D. Polyunsaturated fatty acids in treatment of acute remitting multiple sclerosis. *Br. Med. J.* 2:1390, 1978.

Millar, J. Double-blind trial of linoleate supplementation of the diet in multiple sclerosis. *Br. Med. J.* 1:765, 1973.

Paty, D. Linoleic acid in multiple sclerosis: failure to show any therapeutic benefit. *Acta. Neurol. Scandinav.* 58:53, 1978.

OBESITY

McCarty, A. The unique merits of a low-fat diet for weight control. *Med. Hypotheses* 20:183, 1986.

Lampam, R. Exercise as a partial therapy for the extremely obese. *Med. Sci. Sports Exerc.* 18:19, 1986.

OSTEOPOROSIS

Stevenson, J. Dietary intake of calcium and postmenopausal bone loss. *Br. Med. J.* 297:15, 1988.

Kanis, J. Calcium supplementation of the diet—I & II. Not justified by present evidence. *Br. Med. J.* 298:137 & 205, 1989.

Breslau, N. Relationship of animal protein-rich diet to kidney stone formation and calcium metabolism. *J. Clin. Endocrinol. Metab.* 66:140, 1988.

Marsh, A. Vegetarian lifestyle and bone mineral density. *Am. J. Clin. Nutr.* 43(3 suppl.):837, 1988.

Bush, T. The adverse effects of hormonal therapy. *Cardiol. Clin.* 4:145, 1986.

Bergkvist, L. The risk of breast cancer after estrogen and estrogen-progestin replacement. *N. Engl. J. Med.* 321:293, 1989.

UPPER INTESTINAL DISTRESS

Editorial—Diet and the peptic ulcer. *Lancet* 2:80, 1987.

Ippoliti, A. The effect of various forms of milk on gastric-acid secretion. *Ann. Intern. Med.* 84:286, 1976.

Kumar, N. Effect of milk on patients with duodenal ulcers. *Br. Med. J.* 293:666, 1986.

Childs, P. Peptic ulcer, pyloroplasty, and dietary fat. *Ann. R. Coll. Surg. Engl.* 59:143, 1977.

Malhotra, S. A comparison of unrefined wheat and rice diets in the management of duodenal ulcer. *Postgraduate Med. J.* 54:6, 1978.

Rydning, A. Prophylactic effect of dietary fibre in duodenal ulcer disease. *Lancet* 2:736, 1982.

Thomas, F. Inhibitory effect of coffee on lower eosphageal sphincter pressure. *Gastroenterology* 79:1262, 1980.

Cohen, S. Gastric acid secretion and lower-esophageal-sphincter pressure in response to coffee and caffeine. *N. Engl. J. Med.* 293:897, 1975.

Price, S. Food sensitivity in reflux esophagitis. *Gastroenterology* 75:240, 1978.

Sontag, S. Cimetidine, cigarette smoking, and recurrence of duodenal ulcer. *N. Engl. J. Med.* 311:689, 1984.

INTERPRETATION OF

LABORATORY TESTS*

BLOOD TESTS

The readings given in parenthesis are reference values for "normal" readings. Laboratories and doctors may differ in their designation of "normals." Please refer to the values printed on your report of specific test results for the ranges accepted by your laboratory and your physician. The tests listed below are performed routinely by many doctors as part of a general assessment of a patient's condition—for example, as part of a yearly physical examination. The usual specimen taken from you in order to provide a laboratory with material for the tests is whole blood (or circulating blood), which is drawn from a small vein in the crook of your arm. Usually two separate tubes of blood are taken from the same needle stick. This little operation is painless and safe.

Metabolic Products from Foods

CHOLESTEROL (130–350 mg/dl)—CHOL is the usual abbreviation for cholesterol, which is probably the most important test you will have. If your cholesterol level is average (210–220 mg/dl), then you run an average lifetime risk for developing some diseases. For example:

Heart attacks and strokes: a greater than 50 percent chance
Breast cancer: a 1 in 10 chance for women
Colon cancer: a 1 in 20 chance, for all people
Gallbladder disease: a 2 in 5 chance, for all people

Only a small change in the blood cholesterol level can result in a significant change in risk of disease. For example, a rise of 60 mg/dl in cholesterol level (200 to 260 mg/dl) represents a five-fold increase in the risk

---

* *Please Note:* These remarks about the commonest laboratory tests and their normal values are incomplete, and should be considered only for your general information and interest. Full interpretation of all test results and the treatment of related diseases must be obtained under the direction of a qualified physician.

of dying of heart disease. The lower your cholesterol level is maintained, the better for your health. An ideal level to aim for is 150 mg/dl or less.

Replacing foods derived from animals with starches, vegetables, and fruits will cause cholesterol levels to fall 30 to 100 mg/dl in most people within three weeks. Even though most of the benefit of a low-fat, no cholesterol diet is seen within three weeks, maintaining this diet over a longer time is necessary to keep your cholesterol low and to help you to continue gaining improvement in your general health. Older people usually have more difficulty in lowering their levels because of the large amount of cholesterol that they've stored in their body tissues. Some people who eat foods high in cholesterol can have a low blood cholesterol level in spite of their diet. They either do not absorb the cholesterol readily or excrete it more efficiently than most people manage to do. Even though these people will have a lower risk of heart disease, they still have health risks from consuming so much cholesterol.

Excreted cholesterol enters the gallbladder and thereby contributes to the production of gallstones (90 percent of gallstones are made of cholesterol) and excessive amounts of cholesterol in the lower intestines are believed to be involved in development of colon cancer. Vegetable oils will cause cholesterol to be eliminated from the body, lowering your risk of heart disease. Unfortunately, however, because this cholesterol is excreted through the gallbladder and into the colon, your risks of developing gallbladder disease and colon cancer are increased the more cholesterol you excrete. Thus, a change to a no-cholesterol diet is not only the most effective, but the safest way to lower your cholesterol level. No foods derived from plants contain cholesterol; but coconuts, chocolate, and palm oil contain enough saturated fats to raise blood cholesterol levels. Oats and beans, because of their plentiful supply of soluble fiber, are noted for their efficiency in lowering cholesterol levels. Some people may need specific medication to reduce their cholesterol levels closer to the ideal.

HDL CHOLESTEROL (above 35 mg/dl)—HDL-Chol is an abbreviation for high-density lipoprotein cholesterol. HDL cholesterol is a fraction of the total cholesterol and has some value for predicting risk of heart disease. HDL cholesterol, commonly called the "good" cholesterol, is an end product of cholesterol metabolism and represents the cholesterol that is leaving the tissues, on the way to being excreted by the liver. People with higher levels of HDL cholesterol *metabolize* their cholesterol faster than those people with lower levels. Since you can't easily change your metabolism, you must focus your attention on the foods you eat. *Total cholesterol is the most reliable test value* for those interested in improving their health. Don't be falsely reassured by a high HDL cholesterol level. Your goal is to reduce your total cholesterol by making changes in your diet, regardless of how high your HDL cholesterol level may be. People on low-cholesterol diets have low levels of HDL cholesterol because of the low level of all the fractions of cholesterol in their blood. (I do not routinely follow HDL levels in my patients.)

LDL CHOLESTEROL (below 130 mg/dl)—LDL-Chol is an abbreviation for low-density lipoprotein cholesterol. LDL cholesterol is a fraction of the total cholesterol and has some value in predicting risk of heart disease. LDL cholesterol, known as the "bad" cholesterol, is the form that is most damaging to the walls of the arteries, leading to atherosclerosis. Change to a healthy diet lowers LDL cholesterol as well as total cholesterol. (I do not routinely follow LDL cholesterol levels in my patients—total cholesterol levels are sufficient. Please distinguish LDL from LDH, which is a liver enzyme.)

TRIGLYCERIDES (35–206 mg/dl)—TRIG is the usual abbreviation for triglycerides, which are the fats in your circulating blood. If your blood is allowed to stand in a test tube overnight, a layer of these fats would rise to the top of the tube (just as fats will in a pot of chicken soup left overnight in the refrigerator). Normally, triglyceride levels increase in the blood after eating, and therefore need to be evaluated after an overnight fast. High levels of triglycerides are associated with heart attacks, diabetes, and poor blood circulation, which can result in chest pains, leg pains, and fatigue. Triglyceride levels are also elevated by drinking alcoholic beverages and by eating simple sugars and most fats. *Even fresh fruits and fruit juices can elevate these levels in sensitive people.* Exercise, high-fiber foods (starches and vegetables), and weight loss will lower triglycerides to healthy levels. (Note that sometimes during the period of weight loss the triglyceride levels may rise temporarily, due to the movement of fats from the fatty tissues into the blood.) The lower your level of triglycerides is, the better your health will be. Certainly, any levels above 200 mg/dl should worry you enough to take action to bring them down.

GLUCOSE (64–116 mg/dl)—GLU is a common abbreviation for glucose, the sugar in your blood. When you haven't eaten for a while, the level is normally between 65 and 120 mg/dl. Glucose will rise after you eat, to around 130 to 150 mg/dl; therefore, this test is best made after an overnight fast. In some people, the body's metabolic processes lose control over the proper disposition of sugar, and glucose levels run higher. This condition is called diabetes. The diagnosis of diabetes is made with evidence drawn from this blood sugar test, and diagnosis is confirmed when fasting values are over 120 mg/dl. Generally, the higher the glucose level, the worse is the disease—and the more ailing is the patient. Most diabetes (95 percent of cases) is caused by a diet high in fats (derived from meats, cheeses, eggs, oils, etc.) and low in fibers (fibers are found only in grains, beans, fruits, and vegetables). Correcting the offending diet will solve this problem for most people suffering from the form of disease called adult-onset diabetes. Exercise will lower blood sugar levels. For obese people, weight loss also helps. Childhood-onset diabetes is a different disease, resulting from destruction of the portions of the pancreas that synthesize insulin. Although proper diet is absolutely essential for these patients, cure cannot be expected from a change in diet. Hypoglycemia is a condition in which blood sugar levels are lower than normal (below 50 mg/dl), causing a variety of symptoms, such as weakness, trembling, and headaches. Another test (the five-hour glucose tolerance test) is needed to make the diagnosis. Both the cause and the correction are found in the diet.

URIC ACID (3.4–8.0 mg/dl)—UA is an abbreviation sometimes used for uric acid, a breakdown product of purines, which are found in larger amounts in protein-rich foods such as meats, seafoods, chicken, cheeses, and beans. Accumulations of uric acid can lead to gout (arthritis) and uric acid kidney stones. Often after a low-purine diet is begun, several months are needed to lower the levels of uric acid in the blood.

Liver Tests

LDH (99–215 U/L), **SGOT** (13–47 U/L), **SGPT** (8–62 U/L)—These are abbreviations for three different enzymes that are released from liver (and other body) cells when they are injured. Gallbladder disease, excess alcohol consumption, certain kinds of medications, and the viruses that cause hepatitis are the most common situations that provoke elevation in levels of these liver enzymes. Fatty infiltration of the liver tissues will also cause injury to the liver and a rise in the level of these enzymes. Avoiding toxic substances and a change to a low-fat diet can help to lower the elevated levels of these liver enzymes.

GGT or GGTP (3–61 U/L)—GGT or GGTP are abbreviations for an enzyme that is released into the bloodstream when different kinds of body tissues are damaged. The test for this enzyme is a very sensitive means of measuring liver damage, and can detect injury caused by alcohol consumption even in very small amounts in some sensitive people.

ALKALINE PHOSPHATASE (16–72 U/L)—ALK PHOS is an abbreviation for the enzyme alkaline phosphatase, which can be released into circulating blood from either the bones or the liver. If it is elevated in children it usually reflects normal bone growth activity. In adults, however, liver and gallbladder disease are common reasons for an elevated alkaline phosphatase level. Bone disease and arthritis can also result in elevations.

TOTAL BILIRUBIN (.1–1.2 mg/dl)—T. BILI is the common abbreviation for this test. Bilirubin is a product of the breakdown of the red blood cells. It is elevated when a large and abnormal breakdown of blood cells occurs, and also when the liver is diseased and unable to adequately excrete it. Many people show a slight elevation (up to 3 mg/dl) that is not necessarily an indication of disease. This normal condition results from fasting overnight. The best indication that this is indeed a normal situation comes from the fact that all the preceding liver function tests (GGT, SGOT, SGPT, LDH) are normal.

TOTAL PROTEIN (5.7–8.0 g/dl)—T. PROTEIN is the abbreviation for total protein, and this represents the amount of all proteins present in the circulating blood. These proteins are made primarily by the liver and by cells in the organs of the immune system. They may be elevated in certain kinds of infections and in diseases of the bone marrow. This measurement is not affected by the amount of proteins you eat.

ALBUMIN (3.6–5.0 gm/dl)—ALB is an abbreviation for albumin, which is a protein made in the liver. The albumin level is lowered in serious diseases of the liver and the kidneys.

GLOBULIN (2.0–3.5 gm/dl)—GLB is an abbreviation for globulin, which is the general name for a large group of serum proteins made by the cells of the immune system for defense of the body against infectious organisms and other harmful agents from outside the body.

Kidney Tests

BLOOD UREA NITROGEN (5–27 mg/dl)—BUN is the abbreviation for blood urea nitrogen, which is a measure of breakdown products from proteins. It is made in the liver and excreted by the kidneys. Diseases of the kidneys can cause the BUN levels to rise, making people feel ill in consequence. Low-protein diets lower levels of BUN.

CREATININE (0.5–1.6 mg/dl)—CREAT or CR are abbreviations for creatinine, a breakdown product from muscle tissues which is excreted by the kidneys. Elevation of creatinine levels usually means kidney disease. Some laboratories do the test only when the BUN level is first found to be elevated.

Mineral Tests

INORGANIC PHOSPHORUS (2.6–4.8 mg/dl)—INORG PHOS and PO_4 are abbreviations for inorganic phosphorus, the level of which increases with the amount of phosphates in your diet. Diets high in dairy products can raise this level. The level of this mineral is most important to kidney patients, and rises with failure of the kidneys.

CALCIUM (8.1–10.7 mg/dl)—CA^{++} is the abbreviation for calcium, a mineral that fulfills many functions in the body. The amount of it in the circulating blood must be keep at a critical level. In most people the calcium level is almost always in the normal range. An abnormal level usually indicates either a laboratory error or a decrease in the amount of albumin protein in the blood because of liver or kidney disease (see ALBUMIN, above). An elevated level could mean parathyroid disease. The level of calcium in your blood does not reflect the amount of calcium you eat.

SODIUM (135–145 mEq/L)—Na^+ is the abbreviation for sodium, a mineral found in large amounts in the body and an important component of foods and of table salt. This level *does not* reflect the amount of table salt you eat. Sometimes the level can be low when a person is taking a diuretic medication for blood pressure. High sodium readings usually mean dehydration—you went without eating and drinking for a long time before your blood test.

POTASSIUM (3.5–5.5 mEq/L)—K^+ is the abbreviation for potassium, a mineral found in large amounts in the body and in foods. Blood levels *do not* reflect your dietary intake of potassium unless you have serious kidney disease. Sometimes the level is low when a person is taking diuretic medication. Blood levels of this mineral must be kept within the normal range, or quick death occurs from heart irregularities.

CHLORIDE (96–110 mEq/H) and **CARBON DIOXIDE** (25–32 mEq/L) —Abbreviated Cl^- and CO_2, respectively, these substances are usually at normal levels in the blood unless people are taking medications. Rarely do they represent a problem, even when slightly outside the normal range. Diuretics often lower chloride levels.

Thyroid Tests

THYROID HORMONES—T–4 (4.5–12.5 ug/ml) and **T–3** are abbreviations for hormones secreted by the thyroid gland. **T–7** and **FTI** are abbreviations for calculations of thyroid activity based on the original T–3 and T–4 values. The hormones produced by the thyroid gland control the body's metabolic rate, and therefore have an important influence on health.

Blood Counts

COMPLETE BLOOD COUNT— This test, abbreviated CBC, is an evaluation of the numbers and kinds of blood cells your body produces. It consists of several readings, the most important of which are the white blood cell count, or WBC, and the hemoglobin (see below). The white blood cells are involved in defense and inflammatory reactions, such as fighting infections, and an elevation in number is an indication that the body's defense system is in action.

HEMOGLOBIN (M-13.8–17.2 gm/dl, F-12.0–15.6 gm/dl)—HGB is the abbreviation for hemoglobin, the oxygen-carrying, red-pigmented, iron-containing substance in the red blood cells. The level indicates the numbers of red blood cells in your body, thus, a low level can mean anemia. Twenty percent of the women in our country have iron-deficiency anemia. Dairy products contribute to this problem in several ways (see ANEMIA, page 308). People showing signs of anemia should be checked for blood loss in their stools, at least.

Urine Test

URINALYSIS— Urinalysis is a check of the urine for evidence of kidney disease and bladder disease, such as stones and infection, and metabolic disease, such as diabetes. The urine is collected in a bottle, then examined by chemical analysis and under a microscope. A normal urine specimen has no glucose, proteins, urobilinogen (present in liver and blood diseases), or bile (present in liver disease) in it. Ketones do appear when someone has not eaten for a while, and may happen after an overnight fast before a blood test. Ketones alone are generally not a sign of disease. A normal urine shows very few blood cells of any kind (less than five per microscopic field). The most important cells found in a urine are leucocytes (wbcs) and erythrocytes (rbcs). The presence of these cells in any quantity is a sign of disease somewhere in the urinary tract. Epithelial cells found in urine are not usually a sign of disease, and most often are introduced by contamination of the specimen with vaginal discharge. Crystals, amorphous mucus, and bacteria are often reported, and yet still do not represent evidence of disease. Casts are usually a sign of kidney disease.

GENERAL INDEX

RECIPE INDEX

If you have a question or any idea you would like to share with us, or if you would like further information about The Mc-Dougall Live-In Program, The McDougall Newsletter, The McDougall Program Audio Tapes, and the previous McDougall books, please call or write:

The McDougalls
P.O. Box 14039
Santa Rosa, CA 95402
(707) 576-1654